Pacific Diaspora

Pacific Diaspora

Island Peoples in the United States and Across the Pacific

EDITED BY

Paul Spickard

Joanne L. Rondilla

Debbie Hippolite Wright

UNIVERSITY OF HAWAI'I PRESS

HONOLULU

The volume editors would like to express special thanks to Karina Kahananui Green, Tupou Hopoate Pau'u, and Shane Siataga for their assistance.

Library of Congress Cataloging-in-Publication Data

Pacific diaspora : island peoples in the United States and across the Pacific /
edited by Paul Spickard, Joanne Rondilla, and Debbie Hippolite Wright.
p. cm.
Includes bibliographical references and index.
ISBN 0-8248-2562-4 (cloth : alk. paper) — ISBN 0-8248-2619-1 (pbk. : alk. paper)
1. Pacific Islander Americans. 2. Islands of the Pacific — Emigration and
immigration. 3. Nationalism — Hawaii. 4. Hawaii — Social conditions.
5. Nationalism — New Zealand. I. Spickard, Paul R., 1950– II. Rondilla,
Joanne. III. Hippolite Wright, Debbie.
E184.P25 .P34 2002
304.8'0996 — dc21   2002018080

Designed by D&G Limited, LLC

Printed by The Maple-Vail Book Manufacturing Group

Paul Spickard offers this book with thanks to
William Kauaiwiulaokalani Wallace III

Joanne L. Rondilla dedicates it
to the memory of Fernando S. Rondilla

Debbie Hippolite Wright gives it to her tamariki
Morgan Wetekia, Karamea Moana, Ihakara Te Rangihau, Taimona John

Contents

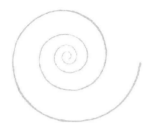

Introduction

Pacific Diaspora?

Paul Spickard

One family migrates from Samoa to the North Shore of the island of
O'ahu in the state (or sovereign nation, depending on one's point of
view) of Hawai'i. Their son goes to Harvard, works in business and state
government, runs for Congress, and serves on the Honolulu city council.
Another family leaves Tonga in the 1970s and establishes outposts in
Auckland, Sydney, Inglewood, and Salt Lake City. They work in construction, small business, and tending children. Their second generation
forms churches and gangs and goes to college. For a quarter century they
remain in weekly contact with one another by mail, then by phone and
jumbo jet, and finally by e-mail and the World Wide Web.

Some Hawaiians leave their islands to go to school or serve in the
army, then find themselves unable to return home because it costs too
much to live there and people from the continental United States have
cornered all the good jobs. They console themselves in exile with spam
musubi, letters from home, and CDs by the Ka'au Crater Boys. Other
Hawaiians remain in the islands and agitate for the return of some form
of national sovereignty to their people. Similar movements of cultural
and political nationalism animate other colonized peoples such as Maori
and Chamorros.

These are just three elements of a vast Pacific diaspora. People of the
islands—of Hawai'i and Guam, Aotearoa and Fiji, Kiribati and Papua
New Guinea, and two dozen other island groups—have been moving
from village to city, from island to island, and back and forth to the industrialized nations of the Pacific periphery, throughout the second half of

Portions of this chapter are revised from a paper given at the Out of Oceania
conference at the University of Hawai'i, Honolulu, Hawai'i, on October 20,
1999.

1

the twentieth century. This is not an entirely new phenomenon. Islanders have been moving around the Pacific for as long as memory recalls, for many hundreds of years. Nor is migration to North America wholly new: In the nineteenth century, islanders worked in the fur trade for the Hudson Bay Company, rushed for gold in California, cut down trees in the Pacific Northwest, and took sail in whaling ships and the sandalwood trade. Yet the velocity and impact of such movements have increased dramatically in recent decades.

This book attempts to represent that far-flung movement of people around the Pacific. Its special emphasis is on the lives that Pacific Island peoples have made for themselves in the United States. Pacific Islander Americans are, as Faye Untalan Munoz notes, "a perplexed, neglected minority."[1] We hope to make the experiences of Pacific Islander Americans known to a wide audience, and to spur others to write about those experiences.

Pacific Diaspora is a collection of essays by a variety of authors—some scholars, some activists, and some merely astute observers. Several of the selections are shortened versions of previously published materials; others are essays commissioned expressly for this volume. The essays are arranged by subject. First comes the question of identity (Part One). Then the book takes up the issue of migration, its impact on island homelands, and connections between various points of the diaspora (Part Two). Part Three traces several ways that culture and social systems have been transformed in the processes of colonial domination and migratory encounter. Part Four is devoted to historic and contemporary issues surrounding gender and sexuality. It is followed by examinations of social problems in family and health care, and the responses made by Pacific Island peoples in diaspora to such problems (Part Five). The final part addresses the history of colonialism and the recent nationalist movement in Hawai'i.

HISTORICAL BACKGROUND

People have been moving around the Pacific Ocean for a very long time: The Pacific diaspora is thousands of years old. Outside analysts (and many islanders under their influence) have in modern times divided the Pacific into three groups of islands and peoples. Melanesia is the name given to a broad band of islands, many of them large and densely populated, stretching from Fiji, just west of the International Date Line, to New Guinea at the doorstep of Southeast Asia. Melanesia is home to hundreds of discrete societies and language groups. North of Melanesia is another band of islands called Micronesia. Micronesia is made up of thousands of

tiny islands separated by wide oceans, yet is more homogeneous culturally than Melanesia. Polynesia is a huge arrowhead-shaped region
stretching from Hawai'i in the north to Aotearoa/New Zealand in the
south, and from Tuvalu in the west to Easter Island in the east. The peoples of Polynesia speak closely-related, often mutually-intelligible, languages despite the vast stretches of ocean across which they range. Most
Pacific Islander Americans, but not all, are Polynesians.

There are several theories as to how people first came to the islands of
the Pacific. Most involve migrations over many centuries, island-hopping
by small boat, small groups of people moving back and forth. The general routes are from mainland Southeast Asia through what is now
Indonesia and the Philippines, thence through Melanesia and Micronesia,
and on to central Polynesia, finally spreading north, east, and south to the
habitable extremities of the ocean. Archeologists and linguists put human
beings and their animals in Fiji and Samoa well before the time of Christ,
in the Marquesas by 300 A.D., in Hawai'i and Easter Island a century later,
and in Aotearoa/New Zealand by 800 A.D.. Apparently there was a good
bit of travel around the Pacific from a very early date, back and forth, so
that there are communities of Polynesians who later went back and settled in Melanesia and Micronesia, for example.

Some migration went just over the horizon, but much of it involved travel
over thousands of miles. Well-stocked expeditions traveled in double-hulled
canoes that held scores of people, employing complex systems of navigation
by stars, wind, and waves. They went to explore and to colonize. Long-range
interregional contact continued, archeologists suggest, as late as 1500 A.D.,
but then it tapered off and outlying island groups like Hawai'i became more
isolated.

Each of the island groups has its own pattern of development during
the time before history was written down and into the modern era. There
was never a golden age when people lived in stable, primitive harmony
with one another and with nature, as some myth-makers would have us
believe. Change was the norm throughout the period of human habita-
tion. The two greatest changes in Pacific history were the initial colonization by the many peoples outlined above, and the sudden coming of
Europeans in the eighteenth and nineteenth centuries.

In the fifteenth century, quite suddenly and for reasons far from the
Pacific, Europeans began to expand outward and discover the rest of the
world. Prior to that time, most of what is generally regarded to be important in human history happened elsewhere, in the richer, more populous
civilizations of the eastern Mediterranean, East Asia, South Asia, Africa,
and Latin America. Just a few generations before Columbus, Europe was
a fringe region, disconnected from and ignorant of the rest of the world.

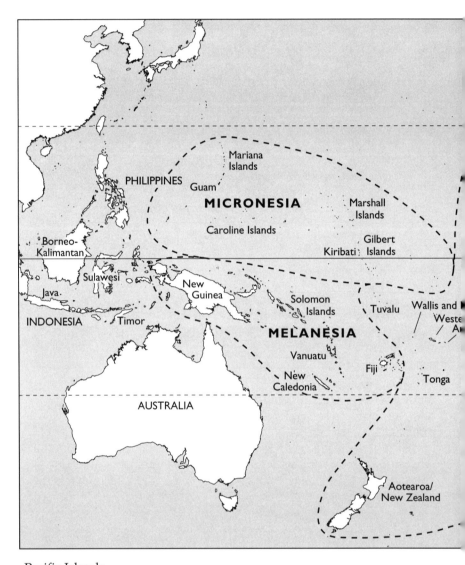

Pacific Islands

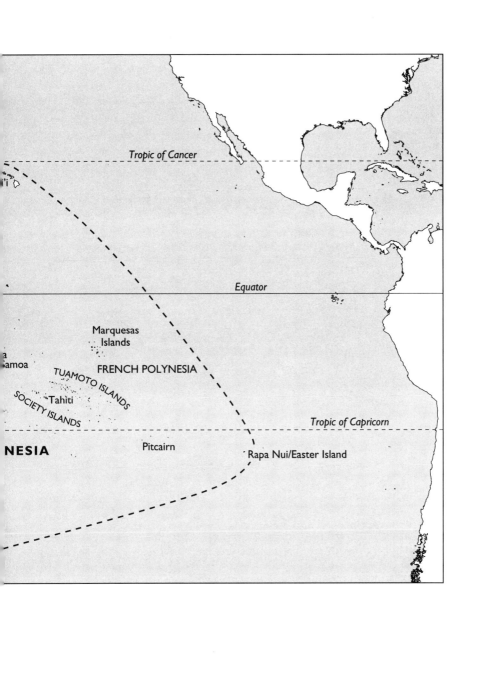

Tropic of Cancer

Equator

Marquesas
Islands

amoa   FRENCH POLYNESIA

TUAMOTO ISLANDS

Tahiti

SOCIETY ISLANDS

Tropic of Capricorn

NESIA   Pitcairn   Rapa Nui/Easter Island

Then things began to change. In the sixteenth century, Spanish voyagers first made it across the Pacific, happened upon some of the people living there, and laid claim to Guam. Two centuries later, French and British sailors came and began to fill in the gaps in the Europeans' map. The most famous of these was Captain James Cook, whose three long voyages between 1769 and 1780 brought most of Polynesia and much of the rest of the Pacific into the purview of Europe.

When Europeans came to the Pacific, some island groups, like Tonga and Hawai'i, were already in the process of coming together to build states that resembled the nations of Europe in size and political integration. Others, like most of Melanesia, continued in political and cultural fragmentation. The stories of the coming of foreigners to various islands are complex and as various as the islands themselves.[2] If there is a pattern, it ran something like this: First there was a sighting of an island or group of islands by a European explorer or trader. Then came a period of sporadic stops by European ships to take on supplies, conduct trade, or learn about the island and its people. The Europeans might involve themselves in local politics or they might remain aloof. Some Europeans jumped ship or were shipwrecked and became for a time part of island society. Some islanders went willingly or under duress on board and sailed away with the Europeans. Some of them came back with tales of a wider world.

In time, European traders began to come regularly to the islands. As their numbers grew, they demanded land and a say in the government of the islands where they resided. Missionaries joined them. Frequently, European diseases such as measles, influenza, and syphilis decimated the population just as iron pots and Christianity were transforming their cultures. Businesses and governments recruited foreigners from Asia to come and work in extractive industries. The governments of the Europeans' home countries became more involved in island politics. Sometimes island factions would play one European power off against another. Other times Europeans came and conquered. By early in the twentieth century, nearly all of the Pacific had been gobbled into European and American imperial systems.

International connections of trade and empire took people out of their home islands throughout the nineteenth century. In the 1840s and 1850s, whaling ships took on several thousand Samoan and Hawaiian sailors, carrying them throughout the Pacific and as far away as North America. In the 1860s, labor agents captured or hoodwinked several thousand Polynesians from various islands into slave labor in Peruvian mines. From that decade through the end of the century, perhaps 100,000

Melanesians went to work under miserable conditions as contract laborers in Australia. Others went from one island area to another: Samoans to Fiji to work on British plantations, for example. Such travel along the sinews of empire continued into the twentieth century, as well.

MODERN MIGRATION TO THE UNITED STATES

That there are Pacific Islanders in America at all is the result of two modern historical forces.[3] One was the American adventure in the Pacific. American missionaries went to Hawai'i in the 1820s. Business people soon followed. They wormed their way into the confidence of the island kingdom's rulers, then overthrew the kingdom in 1893, and succeeded in petitioning to be absorbed under United States sovereignty in 1898, as part of America's first overseas imperial adventure. Thus, the first Pacific Islander Americans were a colonized people, Hawaiian Americans, who eventually became citizens of the fiftieth state. At the same time Hawai'i became a U.S. possession, Guam fell under American sovereignty as a prize of the Spanish-American War. That same year, 1898, America and Germany divided Samoa between them. The United States also claimed two tiny, uninhabited islands, Wake and Midway, as communications stations. Wake, Guam, Midway, and American Samoa were administered by the U.S. Navy, while Hawai'i was administered as a territory by the Department of the Interior.

American involvement in the Pacific expanded during World War II. The American admirals and generals chose to fight that war on Pacific Islands: Guam, Saipan, Bougainville, and elsewhere. The Americans and their Japanese adversaries killed and rendered homeless hundreds of thousands of Pacific Island people. The war severely damaged the economies of Guam and the Solomon Islands, even as it boosted the economic fortunes of Hawai'i, Tonga, and Samoa. Once the war was over, the Americans stayed in the Pacific. The Navy handed Guam and American Samoa over to civilian authorities. Other islands came under United States control: the Caroline Islands (now the Federated States of Micronesia), the Marianas Islands, the Marshall Islands, the Palau Islands (now the Trust Territory of the Pacific). Links of trade, missionary activity, and strategic significance kept Americans coming to the Pacific Islands and opened pathways for Pacific Island people to come to the United States.

The other factor at work in bringing Pacific Islanders to America was a concatenation of social and economic forces that gave rise to waves of migration around the Pacific. The migration took place throughout the twentieth century, but gathered momentum after World War II. It was shaped not just (nor even most significantly) by American colonialism, but by the colonialism of other countries as well: by Japan in Micronesia; by France in Tahiti and the rest of French Polynesia (the Austral Islands, the Gambier Islands, the Marquesas, the Society Islands, and the Tuamotu Archipelago), in New Caledonia, and in Wallis and Futuna; by Britain in New Zealand, Fiji, the Pitcairn Islands, and less formally in Tonga and elsewhere; by Germany in Western Samoa and Micronesia until World War I; by Chile in Rapa Nui/Easter Island; by Australia in Norfolk Island and Papua New Guinea; by New Zealand in the Cook Islands, Tokelau, and Niue; by the Netherlands and later Indonesia in Irian Jaya.

The administrative, military, commercial, and missionary presence of all these outsider nations provided the links along which tens of thousands of Pacific Island people were set in motion. They migrated from village to town within their own countries—as thousands of rural Papua New Guineans have in recent years. They migrated from island to island, so that Marquesans now live in Tahiti, Tongans live in Samoa, and Samoans live in Fiji. And they migrated beyond the islands, primarily to three industrialized, anglophone nations—New Zealand, Australia, and the United States.

Colonialism and quasi-colonialism created the pathways for migration. They also created economic conditions in many island chains that encouraged people to migrate. Since the European and American intrusions, several island nations have entered the world economy as exporters of raw materials and agricultural products and as importers of cars, appliances, and other manufactured goods. In almost no case has the monetary reward of the exports matched the price of the imports. In this situation, Pacific Island nations have had few ways to balance their economies: tourism and foreign aid are two. A third has been the export of people. Pacific Islanders have gone abroad to school and work, sending back remittances that have been crucial to the welfare of their families back home; they have also helped their homelands' balances of payments. At the same time, those immigrant workers have filled a demand in the economies of Australia, New Zealand, and the United States for low-paid, low-skilled, easily exploitable labor.

MODELS OF MIGRATION AND THE QUESTION OF DIASPORA

This book's title, *Pacific Diaspora*, may suggest a particular interpretive slant for some readers. Indeed, we see Pacific peoples who have migrated to the United States as just one part of an international web of migration, a scattering across the globe. But we do not intend to pursue a doctrinaire diasporic interpretation in this book. Rather, we hope to hold several models of migration in tension.

Europeans look at a full moon and see two dark eyes and a mouth: the Man in the Moon. Japanese look at the same moon and see the white space between the dark spots, a round face, erect ears, a fluffy body: the Rabbit in the Moon. Maori see a woman by a tree carrying a gourd for drawing water: Rona, the controller of tides and the calendar. Each set of people is conditioned to see a particular figure in the moon, and each culture has stories about how Rona or the rabbit or the man got to be in the moon. Try it out for yourself. You can see either the man, the woman, or the rabbit, but you can't see all three at once. And once you have committed yourself to one way of seeing, it is hard to shift to another. What a feat of perception it would take to see all three figures at one time!

The preconceived ideas we bring to a perceptual task shape what we see when we get there. The next few pages will consider three ways that scholars and the public have conceived of human migrations, and the effects that these three idea systems may have on the understandings that are generated. One is the immigrant assimilation model; the second is sometimes called a transnational or diasporic model; the third is the panethnicity model. All three are important to our understanding of the lives and experiences of Pacific Islander Americans.

The Immigrant Assimilation Model

The master narrative of the peopling of the United States is a narrative of immigration and assimilation. Until quite recently, nearly all writing on non-native minorities in the United States has viewed them as immigrants after Emma Lazarus's description at the base of the Statue of Liberty: "Give me your tired, your poor, your huddled masses yearning to breathe free, the wretched refuse of your teeming shore." The immigrant model views migrants as participants in a one-way flow of people, transplanted from their unattractive native country and deposited in more fertile soil in the United States.

The classic works on European immigrants to the United States all strike this theme.[4] Oscar Handlin writes of "the uprooted," European peasants who flee poverty or oppression and seek freedom and prosperity in the United States.[5] John Bodnar calls them "the transplanted," emphasizing agency and downplaying trauma, but he, too, is talking about a straight-line train from Over There (which is a bad place) to Over Here (which is good).[6] In this narrative, America is "the golden land."

New York City is "the golden door." San Francisco is by "the golden gate." Ellis Island is "the island of hope" if they let you in, or "the island of tears" if they send you back. What America means to immigrants always goes something like this: "Charles grew up poor on a farm in Austro-Hungary, but then came to America—and ah, the difference! In Europe, he and his family struggled on a little piece of land and had meat 'about once a year.' In America, he and his brothers became skilled workers and independent businessmen."[7]

There has been more than a bit of American triumphalism in this model, with the assumption that prosperity and happiness did not exist in the old place and that they were widely available in the new. The immigrant assimilation model emphasizes not just first-generation enthusiasm for the United States, but also successive generations obliterating their ancestral identities and taking on an undifferentiated American identity. So, analyses of immigrant communities in the second and third generations have often tried to measure the degrees to which they had "assimilated" into non-minority institutions and "acculturated" to the dominant American values and styles of behavior.[8] The pattern is supposed to be that Group B (made up of immigrants) becomes like Group A (the people who really belong in America). Ultimately, the people of Group B enter fully into American society and culture and become undifferentiated members of Group A. Their journey from the Old World to New, from inferior to superior, is complete.

The hegemonic quality of this interpretation is obvious. The task of migrators is to lose themselves and conform to Anglo-American norms. Insofar as anyone maintains a distinct identity, they are not fulfilling the promise of America, and they do not really belong. If others punish them for their difference, it is their fault. The implication of the immigrant model is that, over successive generations, the straight-line train from Over There to Over Here leads on to subjection and ethnic oblivion.[9]

The other problem with the immigrant assimilation model, besides this hegemonic quality in the lives of successive generations, is that it masks some important aspects of the migrant experience itself. It posits, for example, that no one went back. In any town in Sicily in the 1940s one could find men who had gone to America between 1880 and 1920, worked for a while, and then had gone back to Italy. Probably more Serbs and Croats, and certainly more Greek immigrants, went back to their homelands than stayed on in the United States.[10] There are districts in Hiroshima today inhabited largely by the descendants of Nisei, Japanese born in America who went back to their parents' homeland in the 1930s.[11]

Further, the triumphal emphasis on one-way migration and assimilation into the United States has meant that scholars have paid insufficient attention to processes in the places from which migrants have come. Until very recently, no book on Japanese Americans took more than a cursory glance at the history of social change and migration within Japan that formed the pattern and context for migration abroad. Indeed, the going and coming across international borders and oceans can be interpreted most fruitfully, in the Japanese case, as an extension of indigenous Japanese patterns, not as some magical pull of a mythic America.[12] The focus on the U.S. side alone also de-emphasizes the possible existence of systems of international economic and political interaction, such as the involvement of colonized places in an international capitalist market economy.[13] It substitutes a simplified vision of push factors (China is in chaos, there are pogroms in Russia, there is famine in Ireland) and pull factors (America is a great place that has lots of jobs and resources and none of those problems).

The immigrant assimilation model, with its fixation on the American destination, does not enable scholars to make comparisons among migrations from a single country of origin to several different countries of destination. In the first half of the twentieth century, Japanese people went to the United States, Peru, Brazil, Manchuria, and Micronesia, but no book exists in English that compares those various experiences.[14] Similarly, Chinese people have gone to the United States, Singapore, Thailand, the Philippines, the United Kingdom, Jamaica, Belize, Fiji, and Australia. Germans went to the United States, Brazil, and Mexico. Italians went to the United States and Argentina. The immigration model de-emphasizes the connections between those various migrations, the features common to those various migrations by one people, and how they may differ from one another.

The Transnational or Diasporic Model

In recent years, the immigrant assimilation model has been challenged by scholars who have emphasized the diasporic or transnational nature of people movements. People move about the globe in a complex whirl, back and forth and around. The Internet and the World Wide Web have made it clear to all of us what some ecologists and postmodern thinkers understood early on: The world is a connected whole. People, goods, ideas, jobs, corporations, identities, and politics whizz around and around. Chips made in the Philippines make their way into American computers that are sold in India. American parts go into Japanese cars marketed in Europe. Texas cotton is made into cloth in South Carolina, which is then sent to the Dominican Republic to be cut and sewn into garments, which in turn are shipped to New York and London and Dakar to be sold. Guano from Nauru fertilizes lawns and washes clothes in Los Angeles and Copenhagen.[15]

Scholars who use the diasporic model to study migration emphasize connectedness between the sending region and the various receiving regions and comparison of the experiences of migrating people in various locations: of Tongans in Tonga, New Zealand, Australia, Hawai'i, California, and Utah; of Filipinos in Hong Kong, Micronesia, Hawai'i, Yemen, the United States, and Japan.

This is about as trendy as academic work can be. There are (or have been in the past decade) journals such as *Public Culture, Diaspora,* the *Journal of Transnational Studies,* and *Transition* that have devoted themselves to emerging, interconnected, global (or at least transnational) cultural networks. As James Clifford writes in an influential essay, "An unruly crowd of descriptive/interpretive terms now jostle and converse in an effort to characterize the contact zones of nations, cultures, and regions: terms such as *border, travel, transculturation, hybridity,* and *diaspora*."[16]

Some of the signifying about transnational concepts that Clifford laments (which has been known to appear in such journals and others) is just the fuzzy jargon (and, I believe, thinking) of the sloppy end of postmodernism: inventing and throwing off words, whacking concepts up against each other, as much to display one's ability with linguistic pyrotechnics (and thereby attract publishers, achieve tenure, and convince one's students and colleagues of how smart one is) as to illuminate human experience. But some of it is solid scholarship that illuminates experiences that formerly lay in darkness.

For example, Roger Rouse writes on the linked Mexican communities of Aguililla (Michoacán) and Redwood City (California):

> It has become inadequate to see Aguilillan migration as a movement between distinct communities, understood as the loci of distinct sets of social relationships. Today, Aguilillans find that their most important kin and friends are as likely to be living hundreds or thousands of miles away as immediately around them. More significantly, they are often able to maintain these spatially extended relationships as actively and effectively as the ties that link them to their neighbors. In this growing access to the telephone has been particularly significant, allowing people not just to keep in touch periodically, but to contribute to decision-making and participate in familial events from a considerable distance.[17]

That is a new view of Mexicans that the immigrant model could not accommodate.

Xiaojian Zhao takes such thinking into the past, for, as she notes, the condition of diaspora is not new. People in migration have always been linked and have moved back and forth. What is new is that we have a conceptual orientation, the transnational model, that allows us to see that pattern, like the Rabbit in the Moon. Zhao's is a fascinating study of the trans-Pacific Chinese family of the 1930s and 1940s. Adolescent boys for several generations left South China to work in the United States, Hawai'i, and elsewhere. Women and children stayed home. The men would make a trip or two back to China, to marry and sire children, so the family went on for decades, even generations, existing simultaneously on both sides of the Pacific. After World War II, the War Brides Acts were designed to allow American soldiers to bring home, outside racially motivated immigration quotas, women they had married abroad during wartime; several thousand Chinese American soldiers used them to bring over their wives of many years.[18]

If the diasporic or transnational model (I recognize that some would draw distinctions between these terms, and even between "diaspora" and "diasporic," but I will treat them as roughly synonymous) has perspectival and explanatory strength, it is not without its detractors. Perhaps the foremost is Sau-ling Wong, of UC Berkeley's Ethnic Studies Department. She argues against the diasporic concept on essentially political grounds. She cites the centrality of service to communities of color in the mission of her own work and the work of ethnic studies in general. If ethnic studies scholarship is to be useful for much, it ought to empower the powerless. She feels that the diasporic perspective detracts from that purpose. On the one hand, it concentrates on the migrating generation—on first generation Chinese or Samoans, for example, around the globe. In doing so, it turns its attention away from the issues of succeeding generations in any given location. Asian Americans and Asians are not the same people, says Wong, despite the tendency of non-Asians to confuse them. Similarly, one may say that Pacific Islanders and Pacific Islander Americans are not quite the same people, either, though surely they are linked.[19]

Secondly, Wong is troubled by what she sees as an upper-class bias in diasporic studies. She takes issue with the diasporic interpretive leanings of Lisa Lowe[20] and the frequent reference in Asian American studies circles to the international family connections depicted in Peter Wang's film, *A Great Wall.*

> She [Lowe] valorizes "the migratory process suggested by Wang's filmic technique and emplotment": namely, a "shuttling between . . . various cultural spaces," so that "we are left, by the end of the film, with a sense of culture as dynamic and open, the result of a continual process of visiting and revisiting a plurality of cultural sites." . . . I wonder to what extent a class bias is coded into the privileging of travel and transnational mobility in

Lowe's model—and this is a questioning I extend to some other articula-
tions of denationalization. I understand fully that Lowe's "cultural sites"
need not be geographic; however, it is also not entirely accidental, I believe,
that *A Great Wall* is about an affluent Chinese American family of the professional class that can take vacationing for granted and have a comfortable home to return to, even when the father has quit his job. . . . Lowe's
model of identity and cultural formation celebrating is, at least in part,
extrapolated from the wide range of options available to a particular
socioeconomic class, yet the class element is typically rendered invisible.[21]

Such criticism sometimes extends informally to attacks on the class cre-
dentials of scholars who espouse transnational interpretive schemes. I have
heard grousing at ethnic studies meetings that one or another scholar is just
"the spoiled child of a wealthy Third World comprador capitalist who flew
in from the Sorbonne on a jumbo jet and wants to take over ethnic studies."[22] Whining aside, a disproportionate number of people from upper-
class, international backgrounds do seem to inhabit the ranks of scholars
who take a diasporic view, and they may well imagine that their privileged
personal experiences ought to stand as the norm for migrating people.[23]

It might also be argued that the emphasis of the transnational model
on the immigrant generation and connections with ancestral homelands
may jeopardize the well-being of immigrants in racialized states. In the
United States, it is true that there are woeful limitations on the life
chances of immigrants, especially people of color. But there is at least the
countervailing influence of the immigrant assimilation model, which
asserts that anyone born in America is an American and belongs to
America. Contrast that to the situation in places like Germany, France,
and Denmark, where entrenched nativist parties insist that even second
and third generation Turks, Algerians, and Hungarians do not belong.[24]

The Panethnicity Model

Yen Le Espiritu coined the term "panethnicity" to describe a process that
has been going on in the world for a very long time: the lumping together
of formerly separate ethnic groups, frequently in a new geographical or
political setting. Panethnicity was at work when Galitsianers and Litvaks
went to New York and were called East European Jews. It was at work
when Milanos and Sicilianos went to Chicago and became Italians. It was
at work when Irish, German, and Swedish Americans went to California
and became Whites.[25]

Panethnicity was what made Asian Americans out of the children and
grandchildren of Cantonese, Japanese, and Filipino immigrants on the

American West Coast in the 1960s and 1970s. For a long time, outsiders had lumped them together and called them "Orientals," in the mistaken idea that people were the same from Honolulu to Istanbul. Japanese Americans inherited the ugly prejudices that White Americans fashioned originally against Chinese Americans. Filipino, Korean, Vietnamese, and other Americans whose ancestors lived in Asia later inherited those same prejudices and discriminations. Finally, in response to their common oppression, an American-born generation of Filipinos, Japanese, and Chinese began to call themselves by a common name: Asian Americans. Finding strength in numbers, they began to work together to fight their common oppression, and a panethnicity was born.[26]

There are other American panethnicities, of course. African Americans are a panethnicity. People who were abducted from West Africa knew themselves as Igbo or Hausah or Fon or Asante. In America slave owners consciously mixed the peoples and tried to destroy their languages, cultures, and independent identities in order to create a docile work force. By the early nineteenth century they had become simply and panethnically Black. The process was more complex by which hundreds of different people groups became panethnically (if unevenly) Native American or American Indian. And the process by which Mexican and Cuban and Puerto Rican Americans and others are becoming Latinos or Hispanics is still going on.[27]

The panethnicity model, like the immigrant assimilation model, emphasizes the experiences of people in the place to which they migrate—in the present case, the United States. It is similar to the immigrant model in that it tends to focus on the experiences of succeeding generations in the new place, and de-emphasizes connections to places of origin. It is different from the immigrant model in that it does not presume the ultimate absorption of the immigrant people into some amorphous American mass. Rather, it highlights the formation of larger, enduring ethnic collectivities through which people may act together.

The Models and Pacific Island Migration

What then for those who would study the migrations of Pacific Island peoples? Does the immigrant assimilation model, the transnational diasporic model, or the panethnicity model make the most sense? Although I share many of Sau-ling Wong's hesitations about class issues and succeeding generations, it seems to me that the Pacific Islander case is a particularly good example of migration that is fruitfully conceived transnationally.

The first thing one notices when one looks at the history of Pacific Islander migrations is that this has always been a diasporic movement.

Of course, voyagers have been moving around the Pacific for thousands
of years; that is how people got there, movement continued long after the
first settlement of any region, and there is every evidence that migration
was always multidirectional.

European and American colonialism had the effect of channeling migration along the sinews of trade and empire. To take just a few examples,
from the end of the eighteenth century thousands of Hawaiian and Samoan
men took jobs on whaling and trading ships and traveled around the
Pacific. Several hundred, at least, ended up working in the fur trade and
lumber and fishing industries in Oregon, Washington, and British
Columbia. Many stayed on in the places where they went to work, and others returned to the islands.[28] In the last third of the nineteenth century,
nearly ten thousand I-Kiribati went out to work in Tahiti, Samoa, Hawai'i,
Fiji, and Queensland, Australia.[29] Labor recruiters (or were they slave
catchers?) took perhaps 100,000 Melanesians to crushing work in
Queensland in the last third of the nineteenth century.[30] Others were
dragged off to slave conditions in Peruvian mines.[31] Some came back.
Imperial connections also brought hundreds of thousands of outsiders into
the Pacific: Japanese to Micronesia, Filipinos to Guam, Chinese to Hawai'i,
Indians to Fiji, and Europeans and Americans almost everywhere.[32]

The diaspora continues. In the last years of the twentieth century, one
of the most striking features of population in the Pacific is how many
people live in a place that is different from where their ancestors lived.
Lots of the migration takes place within island nations: from Penrhyn to
Rarotonga, from village to town in Papua New Guinea, from island to
island within Kiribati or the Federated States of Micronesia.[33] Other
migration takes Samoans and I-Banaba to Fiji, Niueans to Samoa, and
Tongans to Hawai'i.[34] And there are large movements out of the Pacific
Islands to countries on the edges of the ocean.

Aotearoa/New Zealand has by far the largest number of Pacific Island
peoples among the industrialized nations (see Table I.1).[35] Some island
nations such as Papua New Guinea have maintained the vast bulk of their
people within their homeland. Others, such as Samoa and Tonga, have sent
large fractions abroad. Polynesians and Melanesians of various sorts have
made their way to Australia.[36] And Rapa Nui have migrated to Chile.[37] In
the United States, the largest numbers of Pacific Islanders reside in Hawai'i
and California, but significant numbers reside in Washington, Texas, and
Utah (see Table I.2). In the United States, as in other countries of the extra-
Pacific diaspora, most Pacific Islanders live in or near large cities.

All this movement around the Pacific and beyond is pretty hard to comprehend under the simple, straight-line immigrant assimilation model,
especially because there is so much migration back to the places of origin

(and then forth again, and then back again). Take the case of my friend Tupou. She was born in Tonga three decades ago; at age four went to live in New Zealand; went to elementary and high school in Australia; twice went back to Tonga for about a year each time; attended college in Hawai'i; married and lived in California; then went back to Hawai'i to finish college. Now she lives in California again raising babies, although she aspires to go to graduate school, perhaps in Utah, and then go back to Tonga to live and to serve her people. She has relatives and friends in all those places. She is regularly in contact with them and they with her. All those places are part of one interconnected field of human experience.[38]

Part of what keeps that field connected is a yearning for the home islands.[39] Tupou speaks of Tonga in lyrical, almost mystical terms, as the ground of her identity, even though she has spent only a small number of years actually living in the islands:

> When I speak of Tonga,
> I speak of Me.
> A person made up of multiple identities
> Through my veins flow the blood of various cultures
> But I only identify myself as one from Tonga.
> There, my heart will always stay true,
> For Tonga is my home;
> My island and My taboo.[40]

It is similar for Hawaiians, a people forced out of the islands in large numbers by economic and cultural pressures at home. Kehaulani Kauanui writes of off-island Hawaiians building community in the diaspora, creating political formations that intersect with and support the sovereignty movement at home.[41] They create cultural formations and networks as well. Legendary Israel Kamakawiwo'ole sings to exiled Hawaiians:

> Lover of mine, over the sea.
> Deep blue ocean, waves in motion.
> Where have you gone?
> I look to the sea.
> Some day you come home to me.[42]

Amy Ku'uleialoha Stillman, living in Michigan, writes of hula and mele that are performed in California and bring together hundreds of Hawaiians abroad.[43]

Culture and politics have gone high tech. A host of websites keep diasporic Hawaiians in touch with news of home (and of the episodically victorious Rainbow Warriors), allow them to hear Hawaiian music twenty-four hours a day via computer, buy crackseed, and share perspectives and programs for the independent future of the sovereign Hawaiian nation. Diasporic Samoan youths send tapes, videos, and CDs of cutting-edge hip-hop music from Carson, California, to Honolulu, to Apia, Samoa, and on to Auckland, Sydney, and other points of the diaspora.[44]

One of the objections by Sau-ling Wong and others to the diasporic model is the assertion that most of the people who advocated a diasporic model were themselves members of elites, and that their interpretive schema privileged elite concerns. While that may be true in the main, it does not seem to be true for Pacific Islander Americans. For reasons outlined above, Pacific Islanders are indubitably diasporic, yet most are middle or working class.

If there is a weakness to the use of the diasporic model for Pacific Islanders, it regards the second generation. What will happen to Tupou's children and their children? The vast bulk of the Pacific Islander population that lives outside the Pacific has done so for only about a generation and a half. As the second generation comes of age, it is entirely possible that the island-based, national diasporic formations will not serve as well as they do now.

That is where the panethnicity model comes in. A new identity seems to be on the cusp of being formed in the United States: not Tongan, not Chamorro, not Hawaiian, but Pacific Islander American. In May 2000 the first National Pacific Islander American Conference was held at Brigham Young University-Hawai'i. It may be that such a panethnic institutional formation is a harbinger of a new direction for the peoples of the Pacific Islander diaspora: a common identity as people from the Pacific living in the United States. As with Latinos and Asians, I would not expect the pan-Pacific Islander American ethnic formation to be the only, nor necessarily even the main identity, that an individual holds. For at least a couple of generations, people whose parents were Tongan immigrants may see themselves as two things at once: Tongan Americans and Pacific Islander Americans. But as time goes on that second, panethnic identity is likely to become ever more important.

Cluny Macpherson and Richard Bedford see just such panethnic formation happening among the children of Pacific Islander migrants to Aotearoa/New Zealand. They point to

the emergence of "Pacific" or "PI" world-views and practices. Thus, for instance, to organise a Pacific cricket tournament a group of people from different sub-groups came together to form a common body of rules for playing "Pacific cricket." The result is a game which is not Samoan, or

Table I.1   Pacific Islander Population of Selected Countries

Countries of the Diaspora

Australia	30,000
New Zealand	531,000
United States	365,000

Pacific Island Countries

American Samoa	40,000	Niue	2,500
Cook Islands	17,000	Norfolk Island	2,000
Easter Island	2,000	Northern Mariana Is.	19,000
Fiji	369,000	Pacific Is. Trust Terr.	13,000
French Polynesia	203,000	Papua New Guinea	4,112,000
Guam	34,000	Solomon Islands	340,000
Irian Jaya	1,174,000	Tokelau	2,000
Kiribati	71,000	Tonga	98,000
Marshall Islands	34,000	Tuvalu	9,000
Micronesia, Fed. St.	88,000	Vanuatu	170,000
Nauru	9,000	Wallis and Futuna	12,000
New Caledonia	161,000	Western Samoa	177,000

Source: Fiji, Bureau of Statistics, *Report on Fiji Population Census, 1986. Population Projections for Years 1986 to 2011* (Suva, Fiji: Bureau of Statistics, 1989), 1; Guam, Bureau of Labor Statistics, *Ethnicity Statistics, Guam, 1988* (Guam: Department of Labor, 1988), 1; Robert C. Kiste, "Pacific Islands," *World Book Encyclopedia* (Chicago: World Book, 1991), 15.8; David Pearson, *A Dream Deferred: The Origins of Ethnic Conflict in New Zealand* (Wellington, N.Z.: Allen and Unwin, 1990), 3; United Nations Economic and Social Commission for Asia and the Pacific, *Population of Australia*, Country Monograph Series No. 9 (New York: United Nations, 1982), I.117; U.S. Bureau of the Census, *1990 Census of Population and Housing. Summary Tape File 1C* (CD-ROM), Item: "Detailed Race."

Niuean, or Cook Island but "Pacific." "PI" identities are expressed in new syncretic musics as for instance in the music of Te Vaka, in performance art as for instance in the work of Pacific Underground, in patois and language registers which mark a commitment to belonging, in new clothing and building design.[45]

Will such blending happen among Pacific Islanders in the United States? It is more than possible; it is probable.

It is not likely that Pacific Islander Americans will be absorbed into some other, larger minority collectivity. Since the 1970s the U.S. Census

Table I.2 Pacific Islander Populations in the United States and by Selected States, 1990

Group	Number	Percent	Hawaiʻi	Calif.	Wash.	Texas	Utah	Others
Total	365,024	100.0	44.5	30.3	4.1	2.1	2.1	17.0
Hawaiian	211,014	100.0	65.8	16.3	2.6	1.4	0.7	13.3
Samoan	62,964	100.0	23.9	50.7	6.6	1.5	2.5	14.9
Guamanian	49,345	100.0	4.3	50.8	7.7	4.5	0.3	32.5
Tongan	17,606	100.0	17.5	45.0	2.5	3.6	22.2	9.2
Fijian	7,036	100.0	3.7	81.6	4.2	0.8	0.7	9.0
Palauan	1,439	100.0	24.9	27.6	7.9	5.1	0.3	34.3
Others	15,620	100.0	17.1	32.8	5.5	4.3	3.8	36.5

Source: Herbert Barringer, Robert W. Gardner, and Michael J. Levin, *Asians and Pacific Islanders in the United States* (New York: Russell Sage Foundation, 1993), 275.

has tried to lump Pacific Islanders into the Asian American panethnic group. While Asian American social service agencies and scholarly groups have not been unwelcoming, Asian and Pacific Islanders have so little in common culturally and experientially that the lumping has never taken hold. Throughout the 1990s, Pacific Islander American scholars attended and made presentations at the annual meetings of the Association for Asian American Studies, but it was always with a bit of unease, as if they were guests, not full participants. For the 2000 count, the Census Bureau gave up and recorded Pacific Islanders as a separate panethnic group. Other groups such as Chicanos and Blacks seem even less likely to have a place for Pacific Islanders, no matter that they occupy similar class positions and are neighbors in several western U.S. cities such as Inglewood and Carson, California.[46]

The immigrant assimilation model would expect Pacific Island peoples in time to lose a separate identity entirely, and simply to be absorbed into the amorphous American mass. That may be the fate of some individuals. But it is our guess that, as with Native Americans, Asians, Latinos, and Blacks, a separate Pacific Islander panethnic group identity is likely to last for a very long time.

Perhaps the best thing we can do is to hold these three models in tension, for each illuminates certain aspects of the experiences of Pacific Island peoples in the United States. The transnational diasporic model works well at helping us conceive of and understand the experiences of the immigrant generation. The assimilation model illuminates the experiences of many individual immigrants. The panethnicity model shows us what may be forming as the second generation comes of age. To understand as best we can what is happening in the group lives of Pacific Islander Americans, all three ways of perceiving immigrant experiences are important. As with the rabbit, the man, and the woman in the moon, seeing all three at once is no easy task.

PROVENANCE AND PURPOSE OF THIS BOOK

Pacific Diaspora is the third volume produced by the Pacific Islander Americans Research Project (PIARP).[47] The goals of PIARP are to advance the scholarly understanding of Pacific Island peoples in the United States and to prepare Pacific Islander American students for graduate schools and careers in the social sciences. It was founded in 1991 at Brigham Young University-Hawai'i, and has continued since 1997 in two homes: BYU-Hawai'i and the University of California, Santa Barbara, benefiting from the sponsorship of those two institutions and of the Institute for Polynesian Studies. The editors are grateful to PIARP and the sponsoring

institutions for their support. We are also grateful for the help and
encouragement of several members of PIARP—Blossom Fonoimoana,
David Hall, Emma Hoskin, Dorri Nautu, Alexis Siteine, and John
Westerlund—whose involvement in earlier PIARP projects helped prepare the ground for this book. We wish to thank Amy Varbel for help with
typing, and William Kauaiwiulaokalani Wallace III and Jon Tikivanotau
Jonassen for patient teaching. We are grateful to Masako Ikeda and the
staff of the University of Hawai'i Press for a professional job of publishing. Finally, we also owe thanks to two editors at other houses, Sharon
Yamamoto of the East-West Center Press and Rosalie Robertson of
AltaMira Press, who believed in the project and helped it on its way.

This book is intended to be read as an introduction to historical and
social scientific knowledge about Pacific Island peoples in the United
States, and about parallel experiences elsewhere in the Pacific. We hope it
will be used in courses on American ethnic studies, as well as in history,
sociology, and anthropology courses on the Pacific Islands, and that it
may find a general audience among people interested in the Pacific. This
is a hybrid volume. Most of the selections are sharply edited versions of
previously published articles that have proved useful to the editors in
teaching university students about Pacific Islander Americans. Some, the
contributions written by Melani Anae, Vicente Diaz, Karina Kahananui
Green, Joanne Rondilla, Debbie Hippolite Wright, Davianna Pomaika'i
McGregor, and 'Inoke and Lupe Funaki, are published here for the first
time.

The reader will quickly grasp that there is a great deal more information here on certain groups than on others. We present more material on
Hawaiians than on Samoans, more on Samoans than on Chamorros or
Tongans, and more on those groups than on Tahitians, I-Kiribati, Maori,
Fijians, Palauans, Rotumans, or any other island people. Alas, in these
matters we are prisoners of the state of scholarship. The distribution of
scholarly attention reflects several factors: the relative sizes of the various
island populations in the United States; the length and intricacy of the
relationships between the United States and the respective island countries of origin; the research interests of generations of scholars; and the
priorities of the agencies that have funded such research. We have tried
to select articles representing the experiences of as wide a variety of
Pacific Island peoples as possible, consistent with the themes we wish to
address and our determination to include only items of quality and accuracy.

The themes of the chapters that follow are similarly shaped in part by
the state of scholarship. There is a modest quantity of good-quality published scholarship on identity issues, Hawaiian nationalism, and the emi-

gration experience. Scholarly treatments of cultural transformations, gender and sexuality, and some social problems are extant in small quantities and of uneven quality.[48] This volume does not treat literary or artistic issues, although there is a significant volume of work on those themes. Other topics that we might have wished to include here, such as education and economic issues, have so far not attracted the kind of excellent, brief, well-focused study that we sought in assembling this volume.

Another issue has guided our choices of which pieces to include in this book. We have tried to make sure that the voices of Pacific Islanders and Pacific Islander Americans are well represented here. Some excellent scholarly collections on the Pacific contain almost no writing by the people they study.[49] But we believe that it is important that Pacific people not be rendered silent. Where native scholars address an issue, we have tried to include them. When we have chosen to reproduce the writings of non-islander scholars, we have looked for those who are sensitive to islanders' points of view and who let the reader hear islanders' voices.

We challenge the current generation of students who may read this book to become scholars and investigate all those issues and people groups that are incompletely explored by the essays in this collection. We look forward to the day when the study of Pacific Island peoples in the diaspora, including the United States, is brimming over with excellent studies that carry on and expand the work begun by this book.

NOTES

[1] Faye Untalan Munoz, "Pacific Islanders: A Perplexed, Neglected Minority," *Church and Society* (January-February 1974): 15–23.

[2] For summaries of the first encounters between peoples of the Pacific and Europeans, see, for example, I. C. Campbell, *A History of the Pacific Islands* (Berkeley: University of California Press, 1989); K. R. Howe, *Where the Waves Fall: A New South Sea Islands History from First Settlement to Colonial Rule* (Honolulu: University of Hawai'i Press, 1984); Donald Denoon, et al., eds., *The Cambridge History of the Pacific Islanders* (Cambridge: Cambridge University Press, 1997).

[3] This paragraph and the four that follow, as well as the table of Pacific Islander populations, are taken with some modifications from Paul R. Spickard, et al., comp., *Pacific Islander Americans: An Annotated Bibliography in the Social Sciences* (La'ie, Hawai'i: Institute for Polynesian Studies, 1995), vi–viii.

[4] This theme of one-way migration from bad to good, putting off the old and taking on the new, also is found in the narratives of migration in certain other societies, notably Australia. See, for example, Brian Murphy, *The Other Australia: Experiences of Migration* (Melbourne: Cambridge University Press, 1993); Ronald Taft, *From Stranger to Citizen* (London: Tavistock, 1966); Janis Wilton and Richard

Bosworth, *Old Worlds and New Australia* (Ringwood, Victoria, Australia: Penguin, 1984); Gary P. Freeman and James Jupp, eds., *Nations of Immigrants: Australia, the United States, and International Migration* (Melbourne: Oxford, 1992).

[5] Oscar Handlin, *The Uprooted*, 2nd ed. (Boston: Little Brown, 1973).

[6] John Bodnar, *The Transplanted* (Bloomington: Indiana University Press, 1985).

[7] David M. Brownstone, Irene M. Franck, and Douglass L. Brownstone, *Island of Hope, Island of Tears* (New York: Penguin, 1986), 1, 34, 103, 147.

[8] See Milton M. Gordon, *Assimilation in American Life* (New York: Oxford, 1964).

[9] See Richard Alba, *Italian Americans: Into the Twilight of Ethnicity?* (Englewood Cliffs, N.J.: Prentice-Hall, 1984).

[10] Theodore Saloutos, *They Remember America: The Story of the Repatriated Greek-Americans* (Berkeley: University of California Press, 1956).

[11] Paul Spickard, "Twice Immigrants: Kibei in America and Japan and America, 1910–1950" (paper presented to Japanese American Experience conference, Willamette University, Salem, Oregon, September 18, 1998).

[12] Paul Spickard, *Japanese Americans: The Formation and Transformations of an Ethnic Group* (New York: Twayne, 1996), esp. Chapter Two.

[13] Lucie Cheng and Edna Bonacich, eds., *Labor Immigration Under Capitalism* (Berkeley: University of California Press, 1984); Immanuel Wallerstein, *The Modern World-System*, 3 vols. (New York: Academic Press, 1974–89); L. S. Stavrianos, *Global Rift* (New York: Morrow, 1981).

[14] I understand that such a book is in preparation: *The Japanese Diaspora*, by Michael Weiner, Roger Daniels, and Hiroshi Komai (University of Washington Press, under contract).

[15] Parts of this paragraph are drawn from Paul Spickard, "Christians in a Multicultural America," *Christian Scholar's Review* 24.4 (1996): 479.

[16] James Clifford, "Diasporas," *Cultural Anthropology* 9, no. 3 (1994): 303.

[17] Roger Rouse, "Mexican Migration and the Social Space of Postmodernism," *Diaspora* 1, no.1 (1991): 13.

[18] Xiaojian Zhao, *Remaking Chinese America: Immigration, Family, and Community, 1940–1965* (New Brunswick, N.J.: Rutgers University Press, 2002). The literature on diasporas is growing rapidly. See, for example, Vijay Mishra, "The Diasporic Imaginary: Theorizing the Indian Diaspora," *Textual Practice* 10, no. 3 (1996): 421–447; Robin Cohen, *Global Diasporas: An Introduction* (Seattle: University of Washington Press, 1997); Gérard Chaliand and Jean-Pierre Rageau, *The Penguin Atlas of Diasporas* (New York: Penguin, 1997); Nicholas Van Hear, *New Diasporas: The Mass Exodus, Dispersal, and Regrouping of Migrant Communities* (Seattle: University of Washington Press, 1998); Darshan Singh Tatla, *The Sikh Diaspora* (Seattle: University of Washington Press, 1999).

[19] Sau-ling C. Wong, "Denationalization Reconsidered: Asian American Cultural Criticism at a Theoretical Crossroads," *Amerasia Journal* 21, no. 1 and 2 (1995): 1–27.

[20] Lisa Lowe, "Heterogeneity, Hybridity, Multiplicity: Marking Asian American Differences," *Diaspora* 1, no. 1 (1991): 24–44.

[21] Wong, "Denationalization Reconsidered," 14–15.

[22] Private communication with the author, anonymity requested. I wish it to be clear that the person who said this is not Sau-ling Wong.

[23] Cf. this excerpt from a *National Geographic* cover spread on "Global Culture": "Sophisticated Ladies. They're well-off, well educated, widely traveled, fluent in several languages. Nakshatra Reddy is a biochemist, married to a prosperous businessman in Mumbai (formerly Bombay). Her daughter Meghana (in a PVC catsuit of her own design) is a model and former host on the music video channel VTV. Another daughter models full-time, and a third works for Swatch, the trendy Swiss watchmaker. They are elites, and the global marketplace for goods, information, and style is their corner store" (*National Geographic* [August 1999], 10–11). There may be an ethnic tinge to the division, as well, for many of the most prominent advocates of diasporic views are South Asians, a relatively well-off group in America on the whole, and a latecomer to ethnic studies.

[24] Paul Mecheril and Thomas Teo, *Andere Deutsche* (Berlin: Dietz Verlag, 1994).

[25] Yen Le Espiritu, *Asian American Panethnicity* (Philadelphia: Temple University Press, 1992). For a theoretical view of this and related processes, see Paul Spickard and W. Jeffrey Burroughs, "We Are a People," in *We Are a People: Narrative and Multiplicity in Constructing Ethnic Identity*, ed. Spickard and Burroughs (Philadelphia: Temple University Press, 2000), 1–19. On White racial formation, see Matthew Frye Jacobson, *Whiteness of a Different Color: European Immigrants and the Alchemy of Race* (Cambridge, Mass.: Harvard University Press, 1998); and Paul Spickard n.d., "What's Critical About White Studies?" in *Uncompleted Independence: The Creation and Revision of American Racial Thinking*, ed. Spickard and G. Reginald Daniel (Notre Dame, Ind.: University of Notre Dame Press, in press).

[26] Espiritu, *Asian American Panethnicity*; William Wei, *The Asian American Movement* (Philadelphia: Temple University Press, 1993).

[27] Gary B. Nash, *Red, White, and Black in Colonial America* (Englewood Cliffs, N.J.: Prentice-Hall, 1968); Stephen Cornell, *The Return of the Native: American Indian Political Resurgence* (New York: Oxford, 1988).

[28] Jean Barman, "New Land, New Lives: Hawaiian Settlement in British Columbia," *Hawaiian Journal of History* 29 (1995): 1–32; Janice K. Duncan, "Kanaka World Travelers and Fur Company Employees, 1785–1860," *Hawaiian Journal of History* 7 (1973): 93–111; Tom Koppel, *Kanaka: The Untold Story of Hawaiian Pioneers in British Columbia and the Pacific Northwest* (Vancouver: Whitecap Books, 1995).

[29] Sandra Rennie, "Contract Labor Under a Protector: The Gilbertese Laborers and Hiram Bingham, Jr., 1878–1903," *Pacific Studies* 11, no. 1 (1987): 106; J. A. Bennett, "Immigration, 'Blackbirding,' Labor Recruiting? The Hawaiian Experience, 1855–1871," *Journal of Pacific History* 11 (1976): 3–26.

[30] Edward Wybergh Docker, *The Blackbirders: The Recruiting of South Seas Labour for Queensland, 1863–1907* (London: Angus and Robertson, 1970). See also, for comparative developments within the Pacific, Leonard Mason and Pat Hereniko, eds., *In Search of a Home* (Suva, Fiji: Institute of Pacific Studies, University of the South Pacific, 1987).

[31] Campbell, *A History of the Pacific Islands*, 111.

[32] Mark R. Peattie, *Nanyo: The Rise and Fall of the Japanese in Micronesia* (Honolulu: University of Hawai'i Press, 1988); Leland Bettis, "Colonial Immigration on Guam; Displacement of the Chamorro People Under U.S. Governance," in *A World Perspective on Pacific Islander Migration*, ed. Grant McCall and John Connell (Kensington, NSW: Centre for South Pacific Studies, University of New South Wales, 1993), 265–296; Eleanor C. Nordyke, *The Peopling of Hawai'i*, 2nd ed. (Honolulu: University of Hawai'i Press, 1989).

[33] Mason and Hereniko, *In Search of a Home*; Bintonga Even Tonganibeia, "Kiribati, Development and Internal Migration," in *World Perspective on Pacific Islander Migration*, ed. McCall and Connell, 297–304; P. F. Kluge, *The Edge of Paradise: America in Micronesia* (Honolulu: University of Hawai'i Press, 1991).

[34] Morgan Tuimaleali'ifano, *Samoans in Fiji* (Suva, Fiji: Institute of Pacific Studies, University of the South Pacific, 1990); Hans Dagmar, "Banabans in Fiji: Ethnicity, Change, and Development," in *Ethnicity and Nation-building in the Pacific*, ed. Michael C. Howard (Tokyo: United Nations University, 1989): 198–217; Mason and Hereniko, *In Search of a Home*.

[35] A good place to start for Aotearoa/New Zealand is *Nga Take: Ethnic Relations and Racism in Aotearoa/New Zealand*, ed. Paul Spoonley, David Pearson, and Cluny Macpherson (Palmerston North, N.Z.: Dunmore, 1991).

[36] Helen Morton, "Creating Their Own Culture: Diasporic Tongans," *Contemporary Pacific* 10, no. 1 (1998): 1–30; Richard P. C. Brown, "Do Migrants' Remittances Decline over Time? Evidence from Tongans and Western Samoans in Australia," *Contemporary Pacific* 10, no. 1 (1998): 107–151.

[37] Grant McCall, *Rapanui: Tradition and Survival on Easter Island*, 2nd ed. (Honolulu: University of Hawai'i Press, 1994): 140–160.

[38] She tells her story in Chapter 1 of this volume. See also Albert Wendt, *Sons for the Return Home* (Honolulu: University of Hawai'i Press, 1973); Small, *Voyages*; Dennis A. Ahlburg, "Return Migration from the United States to American Samoa," *Pacific Studies* 17, no. 2 (1994): 71–84; Mason and Hereniko, *In Search of a Home*.

[39] Nancy J. Pollock, "Where Home Is" (paper presented to Out of Oceania conference, Honolulu, Hawai'i, October 20, 1999). Courtesy of the author.

[40] Courtesy of the poet.

[41] J. Kehaulani Kauanui, "Off-Island Hawaiians 'Making' Ourselves at 'Home': A [Gendered] Contradiction in Terms?" *Women's Studies International Forum* 21 no. 6 (1998): 681–693.

[42] Israel Kamakawiwo'ole, "Lover of Mine," on *Iz in Concert* (©1998 by Big Boy Record Company, Honolulu).

[43] Amy Ku'uleialoha Stillman, "Hawaiian Hula Competitions: Event, Repertoire, Performance, Tradition," *Journal of American Folklore* 109 (1996): 357–380.

[44] Examples of Web sites: Hawai'i: Independent and Sovereign (http://www.hawaii-nation.org/index.html); Honolulu Star-Bulletin (http://www.starbulletin.com); University of Hawai'i Athletic Dept. (http://www.uhathletics.hawaii.edu); Na Mele Hula 'Ohana (http://www.namele.org/); Aloha World (http://www.alohaworld.com); Susan J's Hawaiian Music (http://nahenahe.net/susanmusic). The rapid international flow of Samoan hip-hop is described by April Henderson in "Gifted Flows" (paper presented to the Out of Oceania conference, Honolulu, Hawai'i, October 22, 1999).

[45] Cluny Macpherson and Richard D. Bedford, "The Structural Roots of Transformation of Pacific Identity in Aotearoa" (paper presented to the Out of Oceania conference, Honolulu, Hawai'i, October 20, 1999). Courtesy of the author.

[46] For a fuller discussion of the place of Pacific Islanders relative to Asian Americans, see Debbie Hippolite Wright and Paul Spickard, "Pacific Islander Americans and Asian American Identity," in *Intersections and Divergences: Contemporary Asian Pacific American Communities*, ed. Linda Trinh Vo and Enrique Bonus (Philadelphia: Temple University Press, in press).

[47] The others are "Pacific Island Peoples in Hawai'i," a special issue of the journal *Social Process in Hawai'i*, 36 (1994), ed. Paul Spickard, and *Pacific Islander Americans: An Annotated Bibliography in the Social Sciences* (La'ie, Hawai'i: Institute for Polynesian Studies, 1995), by Paul R. Spickard, Debbie Hippolite Wright, Blossom Fonoimoana, Karina Kahananui Green, David Hall, Dorri Nautu, Tupou Hopoate Pau'u, and John Westerlund.

[48] Spickard, et al., *Pacific Islander Americans.*

[49] E.g., Jocelyn Linnekin and Lin Poyer, eds., *Cultural Identity and Ethnicity in the Pacific* (Honolulu: University of Hawai'i Press, 1990).

PART ONE
Identity

"Who am I?" What more basic human question is there than this? Part One takes the reader into the identity dilemmas of Pacific Island peoples in the United States and in other parts of the diaspora from three different angles. In "My Life in Four Cultures," Tupou Hopoate Pau'u tells the story of her life, growing from a child to a young adult in Tonga, New Zealand, Australia, and the United States. This deeply moving personal account raises the question of diaspora that is in the title of this book. Tupou did not "immigrate," leaving Tonga behind and coming on a straight line to the United States, there to assimilate into American life. Rather, she is part of a diaspora. "Diaspora" means "scattering," and that is the pattern of most Pacific Islander migration. Pacific peoples have long been on the move, not from Point A to Point B only, but on to Point C and Point D, then back to Point B, and on again. Tupou went first to Aotearoa/New Zealand, then to Australia, then back to Tonga, back to Australia again, to Hawai'i, back to Tonga, back to Hawai'i, and to the continental United States. Each of those places is part of her story, not just in her past but in her present. Tupou is an American, and an Aussie, and she is most profoundly a Tongan.

Pacific Island peoples, in the islands and in the United States, are a mixed multitude. There are Samoans in Fiji, Tongans in Aotearoa, I-Kiribati in Chuk, Chamorros in California. But they are mixed further in the sense that many islanders have multiple ancestries. In "Pacific Islander Americans and Multiethnicity: A Vision of America's Future?" Paul Spickard explores the ways that Pacific Island people in the United States have handled their ethnic multiplicity. He examines some theoretical concepts regarding ethnicity, the distinctive features of Pacific Islander American multiethnicity, and the ways that people ground their identity in the midst of multiple options. Along the way he tells the stories of many Pacific Islander American individuals.

Joanne Rondilla presents a thought-provoking issue as she poses "The Filipino Question in Asia and the Pacific: Rethinking Regional Origins in Diaspora." The Philippines has long been viewed as part of Asia, and Filipinos in the United States have been called Asian Americans. Yet Asia is an idea created by Europeans. It has been used to refer to every region and people from the Bosporous to Honolulu. As such, it is so broad as to have little internal meaning. It simply refers to the people who live east of Europe. Rondilla asks, in what sense are Filipinos truly Asians, and in what sense may it be more fruitful to think of them as belonging to the Pacific Islands? She suggests that, both in their home islands and abroad in the United States, Filipinos have as much or more in common with other island peoples as they do with Asians.

CHAPTER 1

My Life in Four Cultures

Tupou Hopoate Pau'u

My name is Tupou Hopoate Pau'u and I am Tongan. However, I have lived in a lot of places where cultural differences and traditions have overshadowed my own Tongan identity. I have lived in New Zealand, Australia, Tonga, and now the United States.

I am the oldest of eight children. I was born and raised in Tonga until the age of four years, in my mother's village of Tokomolo. Religious obligations caused my family's migration to New Zealand just after my fourth birthday. My family received permanent residency in New Zealand not long after our migration there, and it became my home for the next seven years. We spoke only the Tongan language at home, so when I started primary school at Te Papa Elementary, my English vocabulary consisted of only four words: "yes," "no," "hello," and "goodbye." I still remember distinctly my first day at school and the humiliation that awaited me on that day. For the first time in my life I experienced feelings of rejection, of being afraid of the White man, and insecurity about my new surroundings, culture, place of residence, and the people that inhabited my new world.

It was lunch time, and my teacher asked a White girl named Kerry to befriend me. Kerry invited me to eat lunch with her and with her friends, who were also White. I unwrapped my lunch slowly. From the corner of my eye, I could see the people surrounding me, smiling, and pointing in my direction. I did not have to speak English to know that behind the smiles that they were trying to hold back were fits of laughter directed towards me. I felt my face growing hot and I wanted to, but could not, cry. Suddenly, there came the most deafening laughter. I looked toward the direction the laughter was coming from, only to meet the mocking glares of strange faces. There above the stares, pointing down at me, stood a boy who repeatedly said, "She wraps her lunch with newspaper," in between fits of laughter. I had just turned five years old; this was my first day at this school and I wanted to die. More so, I just wanted to get

---

This essay was previously published in *Social Process in Hawai'i* 36 (1994): 5–15.

up and beat this dude up. Realizing that my wrapping was different from everyone else's because everybody kept pointing at it, I did not have to speak English to understand what they were making fun of. Frustration at the growing crowd and the humiliating circumstances formed tears that rolled endlessly upon my cheeks. I got up and ran all the way home. The emotions of this experience were new to me. It made me realize that I was different. It was not a difference that came with skin color or physical appearances, because most of the students at this school were Polynesians (although it was a White group that humiliated me). It was a difference in lifestyle and accepted norms. Because of these differences, I felt frustration about many things: wrapping my lunch in Glad Wrap or foil rather than with newspaper; wishing that I had blonde hair and blue eyes; despising the thickness of my own hair and its curliness; being unable to wear the latest "in" clothing that the other students were wearing. Actually, in the beginning, I really did not have a sense of style. I did not know that some clothes were more accepted than others. To me, everything I had on, especially my new dresses and bell bottom pants from the second-hand and Salvation Army stores, were the best there was. I did not wear any of these out-of-style fashions back in Tonga, so to me this was "in."

However, experience proved me wrong again. During a class picture-taking session in my third-grade year I realized again I was different. I still remember the picture clearly. First of all, what I wore caused me to be isolated from the other students. I had worn an ankle-length checkered black and white dress that was very old fashioned. Not only that, I had let my hair out. It was so thick that in the picture it covered the faces of the two people at both of my sides. My teacher, looking at the picture, commented while pointing at me, "Who's this African?" The class laughed and I felt so hurt. I hated myself. I felt ugly; I hated my hair; I hated who I was because I was different and as much as I tried to be accepted into this society, I found myself always at a dead end. I tried hard to be accepted, but my rewards were mockery, laughter, and tears.

My New Zealand upbringing let me know that I was different. I could not understand why it was so hard for them to accept me. Because of this, I had a harder time accepting myself. I believed that because I was a Tongan, I was no good and had no value to my society. This became, without my awareness, the beginning of many years of my search for an identity.

After seven years in New Zealand, my family migrated again, this time to Australia. We moved for economic reasons, as well as to join members of our extended family. I was almost eleven during this migration and my English vocabulary had extended beyond four words. In fact, by now it was my Tongan vocabulary that amounted to only about four words. I could understand what was being spoken to me in Tongan, but I could barely speak it. As a Tongan in Australia, I found myself being woven into the fabric of British colonization. Experiences in Australia left me antagonistic toward my own culture, people, and heritage. I came to reject any parts of me that could be identified as Tongan while praising the White people's world, for their educational systems that I learned in and for their foods that tasted better (so I thought) than the taro and *lu pulu* served at home by my Mum. I found myself always desiring McDonald's or Kentucky Fried Chicken.

I struggled for racial equality in the only society that I knew, but I met many setbacks and frustrations. For example, to feed a growing family, my parents entered the work force as unskilled laborers. This meant that, to make ends meet, we as children were expected to help out by working too. These times made me reject my culture more. I felt that maybe if I had not been born a Tongan I would not have to struggle and work. Maybe if I had been born White, my parents could be lawyers or doctors who could provide more for our family's needs, so I would not have to go to work with them. But that was not my lot in life.

My Mum worked three jobs at that time. I remember after school we were expected to help her with one of her jobs, where she was a janitor at a primary school near our home. We were expected to come straight home after school, change, and go over to help her. We dusted, we swept, we cleaned toilets and mopped floors, while children from our neighborhoods stared with mockery. I felt ashamed at doing this. Although other children did work doing paper runs, yard work, and other jobs, in my eyes I was the only one working. Only my family worked hard, because we were not White and because we were Tongan. These experiences made me really unhappy. I kept thinking, "Why didn't my parents just stay back in Tonga and raise us there so that we wouldn't have to go through all this unhappiness?" However, as a solution to our dilemma, my mother would always give us sermons about studying hard in school so that we would not have to go through the hurts and pains that she endured. This to me was not a reality that could be easily reached. I did not like this type of talk. I was anxious for an immediate solution, and an educational career was not the solution to my sorrows in Australia.

My experiences with work in this manner made me feel inferior toward all White people. I viewed them with such esteem and as having such great status that I could not begin to compare myself to them and I felt my inadequacy within their realm. This began a period of envy and admiration for the White people's world. At the same time I rejected my own culture the most, because I believed that everything would be better if I were not a Tongan, but rather an Australian, whether it be my clothing, my friends, the food that I ate, or the places that I went. I wanted so badly to be White. Yet all I needed to do every morning was to wake up and look into the mirror to realize that I was and will always be Tongan.

This fact was made real to me by a young man named Paul. I was ten years old. I remember how my sister Lisia and I endured a full year of racial comments by this person. Every day after school, we would pass him on our way home. From the other side of the street he would always say aloud, "You niggers go back to where you came from." This was ironic, for I was fairer then he. He was two years my senior, making him four years older than my sister. We both were hurt by his racial ignorance and abuse which left us many times crying upon each other's shoulders.

I began to think that no matter how hard I tried to fit into this society I would never be accepted. Whites, from my point of view at this time, were classified as autocratic rulers. I felt that to be accepted into their world, I had to submit to their tyranny and snobbery, that as a minority class I had to bribe them, flatter them, and court their favors. However, this thought was extremely distasteful for me and certainly I had no intention of trying to pacify this fool who had insulted me with such names. "I am not a nigger. I am a Polynesian," was my silent and unheard cry. I felt really insulted by the word "nigger." Yet, these experiences did not make me want to become any more Tongan. I still rejected my culture, because it was my Tonganness that had given me all these hard times.

The conclusion that my sister and I came to was that this young man needed a punch in the nose, which is exactly what we gave him. Enduring his comments no longer, we just charged at him one afternoon after school and my sister gave him a bloody nose. We never did hear another mean comment from him again, let alone see him, because from that day forward he decided to take another route home. The sad thing about this whole experience was that we had to resolve the problem through violence.

This encounter had me questioning myself and the fact that I was Tongan. I was not a "Blackie," as some kids called me, neither was I a "nigger," but yes, my skin color was different. I could not understand why the Whites would not accept my color, because I had accepted their Whiteness. These experiences made me feel that being a "non-White" made me less of a human being.

In searching for comfort amidst my conflicts, I stopped attending any Tongan functions. I made White friends and associated with them in a White social life. I became blood sisters with a White girl named Melinda Bentley. We became best friends and we did everything together. We had our birthday parties celebrated together, we ate together, we played together and would not go places without each other. Thus, I tried really hard to assimilate into the White man's world. Being with Melinda made me feel that I had accomplished this. Still, many times—especially at school—I knew I was different. When boys would come and talk to us, a majority of them would speak to me only because I was Melinda's friend. Other than that, they could not have cared less about who I was. I was also very shy amongst them, so that as soon as they started to talk or ask me questions, I would just become so silent and think of an excuse to leave them. I was lost. I didn't want to be a Tongan, I wanted to be a White girl, yet I could not act like a White girl in certain ways because my Tongan culture would not allow me. I did not realize that it was my Tongan upbringing at home that made me non-talkative to boys. I just thought I was shy.

Life did not get any easier. I had reached a stage where I really did not know who I was. I had lost my identity and I did not know where else to turn. However, my parents knew the hard times I was going through. They decided that I needed to go to Tonga. Here I was, at thirteen years old, rejecting everything about me that was Tongan, and they wanted to take me to Tonga? They had to be kidding. I rejected the proposal, but they were not kidding. I arrived in Tonga in December 1981.

My mother took me to Tonga and left me at a boarding school for one year. Whether they were inspired to make this decision on my behalf or not, I will always be grateful to them. My life was never to be the same after my one-year experience in Tonga.

I remember clearly the day my mother left me at the dorm. I clung to her like a little child, and all she did was release my hands from around her neck and tell me to learn the Tongan way and be humble. After that she turned and walked away. I was to not see her again until I returned home the following year. My dorm mother took me inside and showed me to my room. While walking through the hallway, I noticed all the girls were outside in the hallways studying. No study was allowed inside the rooms. We walked past this very dark girl and I knew she was not Tongan because she looked different (later I learned that she was from the Gilbert Islands). She was on her hands and knees, crawling around the floor—swatting flies, it seemed to me. I thought she was eating them, too. I got really scared seeing this, and was afraid for my own life, thinking that maybe they were cannibals. Later I was to learn that she was only killing mosquitoes. As I got to know her, I found her culture and people were the most humble and friendly of all in the dorms.

On March 3, 1982, Cyclone Isaac hit Tonga, destroying its many crops and homes, leaving a lot of my people homeless and hungry. Everybody came together throughout the whole island and helped each other out. As a matter of fact, I remember enjoying myself that day. Just before the cyclone hit Tongatapu, during the harsh winds and rain, I was running around outside with my Gilbert friends underneath the coconut trees collecting coconuts, watching carefully that coconuts would not fall on my head.

This experience made me realize the Tongan way: *Koe Tonga Mounga Ki He Loto.* Despite the destruction that this cyclone brought to Tonga, the only mountain a Tongan needed to claim was his heart. The cyclone had brought only hardship and destruction, but they were nothing because of the strength within the Tongan heart. Nothing was impossible. I watched and admired my people working together to build huts for families and working at each other's plantations in order to provide food. I saw how the young people never answered back to their elders and showed them respect. I witnessed how many families with barely sufficient food for their needs were willing to give it away to others who needed it more. I learned to have respect and reverence for the Sabbath Day because the Tongan Constitution requires keeping the Sabbath. I came to love our national anthem of *Koe 'Otua Mo Tonga Ko Hoku Tofi'a*—translated, this means "God and Tonga are My Inheritance." I was learning, I was accepting my culture, and I was loving myself.

I realized that, in Tonga, work was not to enslave a person, but to teach one responsibility. That was why my parents made us work when we were young children. In fact, I was not the only one working. Many of my peers in Tonga were working, too. This was evident in the dorm life that we lived.

Every Saturday was our working day. We rotated days of cleaning our own bathrooms and toilets. We weeded our own gardens, prepared our own foods, and washed our own dishes. This was not a paid job. We were expected to do this. Not only that, we had to go out into the plantations too, tending the crops and picking up coconuts. We were taught discipline and the rewards of hard work: food for our nourishment and a sense of self-satisfaction for a job well done. I remember laughing loudly during one study period—a violation of dorm rules. One of the prefects of the dorms put my name down with a couple of other friends on the toilet cleaning list. I did not feel humiliated. In fact I had so much fun cleaning those toilets with my friends that we decided to clean the bathroom, too. No one mocked us, because everybody had to do the job eventually, so I did not feel that I was being laughed at or put down. The self-rejection and hate for my culture were slowly vanishing and I actually found myself smiling.

When my year in Tonga was over, going home was so hard. I remember calling home to my parents and asking them to please keep me in

Tonga for one more year, but they could not. As I said my goodbyes on that day I felt like my heart was breaking. I knew I would miss my people and the feelings of security and self-confidence that I had felt amongst them. I had found an identity: I was a Tongan, and boy, was I proud! I finally found who I was in the culture of giving amongst my people. I knew the true meaning of *fetokoni'aki:* giving without expecting anything in return. I grew to respect the tales of the past and the traditions of my family. I had a great love for my extended family and felt humbled by their simple ways of living. Although it was only a Tongan hut that I was born in and lived in during my visits with my family, this was home. This was my inheritance. This was my *tofi'a.* I grew to understand the depth of the words, "There's no place like home." This was my home and it meant more than just a place to live. It meant that, when I finally took the time to look inwardly in the mirror at the image that was staring back at me, I saw somebody who was worthwhile. I saw a person with a culture, full of rich traditions and virtuous morals. I had found a genuine smile. I vowed to myself on my flight back to Australia to teach and educate all my friends and family about my Tonga, my home.

After arriving back in Australia, I started school again. Racial discrimination resumed, and it hurt me. However, it did not matter as much, because I knew that, back in Tonga, I had a culture and a people that accepted me and loved me for who I was. Upon enrolling in my classes, the Deputy Headmistress read my transcripts and registered me in the top science, math, and English classes for my year. In my math class, however, I just seemed to have a hard time with my teacher. She picked on me continuously, not only having me answer questions that she knew I would not know, but also always making sure to embarrass me in the process. I was expected to always call her "ma'am" every time I answered a question or asked for help (which I hardly did anyway). The girl whom I sat next to asked me one day why Mrs. Walton picked on me all the time. I just responded, "Because of my color," and left it at that. After a term with her, she recommended moving me to the intermediate class, because she said I could not cope with the work. In fact, it was not the work; it was the teacher that I could not cope with. Thinking about her today hurts me and still promulgates bitter feelings.

Experiences like this made me shrink from speaking out in my classes. I felt that if I were to express my feelings, I would be made a fool of and students would laugh at me. However, during my geography class one day, my teacher helped me speak up for once. It was a discussion about Third World countries. He mentioned that Tonga was a Third World country and looked in my direction as if challenging me to speak. There was a pause and I felt uncomfortable. I replied that, while Tonga may be

Third World in terms of economic and technological advancements, when it comes to culture and traditions, its morals and richness are incomparable. He sternly replied that those things were not important. I said they were, because if the class is only going to learn about the poverty of my country then they will never appreciate the values of my culture.

After my remarks, he sent me out of the classroom to stand in the hallway. This was a punishment for talking back to him. The smirks and smiles of my classmates reminded me of the experience with my newspaper-wrapped lunch. I turned to look at my classmates and then back at my teacher, and I remarked, "You're just prejudiced." Fire reddened his face as I slammed the door behind me. This time I was not crying, but rather very satisfied with myself. I felt triumph over myself in accepting my culture finally and fighting for my right of identity. Moments later he came out and gave me a sermon about manners, nothing I have cared to carry through with me into this life now. Seeing my stubbornness, he sent me down to the principal's office. Much to the teacher's surprise and mine, the principal understood the situation from my point of view, and allowed me to give a presentation on Tonga in each of the geography classes at my level.

Thus, my promise on the plane from Tonga was beginning to be fulfilled. Tonga was to be taught to a White man's society. It did not matter if my presentation was accepted or not. What mattered was that the gap of inequality was slowly being bridged between my culture as a Tongan and my lifestyle as an Australian. I learned a very important lesson from this: I realized that, as the Australian culture was rejecting me, I became a stronger person. The more they threw up walls against me because of my color and difference, the more I became a Tongan. I won in the end because I had the best of two worlds.

In 1989, I went to the United States to further my education. Brigham Young University-Hawaiʻi was a combination of both my Australian and my Tongan experience. It was an American school, but most of the students were Pacific Islanders from many different countries. However, association with my own people sometimes left me unhappy because often I would be labeled *taʻahine fie palangi*. I was often accused of wanting to be a White girl. If by any chance I did not go to one of our Tongan Club activities I would be frowned upon and teased. I would be called an *ulu pupula* person or pig head. The irritating thing was that I knew I could speak Tongan better than even most of these students who came here straight from Tonga. I participated in social events when I had the time; if I did not have the time, then I would not. When I introduced myself anywhere I would always say I was from Tonga. If anybody asked about my accent, I would softly say I was raised in Australia, "but I have a Tongan heart and I'm Tongan all over."

It was not until November 1990 that my grief finally came to an end and I was rightfully accepted as Tongan. I ran as a contestant for a scholarship pageant on campus. In introducing myself on the night of the competition, I said, "I am from Tonga, the land where time begins." I heard cheering and I hoped it was my Tongan friends. I won the title as Miss Na Hoa Pono for 1990-1991 that night, and it was a pretty exciting feeling. However, the real win came when I was finally fully accepted as a Tongan because I did something prestigious for my culture. My peers, when they spoke of me, would now say that I was a Tongan girl.

Yes, I have lived in a lot of places. Right now, if I were to go back in time and change any of my life's stories, the only things I would change would be my complaints and grumbles. Everything else I would keep, because all the hard times have made me who I am. I will graduate next year with a B.A. degree in history and a minor in speech communication, and I hope to go to law school. However, the only degree that counts right now in my life is the B.A. of identity that I have found for myself. I am a person, I am a human being, I am a very proud Tongan, and I am only grateful for a wonderful upbringing in all the cultures that have raised me. To all of these cultures, thank you. To my Tongan culture most of all, *Malo 'Aupito e fanau tama.*

CHAPTER 2

Pacific Islander Americans
and Multiethnicity:
A Vision of America's Future?

Paul Spickard

At a recent basketball game in a schoolyard in Kaneohe, Hawai'i, two players began to argue. As basketball players will, they started talking about each other's families. One, who prided himself on his pure Samoan ancestry, said, "You got a Hawaiian grandmother, a Pake [Chinese] grandfather. Your other grandfather's Portegee [Portuguese], and you mom's Filipino. You got Haole [White] brother-in-law and Korean cousins. Who da heck are you?" The person with the bouquet of ethnic possibilities smiled (his team was winning) and said, simply, "I all da kine [I'm all of those things]. Le's play." This article attempts to explain that interaction. Specifically, it seeks to understand how ethnicity works for Pacific Islander Americans, and what that might mean for other kinds of people.

ETHNICITY IN AMERICA

Throughout most of American history, the rhetoric of race and ethnicity presumed a hegemonic role for American identity. Until the last quarter century, nearly all analytical public discourse, scholarly and popular, pictured ethnicity as something primordial that people brought with them from some other place, which they then lost progressively as they lived in America for decades and generations. In this new country they became, as the ideas were enunciated in the generation of the American Revolution by Hector St. John de Crèvecouer: "The American, this new man, that strange mixture of blood, which you will find in no other coun-

---

This essay was previously published in *Social Forces* 73 (June 1995): 1365–1383.

try. He is an American who, leaving behind him all his ancient prejudices and manners, receives new ones. Here individuals are melted into a new race of men" ([1782] 1912, 64). These words, and the melting pot ideology to which they gave voice, have echoed throughout the history of Americans' thinking about ethnic matters. In the current generation, America has indeed finally become a place where people from all over the world mix and mate, but Crevecouer may not be quite right about the outcome of that mixing for ethnic identity.

In recent decades, another vision of a multicultural America has come to the front. People of color and others who were denied determinative roles in the former rhetoric of race and ethnicity have begun to describe a different pattern of understanding. They have prescribed an America of many more or less permanent cultural islands, to be honored and preserved in their diversity. African Americans, Chinese, Puerto Ricans, Anglos, and many others would all maintain separate identities— whether in harmony or in conflict—far into the future.

MULTIETHNICITY

Most people in fact are descended from multiple, not single ethnic sources. Most African Americans are in fact part European American and Native American, most Jews have some Gentile ancestry, most Scandinavian Americans have some German relatives, and so forth. But the dominant and subdominant paradigms treat ethnicity as if each person had only one ethnic identity. They say, along with census takers and school forms, "choose one box." Thus, a person of African, Native American, and European ancestry has long been regarded—and has regarded himself—as an African American. Even as he may have acknowledged privately that he was descended from multiple roots, nonetheless he identified with only one. Reginald Daniel (1992) refers to this as the "rule of hypodescent": the one-drop rule, whereby Whites and Blacks agree that one drop of Black blood makes one Black. The system was not so clear-cut for other groups; some measure of mixture was acknowledged in the cases of people whose ancestry came from several European sources, for instance. But even then, people tended to see themselves as predominantly one sort of person, ethnically speaking (Spickard 1989; Waters 1990).

In recent years, two things have happened that have caused this to begin to change. In the first place, for about two decades intermarriage across racial as well as religious and national lines has increased enormously. Almost no White American extended family exists today without at least one member who has married across what two generations ago would have been thought an unbridgeable gap. Anglo-American has married Irish, Lutheran has married Baptist; such marriages would have scandalized many families at mid-century, but they scarcely are noticed anymore (Alba and Golden 1986; Anderson 1970; Kalmijn 1991; Lieberson and Waters 1988). No one keeps precise, comprehensive, up-to-date figures on intermarriage. Recent surveys of marriage licenses have shown the rate of Black-White intermarriage more than doubling in the 1970s and 1980s, to nearly one out of twenty-five marriages involving one African American partner (Kalmijn 1993). Similar studies indicate intermarriage by every Asian American group is rapidly rising (Kitano et al. 1984). It has reached the point were even formerly endogamous groups like Japanese Americans and Jews now experience a 50 percent outmarriage rate (Kalmijn 1991; Spickard 1989). Precise, up-to-date intermarriage figures are not now available, in part because the 1990 census reports are coming out more slowly than in previous decades. But no one doubts that intermarriage is on the rise at a rapidly multiplying rate. Because of the increase in intermarriage, a larger number of mixed people has appeared than ever before. In the 1980 census and again in 1990, the fastest-growing ethnic category was "Other," and most such people were probably mixed (U.S. Bureau of the Census 1983, 22, 1992, 3). The cover of a recent special issue of *Time* magazine proclaimed mixed people to be "The New Face of America" (*Time* 1993).

The second thing that has happened to change the discourse of American ethnicity is that, in just the last few years, people of mixed ancestry have begun to claim both or all parts of their ancestry. They claim multiethnicity; they refuse to choose one box (Daniel 1992; Funderburg 1994; Hall 1992). This has gone so far as to result in the formation of organizations of multiethnic persons. Some of those organizations engage in serious lobbying for changes in the census (hence, school forms, etc.) to allow people to check more than one box (AMEA 1993; Multiracial Americans of Southern California 1993). The situation of Pacific Islander Americans can provide some clues to what may lie in store for other American ethnic groups in this ever-more mixed situation.

PACIFIC ISLANDER AMERICAN MULTIETHNICITY

The term "Pacific Islander Americans" is a bit problematic, for, like Asian Americans and Hispanic Americans, Pacific Islander Americans are not an ethnic group, but rather an artificial collection of groups. They appear as a subcategory of the human species in the United States census, on affirmative action forms, and the like, often mixed with Asian Americans, and paralleled by Native, African, Hispanic, and White Americans. Yet almost no person arises in the morning thinking of herself as a Pacific Islander American. Most think of themselves as Tongans (or Tongan Americans), Samoans, Fijians, and so on. A few would recognize the terms "Polynesian," "Melanesian," and "Micronesian" as somewhat larger categories which they have been told apply to them. But those are not indigenous categories, either. They are constructs of northwest European imaginations (Scarr 1994).[1]

Pacific Islanders historically have constructed their ethnic identities rather more complexly than many other peoples. Pacific Islanders have long had a greater consciousness than other American groups of being mixed peoples, of having multiple ethnic identities: Samoan and Tongan, Marquesan and Tahitian, Maori and European, and so forth. They seem more comfortable than other Americans with holding in tension two or more ethnic identities, with being deeply involved in more than one at the same time.[2]

Take the case of William Kauaiwiulaokalani Wallace. Bill is a Hawaiian rights activist and lawyer. When he speaks in public he begins by chanting his genealogy for five minutes and playing his nose flute and drum. As he grew up on the island of Moloka'i, his parents were Hawaiian and his first language was Hawaiian. He dug taro and talked story and knew himself to be completely Hawaiian.

Then at the age of ten or eleven Bill went to live with his grandmother in La'ie on the island of O'ahu. There he found out—much to his dismay, at first—that he was Samoan. He hung out with his Samoan cousins and their friends. He learned some Samoan words, ate Samoan food, and began to feel *fa'a samoa*—the Samoan way. So he was half Hawaiian and half Samoan. But then, on questioning his elders, he found that his Samoan side had relatives in Tonga. And he found that his Hawaiian family went back to Tahiti. So he was Hawaiian and Samoan and Tongan and Tahitian.

Then, as he emerged into adulthood, Bill married a Maori woman from New Zealand. In time, he visited her family and was accorded a position of honor. And he began to discover other pieces of himself. He worked for a couple of years in Samoa, and discovered that his Samoan side included a fair amount of British and some German ancestry, that some of his relatives were members of what some call the *afakasi* class, part-Samoan and part-European. Back in Hawai'i Bill learned that the name Wallace stemmed from a Scottish ancestor. And he found that among his plantation ancestors on Moloka'i was a Chinese man, back some three or four generations. Bill has a pretty clear hierarchy among these identities. The Hawaiian side has organized his life's activities, shaped his values, and determined his identity more than the others. Next comes the

Samoan, although the Maori connection is not far behind. The other ethnic connections are quite dim. He confesses to feeling an occasional twinge of fellow-feeling for each of the peoples that contributed smaller portions to his genealogy, but only the three—Hawaiian, Samoan, and Maori—organize much of his life.

Many Polynesians tell stories like the story of Bill Wallace. Kookie Soliai has five names to represent the four ethnicities she feels. Her full name is Shazzelma Reiko Reremai Ku'uipo Soliai. The first name is a family concoction, but the others bespeak, in turn, Japanese, Maori, Hawaiian, and Samoan ethnicity. Her biological inheritance is equal parts Japanese (maternal grandfather), Hawaiian (maternal grandmother), English (paternal grandfather), and Maori (paternal grandmother), but the English person was adopted and raised in New Zealand, so she does not feel the English connection. Kookie says that her names make her "feel the relationship" to each of her inherited identities, as well as to the Samoan group into which she married. She says she feels completely at home in a room filled entirely with Japanese Americans, and also in a room made up entirely of Maori, as well as in a roomful of Hawaiians.

Features of Pacific Islander American Multiethnicity

Pacific Islander ethnicity is perhaps not unique in the way it is constructed and operates, but it has several features that mark it as unusual. In the first place, Pacific Islander American ethnicity seems to be *situational* (Nagata 1974; Patterson 1975). Dorri Nautu has Hawaiian, Filipino, Portuguese, and several other ancestries. She lives in a mixed community of part-Hawaiians, Hawaiians, and several other ethnic groups, and she is qualified to attend the university on an ethnic Hawaiian scholarship. She identifies herself more than anything else as Hawaiian. But, she says, "If I'm with my grandmother, I'm Portuguese. If I'm with some of my aunts on my dad's side, I'm Filipino. If I'm hanging around, I'm just local. If I'm on the mainland, I'm Hawaiian."

Dorri reports that her Filipino relatives accept her as a Filipina. But they see her (and she sees herself) as a little less completely Filipina than other family members. This is primarily, she says, because she has less cultural knowledge (about food, language, and so forth) than do other family members. Secondarily, it is because she has a smaller historic quantum of Filipino ancestry. Dorri says that her relatives excuse her lack of cultural knowledge because she is not purely Filipina in ancestry or upbringing, whereas they would be critical if a pure Filipina exhibited a similar cultural deficiency. Her Hawaiian relatives, on the other hand, do not seem to make any distinction regarding purity of ancestry. So how

Dorri identifies herself depends on which of her groups she is with—she feels significantly connected with each of her major ethnic derivations, and she is accepted in each of the groups as an insider.

Dorri seems to feel like whichever set of relatives of friends she is with. Lori Atoa reports the opposite situation—being treated as a Samoan by her mother's Idaho Haole family and as *palagi* by her relatives and schoolmates at home in Samoa. Alexis Siteine reports a more complex dynamic in a 1994 student paper:

> [M]y high school friend . . . asked me, "What do you tell people that you are?" My answer was, "It depends on who's doing the asking." I do not choose to sometimes be one thing and at other times another, but I have learned to identify what I think people are really asking. Sometimes they are actually asking, "What makes you the same as me?" Yet, more often it is, "What makes you different?" If asked this question in New Zealand by a non-Samoan, I identify myself as Samoan. If the asker is Samoan, I acknowledge my heritage: "My mother is palagi and my father is Samoan." When I am out of New Zealand and am asked by a non-Samoan, I identify myself as a New Zealander; if a Samoan asks, my answer is the same, but I qualify it with "but my father is Samoan." These replies are generally satisfactory.

These various testimonies also point to some geographical differences. How one thinks about one's ethnicity seems to vary depending on where one is. Dorri Nautu feels "local"—mixed, polyglot, native to Hawai'i but not specifically ethnically Hawaiian—most of the time when she is in Hawai'i. On the mainland she feels Hawaiian, not just placed in that box by others but actively, primarily, ethnically Hawaiian in her own imagination. Some of that may be due to the difference between active and latent ethnicity. When one is with one's ethnic fellows, one seldom thinks about one's ethnicity except on ritual occasions. One just *is* ethnic— behaves in ways that embody the ethnic culture, associates with other ethnic people, and so forth. The time when one feels one's ethnicity more vividly is when one is confronted by a large group of outsiders. Thus, many White people in America imagine they have no ethnicity; yet if they spend an afternoon in Harlem or Tokyo, they are bound to feel their ethnicity quite strongly. So, too, the half-Samoan woman noted above may not feel that identity very strongly while in the company of other Samoans (although an outsider is bound to see them all as being Samoan together); yet her Samoan identity comes to the fore when she is among non-Samoans in Idaho.

The greater recognition of one's Pacific Islander identity when in a contrast situation also may be related to a phenomenon one may observe among Tongans and Samoans in California, Washington, or Utah. Pacific Islanders are more willing to express their multiplicity in an overtly multiple place like Hawai'i than they are on the U.S. mainland. The same person who, in Hau'ula or on the multicultural campus of BYU-Hawai'i, is primarily a Samoan but also admits to some *palagi* and Asian Indian ancestors, in Los Angeles sees herself and is treated only as a Samoan, without the multiethnic consciousness (Misa 1992).

Even farther afield from centers of Pacific Islander American population, one's Pacific Islander identity may become fuzzier, not necessarily in one's own mind but in the minds of the people around. In several western metropolitan areas, most non-Pacific people know that there are Samoans and Hawaiians, and they may know that there are Tongans, although other groups such as Fijians, Marshall Islanders, and I-Kiribati are beyond their ken. Elsewhere in the United States, Pacific Islanders are frequently mistaken for someone else. A couple of years ago, on a plane from the West Coast to Illinois, a curious passenger leaned across the aisle and asked Debbie Hippolite Wright, "What tribe are you from?" assuming she was a Native American. When she told him she was not a Native American, he replied, "Oh, you must be Mexican." When she told him she was flattered, but she was not that, either, he said, "Well, what *are* you?" He had never heard of Maori, but ultimately he was comfortable with the label "Polynesian." Hawaiians are Polynesians and he knew about Hawaiians.

Another feature of Pacific Islander American multiethnicity is the common practice of *choosing one* from among the available identities for emphasis, at the same time holding onto other identities. Thus, Bill Wallace and Dorri Nautu are many things, but they choose to be mainly Hawaiian most of the time. Debbie Hippolite Wright is English and French in part, but chooses to be Maori in her primary identity. Jon Jonassen is Rarotongan and Norwegian and several other things, but is vociferously a Cook Islander.[3] Lori Atoa is Samoan and *palagi*, but chooses Samoan, because she grew up in Western Samoa and because she feels she looks more Samoan. Tupou Hopoate Pau'u has ancestors from Germany, Portugal, England, Fiji, and Samoa, but she is militantly Tongan even as she acknowledges the others.[4]

The choice of which identity to emphasize can shift in the course of one's life. Kookie Soliai says she feels more strongly Maori than anything else in her heart. But when she lived on the mainland she identified herself as Hawaiian because that was easier for a lot of people to figure out, and because it gave her a bond of sisterhood with other islanders far from home. Back in Hawai'i, she identifies publicly as part-Hawaiian despite her greater psychic affiliation with her Maori heritage, for reasons both political and financial (there are tangible benefits to being Hawaiian).

A final feature of Pacific Islander American multiethnicity is that the group tends to admit individuals who have mixed ancestry on more or less the same basis as people who have pure ancestry. That is not always the case in the Pacific, as indicated by the ridicule heaped on *afakasi* in Samoa. But it seems to be true of Pacific Islanders in America. There is little residue of the Samoan pure-blood/half-blood split in the United States, either in Hawai'i or on the mainland. The same is true for other Pacific Islander groups in the United States. Dorri Nautu is accepted by both Filipinos and Hawaiians, although she is treated a bit more specially by the Filipinos on account of her mixture than by the Hawaiians. The difference in her reception is probably partly because Hawaiians and other Pacific peoples see themselves as fundamentally mixed peoples, whereas Filipinos and other Asians see themselves each as more purely one thing. It may also be because Pacific Islander American ethnicity focuses not on the boundaries between groups but on the centers of group ethnicity and the glue that holds the group together—not on who is out but on who is in, and on what they do together.

Defining features, then, of Pacific Islander American multiethnicity include the following: It is situational, depending on whom one is with and where one is located geographically. People are conscious of and affiliate with multiple identities, but they commonly choose one for primary emphasis. And Pacific Islander Americans, perhaps more than other groups, seem to receive mixed people on more or less the same basis as they do unmixed people.

Bases of Pacific Islander American Multiethnicity

The identity choices of Pacific Islanders who possess multiple inheritances are based on several factors. A person's ethnicity may proceed from any of several bases, and the group seems willing to admit people to membership on the basis of any of several items. One such basis is consciousness of *ancestry*—bloodline, as many would call it. Samoans, especially, talk a lot about the importance of "blood," but all the Pacific Islanders interviewed stressed ancestry as an essential basis of ethnic identity.

In order to identify yourself as a Hawaiian, you must possess at least one Hawaiian ancestor. Being able to trace that ancestor gives you location. As Haunani-Kay Trask writes:

> In Polynesian cultures, genealogy is paramount. Who we are is determined by our connection to our lands and to our families. Therefore, our bloodlines and birthplace tell our identity. When I meet another Hawaiian, I say

I am descended of two genealogical lines: the Pi'ilani line through my mother who is from Hana, Maui, and the Kahakumakaliua line through my father's family from Kaua'i. I came of age on the Ko'olau side of the island of O'ahu. This is who I am and who my people are and where we come from. (1993, 1)

Most Hawaiians do not begin their conversations in Pizza Hut by reciting their entire genealogies. But if one is meeting someone in an only slightly more formal way—if one, say, is being introduced to the aunt of one's friend—then the conversation is likely to begin with each person telling the other about who their relatives are and where they are from, until the two people arrive at a point of recognition, where each can place where the other is located among the Hawaiian people. And reciting the genealogy is something that the Ali'i, the Hawaiian nobility, are said to have done of old; the memory of that act anciently performed resonates for many modern Hawaiians. Like Hawaiians, Maori in New Zealand are likely to introduce themselves on formal occasions by means of a genealogical chant.

It is probably true that the idea of blood as the carrier of identity is not native to the Pacific; in fact, it seems to have come quite late—as late as the 1870s in Hawai'i (Jonassen 1993; Kame'eleihiwa 1992; Wallace 1993). And the idea of blood quantum, of calculating percentages, is found only in Hawai'i, and can be traced to American government impositions from the 1920s onward. Genealogy is nonetheless a very old Pacific imperative. The Kumulipo and other ancient chants recite long genealogies that give location and substance to the Hawaiian people (Beckwith [1951] 1972). Lilikala Kame'eleihiwa expounds upon the importance of genealogies to Hawaiian identity:

> The genealogies *are* the Hawaiian concept of time, and they order the space around us. Hawaiian genealogies are the histories of our people. Through them we learn of the exploits and identities of our ancestors—their great deeds and their follies, their loves and their accomplishments, and their errors and defeats. Even though the great genealogies are of the Ali'i Nui and not of the commoners, these Ali'i Nui are the collective ancestors, and their *mo'olelo* (histories) are histories of all Hawaiians, too. Genealogies anchor Hawaiians to our place in the universe. Genealogies also brought Hawaiians psychological comfort in times of acute distress. [T]heir genealogy is comprised of the character of their ancestors. This is the sum total of their identity. From the Hawaiian view, it is pointless to discuss the actions of any character in Hawaiian history without a careful examination of his or her genealogy; without their identities the account would be unintelligible. Ancestral identity is revealed in the names that Hawaiians carry, for

the names of our ancestors continue as our names also. Names of the Ali'i Nui are repeated for successive generations to enhance and share the honor of the original ancestor. In this process, the name collects it own *mana* [power, spirit, authority, identity] and endows the successor who carries it. It is said that the name molds the character of the child. It is as if the Hawaiian stands firmly in the present, with his back to the future, and his eyes fixed upon the past, seeking historical answers for present-day dilemmas. (1992, 19–22)

This celebration of the mystic chords of memory is perhaps as important as the actual content of the genealogical account in gluing together Hawaiians as a people.

There is something incantatory about certain ethnic political speech. It is as invigorating to ethnicity when a Pacific Islander American politician recites the history of abuse that her people have suffered, as when an island spiritual leader chants a genealogy. The ground of ethnicity in this case is almost rhetorical: It is publicly remembering. Like Thomas Jefferson's recitation in the U.S. *Declaration of Independence* of the dastardly deeds done by King George, such a catalogue of wrongs galvanizes the slumbering feeling of a people. Thus, for example, it is essential to the reawakening of Hawaiian political identity that Haunani-Kay Trask (1993) begin her book on Hawaiian nationalism by recounting the wrongs done Hawaiians by Americans and others. It is true history, but it is more than that: It is the act of rhetorically, publicly remembering, and thus it serves to strengthen the ethnic bond.

On a more prosaic level, who one's relatives are constitutes an essential ingredient in one's identifying with and being accepted by a Pacific Islander American group. If you have relatives in a particular Pacific Islander American people, then you are a legitimate member of that group. As a mixed New Zealander, Alexis Siteine, puts it: "Maoris seem to have adopted the 'one drop' rule about themselves: If you can claim any Maori ancestor, then you are part of the *tangata whenua* (people of the land). The members of the Maori club [in school] then, ranged in appearance from the blonde, blue-eyed, freckled variety to dark-haired, dark-eyed brownness."[5]

Much of what happens that is ethnic happens within the extended family. Almost all community ceremonies and obligations are organized on a family basis. The place, above all others, where Tongan or Fijian or Samoan culture is passed on is in the *family*. As Lori Atoa put it: "In the Samoan way of life, the extended family is first priority. Anytime there is a crisis in the family, we are always ready to give whatever is needed. The aunts and cousins on the Samoan side were always around to follow through on straightening us out. There again, we were totally exposed to the Samoan way of doing things." Among Maori, both in New Zealand

and in the United States, it is not just ancestry or phenotype, but ties to the tribal sacred space, the *marae,* that give one ethnic location. Nikki Mozo ended a 1993 student paper with the following declaration of her identity, based on genealogy and family ties:

> I am of the proud Ngati Kahununu tribe, who sailed the mighty Takitimu canoe and arrived on the islands of Aotearoa which is commonly known today as New Zealand. My marae was built at Nuhaka during the second world war in memory of our proud warriors of Ngati Kahununu. The river my people lived from is called Nuhaka. The mountain that my people lived on is called Momokai, which stands to the west of my dad's, my grandfather's, and his father's village tucked in the quiet peaceful valleys of the hills. My name is Nicolette Roimatta Mozo and I am a Maori.

The family tie does not necessarily have to be genetic in order to be powerful. Ricky Soliai (Kookie's husband) is biologically Hawaiian-Tongan-Irish, but his father was adopted and raised by a Samoan family. Ricky regards himself as full Samoan; his family and other people—Samoans and non-Samoans—treat him as a Samoan without qualification, and he insists on raising the couple's children as Samoans only, despite their strongly Maori-Hawaiian-Japanese mother. Contrast that to the situation of a lot of other interethnic adoptees—African Americans raised by White families, we call some of them, or Korean babies in Swedish American families (Ladner 1977). Growing up, everyone thinks of them as interracial adoptees, not as natural members of the group of their adopted parents. On reaching their teen years, many such people go searching for their ancestral roots (there is in fact a thriving industry that puts Korean youths from the American Midwest in touch with the land and culture of their biological ancestors). There seems to be less of this in the Pacific Islander case. One's adoption into a particular Pacific Islander ethnic group seems to entitle one to a more complete membership in that group than is the case with other American groups.

Bill Wallace's experience suggests that you may be able to marry into another ethnic group, although Dorri Nautu's and Kookie Soliai's experiences suggest that perhaps identity acquired through marriage is less strong than identity that comes from the home of your childhood. There is also a possibility that Hawaiians may be more accepting of outside infusions than other peoples for identifiable historical reasons. Bill Wallace points out that, in the middle of the nineteenth century, "With the Hawaiian people dying out, the kings brought in people from the Pacific

Rim—Chinese, Japanese, Koreans—to try to restock the Hawaiian blood." Whatever the case in specific historical situations, and whether or not people may marry into or be adopted into specific ethnic groups, it remains clear that the family is one of the primary bases of Pacific Islander American ethnicity.

Equally important with bloodlines and family connections in determining Pacific Islander American ethnicity is *cultural practice*. One is Tongan because one behaves like a Tongan, speaks the Tongan language, has a Tongan heart. 'Inoke Funaki (1993), in a moving personal exploration of "Culture and Identity in the Pacific," finds Tongan identity in *"fe'ofo'ofani"* (brotherly love), in "family spirit," in "willingness to help each other," in "kindness and neighborly generosity," and in the "art of living together in harmony and peace." One is Samoan because one speaks Samoan and one understands and lives *fa'a samoa*. Many Pacific Islander Americans would argue, indeed, that language is the *sine qua non* of ethnicity, the essential variety of cultural practice, because so much that is powerful is shared through language. Cy Bridges, keeper of things Hawaiian at the Polynesian Cultural Center, can talk long and movingly about the cultural bases of the Hawaiian way—about the daily practices and the heart qualities that (if one exemplifies them) declare one to be a Hawaiian.

Another basis of Pacific Islander American ethnic connectedness is one's relationship to *place*. In Hawaiian, it is the *aina*, the land, and one must *malama aina* (care for the land). The caring is reciprocal, for the land also cares for the people, and the relationship is a deep, family bond. Leaders of the Hawaiian cultural and political renaissance of the past two decades have stressed the importance of reclaiming the *aina* above almost everything else (Trask 1993). But it is not only ethnic nationalist politicians who revere the land. Elderly Hawaiians of no particular political convictions speak of feeling roots reaching down through their feet, deep into the earth of their islands. The stories of Auntie Harriet Ne (1992), which resonate for Hawaiians of many political persuasions, speak intimately of the land and its inhabitants, animals and *menehune* as well as humans.

Pacific Islanders of other derivations also celebrate their ethnicity by reference to place. Tupou Hopoate Pau'u, a Tongan raised in Australia who now lives in California, fled her Tongan ethnicity until her mother forced her to return to Tonga. She now speaks in hushed tones of her first encounter with the village and the hut where she was born, and the intense love for her people and her culture that grew from that encounter to become one of the central forces of her life (see her story in Chapter 1, "My Life in Four Cultures"). She later wrote a poem to express the depth of her commitment. It read in part:

When I speak of Tonga,
I speak of Me.
A person made up of multiple identities
Through my veins flow the blood of various cultures
But I only identify myself as one from Tonga.
There, my heart will always stay true,
For Tonga is my home;
My island and My taboo.

Pau'u's subsequent life choices—to work as a missionary in Tonga, to attend a university made up mainly of Pacific Islander students, to marry a Tongan American, to live in a Tongan community in Southern California, to become a lawyer so she can serve her people—have all stemmed from her experience of that intensely Tongan place.

Not all Pacific Islander Americans have had personal contact with places that symbolize their ethnicity. But nearly all have heard about such places from their relatives, and the collective memory of those ethnic places is a powerful reinforcer of their ethnic identity.

At least these bases, then—ancestry, family, practice, and place—seem important determinants of Pacific Islander American ethnicity. Jocelyn Linnekin, Lin Poyer, and several colleagues (1990) have asserted that cultural identities in the Pacific are mainly "Lamarckian"—that is, they proceed from the notions that "acquired characteristics are heritable" and "shared identity comes from sharing" (1990, 9–10). They would differentiate between such Pacific identities, based, they say, in practice, and what they call "Mendelian" models of ethnicity based in kinship or bloodline. Linnekin and Poyer may be right about ethnic identities in some parts of the Pacific. But as far as ethnicity constructed among Pacific Islander Americans in Hawaii and on the U.S. mainland, Linnekin, Poyer, and their colleagues go too far. Yes, group identities among Pacific Islander Americans are based on place and practice. But they are also based profoundly on ancestry and family connection. Linnekin, Poyer, and their colleagues argue that blood is not the issue; in the crassest meaning of that term they may be right. But while it may be argued that the blood-quantum approach of some Hawaiians, for example, to participation in Hawaiian sovereignty was picked up from White American cultural definitions, nonetheless, every Pacific Islander American people of whom we have much knowledge has a strong sense of blood, of lineage, of clan connectedness, of history as a basis for identity and group membership.

CONCLUSION: MULTIPLE ETHNIC CENTERS

Nearly all American and European ethnic thinking is about boundaries. Perhaps no writer on ethnic theory has been so frequently and reverently quoted as Fredrik Barth; his very influential book on the subject, called *Ethnic Groups and Boundaries*, says in part, "The critical focus of investigation from this point of view becomes the ethnic *boundary* that defines the group, not the cultural stuff that it encloses" (1969, 15). Since Barth wrote that, no one seems to have doubted that boundaries are the important things about ethnic groups. Barth may be right about ethnicity in some other contexts, but his ideas will not work for Pacific Islander American ethnicity. The boundaries surrounding Pacific Islander American ethnic groups are not very important at all. Pacific Islander Americans have inclusive, not exclusive, ethnic identities. What is important for Pacific Islander American ethnicity is not boundaries but centers: ancestry, family, practice, place. If one qualifies for acceptance at the centers of ethnicity, then one is of that ethnic group, no matter to what other ethnic groups one may also belong.

In a multicultural age, maybe this is a better model of ethnicity than any other. Pacific Islander Americans are in some ways a model of what is happening to America at large.[6] The American people are becoming a people of multiple identities. We are, at last, biologically fulfilling de Crèvecouer's vision of a mixed America, but we are not melting. Instead, we are becoming vividly multiethnic within each person (Root 1992). Some other American ethnic groups are beginning to face up to this multiethnic reality. It used to be (and still is for the Orthodox) that to be a Jew one had to be either a convert or the child of a Jewish mother. Now, mindful of dwindling numbers in an era of 40 percent outmarriage or more, not a small number of Reform Jewish synagogues are holding "Get to Know Your Jewish Roots" classes and encouraging anyone who can identify a Jewish ancestor to consider joining the faith. In similar fashion, where a generation ago the small number of mixed offspring of Japanese American intermarriages were shunned by Japanese American community institutions, now one sees their pictures in Japanese community newspapers quite regularly, and their numbers are quite large (Spickard 1989). Pacific Islander American formulations of multiethnicity are especially fruitful for understanding ethnicity as it is emerging in the United States.[7]

Nearly a century ago, W. E. B. Du Bois expressed a tension of duality.

He would not admit to racial duality, to feeling his White ancestry at the same time he felt his Black ancestry. The tension DuBois expressed was between race and nation. But his words provide a picture of an earlier era's torment when struggling to come to terms with multiple identities (Du Bois 1897): "One ever feels his two-ness—an American, a Negro; two souls, two thoughts, two unreconciled strivings; two warring ideals in one dark body, whose dogged strength alone keeps it from being torn asunder." Now, for Pacific Islander Americans at least, it seems possible to reconcile two or more ethnic identities in one person, without torment, and without one being subordinated to the other. Perhaps what is needed in our era is an understanding of ethnicity that does not presume that a person must check just one box. Perhaps, by focusing as Pacific Islander Americans do on the centers of ethnicity, and not on boundaries between groups, we can better prepare ourselves for an age when most if not all of us will be biologically and functionally multiethnic.

NOTES

[1] Although many anthropologists, at least, would assert that these labels do sort languages into meaningful divisions (Crocombe 1984, 1993).

[2] This multiple ethnic consciousness has something in common with *mestizaje*, mestiza consciousness, which Anzaldua (1987) talks about in *Borderlands/La Frontrera: The New Mestiza*, and more generally with the Mexican consciousness of being a mixed people (Steiner 1970), even *la raza cósmica* (Vasconcellos [1925] 1979).

[3] In Jon's case, he has ancestry in several of the Cook Islands, and he emphasizes the national Cook Island identity over any specific island tie. His secondary allegiance is to a pan-Pacific Islander identity, rather than to any of his European stocks.

[4] An extreme—in fact, an unusual—case is that of a student in a course on Asian and Pacific Islander ethnic issues. When the class went around the room sharing the multiplicities of their backgrounds, her answer was an emphatic "I'm half Hawaiian!" and she would say no more. Throughout the whole semester she would not budge, would not admit any significance attaching to anything that might be in the other half, although she admitted the other half existed. For reasons social, ideological, and perhaps political, she would speak only of her Hawaiian side. But this student was an extreme case; most Pacific Islander Americans will admit their multiethnicity even as they choose to emphasize one aspect of their ancestry.

[5] John Harré makes much the same point in *Maori and Pakeha* (1966). I am indebted to Nikki Mozo for the insight.

[6] Some may argue that Pacific Islander Americans are not a model for much of

anything; a critic of an earlier version of this article did just that. That person observed that most of the data for this paper came from Hawai'i and asserted that Hawai'i is so different from other places that it is a lousy example of anything except exceptions. The critic contended that ethnic relations in other places are much more conflictual, more categorical, more hostile than those relations in Hawai'i. I must disagree. Hawai'i is far from an interracial paradise. Every interpersonal encounter in Hawai'i is carefully calibrated in ethnic terms. A conversation between two Haoles is different from a conversation between a Haole and a Korean on the same subject, and very different again from a conversation between two Samoans. There is quite a bit of interethnic stereotyping and hostility in Hawai'i, between Haole and Hawaiian, between Japanese and Samoan, between Filipino and Korean, and so on. What is different about Hawai'i—and what makes it not a bad model but a particularly *good* model for America's apparent future—are two things: (1) it is multicultural in the extreme, as America is becoming; and (2) in Hawai'i, as among Pacific Islander Americans generally, the consciousness of individuals and groups that they are multiethnic is very strong.

[7] There is, of course, the possibility that politics may intrude and current trends toward multiethnicity will be reversed. Sarajevo was not long ago thought by some to be a fairly happily multicultural place, and now it is an interethnic war zone. But despite the power of continuing racial oppression in America and the strength of regional political trends such as the sovereignty movement among Native Hawaiians, the United States is in my judgment quite far from the sort of ethnic division and warfare currently to be seen in the former Yugoslavia and the former Soviet Union.

CHAPTER 3

The Filipino Question in Asia and the Pacific: Rethinking Regional Origins in Diaspora

Joanne L. Rondilla

"What is Asia?" I ask my students. They stare at me blankly, as if I am unspeakably stupid. Finally one answers, "The largest continent." "So what's a continent?" I ask. A discussion ensues that has no resolution, because none of us has a very clear idea of what a continent might be. At least, we cannot come up with a single definition that fits all the things we think to be continents.[1] Turning back to the subject of Asia, I draw a freehand map on the board, then take a piece of chalk and start drawing a line from the east toward the west. "Let me know where Asia starts," I say. Some start shouting when I reach Hawai'i, others the longitude of Japan, others China. "Let me know when I reach the end of Asia." Some speak up when I reach China's western border, some Afghanistan, others the Caspian Sea, Syria, Turkey, or even Tunis.

"If we can't decide for sure what the borders of Asia are, what holds it together?" I ask. What is it that Japanese have in common with Turks, Chinese with Bengalis, Balinese with Tibetans? Not much, it turns out, except that Europeans have lumped everything from the Bosporus to Honolulu together into one vague mass for a very long time. Herodotus may have been at the root of this lumping, when in the fifth century BCE he wrote about a clash between a polyglot Persian army and ragtag bands of Greeks as a titanic battle between East and West. Each person on the Western side was an individual with a story and a personality, heroic or craven. There were no persons on the East, just a faceless horde.[2]

That notion of a unified, or at least undifferentiable, East has lasted in European and American thought down to this day. Edward Said called it "Orientalism."[3] The term "Asia"—the region to which "Orientalism" was applied—stood, in the beginning, for the Roman province of Anatolia, the greater part of modern-day Turkey. But that area east of the Dardanelles stretched in the European imagination past Bangkok to the western shore of the Pacific. Everything in that huge zone was supposed to have been the same. Karl Marx wrote of an "Asiatic mode of production" and his disciples never questioned the notion that people all over Asia were given over to a common pattern of economic enterprise that was not shared by outsiders.[4] Emile Durkheim wrote of "Oriental religions" as a common experience separate from and more primitive than Mediterranean religions.[5] Karl Wittfogel wrote about the inevitable shape of politics in all of Asia as "Oriental despotism."[6]

American Orientalism is a bit different from British or French. European Orientalism comes from historical and imagined encounters with Islam, Arabs, and Turks; their supposed characteristics are then written across the peoples of the rest of the continent. The American version of Orientalism started with those sources in the late eighteenth and early nineteenth centuries, but soon it took on a westward gaze across the Pacific to China and Japan.[7] From this angle the peoples of the Pacific were thrown into the Asian mix. In the last decades of the twentieth century and into the twenty-first century , terms such as "Pacific Rim" and "the Asia Pacific" gained currency. The precise meaning of such conceptual agglomerations of disparate peoples was seldom questioned.[8] Even when the issue came up, almost no one asked whether the Pacific belonged in the same category with East Asia.

I am not exactly arguing against the concept of Asia, for it does have some meaning. In fact, it is a powerful idea that has had enormous effect on history. During the Second World War and later during Korea and Vietnam, the American public heard constantly that "life is cheap in the Orient." There is little doubt in my mind that Americans' belief in the truth of that statement underlay many of the bad decisions of American policy makers regarding the conduct of those wars, and in later conflicts in the Arab Peninsula.[9] In a contrary direction, because people as disparate as Koreans, Chinese, Filipinos, and Bengalis have suffered a common Orientalization and oppression, the concept of "Asian American" has been a useful organizing principle for self-defense in the last third of the twentieth century.[10]

But while I see some utility in the idea of Asia, I am pretty sure that it does not describe anything like a single field of human experience. Using such a broad concept masks so much more than it illuminates, particularly when one thinks about some of the places on the margins of the traditional concept of Asia. Such a place is the Philippines.

Historical accounts, atlases, and works of cultural geography list the Philippines as part of Southeast Asia. The islands that lie in the waters of the Pacific stretch from Rapanui (Easter Island) on the east to Java and

Kalimantan on the west. Yet the European traditionalists who drew this map saw only their own constructions: Polynesia, Micronesia, and Melanesia. The Philippines (and Indonesia) are invisible.

Because the Asian idea is so powerful, when Filipinos go abroad, they are regarded as Asians abroad. In the United States they are counted as Asian Americans, and in fact some Filipinos were important actors in creating the idea of an Asian American panethnicity and elaborating pan-Asian American institutions. Yet I believe that, historically, the Philippines has stronger ties to the islands of the Pacific than to Asia. Language, culture, and migrations link the Philippines to Micronesia, primarily the Mariana Islands, and also to Melanesia. Colonial experiences at the hands of Spain, the United States, and Japan suggest comparisons with parts of Micronesia, Hawai'i, and California. Among Filipinos in the United States, although there are meaningful similarities to the experiences of Chinese and Japanese Americans, equally fruitful comparisons with and connections to Hawaiians, Samoans, and Chicanos have been obscured by the pan-Asian American identification.

In this paper I hope to suggest a new way of thinking about the map of the western Pacific that would include the Philippines in a more meaningful historical and cultural orbit, as part of the Pacific Islands fully as much as it is part of Asia. I also intend to lay out some of the historical experiences of diasporic Filipinos in the United States that might serve to place them in a pan-ethnic coalition, at least part of the time, with Pacific Islanders or Chicanos rather than with Asian Americans.

DIASPORIC FILIPINOS AND PANETHNIC IDENTITY

As a Filipina from Guam who was transplanted to California, something interesting happened to me on the twelve-hour plane ride from Guam to Hawai'i to California. I went from being a Filipina from Guam to becoming an Asian American. The term "Asian American" is still something that I do not quite understand. As I continue to formulate the ideas in this paper, I am still confused by the Filipino question in Asian America, particularly because of my upbringing. Over the years I found that regardless of where one was raised, Filipinos I have encountered have been asking themselves the same thing.

The main focus of the remainder of this paper is to examine Filipinos in regards to Asian and Pacific Islander American political coalitions. In Asian America, Filipinos are placed in a coalition with which we cannot affiliate wholeheartedly. Our issues are often ignored and we are constantly questioning and being questioned as to whether we belong in Asian America. On the other hand, Filipinos have a significant historical and political relationship with Pacific Islanders that needs to be explored.

Before I continue, I want to make clear that the issues I bring up are in no way meant to disregard or disrespect the coalitions between Filipinos and other Asian American groups such as Chinese and Japanese Americans. Throughout history, these coalitions have made great strides working together in struggle against the racist structures around us.[11] In addition, the ideas in this paper are not meant to explain or justify how Filipinos might appropriate Pacific Island culture. Instead, I want to point out our common history and struggle. By examining this, we can begin to understand why Filipinos and Pacific Islanders need to use these connections to build a coalition together.

This is a preliminary formulation, designed with the hope of spurring discussion of the question: Are Filipinos Asian Americans or are we Pacific Islanders, and what are the implications of either formulation? I hope we can begin to ask ourselves what are the things that push us toward a specific political alignment and how can we re-create these coalitions.

BECOMING ASIAN AMERICAN

Before the 1960s, the concept "Asian American" did not exist. Different ethnic groups whose ancestors were from Asia saw themselves as separate, distinctive groups. Non-Asians, specifically Whites, tended to lump Asians into one group, as illustrated in the term "Oriental."[12]

In response to that lumping, the leaders of the Asian American movement of the late 1960s created a panethnic identity—"Asian Americans"—to counter Orientalism.[13] As Asian Americans, Chinese, Japanese, and Filipinos organized to illustrate unity, create strength in numbers, and achieve political recognition. The Asian American movement was bound by the idea of yellow power. As described by activist Amy Uyematsu, yellow power meant to seek "freedom from racial oppression through the power of a consolidated yellow people."[14] Becoming Asian American meant creating unity among peoples who originally saw themselves as separate. Yellow power represented the tie that bound these people. At the same time, yellow power also became a dividing line. The Chinese and Japanese took center stage partly because the Asian American movement began as a college student movement. At this time, there were few Filipinos in college and fewer were middle class. Filipinos immediately rejected this idea because they felt it excluded them.[15] Filipinos considered themselves to be brown—not yellow.[16] Although this seems to be a petty distinction, yellow power pointed out who dominated and who sat in the margins of Asian America. Filipinos took part in the Asian American coalition, but as junior partners.

QUESTIONING ASIAN AMERICA

In response to Chinese and Japanese dominance in Asian America, Filipinos introduced the Brown Asian concept in 1970.[17] The Brown Asian is a concept that demanded inclusion of brown people (particularly Filipinos) in Asian America. By 1972, Pacific Islanders were also being grouped along with Asian Americans. This happened largely because non-Pacific Islanders, specifically Whites, did not really think about Pacific Islanders. Classifying them as Asians was the most convenient place to put them.[18] The problem is Pacific Islanders have no cultural ties and no common ancestry with Asians. They do not have a common—nor even a related—indigenous culture, language, or family structure. They do, however, have a related history of oppression in America.[19] This history was the basis for Pacific Islanders (particularly Hawaiians, Guamanians, and Samoans) to politically align themselves with Asian Americans.[20] Activist Lemuel F. Ignacio explains, "Joining forces gave Asian Americans and Pacific Islanders more power in dealing with power structures in this country."[21]

The addition of Pacific Islanders to Asian America also added another layer to the Brown Asian concept. Filipinos and Pacific Islanders found themselves in the same boat—they were marginalized in a coalition that was supposed to represent them. The Brown Asian concept bound Filipinos and Pacific Islanders to what Ignacio described as "the whole strategy and action of the coalition among Asian American and Pacific Island peoples."[22] In April 1972, The First National Conference on Asian American Mental Health was held in San Francisco.[23] At this conference, there were different caucuses that allowed smaller Asian and Pacific Island groups to voice their communities' concerns. Initially, a Brown Asian caucus was formed to represent Filipinos, Guamanians, Hawaiians, and Samoans. However, in the interest of representing the different individual groups, the four groups made separate presentations. The Filipino caucus asserted the Brown Asian concept. Guamanians, Hawaiians, and Samoans advocated the same concerns as Pacific Islanders. Ignacio further explains, "This new ethnic thrust in the conference led to the Asian American and Pacific Islander movements taking a major turn in its course. The Brown Asian and Pacific Islander dimension became prominent."[24]

These groups banded together to assert their issues and identities very early on in the Asian American movement. They did not hesitate to be critical of a coalition that was created to represent them, but that had failed to include them in any meaningful way. Unfortunately, this assertion has not carried on since 1972. No one re-created the coalition or political structure to assert the needs of Brown Asians and Pacific Islanders. Today, Filipinos and Pacific Islanders are still classified as Asian Americans, yet their issues are not a priority within that coalition. Almost all prominent leaders and scholars of so-called Asian Pacific Islander America are descendents of people from mainland East Asia. Filipino and Pacific Islander voices go almost unheard.

Yet the desire for Filipinos to reassert their unique identity in Asian American politics continues. As activist Tony Ricasa explains, "There is a sense of feeling that Japanese and Chinese have gotten a piece of the pie that Filipinos are not getting . . . . Filipinos believe in coalition with other Asian Americans. They understand its strength. At the same time, they don't feel the coalition is benefiting them."[25]

An example of this is Asian American Studies, which was born out of the Asian American movement. As evidence that Filipinos are still marginalized within Asian America, Filipino Studies still holds second-class status in Asian American Studies. Compared to Japanese and Chinese Americans, there is a lack of interest in researching Filipino issues surrounding language, culture, identity, and history.[26] There are few opportunities for writers to publish and there are few publications by Filipino writers. There is also a lack of commitment to hire Filipino faculty on the collegiate level. UC Santa Barbara is home to one of the largest and most firmly established Asian American Studies departments in the nation. In a curriculum of forty courses, there is no emphasis on Filipinos, with the exception of one course that the faculty has to stretch to offer once every two to three years.[27] In fall 2000, Professor Jon Cruz, a Filipino American, began his tenure as the department chair. Hopefully, his presence will add a greater commitment to smaller Asian American communities such as Filipinos, Thai, Vietnamese, and Pacific Islanders.

Furthermore, in Asian American Studies Filipino American history is viewed in relation to the dominant Asian American groups—such as the 1920 labor strike in Hawai'i, where Japanese and Filipino laborers joined forces against the sugar plantation owners.[28] What Filipinos do not learn in greater depth is how our history frequently has gone against the grain of the histories of the other Asian American groups. Filipinos did not align themselves only with other Asian groups. Filipino farmworkers often worked in alliance with Mexican farmworkers, for instance in the 1933 El Monte Berry Strike where Mexican and Filipino laborers went on strike against Japanese growers.[29] We do not learn about cultural differences such as our family structures. Filipino family structures are still influenced by a pre-European matrilineal family structure, whereas other Asian American family structures follow Confucian family systems, which are patriarchal. We do not learn about the complicated nature of our colonization, first by Spain and then by the United States, and how that affects us today. Only the Philippines, of major Asian nations sending migrants to America, was a U.S. colony.

As Asian Americans, consideration of our concerns has been limited because we are overshadowed by the dominant Asian American groups. For instance, because of the Asian American identification, Filipinos are not seen by the larger society as an underrepresented minority group. In 1986, the University of California system decided not to recognize Filipinos as a special target group for affirmative action because, as Asian Americans, we were supposed to be doing well. What this failed to recognize was that we have lower university retention rates than other Asian groups. Further, our admissions rates are dropping. In 1991, the Filipino acceptance rate at UCLA was 39 percent. In 1996, that number dropped to 26 percent.[30] The policies of the University of California and of the wider society do not recognize these issues because they see us simply as Asian Americans, who, they believe, are uniformly doing well.

Filipino numbers are currently growing. The 1990 census reported roughly 1.4 million Filipinos in the United States; recent estimates suggest that number will go up to 3 million in the 2000 census. In California, Filipinos are the largest Asian ethnic minority group.[31] It makes no sense for Filipinos to be marginalized within a racial group where we are becoming the largest ethnic component. Therefore, we need to shift away from the old ways in which we are defined. Asian America was born reflexively out of Orientalism, a purely colonial concept. In rebuilding coalitions, it is important to let go of how outsiders have defined us. We need to redefine who we are and how we identify ourselves, based on what is most important to us. This will entail re-evaluating the lines between Asia and the Pacific, the lines between Polynesia, Micronesia, and Melanesia, the lines between who is an Asian American and who is a Pacific Islander. It is time we created our identities and coalitions on our own terms. We need to align ourselves with people to whom we have a common tie. This is why Filipinos need to examine their links to the Pacific and with Pacific Islanders.

THROUGH THE PACIFIC ISLANDER LENS

The ties between Filipinos and Pacific Islanders run far and deep. We share a common culture from before European contact, we have a similar colonial history, and the ways in which we have had to deal with the effects of colonization are closely related. Although the details vary from island to island, the general story is the same.

Consider the relationship between the Guam and the Philippines, who have prominent historical and cultural links. Both pre-colonial societies were matrilineal and they shared a common linguistic origin, a common ceramic tradition, and common navigation skills.[32] Guam, like the Philippines, underwent 300 years of Spanish colonialism, followed by American colonialism as a result of the Spanish-American War. This was followed by Japanese occupation during World War II, then by a return to American colonization in the post-war era.[33] The two nations' histories diverged only in recent decades when the Philippines gained independence and Guam became a U.S. territory.

Military presence, educational opportunities, brain drain, and the search for a better life have affected Pacific Island immigration to the United States. By enlisting in the military, Guamanians, Hawaiians, and Samoans were able to leave their homelands and eventually settle in communities around military bases, such as Long Beach, San Diego, Honolulu, San Francisco, and Seattle.[34] Increased opportunities in attaining higher education degrees and a lack of job opportunities at home have made settling in the United States and other parts of the world appealing to islanders.[35] Filipinos had the same experiences when they joined the military to leave the poverty of the Philippines and eventually settled in the United States, in these same cities.[36]

Pacific Islanders in the diaspora maintain strong interdependent relationships to their homelands: Although they no longer live there, there is still a strong connection to home.[37] This is illustrated through remittances, which help reinforce kinship and economic ties between islanders at home and in the diaspora. It is typical for Pacific Islanders to send money home and help someone move out of the islands. For example, Samoa received $33 million during the first 11 months of 1997.[38] The Philippine economy also depends on remittances for survival: In 1994 $800 million was sent to the Philippines via bank transfers from families in the diaspora.

Caught as we are in the complicated web of colonialism, the struggles in our island homelands are related as well. Throughout the Pacific, islanders are fighting to keep and maintain ancestral lands to benefit the indigenous populations. They are constantly fighting a foreign military that imposes itself on the land and people, as well as corporations who insist on developing land to build hotels and luxury tourist spots, arguing that the developments will pump money into the economy. Pacific Islanders have to pay the price for all this. Their natural resources are being depleted. Indigenous populations are being driven off their land and livelihood and forced into homelessness.[39]

These things are happening in the Philippines as well. Recently, the Philippine government approved plans to build a world-class luxury tourist area in Hacienda Looc.[40] Hacienda Looc is home to 10,000 farmers whose livelihoods are rooted in the area. Everything they live on—particularly food and shelter—comes directly from the land. When the developments begin, these 10,000 people are going to be displaced. Their only hope of economic survival is to move elsewhere or to work in the newly built tourist areas.[41]

CONCLUSION

The common ties between Pacific Islanders and Filipinos are many. Therefore, it makes sense that we start to build a coalition together, because we are in the same struggle. We are fighting for the same issues against the same enemy. However, the lines between Asia and the Pacific, between who is an Asian American and who a Pacific Islander, keep us from seeing each other's issues eye to eye. The lines drawn by outsiders are keeping us apart and now the lines need to be rearranged. We need to redefine who we build coalitions with. The basis of how we do this needs to be on our terms—not on the terms of the colonizer.

NOTES

[1] See Martin W. Lewis and Karen Wigen, *The Myth of Continents: A Critique of Metageography* (Berkeley: University of California Press, 1997).

[2] Herodotus, *The Persian Wars*, trans. George Rawlinson (New York: Random House, 1942).

[3] Edward Said, *Orientalism* (New York: Random House, 1978). See also Carol A. Breckenridge et al., eds., *Orientalism and the Postcolonial Predicament: Perspectives on South Asia* (Philadelphia: University of Pennsylvania Press, 1993); Barbara Harlow and Mia Carter, eds., *Imperialism and Orientalism: A Documentary Sourcebook* (Oxford: Blackwell, 1999); Kalpana Sahni, *Crucifying the Orient: Russian Orientalism and the Colonization of the Caucasus and Central Asia* (Bangkok: White Orchid Press, 1997); Ziauddin Sardar, *Orientalism: Concepts in the Social Sciences* (Buckingham: Open University Press, 1999); Jane Schneider, ed., *Italy's 'Southern Question': Orientalism in One Country* (Oxford: Berg Publishers, 1998).

[4] Anne M. Bailey and Joseph R. Llobera, eds., *The Asiatic Mode of Production* (London: Routledge and Kegan Paul, 1981); Timothy Book, ed., *The Asiatic Mode of Production* (Armonk, N.Y.: M. E. Sharpe, 1989); Stephen Porter Dunn, *The Fall and Rise of the Asiatic Mode of Production* (London: Routledge and Kegan Paul, 1982); Lawrence Krader and M. M. Kovalevskii, *The Asiatic Mode of Production: Sources, Development, and Critique of the Writings of Karl Marx* (Assen: Van Gorcum, 1975); Marian Sawer, *Marxism and the Question of the Asiatic Mode of Production* (The Hague: Nijhoff, 1977); Ferenc Tokai, *Essays on the Asiatic Mode of Production* (Budapest: Akademiai Kiado, 1979).

[5] Emile Durkheim, *Elementary Forms of the Religious Life* (1915; reprint, New York: Free Press, 1965).

[6] Karl A. Wittfogel, *Oriental Despotism* (New Haven, Conn.: Yale University Press, 1957).

[7] Fuad Shaban, *Islam and Arabs in Early American Thought: Roots of Orientalism in America* (Durham, N.C.: Acorn Press, 1991); Sheng-Mei Ma, *The Deathly Embrace: Orientalism and Asian American Identity* (Minneapolis: University of Minnesota Press, 2000); Robert G. Lee, *Orientals: Asian Americans in Popular Culture* (Philadelphia: Temple University Press, 1999); Stuart C. Miller, *The Unwelcome Immigrant: The American Image of the Chinese, 1785–1882* (Berkeley: University of California Press, 1969); Alexander Saxton, *The Indispensable Enemy: Labor and the Anti-Chinese Movement* (Berkeley: University of California Press, 1971); James C. Thomson et al., *Sentimental Imperialists: The American Experience in East Asia* (New York: Harper and Row, 1981).

[8] Two exceptions are Arif Dirlik, ed., *What Is In a Rim? Critical Perspectives on the Pacific Region Idea* (Boulder, Colo.: Westview Press, 1993); Dennis O. Flynn et al., eds., *Pacific Centuries: Pacific and Pacific Rim History Since the Sixteenth Century* (London: Routledge, 1999).

[9] John W. Dower, *War Without Mercy: Race and Power in the Pacific War* (New York: Pantheon, 1986).

[10] William Wei, *The Asian American Movement* (Philadelphia: Temple University Press, 1993); Yen Le Espiritu, *Asian American Panethnicity: Bridging Institutions and Identities* (Philadelphia: Temple University Press, 1992).

[11] Wei, *Asian American Movement*.

[12] Espiritu, *Asian American Panethnicity*, 19–20.

[13] Ibid., 20.

[14] Amy Uyematsu, "The Emergence of a Yellow Power in Asian America," in *Roots: An Asian American Reader*, ed. Amy Tachiki, Eddie Wong, and Franklin Odo (Los Angeles: UCLA Asian American Studies Center, 1971), 9–13.

[15] Espiritu, *Asian American Panethnicity*, 32.

[16] Lemuel F. Ignacio, *Asian Americans and Pacific Islanders: Is There Such an Ethnic Group?* (San Jose: Pilipino Associates Inc., 1976), 84.

[17] Ibid.

[18] Paul R. Spickard, "Who is an Asian? Who is a Pacific Islander?: Mono-racialism, Multiracial People and Asian American Communities," in Teresa Williams Leon and Cynthia Nakashima, eds., *The Sum of Our Parts: Mixed Heritage Asian Americans* (Philadelphia: Temple University Press, 2001).

[19] Ignacio, *Asian Americans and Pacific Islanders*, 89.

[20] In reality, the relation is based on both groups being oppressed people of color in America. This relationship is not bound with anything more substantial, and so the Pacific Asian coalition might equally well include Blacks, Latinos, or Native Americans.

[21] Ignacio, *Asian Americans and Pacific Islanders*, xvi–xvii.

[22] Ibid., 108.

[23] Ibid., 135. It is important to also note that funding for this conference came from the National Institute of Mental Health (NIMH). The purpose of this conference was to address Asian American and Pacific Islander community concerns. It has nothing to do with psychological issues.

[24] Ibid., 141.

[25] Espiritu, *Asian American Panethnicity*, 79.

[26] Russel C. Leong, "Beyond 'the lahar of coalitions': Filipino American Studies at UCLA," *Amerasia Journal*, 14.2 (1998), vi.

[27] This course is taught so rarely because the department has difficulty finding someone who can teach the course.

[28] Ronald Takaki, *Pau Hana: Plantation Life and Labor in Hawaii* (Honolulu: University of Hawai'i Press, 1983), 164–176.

[29] Ronald W. López, "The El Monte Berry Strike of 1933," *Aztl[acute]an* 1 (1970): 101–112.

[30] Jonathan Okamura, *Imagining Filipino American Diaspora: Transnational Relations, Identities and Communities* (New York: Garland Publishing Inc., 1998), 48–49.

[31] E. San Juan Jr., *From Exile to Diaspora: Versions of the Filipino Experience in the United States* (Boulder, Colo.: Westview Press, 1998), 2.

[32] Vicente Diaz, "Bye Bye Ms. American Pie: The Historical Relations Between Chamorros and Filipinos and the American Dream," *ISLA: A Journal of Micronesian Studies* (Rainy Season 1995): 149, 151.

[33] Vicente Diaz, "Into the Sunset (Boulevard): Tracking the Disturbing(ly) Familia(r) in Southern California." Conference paper presented February 11–12, 2000, University of California, Santa Cruz.

[34] Faye Untalan Munoz, "Pacific Islanders: A Perplexed, Neglected Minority," *Church and Society* (January–February 1974): 15–23.

[35] Ibid.

[36] Yen Le Espiritu. *Filipino American Lives* (Philadelphia: Temple University Press, 1995), 14–16.

[37] Epeli Hau'ofa. "Our Sea of Islands," *The Contemporary Pacific* (Spring 1994): 157.

[38] Pacific Islands Report: http://pidp.ewc.hawaii.edu/PI Report/1998/February/02-06-05.html

[39] Haunani-Kay Trask, *From a Native Daughter* (Monroe, Me.: Common Courage Press, 1993).

[40] Kilusang Magbubukid ng Pilipinas, "Hacienda Looc Peasants Hit Malacanang Order" (Press release. August 17, 2000. http://www.golfwar.org.).

[41] Matt DeVries and Jen Schradie, "The Golf War" (VHS, 1995).

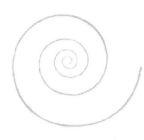

PART TWO
Leaving the Islands

In this part, four authors examine the processes that have taken island people away from home, working from the point of view of the islands themselves. These pieces help the reader see similarities and differences between the experiences of people who came from different island groups and went to different places.

In "Paradise Left?" John Connell takes a demographic and economic look at the region as a whole and asks what drives people to leave the islands and what effects migration has. He lays out the political and economic forces that have caused many people to leave their home islands and move elsewhere within the Pacific and beyond, and that have encouraged them to choose particular destinations. He examines a number of factors that affect Pacific Islander migrations, such as gender selectivity, education, and agricultural change. He describes some issues tying islanders abroad to their homelands, such as remittances and return migration.

Moving away from economic to psychological and cultural issues, Asesela Ravuvu investigates "Security and Confidence as Basic Factors in Pacific Islanders' Migration." Ravuvu is the first author in this anthology to write on the basis of research in Melanesia, in this case Fiji. He helps the reader imagine the fear with which island migrants confront the prospect of migrating and their new surroundings, and the ways they cope with strangeness. He examines a number of factors that help migrants adjust successfully and suggests things that host societies can do to help make the transition successful.

Wendy E. Cowling takes the reader to Tonga in "Motivations for Contemporary Tongan Migration." She describes the Tongan migration overseas, to Australia and other outposts. The bulk of her contribution is a detailed discussion of the roles of custodian/brokers and family networks in selecting people for migration, choosing their destinations, monitoring their activities abroad, and facilitating the sending of remittances. The picture that emerges is of a multinational network tying Tonga together with several points in the diaspora. Cowling also attends to ways that emigration has affected the society of Tongans who remained behind.

Craig R. Janes tells the story of Samoan migration to California in "From Village to City." He outlines the historical factors that gave rise to the movement of Samoans to the United States in the aftermath of World War II. He describes *fa'asamoa*, the Samoan way of life in village and extended family. And he shows how migration worked out in individual lives by recounting the stories of three Samoan migrants.

CHAPTER 4

Paradise Left? : Pacific Island Voyagers in the Modern World

John Connell

In the remote microstates of the South Pacific, prospects for economic growth are unusually limited. Hence the now widely perceived dispari- ties in economic welfare between the Pacific states, especially the small- est states of Polynesia and Micronesia, and the fringing metropolitan nations have contributed not only to substantial migration but also to increasing pressures for further migration. So extensive has this migra- tion become that some of the greatest concentrations of Pacific Islanders are in cities such as Auckland, Honolulu, and Los Angeles rather than in the South Pacific. Some of the smallest states have more islanders over- seas than at home, and currently populated small states and islands are likely to experience future depopulation. As emigration continues, small and vulnerable South Pacific states, in a region of unprecedented strate- gic significance, have become irrevocably a peripheral and dependent part of a wider world.

A conventional image of the South Pacific (especially Polynesia) is of island paradise where an idyllic existence in conditions of "subsistence affluence" (Fisk 1966) is widespread. This perception of the region is cer- tainly not the view from within the South Pacific, at least as reflected in the steady outflow of migrants from the region. In many areas, "changes in natural trends due to declining mortality, the impact of the family planning program, and fertility decline from many causes are overlain completely by migration" (Brookfield 1980, 185). Small islands and small island-states are "beautiful but not places to live" (Bedford 1980, 57). Many aspects of social and economic life on the smaller islands of the South Pacific are affected and organized by migration; it is unlikely that this will change in the future. It might even be said that the Polynesian

This essay was previously published in *Pacific Bridges: The New Immigration from Asia and the Pacific Islands*, edited by James T. Fawcett and Benjamin V. Cariño (Staten Island, N.Y.: Center for Migration Studies, 1987), 375–404.

states are characterized by international emigration, the Melanesian states are characterized by internal migration (although across significant language and cultural boundaries), and the Micronesian states are experiencing both patterns of migration along with some immigration of migrant workers.

THE SOUTH PACIFIC REGION

The South Pacific region, as defined here, includes some twenty-two states and almost a thousand language groups; it is an area of exceptional geographical, cultural, and economic diversity. The region includes only 550,000 square kilometers of land amid 30 million square kilometers of ocean. It has three indigenous population groups—Melanesians, Polynesians, and Micronesians—and recent immigrants have included Europeans, Indians, and Chinese. The pattern of political organization in the region is also diverse. Many of the larger countries are independent, notably those of Melanesia; the exception is New Caledonia, which remains a territory of France but has a strong independence movement. In Micronesia only Kiribati and Nauru are independent; in Polynesia Western Samoa, Tonga, and Tuvalu are independent. Both American Samoa and Guam are territories of the United States. In Micronesia the Northern Marianas is a commonwealth of the United States, and the constituent states of the U.S.-administered Trust Territory of the Pacific Islands are in varying stages of negotiating self-government in "free association" with the United States. Both Wallis and Futuna and French Polynesia are overseas territories of France. Tokelau is administered by New Zealand, whereas the Cook Islands and Niue are self-governing in association with New Zealand. Pitcairn Island remains a British colony. The variety of political structures has major significance for international migration.

With the exception of Papua New Guinea, all the states in the region are extremely small, in both population and land area, although some countries have very large Exclusive Economic Zones. Economic and political jurisdiction over vast ocean areas has increased the economic and strategic significance of the region. Great distances separate countries and island groups within countries. Smallness, isolation, and fragmentation impose constraints on their development strategies. Even in the larger states, the small size of the domestic market has hampered the development of import substitution industries, and only Fiji has a substantial industrial sector; consequently there is a high demand for imports and a consequent necessity to generate increased exports, but also considerable trade imbalances. In the case of the atoll states particularly, an extremely restricted physical environment severely limits the range of productive opportunities.

A negligible share in most commodity markets gives the island countries a weak negotiating position. Their economies are small, open, largely dependent on agricultural production and fisheries, and vulnerable to international economic changes. In the last few years, falling world prices for many basic commodities have seriously weakened the economic situation of most island-states. Some of the smallest states, especially the politically dependent territories, also depend on aid, principally from Australia, France, and the United States.

The significance of the agricultural and fisheries sector lies in its actual and potential contribution to employment, incomes, and welfare (specifically nutrition and health). Yet the fragmentary available figures suggest that the agricultural sector has performed poorly in recent years. Although most of the island-states' populations work in agriculture, usually combining subsistence and cash-cropping activities, some states have experienced an actual decline in food production per capita. Imports of foodstuffs, some of which can be produced locally, have increased in quantity and variety. Exploitation of the extensive fishing resources by developed nations has had limited benefit to the island-states. Yet fisheries have a greater unrealized economic potential for most countries in the region than any other sector of the economy.

Most nonagricultural employment in the region is in the services sector, concentrated in the government. Nowhere is this more apparent than in the constituent states of the Trust Territory of the Pacific Islands and some other dependent states, where productive employment constitutes a small proportion of the total employment. Throughout the region there has been a shift in the labor force from the agricultural to the services sector. Economic recession at the start of the 1980s severely restricted the growth of new employment opportunities, and in many countries a growing problem has been urban and especially youth unemployment. Compared with other parts of the Third World, however, the region has high levels of income and welfare (health, education, social services, and nutrition). Although Western Samoa, Tuvalu, Kiribati, and Tonga are all included within the United Nations group of Least-Developed Countries, their development situations are no worse than those of other small Pacific states.

The larger independent Melanesian countries—Papua New Guinea and the Solomon Islands and, to a lesser extent, Vanuatu and Fiji—have more diverse economies, are much less vulnerable to fluctuations in the external economy, and hence have the best prospects for development. The dependent territories, especially the American territories, tend to have a narrow economic base, although they are supported by apparently long-term political agreements and external development assistance. The independent states of Kiribati and Tuvalu experience severe problems in maintaining basic subsistence levels for their dense populations; continued aid and emigration appear to be the only feasible solutions for them (Connell 1985a).

Thus the region remains on the extreme periphery of the global economic system, to the extent that:

> The Pacific Island countries show all the signs of "underdevelopment" and "dependency": their economies are export orientated; there is little autonomous industrial development, political, public service, and private sector elites have a vested interest in the maintenance of present patterns of aid and development; foreign-owned companies have made handsome profits and still dominate some sectors of the economy; urbanization is running ahead of urban employment; most people are peasant producers with only a partial involvement in the cash economy. (Macdonald 1982a, 57)

Despite these similarities, the countries of the region have had quite different economic and political pasts. Their population structures, migration experiences, and development plans reflect some of their differences.

The populations of most South Pacific states are now as large as they have ever been, and despite recent declines in fertility, the growth rates in most countries remain high. The current population growth rate for the South Pacific as a whole is around 2.5 percent a year, by world standards a high rate. For some observers it suggests the prospect of a Malthusian crisis as population outstrips resources. (See, for example, Fairbairn 1982). The postwar demographic pattern in most countries of the region has been one of continued high or only recently declining birthrates combined with substantially lower death rates; the onset of the demographic transition has produced rapidly growing populations in many areas, especially in parts of Melanesia and Micronesia. In most parts of Polynesia, natural increase is very high, but population sizes are stable or declining as emigration siphons off the excess numbers. Higher life expectancy has resulted principally from a drop in infant mortality, and the decline in mortality has generally been accompanied by an epidemiological transition from infectious and parasitic diseases to chronic noncommunicable diseases.

Several countries in the region have responded to high fertility levels with family planning policies and programs. In the 1970s, Fiji achieved such a substantial reduction in fertility levels that its program, with that of Singapore, was regarded as a model for the Third World. In recent years there have been indications not only of increasing fertility levels and declining contraceptive acceptance rates, but also of considerable national and individual resistance to family planning programs, especially in Melanesia. Thus a critical development issue for the region is that of maintaining, let alone improving, present standards of living in the face of rapid population increases.

CONTEMPORARY MIGRATION FROM THE SOUTH PACIFIC

International migration to the metropolitan nations on the fringes of the Pacific is primarily a Polynesian phenomenon. Many people from Niue, the Cook Islands, Tonga, Western Samoa, and American Samoa have moved either to New Zealand (whence some have gone on to Australia) or increasingly, as the New Zealand economy has stagnated and immigration restrictions have become tighter, to the United States. For the smallest states—Niue and the Cook Islands (and also American Samoa, Pitcairn Island, and Tokelau)—movement has been particularly dramatic since less than half the indigenous population remains. Only the Cook Islands, Niue, and Pitcairn are consistently losing population, however. In the largest countries of Melanesia emigration has nowhere reached such proportions: The larger countries are independent, rather than associated states, hence metropolitan immigration laws exert some control, and their economies are more viable. Two other significant migration streams to metropolitan nations are, first, that of Fiji Indians who are moving primarily to Canada and, to a lesser extent, to the United States; and, second, that of Chamorros (from Guam and the Northern Marianas) who are moving to the United States. Political status affects migration in that the nationals of the Cook Islands, Niue, and Tokelau are New Zealand citizens and may move there freely. Similarly, American Samoans, Guamanians, and Northern Marianas islanders are free to enter the United States. The widespread migration from these states hints at the role of legal restrictions in constraining emigration from the South Pacific region.

Within the South Pacific, significant international migration movements also occur. Polynesians have moved from French Polynesia and Wallis and Futuna to New Caledonia, although in both cases this movement has been particularly reversed since the end of the "nickel boom." A second important movement is that of i-Kiribati and Tuvaluans to

Nauru. Although some regional population movements exist elsewhere, they are minor in number and significance. In every case the opportunities for international migration movements are increasingly directed outward. The scale of international migration currently appears to be more closely determined by the vicissitudes of the international economy (and specifically that in the United States and New Zealand), rather than the domestic island economies. It is also affected by the legal restrictions placed on international migration by the metropolitan nations, restrictions that are likely to be partly determined by the international economic situation. Thus the scale of future international migration is unpredictable. However, the signing of the Compact of Free Association between the former entities of the Trust Territory (Palau, the Marshall Islands, and the Federated States of Micronesia) allows free movement between those states and the United States. Although distance, language ability, and skills place Micronesians seeking American employment at a disadvantage, it is likely that outmigration will increase substantially within the next decade because local economies are particularly impoverished (Schwalbenberg 1984). Beyond this, it is now unlikely that the Australian government will relax its restrictions on migration from the South Pacific. In every case the structure of migration will continue to be essentially determined by political and economic forces in the metropolitan nations.

The major influences in international migration are economic even when social forces are also significant. Migration is primarily a response to inequalities, both real and perceived, in socioeconomic opportunities that are themselves a result of dependent or uneven sectoral and regional development. Migration has been largely a function of the effective penetration of peripheral capitalism, the imposition of colonial administration, and perceptions of relative deprivation. But social influences on migration are also important, such as the desire for access to education and health services, and also as one element of the rite of transition to adulthood.

Family migration, often initiated by the male, now predominates, and sex ratios in most areas are balanced. As elsewhere, migration is generally characterized by the movement of young men and women, a situation that has contributed to transferred high fertility and dependency rates in some areas. Just as economic and social influences on migration cannot be easily distinguished, nor can the economic and social impacts of migration in the small states of the region.

Radical changes in expectations about what constitutes a satisfactory standard of living, a desirable occupation, and a suitable mix of accessible services and amenities have been a major cause of migration.

Aspirations now almost always involve the availability of imported food and other goods and access to schools, hospitals, and even modern entertainment—all of which demand cash income. In parallel with changing aspirations and the increased necessity to earn cash, agricultural work throughout the Pacific has been losing prestige. Hence the limited participation of young men in the agricultural economy is declining further. Changes in values, following increased educational opportunities and the expansion of bureaucratic (largely urban) employment within the region, as local employment opportunities have not kept pace with population growth. These changes have also contributed to the widening gap between expectations, which are themselves continually being revised upward, and the reality of limited domestic employment and incomes.

In some countries, education is oriented to the needs of migrants in their destinations rather than at home and hence proves a catalyst to migration. In Kiribati, for example, attempts to introduce vocational education in community high schools have been strongly opposed by parents concerned that their children will be unable to obtain bureaucratic employment. Moreover, many educational systems, notably those in U.S. territories, inevitably result in disdain for rural life because "the exclusion of traditional skills and knowledge from westernized school curricula in many developing countries amounts to a constant tacit assumption that such things are not worth learning" (Johannes 1981, 148). Tertiary education is usually undertaken outside the home country, especially in the smaller states, a factor contributing to emigration. Consequently, "migrants seek in the West access to material goods, jobs in the industrial sector, better education for their young, and social mobility in a society they have believed free of the traditional barriers of rank and family status that made such mobility difficult at home" (Shore 1978, xiii). The experience of the wider world, its values, and its material rewards further underlines the migratory experience.

THE IMPACT OF MIGRATION

Migration is both a catalyst and a consequence of social and economic change, and no society and few individuals in the South Pacific have been untouched by its influence. Few of its effects can be reviewed in any detail in this chapter, although migration has had a major influence in other spheres, such as politics, religion, nutrition (Connell 1984a), health (Connell 1987), and the lives of women (Connell 1984b). The present focus on the relationship between migration and demographic and economic change emphasizes issues relevant to the future status and structure of international migration in the region.

Sex Selectivity

Sex selectivity in migration has implications for demographic change. There is much evidence that when men were the primary migrants, the birthrate was slowed; in some areas, such as Rotuma, migration was even regarded as one means of family planning (A. Howard 1961). Recently, more balanced sex ratios in migration and the demise of long-term labor contracts have limited the impact of migration on fertility (and reductions in infant mortality) that counteract any population decline following migration (Connell 1986). Indeed, in large parts of Polynesia natural increase is very high and international migration has proved to be a safety valve. The general argument that return migrants, through their contact with "modern" values favoring small families, induce lower fertility and thus reduce population growth in rural areas (see Standing 1982, 23; Simmons, Diaz-Briquets, and Laquian 1977) is not validated in the South Pacific. The extent of emigration, and the strong influence of Christianity have all encouraged high fertility. The direct effect of migration on fertility levels in the region is now generally limited.

The major effect of migration on fertility in the region is through the transfer of fertility from one part of a country to another (usually from rural to urban areas) or outside the country. One result of this transfer is that migrants, and especially children born outside the home village or country, increasingly lose their native identity, experience problems of ethnicity, and, perhaps most important, find that they have only minimal residual claims to land and hence development opportunities in their home areas. This loss is exacerbated where marriages are increasingly across language boundaries and ethnic and cultural groups. Since alien birthplaces and loss of linguistic ability necessarily discourage return migration, transferred fertility is a major influence in the permanence of migration.

Education Selectivity

Throughout the South Pacific it is possible to demonstrate that it is the most educated who migrate first and, moreover, that many migrants have left rural areas to take advantage of superior urban and international educational facilities. These two factors of migration reinforce each other, so that the bias is likely to be maintained (Connell 1980, 6). Invariably, migration results in the loss of the most energetic, skilled, and innovative individuals, and this loss is not compensated either by remittances or by any other trickle-down effect from urban and national development. In some small states the brain drain has been excessive: The

Cook Islands, for example, lost more than half of its vocationally quali-fied population in the single decade of 1966–1976 (Cook Islands 1983, 23). The ubiquity of the education bias, despite the short history of formal education in parts of the Pacific, suggests that it is likely to continue (see Hezel 1985). The combination of changing aspirations and the migration of the more educated young contributes to a brain or skill drain from national peripheries and from small states, perhaps ultimately worsening the welfare and bargaining position of those places.

Agricultural Change

There are complex and substantial variations in the impact of migration on the agricultural system. These differences derive principally from the extent to which the agricultural system depends on male or female labor, the length of absence of migrants, and the extent of compensatory remit-tances that may be used to hire labor or machinery (Connell 1986). When migration takes place in a rural area characterized by low and perhaps diminishing returns due to population pressure on small landholdings, the reduction in population hypothetically can reduce any tendency toward diminishing returns and raise the productivity of rural labor. In the Pacific area, however, population pressure on resources is generally modest and the potential for mechanization is limited, so that rural land is subsequently worked by a smaller remaining population without an increase in productivity. Apart from the few states with declining popu-lations, increased food production or purchases are required to support the growing population. Of seven larger Pacific countries (Fiji, French Polynesia, Papua New Guinea, Solomon Islands, Tonga, Vanuatu, Western Samoa), over the period from 1965–1978, only Papua New Guinea actually increased its food production at a rate greater than that of the population increase. The others suffered declines in their per capita food production, resulting in less food being available and greater com-pensatory imports (Yang 1982), although such trends were only partly related to migration. During this transition, agricultural systems have gone from "subsistence affluence" to "subsistence malaise" (Grossman 1981) and local economies have gone from "village subsistence" to "mon-etary subservience" (Thomson 1976, 166). In much of Micronesia and elsewhere, whole socioeconomies have gone from subsistence to subsidy. Again, these trends have been strongly influenced by attitudinal changes, with discontent contributing to a downward spiral of the local economy.

A further result of the limited availability of labor and labor-saving technology has been a general decline in the use of marginal and distant land. In parts of Fiji, migration in the 1950s had already resulted in a declining area of cultivated land (Ward 1961, 270). Where a cash inflow from remittances or wages is considerable, some components of the agricultural system may simply be abandoned. Thus, in the Cook Islands regular remittance payments appear to encourage many middle-aged and elderly people to abandon full-time agricultural activities and become dependent upon remittances (Curson 1979, 193–194); but only in exceptional circumstances, such as in parts of American Samoa, Micronesia, and Nauru, has subsistence agriculture effectively disappeared.

In some parts of the Pacific, especially in the smaller states, opportunities for productive investment in the agricultural economy range from severely restricted to virtually nonexistent. In these situations, typified in wholly atoll states like Kiribati, the Marshall Islands, and Tuvalu, conditions are such that "every migration creates greater consumer wants and diminishes the chance of satisfying them at home" (Wallman 1977, 111); lands are neglected and the idea of achieving self-sufficiency becomes more and more implausible. Even on larger islands, such as Western Samoa, it could be argued that migration is "a far more lucrative investment than anything available in the village" (Shankman 1976, 71) principally because of the lack of land, the unavailability of cash crops other than copra, and remoteness. In these conditions, income can be invested only in increased, if not necessarily improved, consumption. Moreover, if out-migration from small islands decreases, as is likely in the case of Tuvalu (because of declining employment opportunities in Nauru), cash incomes will fall; and although the subsistence sector should be able to support the increased population, cash crop production (of copra only) is likely to fall as coconuts are eaten rather than sold (Chambers 1975, 103), thus reducing the quality of life. Capital investment in agriculture is most appropriate to the larger islands; in the smaller atolls especially, the conservative use of income reflects the lack of productive investment opportunities.

The process of agricultural decline that has gone on elsewhere, as in the smaller Caribbean islands (see Manners 1965, 186), is being replicated on the small islands of the Pacific, especially on those where international migration has been common. Niue is characterized by "dynamics of dependence." Many of the potential innovators in agriculture have migrated, and farmers have shortened their time horizons, believing that there is little point in planting coconut trees if they bear fruit when the owner has migrated, when he has a smaller family to support or inadequate labor to maintain the plantation (Pollard 1978, 82). Overall, then, migration and migrants' remittances have contributed to the disintensification of the traditional agricultural system (Brookfield 1972, 1984) that has followed the expansion of cash cropping.

Although increased urban demand might have been expected to stimulate rural production, rapid urbanization is exacerbating these trends in the South Pacific. Earlier wants have become needs, and purchases must be partially financed by migration to wage employment. The shift away from production has been followed, more slowly and less obviously, by a decline in exchange and reciprocity. A parallel trend is the growing segregation of work from private life and the separation of public and private spheres of activity. The establishment of capitalism, along with the emergence of cash cropping, wage labor, migration, and greater individualism within nuclear families, has tended to separate families from the community and women from men. Such trends are universal.

Remittances

The absence of migrants is usually balanced by some form of resource transfer from migrants to kin in the areas of origin. Such remittances, which maintain social ties and act as insurance premiums for migrants, are used principally to repay debts, finance migration moves for kin, and purchase consumer goods, including housing. Their use reinforces a traditional set of values. Thus migration, emerging out of inequality, may reinforce, rather than conflict with, the social hierarchy. Moreover, overseas migrants often have conservative attitudes toward development in their home areas; many Palauans in Hawaii have argued that it is important "to limit outside influences and hold onto traditional ways" (Vitarelli 1981, 22), and so remittances are aimed at conserving that tradition. The economic role of remittances has been discussed in detail elsewhere (Connell 1980, 1986). In some of the poorer parts of the region, including Kiribati and Tuvalu, migrants are "sending home part of the means of subsistence. This is quite a different pressure on urban incomes from one where gifts to people at home are luxuries and the timing of them [is] more or less immaterial to the recipients" (Morauta and Hasu 1979, 31).

The dependence on remittances is equally great, if not crucial to subsistence, in numerous parts of the South Pacific characterized by high levels of internal or international migration. Despite contributing to inflation, especially in the larger Polynesian countries, remittances have raised living standards and eased national balance-of-payment problems; they have also contributed to employment, especially in the construction and service sectors. In some small states and on a number of islands, remittances constitute more than a quarter of the total income in normal circumstances (Connell 1980, 1986) and in exceptional conditions (as in the aftermath of cyclones) and places (some outer islands of Kiribati and Tuvalu and many villages elsewhere) may constitute more than double the proportion. The resultant dependence on remittances has reinforced the belief of individuals, households, and states in the necessity for continued migration. Indeed, increased demand for imported consumer goods can usually be met only by further migration where little of the remitted income is invested in economic growth.

Remittances and the elitist and consumer-oriented ideas of return migrants contribute to increased demands for high levels of consumption and welfare, although neither remittances nor return migrants may make significant contributions to increased production. Rising expectations in the wake of independence for many states in the 1970s and growing materialism have exacerbated the shift from production to consumption, the decline of exchange, and an increase in social tensions. The spreading taste for commodities has influenced work habits. For many in the South Pacific, the largest cities and the metropolitan countries exercise the same allure, offer the same sense of future, and apparently validate migration.

Return Migration

Since migrants are generally younger, less traditional, and better educated than nonmigrants, they have a considerable potential for contributing to economic and social development in their villages and countries of origin. Elderly migrants, however, are unlikely to be interested in development opportunities; in Wallis and Futuna, where by the 1970s the islands could be described as "holiday islands and havens for the retired" (Roux 1980, 174), return migrants have done so because of limited success abroad. This tendency is best documented in the case of American Samoa, where those who returned valued their family ties and the customary social organization of Samoa but also had been unsuccessful in some respect—usually in gaining long-term employment—in their adjustment to the U.S. economy and society (Lyons 1980). Both nostalgia and reaction to discrimination also play a part. The available evidence suggests, however, that in comparison with situations elsewhere, return migration is limited and confined largely to "failures" or the retired. Moreover, the more successful return migrants tend to remain in the towns. Despite stated intentions, "it is probably unrealistic to expect more than a tiny fraction of those who have already escaped from the rural areas to ever go back. Many will want to go back but only provided that 'want' is never put to the task" (Crocombe 1978, 52).

All too often return migration is perceived as an admission of failure. Hence Shankman (1976, 96) states bluntly that "Polynesian migrants do not return except for visitations, once they are overseas and have attained a degree of security." The limited extent of return migration is in part due to the great differences in income levels in Polynesia and in metropolitan nations and in part due to the difficulty of obtaining skilled jobs and the reluctance of return migrants to work in the agricultural sector. Consequently, widespread intentions to return may have more to do with nostalgia for the past than with a real plan for the future (Pitt and Macpherson 1974, 16). In general, despite occasional pressures on migrants overseas and occasional incentives from within the South Pacific, the volume of return migration is small.

Where rising expectations are combined with increased pressure on rural resources and static job opportunities in the formal sector, migration from rural areas is more likely to be permanent; this permanence may be in urban areas (and there are now third-generation urban residents in the South Pacific) or in metropolitan nations. In the United States, and certainly elsewhere, a significant number of ethnic Pacific Islanders are unable to speak, or at least speak fluently, the language of their home country (Levin 1985). This lack of facility is inevitably a deterrent to return migration, of either children or their parents, since all are embarrassed by the prospect of "young Samoans returning home and unable to speak their own language" (Emery 1976, 16). Such children are almost inevitably destined for an urban and international future.

The extent to which the impact of return migration is positive is doubtful. Although Pitt (1970) has argued that skills obtained from migration are valuable in the case of Western Samoa, considerable doubt exists about the transferability of skills obtained overseas to an economy like that of Western Samoa, where wages and salaries are much lower than in metropolitan countries. It appears that those who have the skills most in demand in Western Samoa concluded that there were four principal reasons for nonreturn. First, local businesses succeeded only rarely despite numerous attempts—partly because commerce was poorly understood and also because the social power of the *'aiga* (extended family) ties eroded profitability. Second, wages and fringe benefits in Western Samoa were very low; third, New Zealand-born children had trouble adjusting to Western Samoa and hence parents were reluctant to return with them; and, fourth, the gerontocratic social organization limited individual aspirations (Macpherson 1983). Moreover, in Western Samoa and other island states there is much evidence that actual return migrants are a "source of dissatisfaction with village life and the predominantly subsistence economy" despite, or more probably because of, the status they have gained from migration (Meleisea and Meleisea 1980, 37). They introduce new discontent, values, and aspirations; do not settle long themselves; and induce others to follow their lead.

Nevertheless, in recent decades return migrants to the countries of the South Pacific have included many of the principal political leaders in the region, including most of those who took a significant part in negotiating independence for their states. Return migrants to the Cook Islands include its three successive premiers (Albert Henry, Geoffrey Henry, and Tom Davis) and elsewhere in the region most political leaders have experienced education, training, and even employment abroad. For the molding of a political elite, the overseas experience has been vital. So, too, this return migration critically influences values; for many Cook Islands politicians, for example, "their life-style tends to be European in private and Maori in public" (Crocombe 1979, 54). These are the marginal men who were once the proponents of modernization and change. Those who might be future political leaders are now less likely to return, a situation that both emphasizes the conservative politics from the South Pacific and channels the frustrated away from inflexible systems of social and political stratification (as, particularly, in Tonga and Fiji).

Moreover, potential return migrants may face competition at home for the limited employment opportunities available and opposition from those who fear losing their jobs. For example: "Samoans who stayed at home will have taken over unused resources, especially in areas of rising population. Many rural Samoans feel that the migrants should not come back for long periods though they are welcome as visitors" (Pitt and Macpherson 1974, 15). The same attitudes are present in Niue and the Cook Islands. There are then few social, political, and economic incentives to return and, sometimes, not even the security of subsistence.

Many of the more positive comments on the impact of migration date from an earlier era when migration was less common, it was predominantly circular (thus producing a high level of remittances since return was almost certain), and there was no real demand for skilled labor in the region. Restless young men could earn money overseas, invest in the village, and return as responsible citizens. But the current context of migration is quite different. Whereas early migration was prestigious, it is now too common to be so. It has also produced a socioeconomy dependent upon migration. Expectations have risen and are increasingly difficult to meet within the confines of small national economies. Migration is thus viewed less as a means of diversifying economic risk within households than as a permanent transfer of human resources elsewhere. Migration is no longer so likely to be circular.

TOWARD A NEW DIASPORA

Undoubtedly, international migration has been a major benefit to destination countries, but for countries of origin the outcome is less clear. The prevalent use of remittances, the lack of economic growth, the failure to restructure economies, and the form of social change encouraged by emigration suggest minimal benefits at best. The impact of international migration in the migrants themselves, especially on their personal values and attitudes, is wide-ranging. On the positive side are the potential for gaining higher wages, education and other welfare benefits, experience, and new skills. Though there are social and psychological costs in the course of this acquisition, the conclusions suggest that many migrants benefit, although their children may be less fortunate. Because of limited return migration, the marginal value of many acquired skills in the sending countries, and the social conflicts between migrants and home societies, not all individual gains become gains for the sending countries.

At a national level, some evidence suggests that the source countries may suffer no net loss from high levels of emigration in the long run. Citing the case of a number of small countries, Blazic-Metzner and Hughes (1982, 96) conclude that "the benefits nevertheless appear to exceed the costs for both individuals and countries." They note, however, that "the literature on this subject is large and emotive" (101) and not wholly conclusive and that benefits will not occur if "the country concerned follows foolish policies" (95). In the case of the small South Pacific states, few are large enough to have effective development policies. Consequently, international migration is often viewed as a significant source of income, as a safety valve that reduces pressure on national governments to provide employment opportunities and welfare services, and as a means of satisfying rising aspirations among political minorities and the poor and unemployed. Concern focuses on specific issues such as the brain or skill drain, or, in the case of Niue, Pitcairn, and the Cook Islands, the overall population decline.

The safety-valve effect, limited economic growth, and arguments in favor of individual freedom of movement have created a steady migration from many countries. Constraints on international migration are posed by the destination countries rather than the source countries. International migration has thus become a substitute for development rather than a short-term support for increasing the effectiveness of national development efforts. Moreover, if migration were to become more restricted, and national socioeconomies were not restructured, the benefits would be even less apparent because of the inevitability of declining remittances in conditions of rapid population growth.

While international migration has had both positive and negative effects in the South Pacific region, the significance of the positive effects (notably increased standards of living) must be contrasted with the limited development potential of many countries in the region and their failure to achieve significant economic growth. The possibilities for agricultural and other forms of development vary substantially within the Pacific.

Most countries in the South Pacific cannot guarantee perpetually unlimited migration and access to metropolitan countries; however, some, such as Kiribati, and Tuvalu, now have effectively no outlets (other than Nauru in the short term) and, paradoxically, it is in those countries that a migration-based development strategy appears to be almost the only viable option. Even in the 1890s, labor migration was "the only alternative to starvation" (Macdonald 1982b, 53). In light of concern over the impending closure of the Nauru phosphate mines, a recent review of Australian aid gave particular emphasis to the special needs of the small states in the South Pacific. The executive summary attached sufficient importance to the problems of Kiribati and Tuvalu to give them a significance denied to all other states except Papua New Guinea. The review argued that Australia should "go beyond traditional ideas of aid" (Australia 1984, 181) to provide a special immigration quota for two countries with which Australia has hitherto had few ties. As in the case of the Asian Development Bank survey, external perceptions increasingly recognize the need for international migration from the South Pacific—a recognition that is likely to stimulate further pressures from other countries and reduce the dynamism of more self-reliant development initiatives.

In his introduction to an analysis of the impact of migration on Western Samoa, Shankman (1976, 17) makes the sweeping statement that "there are no examples of countries that have developed through migration and remittances." The historical validity of this argument is highly doubtful, and in countries like Kiribati and Tuvalu, though migration may not have contributed greatly to development, it has certainly prevented nondevelopment. The principal advantages from international migration follow short-term or seasonal migration, but as migration becomes more pervasive and long-term these benefits may be reduced as dependence and uncertainty increases.

Concern over future metropolitan restrictions on immigration and issues of national pride and independence have produced a minority interest in the achievement of economic development in a more self-reliant context, possibly associated with a transition to low fertility. The economics of self-reliance have been considered elsewhere (Connell 1986; Seers 1983). In most states of the South Pacific, movement toward the self-sufficiency that reduction of migration and remittances implies would be difficult and painful. In many places aspirations are firmly directed toward the acquisition of modern goods. As has been argued for the small island of Rotuma, "with the prestige given to 'foreign' goods, it is doubtful, therefore, that Rotumans would *want* to be self sufficient, even if it were a possibility"

(Plant 1977, 174). In Tikopia, "from such a level of dependence on imported goods it becomes difficult to retreat without unease and a sense of deprivation" (Firth 1971, 69). In Ponape, too, villagers are not interested in adequate subsistence or even the "right to subsistence," but rather desire "continued and increased access to the goods and prestige provided by employment" (Petersen 1979, 37). These values from different parts of Polynesia and Micronesia are exceptionally widespread and attest to the serious local problems attached to even marginal movements toward greater self-reliance.

The limited prospects for economic development within the South Pacific are likely to be increasingly influenced by global economic cycles and the peripheral position of the region in that economy. Most economic forecasts for Third World countries in the next decade suggest a bleak future for the states of the South Pacific, although the states' isolation, their tenuous links with the international economy, and the strength of their subsistence sectors are likely to continue to dampen the regional impact of fluctuations in the world economy. Because of their growing dependence on depressed world markets, "the inherent vulnerability of Pacific island economies has become increasingly apparent" (Polson 1983, 21; see also Tisdell and Fairbairn 1984). The traditional export crops of the region are less able to support Pacific Island populations and governments at their current expenditure levels, let alone support economic growth and the rising expectations of potentially growing populations. Even where there has been mining development, low market prices have prevented substantial gain. Owing to these economic trends, the South Pacific states have become increasingly dependent on the global economy for aid, trade, private investment, and, ultimately, migration. Their economic and cultural dependence will determine future trends in migration.

Virtually throughout the South Pacific, islanders have mobilized colonial ties to emigrate to the metropolitan countries; small states like American Samoa, the Cook Islands, Niue, and Tokelau have more islanders overseas than in their own countries. In larger Polynesian states the same trend exists, and the Micronesian states are likely to approach a point where Micronesian residents of the United States may outnumber the "folks back home" (Marshall 1979, 10–11). There has already been significant migration from Palau (and Guam and the Marianas) to the United States, and this movement is likely to be followed by more extensive migration from other parts of Micronesia (Connell 1985b). The more often such choices are taken, the more difficult they will be to avoid for future generations of Pacific Islanders as the focus of life moves ever outward.

Individual aspirations in the South Pacific are as much focused on emigration now as they have ever been; there is no apparent reason why this focus should change. Despite the initial costs of migration, migrants usually reach the living standards of the host countries, or at least of the less affluent within those countries, within a generation or so. Long waiting lists for emigration and illegal migration demonstrate a large pent-up demand. Examination of development plans, policies, and practices in the "soft states" of the region further suggests that future economic development is unlikely to stimulate increased income and welfare levels in a equitable manner or to generate significant increases in wage employment. Moreover, not only is there no real opposition through policy to sustained emigration overseas, but in many states policies actually favor labor migration and emigration.

Most migrants from the South Pacific, including some of those with skills, are in the secondary segment of the labor force of the metropolitan destination countries (mainly New Zealand and the United States), where social, institutional, and economic barriers prevent movement into the primary segment. Most Pacific Islanders remain in unskilled jobs with low wages (Levin 1985), unstable tenure, poor working conditions, few benefits, high employment, and little unionization. Hence, migrants from the region, whether temporary or effectively permanent, continue to function essentially as guest workers. As metropolitan economies are restructured and rationalized, the "secondary sector is most likely to experience a decline in the demand for labor" (Gibson 1982); immigration policies of the metropolitan countries are therefore tending toward greater severity toward migrants and skill bias. While global trends suggest increased national opposition to international migration—as a political response to social and economic problems associated with high levels of unemployment—evidence from the principal destination countries for South Pacific migrants suggests that future policies are unlikely to discriminate further against the South Pacific states and that familial ties may enable Pacific Islanders to increase their immigration even if metropolitan immigration laws are strengthened.

As they have done for more than two decades, many Pacific Islanders, especially Polynesians, see emigration or overseas employment as a means of escaping limited domestic economic opportunities and maximizing their household development options. The voices of those who urge more self-reliant development strategies or those who contemplate with nostalgia enclosed village or island communities with their assumed immutable order are lonely voices in the wilderness; it is the new diaspora that extraordinarily rapidly has come to characterize the contemporary South Pacific. One of the last regions of the world to be settled has entered a period of potential population decline.

CHAPTER 5

Security and Confidence as Basic Factors in Pacific Islanders' Migration

A. Ravuvu

FEAR OF THE UNKNOWN OR STRANGE WORLD

Many of us are too cautious or frightened to move into the unknown. According to beliefs of many Melanesians, Polynesians, and Micronesians, the unknown is dangerous, the abode of ancestral spirits and other cosmological entities. The spirit world is generally *tapu* or avoided by people if they want to live long and enjoy life. Thus, the strange or unknown world is feared and sanctified to the extent of being prohibited or *tapu* to mortal beings. No wonder the old women back home used to wail loudly and cry when we were sent to boarding schools far away from our isolated homes. To disappear into the unknown is tantamount to nonexistence or death, however temporary it may actually be. For no one knows for certain whether one is going to return. Every time I went back to boarding schools, the elders of my clan and other villagers would offer *yaqona* to the ancestral gods through our chief, requesting their protection and assistance so that the journey to and from school would be safe, and that they would protect me from the evil acts of others, both mortal and immortal. Thus, the unknown for many Pacific Islanders is the world of strange people with strange habits and customs that are difficult to come to terms with. To venture into such a world involves a great deal of risk-taking. This requires courage, a personal quality that can be appropriately developed only in a positive frame of mind common to societies in which the members believe in themselves rather than other extraneous or supernatural powers to effect their needs and fulfill their aspirations.

This essay was originally published in the *Journal of the Polynesian Society*, (1992): 329–341.

In many traditional Pacific societies, the strange and unknown world is the domain of males, those who were thought to have strength and confidence to face the odds likely to be met. The female arena is the known, the less dangerous, usually domestic surroundings. For instance, deep-sea fishing and hunting in dense forests are men's tasks, whereas women fish on shores and surrounding reefs. Women's sphere of activities is generally around the home, unless they are secure and confident enough to move beyond the domestic scene, and this is often done in groups or with men to provide protection. The group provides a sense of security and the larger the membership of the group the more confident and secure are the members.

GROUP SECURITY

It is important to understand that confidence and security among Pacific Islanders are acquired through membership of a kin group or otherwise. Members of the group cooperate and depend on one another for survival. The group provides security and confidence to members, and to be alienated from the group is a psychologically traumatic experience. Thus, individuals often make economic sacrifices in order to maintain group membership and attendant social and political ties.

Moving away from the support and protection of the group, a Pacific Islander often finds himself/herself helpless and isolated, so that insecurity or lack of confidence in oneself to succeed in a new surrounding makes life intolerable. The person becomes homesick and, unless he/she finds a known acquaintance, the return home to the group is not only inevitable but an urgent priority.

It is not unusual for Pacific Islanders, as it is for others, to move and settle far away from the home base where there are already people of their own kind or others whom they know. The earliest settlers or migrants provided security and confidence for the newcomers and even encouraged or assisted them to settle down. Thus, Pacific Island migrants generally venture only where others of their kind have already settled and from whom they quietly hope to receive assistance and protection from the threats posed by an unfamiliar environment. The earliest migrants and settlers, themselves feeling isolated at times, are also pleased to see newcomers and often urge them to stay on. (But, when there are plenty of one's own kind, and times are tough, the opposite may be the case.) This adds more security and confidence against the threat of the majority indigenous group. If the place and its people far away are well known and liked, and the journey to and from is easy and safe, it is thus less threatening to those intending to make the visit. There are also Pacific Islanders doing military service overseas in Britain, America, United Nations peacekeeping forces in Cambodia, Lebanon, etc., enjoying their work in an alternative form of security provided by being in the military forces of other nations.

RELIGION GIVES CONFIDENCE TO MOVE

Through European missionaries, Pacific Islanders were introduced to a new religious faith with a Christian God that could protect them not only from ill-doings by their own kind, but also those of the white men. To adopt the European god was also to acquire its power and, thus, the security and confidence to venture out into the distant unknown, as the Europeans had. Armed with the belief in the power of the Christian God, it was not too difficult to get Pacific Island men to move into the unknown and strange world spreading Christianity to its inhabitants. In the Pacific, the first to be Christianised were the Eastern Polynesians of Tahiti, followed by those in the Cook Islands, Samoa, Tonga and Fiji and, subsequently, Vanuatu, the Solomon Islands and Papua New Guinea, in that order.

Christianity provided a new, wider cultural base for understanding; protection and security were derived from acquiring the Christian technology of both software and hardware. Christian teaching and education provided strength and confidence for Pacific Islanders to move and settle first among neighbours of their own kind, then among more distant Pacific Islanders. Tongans, Samoans, Cook Islanders and Tahitians were the first to move into other worlds as Christianity progressed westward. Later, it also encouraged movement or migration among Melanesians. The last, but most important, move was to the sources where their new Christian God was perceived to have been originated—the metropolitan countries populated by whites of European descent. Pacific Islanders began to feel accepted by others and to feel secure and confident in interacting with them because they now shared a common religion. In fact, as well as in Australia, New Zealand, the United States of America, Philippines, Latin America, the Caribbean and beyond.

KNOWLEDGE IS POWER

Western-type formal education acquired within or outside one's own cultural context also provides power and strength to enable one to overcome one's fear of the strange world. Such education makes it easier for a person to cross intercultural context. Through adopting a Western-type education system, Pacific Islanders have acquired a great deal of knowledge and even curiosity about the outside world, in particular, that of our colonial masters.

Apart from Pacific Islanders who were forcibly resettled in other coun-tries for one reason or another by colonial powers, overseas education in nearby metropolitan countries such as New Zealand and Australia became another source of strength or power that provided security and confidence to those who had acquired such an opportunity.

A new difficulty, however, is that while the balance of power in the Pacific shifts toward Japan and its neighbours in Northeast Asia, our peo-ple are not adequately preparing themselves to meet this new challenge and to deal with these new powers. Whereas most of us now have some knowledge of English and of European culture, we have almost none of the languages or cultures of these countries that are likely to dominate the Pacific Islands in the years to come. This is not to reject English or English-speaking peoples, but to realise that, for the future, such a reali-sation alone is not enough.

SEEING IS BELIEVING

Knowledge about other people and other lands provides power and strength for one's personality in relation to others who do not possess it. Such knowledge is acquired through education derived from listening to stories and news about other people and lands, looking at pictures, movies, visitations of various types. There is, more and more, a constant flow of Pacific Islanders between Polynesia and Australia, New Zealand and the United States of America. And Micronesians above the equator move freely between their homelands and North America. But, even from the most isolated islands throughout the Pacific, we find I-Kiribati and Tuvaluans working on German ships, ni-Vanuatu on Taiwanese ships, Fijians in peacekeeping operations in the Middle East, Cambodia, Afghanistan and in the oil industry in the Arab countries. And there is a constant flow of people from throughout the Islands on training courses or attending conferences round the world. Their observations and expe-riences filter back to the most remote village, building up a picture (how-ever accurate or inaccurate) of which places are safe and which are dangerous, which are the source of money and which are poor. And with it is built up a network of contacts that others may use. With such expe-rience, power over the unkown is acquired and one's confidence is so enhanced that the potential migrant acquires security and confidence in facing the new world.

Fascination with what the outside world is like becomes a driving force that also drives Pacific Islanders to move, not only to satisfy curios-ity, but also to seek new opportunities and even to enhance their status at home. Initially, these adventurers were men whose masculinity and sense of conquest needed to be satisfied and their strength proved once and for all. Now, from Polynesia and parts of Micronesia, women travel in equal numbers, though not generally quite so far afield. For Melanesia and Kiribati the travelers are still mainly men.

With better communication, Pacific Islanders have become more aware of their problems in relation to the rest of the world; they perceive themselves as falling further behind in economic and social development. Even within the Pacific Islands, improved communication and better transport have increased movement of Island populations, so that the drift from the rural underdeveloped areas to the urban centres and port towns like Tarawa, Suva, Port Moresby, Honiara, Apia, and Nuku'alofa has become a major problem for these Island nations. This has given rise to increasing unemployment and other related social problems. Once in the urban centres, knowledge of the outside world is brought closer to them, through movies, television, videos, newspapers, radios and visitors. Experiences gained from living and working in an urban setting provide a new sense of confidence in handling the other world (but often reduced confidence about one's own), and additional motive to move further afield in search of better opportunities or the fantastic lifestyle portrayed by the mass media, overseas tourists and returned migrants.

Interaction with foreigners and tourists adds more understanding of the outside world. Cultural boundaries are, at times, blurred. Marriage across cultural boundaries, unthinkable a few decades ago, also takes place and increases. City and town lifestyles add more to the new acculturation process which develops most strongly in the character of urban dwellers. The urban dwellers of Pacific Island port towns provide proportionately more of the pool of migrants for overseas destinations such as New Zealand, Australia, Canada and the United States of America. Thus, the urban centres and port towns of the main islands of the Pacific countries act as a re-socialising agent for the outside world which has some cultural similarities with its local counterparts.

URBAN AND RURAL CATEGORIES

Among Fijians and other Pacific Islanders, to be an urban dweller is progressive, and to acquire a residential lot in the city is an achievement. City dwellers, because of their earning power and access to other modern amenities not readily available in the rural setting, often exude a quiet superiority when in the company of their rural kin. Although the rural folk often pride themselves as the people of the land who are maintaining their traditional identities and greater independence from being totally controlled by the pressure of the monetised or market economy, they feel deprived of the services and modern technological benefits which many urban dwellers enjoy. They, thus, have an inferiority complex in relation to the city dwellers who often boast about their comparative sophistication and advantages.

When a person is observed to be unsophisticated or not smart enough in complying with the norms or expectations of urban living, he or she is labeled as *"nako"* (of the village) or *"kaicolo"* (of the outback or interior) in Fiji, *"kainibuki"* (someone behind) in Kiribati, *"ai motu"* (of the outer islands) in Tonga, *"tufanua"* (without manners) in Samoa, *"bush kanaka"* in Pidgin, and so on. On the other hand, anyone who is smart and not shy, forward and who expresses himself in English and puts on fashionable clothes, shoes and make-up, is considered as urbane, of the city and big world, smart and cosmopolitan, cultivated and advanced, refined and European-like, even though a good number of such people possess hardly any such qualities. Nevertheless, because they are town dwellers, just as we perceive the whites, all of whom we believe, either rightly or wrongly, to have all the good things in life and, in particular, the money with which one can purchase any items one can think of in this world. Thus, increasingly, Pacific Islanders move to the towns and the cities where they hope to acquire the good and novel things which their rural life-styles cannot provide. Once in the city, they realise that work has to be done to maintain the newly acquired life-style; some just do enough to enjoy some aspects of the new life, but many others become hangers-on, street people or roamers, parasitic on others and living a hand-to-mouth existence.

Once established in the cities, many find it hard to return home empty-handed and, thus, the stay is prolonged and their sense of place or attachment to the home base weakened. Remittances in kind or cash, which may have been sent frequently to relatives back in the village, also diminish as time goes on. Although the pressure on some Island migrants to return home is great at times and many say they will return, only a few have really done so. With the migrant feeling more secure and confident in handling city life, and having become established in new social groups, clubs and organizations which in turn act as a form of socio-economic security of life insurance, the home base is usually remembered but decreasingly depended upon for the provision of security and confidence. Almost all feel confident to go back home only for a visit. Some return permanently if they have acquired enough economic gain and social status to place them well beyond those living back in their original villages. They have to display to their village folk evidence of achievement, to show that their absence from the village was worthwhile and beneficial, not only for the returning migrants but for the various relatives as well. One is expected to share generously (usually for short-term consumption) the accumulated wealth which could be invested wisely for the individual and the community.

Thus, the drive to improve oneself socially and economically by moving into towns, together with the differential perceptions and status accorded to townsfolk as superior, modern, progressive and more efficient than villagers, also become important factors for migration. The rural dwellers often develop an inferiority feeling of being behind the times, traditional, and deprived of the most efficient means of earning a living, however costly it may look. This catalyses the gathering of personal strength and confidence to move into towns or overseas, to achieve the status and economic benefits they are assumed to offer.

FROM PACIFIC ISLAND PORT TOWNS TO METROPOLITAN CITIES

The East Polynesians and then the West Polynesians were the first to migrate in large numbers to New Zealand, Hawai'i, and the west coast of the United States. Tahitians, Cook Islanders, Niueans, Tokelauans, Western Samoans and American Samoans now live in metropolitan cities such as Auckland, Wellington, Honolulu, San Francisco, Los Angeles and some as far as Paris. Niueans and Cook Islanders have free access to New Zealand. American Samoans and most Micronesians have free access to Hawai'i and the United States. Western Samoans are allowed to migrate to New Zealand on an annual quota system, and the Tongans may work there on a six-month basis for many years. Sydney today has tens of thousands of Pacific Islanders. Although Australian and New Zealand citizens are allowed free access to each other's countries, not all Islanders do. All Cook Islanders, Niueans, Tokeluans, and some Samoans have that right, as do all persons of Island heritage born in those countries, but those born elsewhere need visas to travel between those two countries.

Again, those Pacific Islanders with determination and self-confidence who were prepared to take the risk of leaving an established and familiar environment for an unfamiliar one were the first to make the move to metropolitan cities, which they perceived to offer more opportunities. These pioneer settlers became the source of encouragement and security for the next wave. Such moves brought about further alienation from traditional village-based culture but with a compensatory increasing understanding and confidence to face a new and broader cultural context than ever before. Thus, the once strong sense of attachment to their traditional land and home bases is being diminished to the extent that some migrants try to ignore or forget their own identities by claiming and adopting those of others to whose life-style they are aspiring. But often this is too difficult to achieve. The original home base, thus, continues to be a source of security and confidence and a place to return to (at least in one's dreams!) when the going gets hard.

Melanesians and Micronesians began more recently to migrate in large numbers to metropolitan cities. In the past, large groups of them were taken by force and deceit to work in plantation colonies of the then colonial powers. Today, some have yet to recover fully from their fear of past atrocities of the blackbirding and labour trading days. Since they were also the last to be Christianised and to receive Western formal education in the Pacific, not many have ventured far afield and settled in foreign countries. Most of those few who have migrated from their home countries are professionals who achieved the highest educational standard in the Western formal school system. This educational experience provides them with the confidence and security to move out and interact with other people in the metropolitan cities of Australia, New Zealand and the United States of America, and in the cosmopolitan port towns of South Pacific Island states.

With Pacific Islanders increasingly acquiring higher professional skills and qualification, it can be assumed that most of them will aspire to eventually migrate to metropolitan countries where their qualifications and skills will be in demand and appropriately rewarded. (However, some Pacific Islanders will prefer to remain behind and attempt to transform their countries into one where they can be positively employed. Most Guamanians, American Samoans, Norfolk Islanders, Pitcairn Islanders, Cook Islanders, Niueans, Tokelauans, Wallisans and Futunans have already done so. Other Micronesians now have the northern outlet to the United States of America, but Melanesians at present have nowhere they can go in significant numbers. This will make Melanesia a different world from Polynesia and from most of Micronesia.)

Once Pacific Islanders enter metropolitan cities and establish themselves, they are perceived in their home countries as lucky people who have made it into the big world; even if they have no jobs but live on the dole, since this gives a higher income than most employment at home. Who would know of their failure from far away at home? Living in Australia, New Zealand, the United States of America, Canada and even Britain sounds fantastic to most Pacific Islanders. It overrates the position of the Pacific migrants in those countries who are often looked down upon by earlier migrants long established in the economic and political sectors of such countries. Pacific migrants are often used as scapegoats for increasing social problems even when they consist of only a small percentage of the total population of the city in which they stay. Although the unskilled Pacific migrants are usually employed to do the dirty and menial tasks which no one else will do, they are generally left to their own devices and receive little public appreciation for the work they are doing. Worse still, if they are overstayers or illegal migrants, they have to be on the run while trying simultaneously to be employed.

NEED FOR POSITIVE PLANNING FOR PACIFIC ISLANDERS' MIGRATION

There is a dire need for an assertive, positive resettlement policy for Pacific Island migrants. Using such a policy, the colonial system had worked and was effectively maintained. But now, this positive resettlement needs to be by operation. The best qualities within the system are to be reactivated not only for the sake of maintaining the commonwealth or the capitalist economic alliances, but, more important, also for the achievement of equal opportunities and equitable distribution of wealth and power.

LABOUR EXCHANGE

It is now imperative that some labour exchange policies among Pacific Island countries be formulated and implemented. It is important for Australia, New Zealand and other Pacific Island states to review their immigration policies so that the less fortunate are given more opportunities to be exposed to new ideas and techniques and to develop themselves further. It has been observed that migrants from an underdeveloped situation moving to a more developed one generally work hard to establish themselves economically in order to gain social and political security. Labour exchange among Pacific Island states is now a necessity not only for developing confidence and security, but also for commercial entrepreneurship and the maximum use of surplus manpower resources available in some of these Island countries. Through such labour exchange schemes, cultural contact is enhanced. This leads to a better understanding and increasing confidence in oneself and, thus, less fear of others. Yet it is important that such labour exchange is arranged through Government channels. Shortage of either unskilled or skilled labour can be supplemented by surplus resources available in other countries in the Pacific region, but care must be taken that workers are not exploited or mistreated by their employers.

INTERCULTURAL COMMUNICATION

Although such work schemes provided some cash to take back home for communal development programmes, they hardly provided enough for the improvement of living standards back home. Furthermore, little new skill and knowledge of a developmental or technical nature was gained by such types of work. But one thing definitely had been gained from such overseas work experience: confidence and boldness to return a second or third time on an individual basis. Perhaps they never returned home the fourth time. By this time, the person had acquired adequate knowledge and experience to beat the heat and to survive in the new setting. Knowledge is power and, thus, provides the individual skill and confidence to adapt to new situations and to establish oneself among others with whom one has little cultural affinity initially. This is the same process that has occured to other peoples also, but it is the Pacific Islands migrants or the Asians, for that matter, who have often been singled out and negatively labelled as overstayers or illegal immigrants in white-dominated contexts when their visas expired. This is because they are culturally and behaviourally more visible than others.

To most people living in Melanesia, and in some parts of Polynesia and Micronesia, the immigration policies of metropolitan countries, which are the centres of our past colonial rulers, have appeared very negative and restrictive. Such policies restricted the opportunities for many Pacific Islanders to be exposed to the outside world after they had been partly acculturated by past colonial rulers who left behind social, political, economic and religious systems which cannot be effectively supported by the local infrastructures of these Pacific Islands states.

It is unfortunate that, now, when Pacific Islanders feel increasingly confident and secure about moving farther afield to develop themselves and acquire new skills and opportunities, now that international peace and security have been achieved and maintained, now that travelling has become much more efficient and safe, they find that certain categories of Pacific Island migrants have increasingly restricted entry into such developed countries through immigration laws and policies which tend to discriminate against them.

Only those Pacific Islanders who have certain skills and higher qualifications needed by the countries to which they wish to migrate have some chance of being accepted and allowed to settle in those countries. This has a retrogressive effect on the Islands, because it takes away from those Pacific Island countries the few qualified and skilled people, which they most need for their development, and leaves behind people with few skills and qualifications. This is a worse form of resource exploitation than any ever alleged in the colonial history of Pacific Islands. The few qualified Pacific Islands people, trained with meagre resources, are attracted away from the Islands by better salaries and conditions offered by the more developed countries. This phenomenon is also occurring in New Zealand and Australia as skilled and highly qualified people from those two countries are attracted to Europe, the United States of America, and to some Asian countries such as the Middle East and Japan.

Pacific Islanders were resocialised by their past colonial rulers to a new way of life, and today they have continued to emulate them and to be dissatisfied with what they have and sometimes with themselves. They want to develop and improve themselves to be like others in developed countries. Constantly reminded by the developed countries and aid donors that they are still poor and underdeveloped, they are, however, often placed in a dilemma regarding whether to take action to liberate themselves from traditional beliefs and practices which are often used as an excuse for their lagging behind others, or to adopt the new way and life-style brought about by developers but lose their cultural heritages and identities in the process. To overcome such dilemmas, some now aspire to the developed world in the hope of becoming developed or even to share in the wealth but, unfortunately, many more want only to enjoy a fantastic life and to be considered developed back home even if they have become street people of Sydney, Auckland, Honolulu or Los Angeles and San Francisco.

Today, the increasing population has meant competition and rivalry for scarce resources, such as wage employment, within and among the small Pacific Islands states. But, instead of our developed neighbours opening their doors for us to share some of the remnants from the tables of the wealthy, they now have an increasing number of locks on their doors and put different types of prohibition signs on their gates. Economic embargoes are often imposed when small Pacific Island countries misbehave or work toward equitable trade and power distribution. At times, these big ex-colonial brothers become paternalistic and domineering, and can only be rebuffed by the claim of interfering with one's sovereignty. Nevertheless, such confrontation, increasing constant contact and understanding of the outside world through education, trade and commercial activities provide Pacific Islanders with more confidence to negotiate their case on equal terms with foreigners. Through the maintenance of international peace and security, and with the availability of cheap, safe and fast means of communication and transport, more Pacific Islands peoples will be on the move, settling in other countries where they feel confident and secure to prosper in life. There is, however, a small degree of reverse migration among Samoans, Cook Islanders,

Tongans and others. Such people are either failures, or successes affected by economic depression in Australia and New Zealand and looking for some security back in the original home front.

The problems faced by the Pacific Islands today are generally historical and sociological in nature. They are the results of the interfacing of various and cultural systems through time whereby the technologically powerful dominates over all others. A sympathetic, sensitive and cooperative approach to the problems and issues of Pacific Islands migrants is very important and essential. Such an approach must provide them with the opportunity to develop themselves and settle with less fear and hassle in the new situation to which they are aspiring and where they are likely to stay either temporarily or permanently. Everyone is looking for a society in which he or she can live in peace and security, and be given the opportunity and the support and training to prosper and enjoy life.

CHAPTER 6

Motivations for Contemporary Tongan Migration

Wendy E. Cowling

Migration can be seen as a process in which large numbers of individuals and families begin to write a new history for themselves. The initial act of leaving one's parents, family, neighbourhood, society and culture, and adopting a new life- and work-style is a crucial one. Only a small proportion of people who enter a migration process, or who have participated in major migration movements in the past, have had a clear perception of what they were going to encounter, or the extent to which their lives were going to change. While it is very likely that a large proportion of the individual migrants are the forerunners in a migration which will ultimately involve other members of their kin network, they are not usually able to foresee this at the time.

Leaving aside the effect of wars in creating large numbers of refugees, it must be recognised that throughout the world most large-scale migratory moves during the past twenty-five years have primarily been the movement of labour. In the 1960s internal migration in many of the then less developed countries in Latin America and in Asia and Africa was seen as a necessary function in the development process.[1] Little of this rural-urban migration was organised or controlled by governments. Most rural-urban migration was precipitated by rural poverty, landlessness, and to some extent was influenced by development decisions and aid or funding decisions made by developed countries and international organisations, for the new industrial development tended to be located in cities.

International migration has tended to be much more controlled, particularly by developed economies in Europe and by countries such as Australia and New Zealand. In the period immediately following the Second World War, both Australia and New Zealand found they needed

This essay was previously published in *Tongan Culture and History*, edited by Phyllis Herda, Jennifer Terrell, and Niel Gunson (Canberra: Australian National University, 1990), 187–205.

more people to fill the gap left by the low birth rate prevailing during the economically depressed 1930s. Much of this labour was needed to undertake work in development projects and in the expansion of industries and manufacturing. Most of the people in the initial stages of the post-war migration programme were recruited and sponsored from Great Britain, and from the large numbers of northern European "Displaced Persons."[2] Considerable numbers of southern Europeans entered Australia unassisted by the Government, having been sponsored by family members resident in Australia.[3] The "family reunion" immigration programme has continued as an important contribution to the total annual migrant intake in Australia, although it is subject to changes in government policy, and in recent years has been severely curtailed in favour of a more selective migration programme.

During the four decades since the end of the Second World War, emigration by Pacific Island people has been one of the major factors and influences in determining the economic, social, and political situation of the region.[4] Bertram and Watters have identified a number of island states in Western Polynesia as "Mirab economies or societies" meaning that a society and its economy are shaped and affected by out-migration, by funding from the remittances of their overseas migrants, by aid from a variety of government and non-government agencies, and by the model of bureaucratic administration which has been developed, influenced by a British-derived colonial model. Income from external sources, that is, from remittances from expatriates and from aid donors, far exceeds that earned from internal sources, including exports.[5] Bertram and Watters' work covers the Cook Islands, Niue, Tokelau, Kiribati, and Tuvalu, but their theory and model can also be applied to Western Samoa and to Tonga.

In Tonga, village-based subsistence agriculture is still an important contributor to the sustenance of much of the population. However, there are problems in relation to access to and availability of land suitable for subsistence agriculture, with a paradoxical situation of under-utilisation of land due to uncertainty about ownership and use rights, or loss of much of a village's younger male labour force due to internal or external migration.

Each island group in the South Pacific has a different migration story. As will be seen the Australian connection with Tonga is of long standing, but what is most relevant is the on-going effects of the New Zealand negotiation of short-term contractual agreements for labour power with Tonga and Samoa in the early 1970s. The contract terms were not long enough for workers any longer, so many Tongans and Samoans overstayed, consequently coming into conflict with the New Zealand immigration laws. In 1975 this led to dramatic confrontations between police and overstayers.[6] This history encouraged some Tongans resident in New Zealand to move on to Australia, which became an increasingly desired destination for people seeking out-migration opportunities.

New Zealand offered a classic demonstration of the use of migrant labour as a secondary, or replacement force.[7] Where industrial enterprises are somewhat moribund, without capital for re-structuring or the purchase of new technology, there is a tendency to employ migrant labour to replace local workers who have gone elsewhere seeking higher wages and better conditions. Conversely, an increase in some industries has led to the de-skilling of much of their workforce. Again, local workers may move elsewhere to be replaced by unskilled migrant workers.

The pattern in New Zealand and Australian industry has been similar. In Australia manufacturers of goods such as food items and cars, the demand for which is subject to seasonal or market fluctuations, tend to utilise casual and part-time labour, in preference to full-time permanent workers, and the workforce usually includes a large number of migrants and women, migrant and Australian-born. Enterprises in the service sector, characterised by low wages and difficult working hours or conditions, for example transport services, hospitals, hotels and restaurants, also utilise migrant labour. World-wide, clothing manufacturers and manufacturers of small items utilise the system of out-work whereby piece workers are paid very low rates for their sewing, or the assemblage or packaging of goods. In Australia large numbers of migrant women have been recruited for this work, including recent arrivals such as the Tongans and Cook Islanders.

TONGANS IN AUSTRALIA

The Tongan migrant presence up until 1985 tended to be almost invisible to the majority of the Australian population. They have not experienced much overt racism and hostility such as that offered to groups like the Indo-Chinese. This is due, in part, to the fact that they were not seen as permanent migrants and in part to the romantic view of the Pacific held by many Australians. In addition, most Tongans are committed to goals which encourage assent to a work ethic, making them valuable employees. Wages in Australia are much higher than in Tonga, so people accept the problems and sacrifices inherent in shift work, uncongenial factory or work environments, and even exploitation, as the working period is often considered or intended to be short. They may, during the early period of their stay in Australia, accept below-average wages. Networking by Tongan migrants through church, family, or friendship contacts frequently enables the placement of workers and the communication of information about work availability, "better" jobs, opportunities for temporary work, and more acceptable wage levels.

From the 1950s to 1970, only a small number of Tongans had permanent residence in Australia. Most of these were women who had married Australians, following nursing or teacher training in Australia, or who had met and married Australians or other Europeans in Tonga. There were also a small number of wholly Tongan families resident in Australia, but they were scattered, and often had little contact with each other. During this period there was always a small group of Tongan students, royal, noble, and élite, attending school in Methodist church schools, particularly in Melbourne and Sydney.

There were strong sentimental links between Tongans and Australia because of the Australian Methodist Church's relationship with the Free Wesleyan Church of Tonga. Contact between missionary families from Australia and Tongan families was often maintained on the return of the missionaries to Australia. In the 1950s, the Australian Methodist Church sponsored Tongan women to train as nurses at a Church-operated hospital in Sydney, where they also maintained a hostel for Tongan students. Hence, during this period, many of those Tongans who sought permanent residence in Australia had church connections and support. The Methodist links were often an influential factor in choosing Australia as a place of residence, whether temporary or permanent, as the rate of Tongan migration increased from 1970.

The year 1970 can be counted as the beginning point of a steadier flow of Tongan immigrants, many of whom entered Australia following residence in Fiji or in New Zealand. In the early 1970s a small community of Pacific Islanders began a regular combined Methodist church service in central Sydney. In 1974 the Methodist Board of Missions in Australia and the Pacific Islander Methodist community, comprised mainly of Tongans, Samoans, Rotumans, and Fijians, sent a request to the Pacific Island churches for a Pacific Islander minister. This congregation continued to function as a united body until 1986, when ministers began to be appointed to work with congregations comprised solely of Tongans, or Samoans, or Fijians or Rotumans. The funds for the support of these ministers were raised by their respective communities. There are also a number of Tongan church congregations in cities on the eastern seaboard linked with Methodist-derived churches in Tonga and New Zealand, the Congregationalists, the Assemblies of God, the Mormons, and the Seventh Day Adventists, also have Pacific Islander congregations.

By 1975 the number of Tongan residents in Australia had grown considerably, and it has continued to increase from that year. This was largely due to the cessation of the contract worker scheme agreement between New Zealand and Tonga and Samoa, when Australia came to be seen as a possible source of employment. In the late 1960s and early 1970s, tourist visas were relatively easy to obtain for people from the Pacific, and the permanent Tongan population included legal residents and an increasing number of overstayers. The status of some of the latter was eventually legalised during Australian government amnesties in 1974, 1976, and 1980. In 1981 a small "permanent population" of Tongans (almost 1,500) was recorded in the Australian national census as resident in Sydney. This was the first time the Tongan community was counted separately from a category of residents originating in "Oceania." The figure is not an accurate record as numbers would have been recorded as being New Zealander in origin, and many overstayers encouraged their hosts not to include them in household enumeration. By 1985 the Tongans were classed by the Commonwealth Department of Immigration and Ethnic Affairs as an "emergent population." A small amount of welfare assistance was directed by this Department to the Tongan community to fund a part-time Tongan welfare worker in Sydney.

By the end of 1986 there were approximately 8,000 Tongans in Australia, with an estimated 6,000 resident in the Sydney metropolitan area.[8] The major portion of the population is concentrated in Melbourne, Sydney, and Brisbane, with small communities in Canberra-Queanbeyan, Newcastle, and Wollongong. At least one third of this population is comprised of children and elderly relatives, including parents of non-working age. The Tongan communities in these cities, particularly those connected with major denominational church congregations, comprise large family networks. Members of these churches and kin networks also maintain additional formal and informal connections based on their village of origin, school attended in Tonga, *kava*-drinking groups, workplace, and, to a lesser extent, their residential location in Australia.

MIGRATION AND CONCEPTS OF THE FAMILY

In the past the aspect of love (*'ofa*) which encompassed the notion of love as "caring" (*'ofa*) underpinned the Tongan custom known as *fetokoni'aki*, the sharing of things, particularly of food, not just among family members but with those who requested it.[9] This value is still incorporated in the ideology of the family in Tonga.[10]

The prevailing ideology of the family (*fāmili*) is that it should function as a supportive self-improvement group. The family is the provider of everything for the individual, both physically and emotionally. Members of a family are said to "belong to each other." They should operate in a spirit of mutual love, caring for each other. This is known as *fe'ofo'ofani* in Tongan. The Kingdom of Tonga, in the ideal, is the *fāmili* writ large. The word *kāinga* is now used less frequently for the kin group related to the individual through his or her maternal and paternal grandparents. *Fāmili* has come into more common use. Tongans frequently use terms such as "the nuclear family" and "the extended family," acquired from Social Studies classes in school and from the media, to differentiate between the two types of relations. Although disputes may occur among *kāinga* members over land, resources, inheritance, or marriage choices, or some members of one generation in a family may compete for the affection and loyalties of nieces and nephews, a united front is presented to the stranger: "In our *kāinga* we regard and treat everyone as the same."

One of the crucial factors in the acceptance by Tongans of overseas migration is the historical fact of the internal migration which has taken place for several generations, influenced by the Tongan commitment to the education of children. In the past, as in the present, people moved from Ha'apai, Vava'u, 'Eua, and from Tongatapu villages distant from Nuku'alofa, to enable their children to attend church or government high schools in the capital.[11] Husbands and wives accepted long periods of separation from each other, or from their homes, in order to give their children what they considered was the best start in life. There is now a high Tongan literacy rate, but there is very little waged work available for school leavers annually entering the employment market. A contributing factor is that the education system has not necessarily given the children skills which would make them employable in the context of a developing economy. There is a limited amount of formal training offered in trades such as mechanics and carpentry or in business skills. The tight job market, and a very competitive tertiary scholarship system, has influenced many families with young children to consider emigrating in order to give the children a better knowledge of English and a "head start" in the Tongan education system on their hypothetical return.

Tongans enjoy children and the notion of large families. Informal adoption of children by close relatives is common. The view that emigration is a likely option for some young family members and the fact that remittances from relatives living abroad help with the costs of a child's support and education have weakened any commitment by many Tongans to family planning. In discussions of family life and the responsibilities of parents and children, many respondents, particularly members of the churches based on Methodism, such as the Free Wesleyan Church, the Free Church of Tonga, the Church of Tonga, and the Tokaikolo Fellowship, invariably linked their ideas on family to ideas of religious duty as did members of the Church of Jesus Christ Latter Day Saints (the Mormons). Replies from respondents frequently matched almost word for word, suggesting that religious teaching on the concepts of the family have been well absorbed. Justifying values and notions on the concept of the family have been abstracted from the Bible and from Christian teaching. Children are said to be "a demonstration of the love of God," and are "a burden for the parents to carry in love." In turn, the children are expected to demonstrate their love and care for their parents.

A few young respondents expressed mild resentment at the expectations of their family and of society in relation to their role and responsibilities within the family network, particularly the economic contributions they were expected to make. They were frequently resentful about the assumption made by their parents of their obligations to institutions outside the family, particularly the major financial contributions elicited from adult church members through the annual Misinale collections in the Free Wesleyan Church, Free Church of Tonga, and Church of Tonga, and the annual collection of the Roman Catholic Church. Major contributions to these collections are also given by church members resident overseas, to supplement family giving at the local level.[12] Overseas Tongan churches also make their own annual collection, which is sent back to Tonga to support the home church. However, the majority of informants considered that parents had a dual responsibility to the church and to the family, and that the prosperity of the latter depended on the keeping of the former.

Both Walsh and Marcus[13] have documented the importance of the family and of kin networks in Tongan life. In a discussion of internal migration in Tonga in the 1960s Walsh emphasised that the individual "belongs more to his family than to a place."[14] Family and traditional values (often one and the same) motivate and direct much of an individual's life, whether the person is a resident in town or village. This process of kin support of an internal migrant still continues, and is perhaps one of the reasons that crime against property has not dramatically increased in spite of the high rate of urbanisation, for few individuals resident in urban areas in Tonga live outside a household arrangement.

The links of a descendant of an internal migrant with the village of his or her parents' or grandparents' origin are often still quite emotionally strong. Many Tongans, although one or two generations distant from residence in a village located outside Nuku'alofa, will still identify themselves by the island group or the district of Tongatapu from which their families originated. For many internal migrants Nuku'alofa was the residence of convenience, where an individual or a number of members of a family had lived in order to undertake waged work or schooling. Availability of town allotments was also a factor in attracting migrants,[15] and the very limited amount of infrastructure improvement due to a lack of development funding being expended on island regions other than Tongatapu motivated people from these groups to move to the capital.[16] The devastation of homes and farmlands caused by cyclones in 1975 and 1982 have precipitated much of the migration from Ha'apai during the past decade.

In the papers published in 1975 and 1981, Marcus concentrated his discussion on the functioning of élite and middle-class family networks which had links between Tonga, New Zealand, and the U.S.A.[17] The use by this group of overseas educational opportunities and overseas links in order to broaden the life and earning opportunities for members of the younger generation has been increasingly emulated during the past decade by families in the prosperous farmer class, and the commoner élite, whose members are well-placed in the bureaucracy, in the Free Wesleyan Church, or as business entrepreneurs. From observation, the functioning of these "estates" and "networks" appears to be informal rather than formal.

MOTIVATIONS FOR TONGAN EMIGRATION

The reason most commonly given by family members remaining in Tonga or offered by those who have emigrated to Sydney was that the move overseas was motivated by the desire to "help the family." The majority of household members interviewed in Tonga in 1986 had at least two members of their immediate family overseas (the largest number for a household was six). These family members were resident in Australia, the United States of America (mainly in Hawai'i, Utah, California, Arizona) and in New Zealand.

While Tongans living in Sydney stressed that they had moved because they needed work, or were landless, or had felt oppressed by the operation of the social system in Tonga, including the sharp class differentiation between nobles and commoners, their relatives in Tonga spoke of the migration of family members as motivated by the desire to "help the family," "improve the standard of living of the family," "contribute to family pride," "upgrade the status of the family," "to gain more respect for the family," "to enable the family to increase its giving to church and village projects," "to demonstrate the love of the children for their parents," or "to assist the development of the Kingdom." The emigration of Tongans, while frequently motivated by notions of assisting the family materially, is also influenced by another important principle of Tonga life, that of the individual choosing a course of action as an independent person: "to please oneself" (a Tongan expression).

In 1987, almost eighty-six percent of a sample of seventy-five respondents interviewed in Tonga stated that family members such as sisters, brothers, husbands, daughters and sons, had emigrated in order "to help the family." They had obtained insufficient income in Tonga to enable them to do this to their satisfaction. The remaining people in this sample group stated that relatives had left because of their desire "to see the world," or for education, or for holidays. This group gave no economic reason for the departure of family members; that is, they considered their household to be self-sufficient. Nevertheless, a number of these respondents received remittances, particularly for special occasions.

Many men in Tonga today have reached sixty years of age without experiencing any regular or long term paid employment, while others have had no paid employment of any kind.[18] It is not unusual to find that a job overseas is the first waged labour a man or a woman has performed since leaving school. A number of those who had left Tonga seeking "better paid work" had been employed in the Tongan Public Service, and included people who were formerly clerks, teachers, policemen, nurses, soldiers, technicians, and tradesmen.

There are paradoxes in the Tongan commitment to "tradition." The desire and pressure to conform to traditional values appears to be strong, particularly on occasions such as the celebrations and funerals of nobility. At these times people resident in the villages and hamlets on the noble's estate will provide food, mats, painted lengths of bark cloth (*ngatu*), and other tributes in their role as the symbolic family of the noble (*kāinga*). However, what sometimes seems to be a great devotion by commoners to their traditional obligations may conceal a considerable amount of self-interest. A client known and seen to be dedicated to serving a noble estate-holder might hope to be rewarded with a sympathetic response when he wants land or assistance in some other matter. I found many Tongans in Australia expressed an unprompted resentment of the domination of society and resources by the nobility and the élite. There was less discussion of class issues in Tonga itself by respondents, but this is not surprising, in that the Sydney residents felt freer to express their opinion on this issue. In addition, many of the household heads whom I interviewed in Tonga were middle-aged and somewhat conservative in their views.

The perception of many Tongan commoners is that there are three ways they can circumvent the domination of the nobility and non-noble élite in Tongan society. One way has been by the encouragement and support of family members to obtain post-secondary education to enable them to become upwardly mobile and penetrate the perceived hold by the noble and non-noble élite on jobs in the bureaucracy. Government jobs provide secure incomes, and some power, through access to decision-making. Some higher echelon public servants are able to utilise their guaranteed income as a basis for expansion of business interests, including the production of cash crops for export. Not only do members of the élite employed in government have financial resources, enabling them to obtain substantial loan funding from the Tongan Development Bank, they also have a network of contacts to enable them to confidently deal with applications for business and export licences, etc. They may also have a spouse engaged in business enterprises or waged work and thus earning an income which enables risk-taking in projects requiring loans.

Out-migration for post-secondary training or to widen job opportunities was available in the period 1950–1975, but for only a relatively small group of people. Favoured occupations for men were the practice of medicine, teaching, administration, trades, and the Christian ministry, with nursing and teaching favoured for women. The number of scholarships sponsored by the Government, the churches, and through aid agreements with foreign governments, has increased, as has the possible range of occupations. Qualifications gained by nurses and teachers in Tonga are not accepted as sufficient for employment in these occupations in Australia, but would enable the holders to gain entry into up-grading or other educational programmes.

The second way for commoners to circumvent domination by the financial and political élite of Tonga is through the temporary migration of some members of a family in order to amass resources which can be used to improve or develop family enterprises in Tonga. If the migrant is married and able (and willing) to shift his whole family, the move is usually justified by a belief that the children will be advantaged by attendance at an English language school. Single men and women (employed and unemployed in Tonga) and deserted wives have also taken up opportunities for short-term wage earning overseas. They are usually funded and sponsored by relatives already resident overseas, who give them accommodations and may help them get work. Women who are qualified teachers or nurses are taking unskilled factory work or work as nurses' aides, cleaners, or fruitpickers, in order to fulfill short-term earning goals. In Australia only a small number of Tongan men and women have obtained white collar work or are in professional occupations as yet. The possibility of extending their opportunities to meet potential marriage partners, whether Tongan or European, has also become an increasingly important motivator for the migration of single women. Short-term stays may be from three months to two years, depending on a person's success in negotiating and extending a visitor's visa, or on their deciding to remain as an illegal overstayer.

The third way to overcome domination by the Tongan élite is to make a permanent migratory move, accepting the possibility that there may be no permanent return to Tonga. Many of the people who see themselves as sojourners will in fact not return, particularly if they can obtain residence rights in their new country. They may revise their future plans, deciding to remain in Australia until a child finishes secondary or tertiary education, or until they themselves amass sufficient savings to begin a small business in Tonga. They may return to Tonga for holidays on a regular basis, and work to recruit other members of their immediate and extended families to join them in Australia.

THE CUSTODIAN/BROKER AND
THE FAMILY NETWORKS

What is now in place is an invisible trapezoid-shaped movement across the Pacific. People, money, goods, ideas, and influences, are in motion virtually all the time. The lines run to and from Tonga, with the main connection points located at Apia (Western Samoa), Pago Pago (American Samoa), Honolulu (Hawai'i), Los Angeles and San Diego (California), and Salt Lake City (Utah). There are also considerable numbers of Tongans in cities and towns in Texas and Arizona. In the southern Pacific the connection points are located in New Zealand, at Auckland, Wellington, and Christchurch, with populations in most of the provincial cities, and in Australia in the capital cities and provincial towns on the eastern seaboard.

Key individual members of these family networks can be found in Tonga, and in Tongan communities abroad. These individuals are important in the family decision-making process which can affect the movements of some family members.

The facilitator, or clearing-house as it were, for decisions and money movements is frequently located in Tonga, resident in Nuku'alofa. This person is likely to have had a higher education, and may have business expertise, with a sound knowledge of how arrangements can be made for travel, for banking, for importing and exporting goods. Overseas, help is often sought from Tongan travel agents, church ministers, or people with some experience of the host society and in handling transactions, to assist in moving money or people. Many of the arrangements are *ad hoc* because the movement of people to other countries depends on visa allocation, and on the financial resources of a family at the time a decision needs to be made.

These key members often have custodianship of family property and land in Tonga. They may be compensated for this custodianship, or for the care of aged parents remaining in Tonga, by substantial gifts from the members living abroad. However, on the whole, the duty is usually more burdensome than profitable. The intermediary's role may involve difficult negotiations or involve time spent in dealing with remittances on behalf of other family members. For example, money may not be sent to a wife by a husband living abroad, but through the agency of the husband's brother or sister, in order that they might ensure the money is spent as the husband wishes.

The work of the custodian/broker in a migrant community can be quite onerous. Some of these people have developed their family helping role into financially rewarding work as a full-time broker for members of the Tongan community, and operate as tax or travel agents. Others have utilised their experience as intermediary between Tongans and the host community to enter the host country's bureaucracy. Others have moved from informal leadership roles to formal ones, such as becoming full-time, unordained church ministers, giving their brokerage role an extra dimension. The notion of a cultural arbiter or broker is well accepted by Tongans. However, the broker is vulnerable to criticisms such as "getting above themselves," "conceited," "showing off," "flying high," or even to accusations of dishonesty and of obtaining too many advantages from their role.

Many "family estates" have been formalised as business enterprises in Tonga in which a number of members of one family, usually siblings or parents and children, are involved and employed. These enterprises may have branches in overseas countries, usually located in a neighbourhood in which numbers of Tongans reside. They usually operate businesses which supply goods and services, such as travel agents, purveyors of vegetables such as yams and taro, and other food lines sought by immigrant Pacific Islanders. Alternatively, a relative in an overseas country will be the chief contact to ensure that the owners of a business in Tonga regularly receive supplies of parts, equipment, second-hand clothing, etc. Tongan businessmen with enterprises in overseas countries will usually keep a network operating whereby they will place relatives or fellow villagers in the business when the newcomers arrive from Tonga. People in managerial or supervisory positions will also act as "gatekeepers" for the placement of new migrants. It is quite likely that in any year a number of family estates will be created by sections of Tongan family networks when a business enterprise is formally established which draws on capital and skills from among members of an extended family.

Children tend to be dealt with somewhat arbitrarily (to European eyes) in the family networks. Small children may be sent as companions to elderly grandparents living abroad, or are returned to grandparents, or aunts, or other relatives in Tonga for long-term care. Nieces and nephews are sent abroad to their parents' siblings, to enable them to attend school. These movements often seem to occur on impulse; for example, someone is returning to Tonga or to the migrant's host country and it is decided that a child should accompany them.

One important area of decision-making may involve the need for an increased investment in the education of younger family members. The number of scholarships available in Tonga for tertiary education abroad is limited, and they may be tied to specific degrees and government departments. While investment in overseas tertiary education may be considered as likely to contribute to the increased prestige and eventual affluence of at least a section of the family, this is not the sole motivation. The personality of the individual and of the individual's parents are important. There will be more cooperation and help given if the young relative is particularly well-regarded and is clearly hardworking. Members of the *kāinga* of both the parents may be called on to contribute towards assisting a young man or woman to study overseas, without any assurance of an immediate return. As the young people of one household, or section of a kin network, complete their education, it is not unusual to find that their parents have assumed responsibility for younger nieces, nephews, and cousins, and that the educated, employed senior cousin will be expected to contribute to their education, or to other projects which will benefit members of the kin set. This expectation of some sort of repayment can place an undue burden on educated and employed young people, for they are frequently expected to contribute financially, physically, and emotionally to maintain at least some of their close kin, particularly parents and brothers and sisters. It is considered shameful not to assist, or offer to assist, close relatives when this help is requested or appears necessary.

The obverse of helping the "good" young members of a family is the view that residence overseas can be an educational and reforming experience. "Difficult" young men—unemployed, bored with village life, perhaps falling in love unsuitably, or getting into trouble occasionally with the police over drunkenness, fights, or for making illegal home-brewed "beer"—will be offered the opportunity to leave Tonga. While they may be sponsored by relatives at home and in the destination abroad, many of these young men keep well away from the activities of the Tongan community. Some of them reform, settle down, perhaps get married, and regularly send remittances home. Others who get into trouble in their new place of residence may find themselves reported to the immigration authorities as overstayers and deported.

WHO GOES? WHO STAYS?

The prevailing ideology of the family in Tonga as a supportive, self-improvement group, in which members are motivated by notions of filial piety and filial duty, while useful as a means of social and political control, is now being utilised by working and middle class commoners as a rationalisation for out-migration, whether temporary or permanent. It is simplistic to say that the motivation for a great deal of Tongan out-migration is the desire for higher incomes and the acquisition of goods, although this is how it is regarded by many members of the Tongan élite. They often have an equally simplistic solution. Ignoring facts such as landlessness, or mal-distribution of land resources, and the large numbers of young people who annually reach the age of fifteen without the prospect of future paid employment, they are likely to state: "All Tonga needs to prosper is for the farmers to work harder."

Many of the people who are electing to remain in Tonga are élite bureaucrats (often with business or farming interests), small-scale and large-scale entrepreneurs and manufacturers, prosperous farmers, and members of noble families. In discussions with senior bureaucrats and with members of the Tongan élite, some have stated that commentators such as myself take too gloomy a view of Tongan out-migration. They point out that it is a voluntary act, one which aims for self- and family improvement. Many of this group claim that people do not *have* to go, that industrious farmers would prosper in time, and that young people with no prospect of paid employment should return to the farm, or to fishing, in order to support themselves. This argument ignores the vagaries of climate and the uncertainties of the internal and export agricultural markets. It also ignores the fact that Tonga is a cash economy in which exchanges in kind for self-maintenance and the economic support of members of an extended family are now virtually non-existent. These exchanges of food and other items among family members have, to some extent, been replaced by the sending of remittances and goods from overseas, some of which are repaid with gifts of Tongan foods and with artifacts, such as mats and painted bark-cloth.

The proponents of the argument that people migrate solely from personal preference, or because they are motivated by acquisitiveness and a desire for self-improvement, tend to ignore the benefits of migration to the Tongan economy through the receipt of remittances. These ensure healthy monetary reserves in Tonga, offsetting imbalances in the area of exports and imports. Remittances enable a considerable number of people to stay in place, to continue to enjoy living in the Kingdom. Remittances are the supplement to the incomes of fishermen and farmers, the surety of the payment of school fees, providing much of the finance for church building programmes. They also supply the means to improve family homes and village amenities. They function as a social welfare system supporting the aged. Many families who are actively farming depend on sizeable contributions from absent members to improve plants and to increase their cropping capacities. Many families in Tonga have electricity, a telephone, and even a video recorder, thanks to the generosity and hard work of sons, daughters, brothers, sisters, and cousins living abroad.

It is true that migration can be seen as a pragmatic response by households and extended families to the need to obtain something more than survival income utilising family labour resources. But for many families and households migration has exacted a great cost in terms of emotional and cultural loss. According to family members remaining in Tonga and resident in the sample of seventy-five households surveyed in 1986, only about 20 percent of the emigrants from those households and families are likely to return to live permanently in Tonga. About 15 percent had returned for holidays since first leaving Tonga. About 10 percent of family members still resident in Tonga, particularly parents of emigrant children, had visited their children or close relatives overseas.

The chain migration process in kin networks is particularly noticeable in the case of the Tongan-American families, some of who emigrated a generation ago. The cost of returning to Tonga for holidays for a family group is very high. In addition, if family members do return to Tonga for a visit, they are expected to bring with them a substantial cash gift and goods. Those family members who had emigrated to America were less likely to return permanently to live in Tonga, but were more likely to encourage the remaining members of the family to emigrate and join them. Familial ties are therefore becoming a major dislodging force. Direct moves from a village residence to an American city are becoming common, causing a noticeable abandonment of family homes and of land in villages. Brothers and sisters of the emigrants and their children are encouraged to make the move in order to ensure their future care and the proper performance of funeral and post-death customs. The death and burial overseas of family members, particularly parents, spouses, and children, more or less ensures that there will be a group of kin permanently residing abroad. The attractive pull of the home community may lessen over time, but not the emotional power of the family, or the emotive power of Tongan identity and loyalties.

Family needs and loyalties are being used as a justification for out-migration by Tongans, while the very act and effect of this out-migration is causing hardship for many nuclear family and extended family units in

Tonga. As in all migratory movements of labour world-wide, undue hardship is being experienced by those who remain at home: women, children, and, to some extent, elderly parents. In many families the wife and children who remain in Tonga have experienced long periods of separation from the husband and father; separation periods of seven to ten years are not uncommon. Desertion of wives and children in favour of beginning a new family unit in the host country is also not uncommon, particularly if the male migrant has not succeeded in obtaining a residence visa. In such cases, if the migrant leaves the host country he will not be able to return. Marriage to a citizen of the host country will enable the migrant to obtain residence rights, but this may mean, at the least, cutting the ties with his former wife. These situations have precipitated emigration by deserted wives who may have few resources on which to draw in Tonga to support themselves and their children. Many of these women say they feel ashamed to ask brothers or parents for long-term support. Many children are then separated from both parents, left in Tonga in the care of the mother's or father's relatives, or because they have been returned to Tonga, or have been left in Tonga to be cared for by relatives. Their return to Tonga may have been due to the disappointment of the parents with the children's non-achievement in a new school system, or concern over the loss of language and cultural identity, or concern over pressure on the children to conform to the behaviour of the peer group in the new society. There have also been clashes with host-country government social welfare agencies over the perceived mistreatment of children by parents. The parents arraigned for beating their children resent what they consider is outside interference in their "right" to discipline their offspring.

The majority of respondents in Tonga stressed how much they missed the companionship of family members living abroad, but it was felt that this sacrifice was worthwhile for both the migrant and their family. It was considered that the people living abroad could "help the family so much more than they could previously." While some family members in Tonga were aware of the fact that increased family prosperity was bought at some cost to the migrant, and to the social fabric in Tonga, they saw little alternative to the continuation of migration. Many of the migrants in Sydney are aware of the total price which they are paying for their improved standard of living and their increased ability to assist their families; others are not. Most philosophically accept their exile from Tonga, work at maintaining their cultural identity, and are generous donors to village, school, church, and national causes in Tonga. They talk of return "perhaps in a few years." Some use this belief in the short duration of their stay to explain why they are not worried too greatly about the possible loss of cultural identity or language among their Australian-born children. They feel this lack will be remedied on their return home to Tonga, not visualising the possible conflicts when adolescents are returned to a different society without a good knowledge of the language, and possibly without a desire to identify with the home culture and mores.

Others are consciously attempting to adjust their child-rearing patterns in order to minimise clashes with their children and with members of the host society due to cultural differences. There is now an increase in the number of Tongan-Tongan marriages in the Australian migrant community, in preference to Tongan-Australian marriages. This is partly due to the increase in the number of kin networks now resident in Australia, with management of the affairs of younger people being more closely supervised or undertaken by their familial elders. However, there is a high proportion of single men in the Australian Tongan community. Some of this group have contracted de facto marriages with Australian women in order to obtain residence rights.

I believe there is a greater possibility of permanent return by members of the Tongan communities living in New Zealand and in Australia than by those living in mainland U.S.A. Many migrants would like to exercise options of split residency between Tonga and Australia, or New Zealand, enabling them to reside in Tonga, but visit Australia or New Zealand to earn capital from time to time. This option is probably only available to those already in the migration process, and who have obtained permanent resident visas in their host countries. A significant number of Tongan men with residence rights in New Zealand are now living and working in Australia with the short term goal of earning enough to assist in the purchase of a house in New Zealand. The Australian government's immigration policy has become more restrictive in recent years, and there is little indication of an intention to ease entry and residence requirements. The Australian government has also resolutely avoided commitment to ideas of "guest worker" contracts. The New Zealand government reviewed its options in early 1987, having been surprised by the large response to the temporary innovation of visa-free entry by Tongans, Samoans, and Fijians.

It has to be recognised that those leaving Tonga are not just seeking personal and family economic goals, but are expressing the belief that they cannot achieve even relatively modest aims in Tonga, such as improved housing or even a clean water supply, without seeking to obtain money from outside the local economy. The Tongan Five Year Development Plans have given only passing attention to the pressing problems of low wage levels, unemployment, and the need for an equitable reorganisation of land distribution. Wage levels in Tonga are very low and appear to be based on an assumption that the worker has family support and access to land on which to grow subsistence crops. This assumption is not correct, particularly in view of the fact that most of the employed members of the population are concentrated in Nuku'alofa, although they may have rights to use land located elsewhere in other island groups. The Tongan government has not tacitly acknowledged the importance of the migrants' remittances to the Tongan economy, nor has it publicly undertaken any serious negotiation with governments in New Zealand and Australia regarding the status of their emigrés.

The Tongan government's decision-making process has moved slowly in response to what are actually very modest desires on the part of Tongans for life improvement, particularly in the island groups away from Tongatapu. Many of the large-scale development choices which are being made seem to be favouring noble and élite developers who hope to profit from a hypothetically increasing tourist trade.[19] There are jobs being generated by the encouragement of local and foreign investment in industrial enterprises, but the wage levels are often exploitative. Few Tongans want wholesale modernisation and it is ironic that the government's slowness of response has precipitated the migration of families to cope with life in cities in advanced capitalist societies such as the United States of America, Australia, and New Zealand.

The Tongan commoners' commitment to the family as a source and motivator of quality of life improvement is exacting an unacknowledged cost economically, socially, and culturally. The values of church and state, which united "tradition" with a Protestant work ethic, emphasising the individual's duty to the family and to the Kingdom, have been well absorbed. However, social relations are inevitably altering. Traditional values implicit in *fetokoni'aki*, which primarily involved the sharing of food within the *kāinga*, are being transmuted into beliefs that love and duty are primarily expressed by the giving of cash. Emigration is seen by many as the only way to attempt to amass large amounts of capital. There is still great deference offered to "tradition" in Tonga and among Tongans overseas. It seems unlikely that the invocation and enactment of tradition as a formula to contain change in social relationships and in social roles and behaviour will be effective against the inexorable influence of the cash nexus.

NOTES

[1] See Todaro 1976, 1.
[2] Between 1947 and 1961, 811,000 males and 661,000 females migrated to Australia, a total of 1,472,000. This includes 171,000 "displaced persons" who entered Australia between 1949 and 1951. See Borrie and Spencer 1965, 16–17.

[3] Collins 1988, 20–24; see also Birrell and Birrell 1987, 51–58.

[4] Cf. Watters 1987, 35.

[5] Bertram and Watters 1985.

[6] See de Bres and Campbell 1975.

[7] Cf. Gibson 1982.

[8] This figure is a "guesstimate" based on estimates by church leaders in Sydney given during interviews with the author in 1985. The Free Wesleyan Church of Tonga, which established a Sydney Parish in January 1986 with a full-time Tongan minister and thirteen congregations, had at that time approximately 2,000 members and adherents. There were an estimated 500–700 members and adherents of the Roman Catholic Church, and 1,000 people connected with the Tokaikolo Fellowship, the Free Church of Tonga, and the Church of Tonga. Other Tongan congregations exist in the Assemblies of God and Seventh Day Adventist churches. There were also a considerable number of people not maintaining church connections for various reasons or not identifying themselves with the Tongan population.

[9] Cf. Kavaliku 1977.

[10] See Kaeppler 1971 and Marcus 1975 for a full discussion of kinship categories and ranking within them.

[11] Cf. Dillon 1983, 51, 52.

[12] The Misinale collection has had an extraordinary history. See Bollard 1975 for a discussion of how and why it began.

[13] Walsh 1969; Marcus 1975, 1980, 1981.

[14] Walsh 1969, 97.

[15] See Dillon 1983.

[16] Cf. Sevele 1973.

[17] Marcus 1975, 1981.

[18] Some older men interviewed who gave their occupation as "farmer" had worked for wages during World War II, or had worked during a long stay in town during the education of their children. One or two, while resident in Nuku'alofa, had taken up occupations in the informal sector, making artifacts for tourists and resuming full time farming on the completion of their children's secondary education.

[19] The Tongan Development Bank encourages development and the improvement of small-scale farming and fishing and other enterprises by a well-administered programme. Larger loans for similar purposes, but on a larger scale, say for boat building, may be funded by foreign aid, the administration of which is handled by the Central Planning Department.

CHAPTER 7

From Village to City: Samoan Migration to California

Craig R. Janes

HISTORICAL BACKGROUND

The forces compelling Samoans to migrate arise out of a long history of colonial encounters with Euro-Americans culminating in the dislocations of the Second World War. Europeans and Samoans became aware of each other for the first time in 1722, when the Dutch explorer Jacob Rogeveen sighted and visited Manua. But it was another century before Europeans came in substantial numbers. In the interim, to be sure, there were the occasional and inevitable arrivals of castaways, beachcombers, and rogues who plagued Pacific island societies in the post-explorer era. But for the most part, Samoa avoided the tragic consequences of contact that befell Tahiti, the Marquesas, and some parts of Micronesia. To most Europeans neither the islands of Samoa or their inhabitants held the same kind of allure as the Polynesian islands to the east. Samoans refused to have much to do with European interlopers; by and large they bore their presence with dignity and tolerance. European contact did little to alter the structure of society until the early nineteenth century, when the first missionaries arrived. This produced a revolution, but a revolution led almost entirely by Samoans and structured in Samoan cultural terms.

Until the beginning of the Second World War, American Samoa was governed by the U.S. Navy with a kind of benign neglect. Local entrepreneurship was not supported; social, educational, and public health services were provided only sporadically and often paid for by the

This essay was previously published in *Migration, Social Change, and Health: A Samoan Community in Urban California* (Stanford, Calif.: Stanford University Press, 1990), 20–43.

Samoans themselves; there were no attempts at social or economic development; and the Samoans were kept isolated, left largely to go about their own business.

But for the most part Samoans steadfastly went their own way and sought their own satisfactions. In both Samoas the changes wrought by a century of Western domination were slight. Samoans tended to take what they wanted from the aliens, but acceded not at all to demands made on them by governments in areas that were not perceived to be their business. As the Second World War approached, it could thus be said for both Samoas that they had survived the worst aspects of Western cultural domination without "losing their numbers, their strength, their dignity, or their zest for a good controversy" (Oliver 1961, 220).

The war had a sudden and profound impact on Samoan society. It was not so much actual conflict that caused this upheaval as the presence of vast numbers of mostly American troops, accompanied by the products of a highly technological society and its monetary largesse. The concentration of American troops was especially high on the small island of Tutuila, which was a major staging and supply depot for American military forces. Within weeks after Pearl Harbor, Tutuila was transformed from a sleepy outpost to a major military installation. Military leaders feared for a short time that Japan might attack Samoa for its harbor facilities, and the U.S. invasion of Guadalcanal was staged in part from the Navy facilities at Pago Pago.

Tutuilans lived in a virtual armed camp where American Marines at one point reportedly outnumbered them. Manua did not share this fate, but was deeply affected nevertheless, for substantial numbers of its young and middle-aged men were drawn to Tutuila to participate in war-related activities. Many worked as stevedores on the docks, and others worked in road building and on construction crews. Nearly 1,000 men joined the "home guard," or a reserve Marine unit called the Samoan Marines (Malini). Schools were closed and buildings commandeered for use as barracks and supply depots, and for other purposes. A paved road was built along the south coast from one end of the island to the other. Roads were also thrown across the steep mountain interior at a few places, bringing remote villages to within a day's walk of the port town of Fagatogo.

The infusion of large quantities of cash into the Samoan economy had direct and long-lasting effects. The copra industry ceased during the war, but an unprecedented amount of money from military-related wage labor found its way to nearly every family in American Samoa. The presence of U.S. troops with little to do but spend money brought a new wave of prosperity to local merchants and provided a ready market for Samoan crafts. The war brought, in no uncertain terms, a monetary economy into American Samoa and left it relatively rich. "The [American Samoan] government's surplus, carefully invested, made it one of the few governments in the world which was more prosperous in 1945 than it had been in 1941" (Gray 1960, 245).

After the war many Samoans returned to their subsistence activities and the world they had known; but Samoans and Samoa would never be the same. Young men who had seen Hawaii and points beyond were anxious to see more of the world. Many members of the Fita Fita and the Malini chose to migrate to Honolulu or California to enlist in the U.S. armed services. For a time the U.S. Marines and Army guaranteed reimbursement of air or boat fare to Samoans who could pass the entrance exams.

Samoans had also acquired a taste for material assets far beyond their ability to pay. Young people crowded into the rapidly growing Pago Pago area looking for wage-paying jobs to satisfy their appetite for American clothes, canned foods, beer, and motion pictures. But falling exports and rising import prices seriously affected the local economy, and the number of wage-earning jobs available to Samoans was sharply reduced. The majority of remaining positions were with the U.S. Navy or supported directly by Navy funds. It became apparent to many future-oriented Samoans that migration to Hawaii or California was the alternative of choice for anyone seeking a job, education, or escape from what some perceived as the chafing confines of village life.

Life in the villages was also affected by rising population. Public health programs that accompanied the war effort improved village sanitation and all but eliminated filariasis.[1] Accessible clinic facilities were established in nearly every district, and Samoans became increasingly aware of the benefits of medical care. The death rate fell from 24 per 1,000 in 1912 to 8 per 1,000 in 1949. The annual birth rate stayed at 40 children per 1,000 through this period, resulting in a threefold population increase between 1900 and 1950, from about 6,000 to nearly 19,000 persons. For the first time Samoans experienced some crowding and a need to expand their subsistence activities. For young men and women, particularly, the competition for positions of status and prestige became fierce. And to those young men who bridled under the authority of the family chief, migration became an attractive alternative to staying at home and pursuing status and prestige along conventional paths (Gray 1960; Lewthwaite, Mainzer, and Holland 1973).

The Navy's decision in 1951 to terminate its operations in Pago Pago and transfer civilian personnel and their families stateside served more than any other to trigger the massive migration of American Samoans to Hawaii and California. With the Navy went many of the remaining wage-earning opportunities. When the last transport called at Pago Pago in

1952 to pick up dependents of military men and civilian employees who had been transferred to Hawaii, authorities were faced with something of a rush: almost 1,000 Samoans embarked for Honolulu to join relatives or to enlist in military service.

By 1960 Samoa was seized by migration fever. It was not just military experience, education, or employment that migrants sought, but something far less tangible. Many people left with nothing else in mind save for the idea that migration was necessary to secure a future for themselves and their families. Gifted young people were encouraged to migrate for further education in Hawaii or on the mainland, and others were simply propelled by the belief that all things in Samoa were inferior to what was to be had on the mainland. By the early 1960s it was clear that migration was becoming institutionalized as a rite of passage for young Samoans. In 1962, for example, the prerequisites for being elected to a chiefly title, especially a high one, had expanded from a knowledge of ancient lore, speaking ability, and political savvy to include education, wage-earning experience and ability, and status as a migrant (Holmes 1964). Consequently, promising young men in line for higher titles went abroad for the requisite education and job experience. One man I met on my trip to Tutuila in 1982 said he had been sent to Fiji to learn skills as a medical practitioner, and then to Hawaii, where he eventually earned a master's degree in sociology. He returned to take one of the highest titles in his district and became one of the most powerful men in the government of American Samoa.

Emigration was so great by 1970, particularly in the productive age categories, that subsistence agriculture nearly disappeared. Income from remittances, local government employment, a growing tuna-canning industry, small-scale entrepreneurial activities, and other wage-earning opportunities had made it possible for many families to purchase much of their food. Today, agricultural labor is universally disdained by young men, and local fisheries have declined because of overfishing. Consequently, most food is now imported from Western Samoa, Hawaii, and the mainland. Canned food and drinks have replaced products native to Samoa. When I observed the market in Fagatogo on several occasions in the summer of 1982, I found very limited amounts of local produce or fish for sale; what little was available was imported from Western Samoa. One man, a migrant who gave me a tour of Tutuila, showed me his now overgrown family lands, saying at one point along the way "someone should really take care of this land, but everybody is in San Francisco. Those who stay here are too busy or too lazy to climb up the mountain. It is easier just to go to the store."

The first migrants to leave Samoa were predominantly young and male, reflecting the large numbers of men who left to join or work for the military (Lewthwaite, Mainzer, and Holland 1973). A military career was not seen as appropriate for young women. By the late 1950s the ratio of men to women migrants had equalized, but the age of the migrants remained young—between the ages of 18 and 30. Though few sociodemographic data on Samoan migration exist, my data suggest that the very first cohort of migrants was mostly made up of single males. Within a few years, by the late 1950s and early 1960s, unmarried young women also came to help their relatives with child care and household chores. This trend continued, though the average migrant leaving Samoa after 1970 tended to be older. I met elderly parents in several households who had recently migrated to live with or visit children and other kin.

In sum, the Second World War worked profound changes on Samoan society. The most evident and lasting effect was the infusion of cash into a subsistence economy. This led directly to what Lewthwaite, Mainzer, and Holland (1973) called a "revolution of rising expectations." Once Samoans experienced the luxuries and freedoms that a cash income provided there was no turning back. When the Navy left in 1951, taking with it the majority of island employment opportunities, the dam was broken. Yet during this time Samoans remained largely committed to those aspects of their culture they considered superior: kinship and family, religion, systems of leadership, and family rituals and events. As they had done throughout their colonial history, Samoans integrated what they liked about the new with what they admired of the old.

To be sure, urbanization and the monetization of Samoan society introduced some cultural variability into American Samoa. The most evident differences are in the political system, due primarily to an erosion of the leaders' (*matai*) authority over their extended families. This is a consequence of descent groups' shifting away from dependence on agricultural land for subsistence, which the *matai* controls, to reliance on wage income. A source of steady cash income gives the wage earner considerable economic and thus political independence. Much of the cultural differentiation that exists today can be traced to the extent to which villages, and within them families, have been incorporated into the cash economy (see, e.g., Ember 1964). Today, as in the past, the center of capitalist economic activity is in the urbanized zone surrounding Fagatogo.

FAʻASAMOA: THE CULTURAL BACKGROUND OF SAMOAN MIGRANTS

The basic social and political unity of Samoan society is the village (*nuʻu*), or in the case of very large villages, the subvillage (*pitonuʻu*). Villages were historically—and are still largely—autonomous. Intravillage conflicts and disputes are adjudicated by councils consisting of titled family heads, or matai. Village-wide associations of young men and women (the *'aumaga* and *aualuma*) cooperate in carrying out local public-works projects, preparing for ceremonial affairs, and feeding and entertaining visiting groups from other villages. Laws and regulations are promulgated by village chiefs, and violations are handled within the village, though the *matai's* reduced political control has limited their powers of enforcement somewhat (Ember 1964). Even in villages that have been incorporated into growing urban areas, the autonomy of the village as a political unit, and more important, as an aspect of individual identity, has remained intact (Hirsch 1958; Holmes 1964; Tiffany 1974).

Most members of an *'aiga* are close cognatic kin and affines, but there are often more distant kin in temporary residence, for people are wont to exercise rights to hospitality and membership in *'aiga* to which they can trace kinship.

Membership in an *'aiga* provides individuals with cooperative use of land; they also have the potential of attaining leadership status, since membership confers access to a title in the *'aiga*. Membership in an *'aiga* is never fixed. Anyone belonging to a local *'aiga* also belongs potentially to many others as well. These may be dispersed throughout several villages. But many potential memberships are not activated because, "it would be most difficult, if not impossible, for an individual to meet the political, economic, and psychological obligations involved in maintaining active memberships in all *'aiga* to which he could conceivably claim consanguinity" (Tiffany 1974, 36). Individuals generally collapse the number of links to other local descent groups by simply referring to relationships as falling on "sides." It is common to hear the father's side of the kindred referred to as the "strong" side (*itu malosi*), and the mother's as the "weak" side (*itu vaivai*), indicating some preference for patrilineality. In actuality, however, people typically activate ties with the local *'aiga* in which they are raised and remain in it unless marriage and/or profit dictates doing otherwise (Holmes 1974; Mead 1930; Shore 1982; Tiffany 1974).

'Aiga are identified with a particular village. Although some members may live elsewhere, the core of the *'aiga*—often centered about brothers—remains in the village, occupying land that belongs historically to its *matai*. The most important dimension of Samoan descent and social organization is that membership in a localized segment is maintained through active participation, and that one's potential membership in other groups is allowed to lapse or remain latent until activated for some purpose. Migration is one way that Samoans use latent kinship ties. Ritual and social activities also bring together, for a time, dispersed members of an

'aiga; most important are rites of passage such as marriages or funerals and formal meetings where successors to a vacant title are chosen by the full kindred (*'aiga potopoto;* literally, "assembling kindred"). All *'aiga* members are bound by mutual rights and obligations that include participation in kindred events and economic or political support when it is needed.

Each local *'aiga* has its own *matai,* vested with the power to make economic decisions affecting the family, particularly the use of land, and to represent the family in the village council and as a spokesman on special occasions requiring formal oratory or a commercial exchange of goods. A highly ranked *matai* may be the leader, symbolically, of the entire dispersed network of cognatically related kin. All *matai* are also hierarchically related to other *matai* in a village political system.

Each title gives its holder control over lands currently under cultivation and within the village where houses are located. The *matai* approves and commissions the building of houses on the village lands he controls. In theory one title may overlap with another in terms of landownership, but in practice residence and use have precedence over theoretical political rights (Mead 1930). *Matai* also have authority over the actions of individuals within an *'aiga.* This authority takes the form of assigning tasks related to feeding the *'aiga* and keeping up the structures and garden lands. Also important are village or ceremonial events in which the *'aiga* participates. Contributions for funerals, weddings, church dedications, and so forth, as well as allocating labor for cooperative village projects, are under the control of the matai. Finally, the *matai* is responsible for the behavior of his descent group and culpable for the delicts of its members.

The title a *matai* holds indicates the kind and extent of power he has in relation to other *matai* in the village and district. Some *matai* are called *ali'i,* which has no exact English translation but is usually defined as "nobleman," or one who possesses the power to command. Others are called *tulafale,* theoretically orators for the *ali'i,* who wield the active "executive power that we [Americans] recognize as explicitly political" (Shore 1982, 59). The categories of *tulafale* and *ali'i* are exclusive; that is, the rank of a *matai* title is determined in relation only to others within the same category. The ranking of the most senior *matai,* of either category, is typically related to historical and/or mythological relationships to, and lines of descent from, a senior ancestor or group of ancestors. "High" titles can often be traced from apical ancestors; lesser titles have more obscure origins and are often defined by their relationship to a senior title in the same *'aiga.*

The principles of cognatic descent give individuals the choice of activating ties to different *'aiga* and thus maximizing their access to economic and political position. The utmost in authority, power, and prestige in this society hinges on its *matai* system. Access to titles is open to most men who possess the motivation, intelligence, personality, and skills for leadership. Although women can and do occasionally hold titles, their power on the whole resides in their ability to veto the election of men to titles. Women participate in the decision-making process.

The village and district hierarchy of chiefs is represented in a formal stylized system of address known as *fa'alupega*. The *fa'alupega* may serve, as suggested by Mead (1930), as a mnemonic for ordering rank relationships based on a hypothetical meeting of a "great fono." However, terms of address are not determinate or invariant, but open to change and restructuring depending on the speaker's purpose and the context in which they are used. *Fa'alupega* remain extremely important to this day, and on the mainland migrants, particularly those in leadership positions, must remember with great accuracy the *fa'alupega* of the many villages and districts that sponsor traveling groups to California and Hawaii. A poorly remembered or presented *fa'alupega* at the conclusion of a welcoming speech is an insult to the visitors and causes the speaker and the group he represents great shame.

Samoan villages are very public places, and it is in the public sphere that Samoans emphasize the proper organization and orderliness of behavior. Individuals are expected to abide by a set of precepts that carry legal and moral force. "In a well-run village, life is *maopoopo* (well ordered), and the lives of its residents are *puipuia* (protected or, literally, 'walled in') by customary institutions" (Shore 1982, 118). Samoans rely on the publicness of behavior to deter antisocial acts and ensure conformity. The public pronouncement of crime and punishment, as well as village gossip, is a powerful instrument for social control and conformity. One of the major changes that occur after migration is the dispersal of *'aiga* members into private, single-family dwellings that are relatively impervious to the prying eyes of other Samoans. Although *'aiga* members are aware of a large portion of their relatives' lives and the church provides an urban setting where gossip and public opinion continue to be powerful methods of social control, individuals have ample opportunity to escape the confines and constraints of the public Samoan world. This appears to be particularly important to adolescents, who by virtue of school and school activities are able to escape the control ("eyes") of their parents and relatives. Public pressures for conformity to ideal behavioral patterns can be expected to weaken substantially with urban living.

In this sketchy account of Samoan culture and society (and often in more detailed accounts), the impression of a fixed and invariant social system may be erroneously conveyed. In fact, Samoan social and political organization is so flexible that despite a half-century of anthropological scrutiny, writers continue to debate and confuse certain basic issues (see Freeman 1983; Shore 1982). These debates appear to stem primarily from the tendency of scholars to fix Samoan social action in space and time, to construct a static and normative view of Samoan social structure. However, as Shore (1982) argues, Samoan social organization is context-dependent; apparent contradictions can often be explained by "looking to the relations" of who is present in a certain situation, and for what purposes. Samoan society also has an open and flexible quality that puzzles outsiders looking to describe some invariant truth about social behavior.

To migrants the Samoan cultural system provides a framework for interpreting urban life and organizing social relations. Although Samoa has changed dramatically since the Second World War, many aspects of Samoan culture remain remarkably strong and vibrant. People learn the history of their titles and *'aiga*; basic principles of kinship are still understood; the formal political system remains largely intact, though functioning primarily on a symbolic and ritualistic level; and the norms and values that inform interpersonal relationships remain the basis of Samoan social behavior. Migrants not only bring this system of knowledge with them but apply it in forging their new communities. They do so in an environment that could not be more different is testimony to their creativity, as well as the at least immediate adaptability of their principles of social organization.

THE MIGRATION PROCESS: PERSONAL STORIES

Migration is often framed as a consequence of factors (primarily economic) distributed along two dimensions: those that push individuals from their societies of origin and those that pull them into specific societies. As we have seen, for Samoans the dynamics of push and pull began with the Second World War (Lee 1966). During and subsequent to the war, rising populations, restricted access to status, and new desires for education, goods, and travel impelled islanders to leave in increasing numbers. Although the characteristics of the migrants have changed over time, the context has remained relatively invariant. These aspects of social demographic change constitute what Mitchell (1959) has defined as the *necessary* conditions of migration. Necessary conditions are not, however, *sufficient* to describe individual acts of migration. For this purpose, let me present three personal histories that highlight the general characteristics of Samoan migration and show how both the process and the personnel have changed over time.

Tausua

When the Second World War began, Tausua was lured, like many other men of his village, to Pago Pago to work as a stevedore. There he came in contact with U.S. Marines just arrived to guard the island. He was so impressed by the uniforms and the stories he heard of the Marines' reputed toughness and courage—attributes Samoan men admire—that when a friend told him that the government planned to organize a reserve outfit of Samoan Marines, he eagerly volunteered. Although Tausua dreamed about going abroad, the Samoan Marines spent the entire war stationed at Tutuila. There they underwent basic training, assisted the Americans with a number of public works projects, and guarded military property. When the war was over the unit was disbanded, leaving Tausua with nothing to do but return home. However, he had met a girl from a nearby village, and for lack of a consistent plan for the future, they chose to marry. The formal ceremony was held in late 1946. The couple moved into the main town of Fagatogo, where Tausua was able to get occasional jobs working for the government or helping local merchants.

During this time Tausua remained attracted to the idea of being a soldier, but he knew that to enlist he would have to find the boat fare to travel to Honolulu. Fearing that once Tausua left Samoa he might never return, his wife was very much against his leaving. Finally in 1951, in the face of Tausua's constant complaining and pleading, his wife acquiesced. He was able to pay his boat fare with wages he received for his stint in the Samoan Marines and was duly inducted into the U.S. Army. Tausua tried to get his wife and children to come with him at this time, but his wife was afraid, saying, "What if something should happen to you? We would be all alone in Hawaii without anyone to help us." After the Korean War Tausua returned to Samoa; this time he succeeded in convincing his wife and children to join him in Hawaii. They arrived in Honolulu in late 1953. In 1956 Tausua left the Army three years later, moved to San Francisco, where he found an apartment in the Hunters Point area, and went to work for a local ship-building company. He was employed there until the late 1970s, when a serious back injury forced him into early retirement. He and his family now live a modest life in a modest house they purchased in Daly City. Tausua helped establish one of the area's largest Samoan Congregational churches, and over the years he has helped many of his relatives establish themselves. At the time of the interview he had just brought over a nephew so "he could get a decent education."

Tausua is typical of many early migrants to Hawaii and the mainland. Most were young, had some experience with the American military, were highly motivated to travel, and were independent and fairly self-reliant. Tausua, his wife, and others like them were the pioneers on whom scores of later arriving relatives, friends, and village-mates depended for initial housing and employment arrangements. For example, another migrant of Tausua's cohort, Enokati, arrived as part of a group of migrant farmworkers in 1949 to pick lettuce for a Japanese grower in the Santa Clara Valley. They had been recruited by another Samoan who had worked for this grower the two previous seasons. On fulfilling his contract for a season's work, Enokati quit and moved to San Francisco, and helped to settle nearly 50 other migrants. In the early days, he claims, "we helped all Samoans, whether we were related to them or not, because there weren't many of us here."

For women, the story is different. Many came with or to join husbands and other relatives. Most of the women I spoke with exercised considerably less control over the decision to migrate than men. For these early female migrants, raising a family in a strange place with few other kin around was sometimes a lonely experience.

Malosi

Malosi always excelled in school and after graduation from the ninth grade, she received a scholarship to the nurse's training facility in Utulei. In early 1946 Malosi left her village of Leone, Tutuila, to live with relatives in Utulei while participating in this training program. Malosi completed her training in four years and then returned to her native village. There she worked for the local dispensary, counseling village women on sanitary methods of food preparation and childcare, treating scores of ailments, referring villagers to the main hospital, and occasionally assisting midwives in the delivery of babies.

In the summer of 1950 Malosi received a letter from a distant relative living in San Francisco, asking her to come and help with a very sick child who needed constant attention. Malosi agreed and arrived in San Francisco in December 1950. Shortly after, she met her future husband. They returned to Malosi's village for the wedding ceremonies but soon returned to San Francisco so that Malosi's husband could join the army.

In recounting those first years, Malosi said. "We're excited about seeing America, about being somewhere where there was indoor plumbing, and electric lights and appliances. It was like a miracle, what we saw. But we were afraid; we lived in the housing projects then, and we tried our hardest to live the American way. We did not want to show our differences. It was much worse when my husband shipped out to Japan and left us alone. I was afraid and lonely. It was just me and my two oldest kids at the time. But then our relatives came from the islands and we started our own church and started acting like Samoans again." Malosi and her husband are the heads of one of the area's largest and most influential extended families, numbering over 75 members.

The stories of Tausua, Enokati, and Malosi are those of exceptionally bright and accomplished individuals, and it seems likely that this first group was self-selected for these traits. Later migrants typically moved to join established family and church networks and did not suffer the same degree of loneliness Malosi describes, or the fear and uncertainty that must affect all pioneers. Relatives and church-mates, initially at least, housed them, fed them, and in some cases provided a ready-made job. Such are the obvious benefits of kin-linked chain migration—benefits that have accrued to most migrant Samoans since the late 1950s.

The story of a young woman, Agalelei, is typical of these later migrants in terms of motivations, the process by which the decision to migrate was made, and experiences subsequent to their arrival on the mainland.

Agalelei

Agalelei was born and raised in the village of Ofu, Manua. She grew up in what she calls a "very traditional" way, of poor parents who had little status in the village. She was the youngest of five children, with three brothers and one sister. She started school late because she had to care for her parents. Only one sister was left in the village when she was growing up, and the two shared the many household chores. In 1962, at the age of 18, Agalelei finished junior high school in Utulei, Tutuila. When she graduated, the 22-year-old Agalelei wanted to do anything but go back to live in Manua. "I was crazy to leave Samoa. All my brothers had gone, and some of my friends and people I knew told me about all the wonderful things over in California. I wanted to see these new places for myself. I thought maybe I could get a better education, too. When my oldest brother wrote me and asked if I wanted to come, well I just jumped at the chance. I was on the plane within a week. I've never regretted it, either. My husband wants to go back; he thinks the life is better there, but me, I don't. There is nothing for me back there. My kids are my future and I'll struggle to keep my kids here and bring them up right with a decent education." Agalelei and her husband lived with her brother and his family until they had a child and moved into a place of their own.

For Samoans of Agalelei's age migration had already become institutionalized. For those with relatives abroad, especially siblings, the move itself was relatively easy: a quick letter to a brother, sister, or uncle, and the fare was arranged. Or a person's mother or father would make arrangements with his or her siblings who had previously migrated, and fares and initial accommodations were made available. In cases such as these, young men and women commonly "repaid" the transportation costs by helping their benefactors with chores and child care or by getting a job and contributing wages to their hosts' household.

This has been the pattern throughout the course of Samoan migration to California. Once the community was established by the first pioneers, relatives flocked to join them. The later migrants differed from the first arrivals, moving into a world rendered less foreign by their kinfolk's experiences and accumulated knowledge. When they arrived, the social landscape was already familiarly structured around small but growing kin groups and church congregations.

More recently two new kinds of migrants have been arriving. The young still come seeking what they perceive as a better future, to be sure, but they are increasingly joined by those who have been affected by the demographic distortions that decades of emigration by young adults have produced in many villages of Samoa. One of these new groups consists of older men and women who come to be with their children and visit their grandchildren. It is common in some areas, particularly in the more isolated villages of Manua, for nearly all the children of a family to have migrated to either Tutuila or the United States. Aging parents thus find themselves without the degree of familial support they had looked forward to and expected in old age. They either migrate on a permanent basis to areas where children have homes or visit for extended periods. Many also migrate for health reasons, encouraged by children to take advantage of what is perceived as a health-care system that is far superior to Samoa's. Once here, elderly migrants are typically dissatisfied with the quality of urban social life—particularly with the physical distances between households that make visiting difficult. As one man told me through his middle-aged son: "There is nothing to do here. I like it better at home where I can walk to the next house and sit with my friends. We make fishing lures and talk. I miss this. Here I just sit and watch all these crazy people on television."

There are, of course, elderly who are "old-time" migrants, but they have lived long enough in urban areas to be relatively comfortable with city life. They will shortly be joined, in any case, by the first cohort of migrants, who are fast approaching old age. Most of these "pioneers" continue to enjoy the fast and busy life of San Francisco, although a few men approaching retirement admitted to me that they might like to return to the islands to live, for they found they wanted to "relax."

The other new kind of migrant group also consists of older people who come to the United States, they say, because nothing remains for them in their villages, even though they prefer life there. *Matai* may have few *'aiga* left in the descent group they lead, everyone having gone to the United States. Fewer young men may be about who are willing to care for the plantation, provide food for the households, and earn cash for necessary trade items. Other, nontitled individuals may face what we call in America a midlife crisis, suddenly finding village life and its rewards unsatisfying in comparison to the urban experiences of friends and relatives. Finally, the loss of a job, political squabbling, or family problems may provide a reason for people to leave Samoa.

One man named Tui, a junior-rank *matai* from a small, fairly remote Tutuilan village, arrived recently to join his sisters and younger brothers, the majority of whom live in the San Francisco area. When asked why he decided to come, he mentioned poor health (filariasis) and a desire to ensure a "good future for my children."

I later interviewed Tui's older sister, a woman who migrated in the early 1950s. She resented her brother's attempts to assert authority over the *'aiga*. She thought it was unfair for Tui to assume leadership because he had not worked as hard as she and her brothers had to "build our lives over here." This kind of criticism was occasionally leveled by long-time residents at *matai* who they said "took advantage of the family."

In the same category is Ioane, who left Samoa in 1970 at the age of 44. Ioane says he migrated because he was tired of working at part-time, poorly paying jobs and farming his family's lands. Knowing that he had no chance for a *matai* title, he asked his brother already established in San Francisco to pay his way over—which he did. A year later, Ioane and his brother pooled their resources to bring over Ioane's wife and eight children. Ioane arrived with only an eighth-grade education, few job skills, and a family of nine to support. In the twelve years that he had been in California, he had only worked one temporary job. His children and his relatives helped where they could to support the household.

Not all recent older migrants are similar to these two men, but there is a noticeable tendency for more recent arrivals to represent a greater potential drain on established households than was the case during the first two decades of Samoan migration. This has not gone unnoticed by the Samoans themselves, and they offer a variety of perspectives and opinions on the problem. Said one young woman, a daughter of one of the first migrants, "Most of the Samoans who come over now go on welfare. They do not have the skills or motivations my parents' generation had when they came over. They have no grasp of how to manage money." A well-established man who migrated in 1959 later told me essentially the same thing:

> In the last ten years more and more Samoans coming over here are going right on welfare. When I first came, nobody did that; it would be a great

shame. [Why do you think this is?] Well, there are many reasons. You know, back home it's an easy life now. The government has lots of money and you don't have to work hard to get it. You just have to know someone. Some of these Samoans also live for a while in Hawaii. You know those Hawaiians, they taught Samoans all about the welfare. When these people come over here they go right on the welfare just like they did in Hawaii. Also, there are a lot of older people coming over here now, people who are too old or too sick to work. The family has to care for these old guys.

The idea that the "easy life" of Samoa contributes to the economic situation of contemporary migrants is an interesting one. What the man had not perceived was that the economy of California had changed significantly between 1960 and 1980, making employment for Samoans and other groups with minimal education and technical skills scarce.

NOTES

[1] A chronic disease caused by a mosquito-borne parasitic nematode, resulting after some time in about 5 percent of the cases in the condition popularly known as elephantiasis.

PART THREE
Cultural Transformations

The Pacific Islanders who have come to the United States are just one part of a vast trans-Pacific net. Samoan migrants to Seattle are likely to have relatives on the north shore of the island of O'ahu in Hawai'i, Pago Pago in American Samoa, Apia in Western Samoa, Auckland, and Sydney. Similar patterns obtain for people from other island homes. Even as islanders have gone abroad, American and other European-derived peoples and cultures have come to the islands. All over this physically vast oceanic web of personal, economic, political, and cultural interconnectedness, cultural transformations have taken place.

Two of the selections in Part Three attend to one particular aspect of life in the diaspora: the matter of assimilation, identity shift, and culture change between the migrating generation and their children, the second generation, who are born in a new place. Helen Morton writes about Melbourne, Australia, in "Creating Their Own Culture: Diasporic Tongans." Morton writes about *anga fakatonga*, the Tongan way. Her primary concern is culture and the ways that Tongan values, family practices, and identity are changing. Not only are some Tongans assimilating to Australian culture, but some are becoming "born-again Tongans" in the diaspora.

Melani Anae writes of the creation of a New Zealand-born Samoan identity in "Papalagi Redefined." She charts the pressures on second-generation New Zealand Samoans affiliated with the Newton Church, on the one hand to assimilate to *Pakeha* (White) New Zealand culture and on the other to retain their parents' definitions of *fa'asamoa*. She finds them making a third way to an identity of their own.

Vicente Diaz stays at home in the islands with "'Fight Boys Til the Last': Islandstyle Football and the Remasculinization of Indigeneity in the Militarized American Pacific Islands," but the islands are changing, too. His concern is not with culture changes that take place abroad, but rather the changes that cross-Pacific colonial connections bring to islanders at home. He focuses on football played by island people in Guam, learned in a quasi-military environment. Football is a public spectacle, a crucible for culture, and a place where manliness is defined, taught, and performed. The coaches of Diaz's Tamuning Eagles were already-colonized Hawaiians who had been brought to Guam on the routes of empire, as well as some Guam residents who had gone abroad, most often in the military. Diaz explores complex transformations in the meaning of island identity (Hawaiian as well as Guamanian), and particularly of masculinity, that play out on and around Guam's football fields.

Hawai'i is the place where American cultural hegemony has been most complete for the longest time. In "The Dynamics of Aloha," George Kanahele takes the reader into the emotional and imaginative life of contemporary Hawaiians through an examination of their most famous value, *aloha*: an ethic of love, caring, sharing, welcome, generosity, and gentleness that is interwoven with family, the land, and the dignity of the Hawaiian people. He examines ways that *aloha* has been appropriated by outsiders and adjusted by Hawaiians in the tourist industry and in everyday life. He also shows the ways that *aloha* continues to undergird many aspects of human relationships in the islands, indeed to provide a cultural foundation for Hawaiian reassertion against colonial domination.

With the final selection in Part Three, 'Inoke and Lupe Funaki turn to Tongans in the United States. They examine the ways that *anga fakatonga* is being transformed over generations in this country. They present an interpretation that will be familiar to devotees of the immigration assimilation model discussed in the introduction to this book. They see the relationship between Tongans and American culture as one of adaptation and compromise on the part of immigrants and their children. They point to elements of Tongan culture that they believe are essential to a thriving Tongan identity and community in the United States. They also suggest ways in which they believe Tongans ought to make compromises with American culture and values in order to lead fulfilling lives in this country.

CHAPTER 8

Creating Their Own Culture: Diasporic Tongans

Helen Morton

I asked 'Ana, a young Tongan woman living in Melbourne, Australia, whether she would describe herself as Tongan, Australian, or both.[1] She replied, "I'd say both. I'm not really Tongan; I am in appearance, but I'm very western because I just don't follow the Tongan culture. I only do what suits me, what I'm comfortable with."

During her primary school years in Australia and her high school years in Tonga, 'Ana's parents encouraged her to speak only English at home, and she did not learn Tongan until she was an adolescent. Her parents did not closely follow *anga fakatonga* (the Tongan way) in her upbringing. Now, as a member of an extended Tongan household in Melbourne, when 'Ana says she wants to do "something to do with the Tongan culture" she means she wants to write about it. She also wants to write about how *anga faka-tonga* is changing in Tonga, in ways as varied as the decreasing authoritarianism of parents and the increased use of plastic sheeting in the production of tapa cloth. Only a Tongan could write about such changes, she says, because outsiders could not really understand.

TONGANS AND MIGRATION

The Tongan diaspora, scattered throughout many nations, has the general characteristics of diaspora identified by William Safran: "a history of dispersal, myths/memories of the homeland, alienation in the host (bad host?) country, desire for eventual return, ongoing support of the homeland, and a collective identity importantly defined by this relationship" (1991, quoted in Clifford 1994, 305).

Tongans are not in exile, as were groups first identified as diasporic (such as Jews). However, conditions in Tonga, such as land shortage,

---

This essay was originally published in *The Contemporary Pacific* 10, no. 1 (1998):1–30.

135

unemployment, and low wages, combined with the increasing cost of living in Tonga and the perceived opportunities for material and educational advancement in western nations, create a situation that makes emigration imperative for many Tongans.

The title of this paper is taken from a comment a Tongan woman made to me when describing the problems some Tongan immigrant children face in constructing their cultural identities. Sela made a triangle in the air, with one corner representing the child and the two other corners representing western Tongan cultures. She indicated the child taking a course somewhere in between these two points, commenting, "He creates his own culture."

Sela was talking of her encounters with disadvantaged Tongan children in Auckland, New Zealand, in families where the parents were so busy struggling against poverty and other social problems that they did not actively teach their children *anga fakatonga*—a Tongan version of the scenario in the movie *Once Were Warriors*. It contrasts sharply with the Tongan migrants I have encountered in Melbourne; yet, as I shall show, they can also be seen to be creating their own culture.

Very little is known of the Tongan population in Australia, although Tonga is one of the main sources of Pacific Islander migrants arriving in this country. Tongans are relatively recent immigrants, with few arriving before the 1970s, and it is unclear how many are now in Australia. The 1986 census recorded that Tongan was spoken by 4,391 persons (Connell, Harrison, and McCall 1991); however, this figure does not reflect the number of persons who identify as Tongan. There are also many overstayers, with Tongans having one of the highest rates of overstaying in Australia (Department of Immigration and Ethnic Affairs 1987, cited in Connell and McCall 1989, 10).

The most important resource networks for Tongan immigrants are the church and the extended family. However, these networks are weakening, and certainly have not prevented many Tongan immigrants from experiencing a range of problems such as isolation from the wider community, unemployment, inadequate housing, marriage breakdown, domestic violence, and alcohol abuse. In addition, the extent to which "traditional cultural values and languages" are retained is highly variable between and within Islander populations. The issue of whether traditional culture is being retained, lost, or adopted is, of course, inseparable from the issue of cultural identity.

TONGANS IN MELBOURNE

The Tongans who have settled in Melbourne are geographically dispersed, far more than in many other cities with populations of immigrant Tongans, such as Sydney, Auckland, or Salt Lake City. My estimation, based on the available statistics and my own data collection, is that approximately 2,000 Tongans live in Melbourne. This relatively small and highly dispersed population retains a sense of community primarily through its churches: there are Tongan congregations of the Uniting Church, the Wesleyan Methodist Church, the Catholic Church, the Church of Tonga, the Tokaikolo Fellowship, and the Maama Fo'ou. Most of these churches have several congregations in different areas of Melbourne, and some are also found in rural Victoria.

The proliferation of churches is partly the result of the population's dispersal combined with factionalism, but also indicates the importance of the church as a social institution for Tongans. Since they first began to settle in Victoria in the 1960s, Tongans have established their own church congregations, often traveling considerable distances to attend. Much of my work had been with a large Uniting Church congregation (hereafter "the Uniting Church"), where the approximately 350 Tongan parishioners come from many areas of Melbourne, some over an hour's drive away. Ministers in Tongan churches are accorded great respect and wield a considerable amount of power, and the differences between the Tongan congregations are determined as much by the inclinations of individual ministers as by differing religious practices.

Considerable rivalry exists between the churches, with some vying to be seen as more "traditional" in Tongan terms and others claiming that their more western approach better assists the settlement process. The Uniting Church straddles the traditional and the modern, holding services in both English and Tongan and combining both Tongan and Australian elements in its activities. This church is of particular interest because it is actively involved in the process of cultural reconstruction and demands a great deal of its members' time and other resources.

This church also holds formal debates, seminars, camps, and discussions with invited speakers, during all of which participants self-consciously reaffirm, contest, and refashion aspects of "the Tongan way." The church places a strong focus on young people, explicitly to address the problems they face in the context of migration, and it employs a youth worker. This focus on youth is common to many of the Tongan churches, such as the Tongan Wesleyan Methodist Church, which has recently sponsored a trainee through the Fijian Bible College specifically to work full-time with young people in the church.

An example of the kinds of activities that are organized is a formal debate held in mid-1995 at the Uniting Church, on whether parents should force teenagers to return home if they tried to move away. Those arguing in the affirmative repeatedly insisted that in Tongan culture children should remain at home until they marry, so forcing children to return home was justified. Those on the opposing side were mainly concerned with how such actions would be perceived by Australians.

The various Tongan churches clearly are not simply places of worship. They provide social opportunities, mediate between immigrants and their new society, and are sites for the reaffirmation and reconstitution of cultural identity.

Despite the explicit discussion of aspects of Tongan culture in the context of many of the activities organized by the church, the parents I have spoken with have denied that the church plays any role in teaching their children *anga fakatonga*. One mother explained, "The church is something for the child to fall back on, you know, it doesn't necessarily teach the child to behave like a Tongan, or in the Tongan custom. I think to learn about the Tongan custom, no, I don't think the church gives them that." Rather, the parents see the church-related activities as being of more practical benefit, in that they keep their children tied to the Tongan community by taking up much of their time and providing an opportunity to mix with their Tongan peers.

Not suprisingly, parents believe that their children learn *anga fakatonga* primarily in the home. Some people insist that Tongans in Australia stick strictly to *anga fakatonga,* while others claim it is being abandoned. I have found an enormous amount of variation, both in the extent to which parents claim to be teaching their children *anga fakatonga* and in their definitions of that concept. Such variations are also found in Tonga. However, in the context of migration, parents seem to make more deliberate choices in this regard.

Anga fakatonga is a concept that embraces all that is said to be Tongan in values and behavior and is therefore often translated as "culture" or "tradition." Yet it is not represented as primarily past-oriented. The Tongans with whom I have discussed *anga fakatonga* are not so much concerned with "creating the past" (cf. Keesing 1989) as with knowing what is right for the present. They are also acutely aware of historical processes; as one minister commented, "We've moved on from our Tongan culture of yesterday, two hundred years ago, to another Tongan culture today."

The cultural identity of younger Tongans seems to be only weakly based on explicit historical identification, unlike, for example, the case with Maori youth. More often, parents tell stories of their own childhoods primarily to stress the advantages their children enjoy in comparison. "The past" in all of its historical transformations remains encoded in many aspects of these children's lives, such as the Tongan dancing and singing they learn, the Tongan clothes many wear to church and important events, and many of the practices they observe at such events, yet it is seldom rendered explicit except in the vague sense of "this is what Tongans traditionally do: this is *anga fakatonga*."

A number of elements are usually identified as centrally important to *anga fakatonga*. Tonga is a highly stratified and status-conscious society, and in any social interaction cross-cutting hierarchies such as gender, kinship, and age determine the differential status of actors. Low-status persons are expected to demonstrate respect and unquestioning obedience of those of high status, and within families the higher status of sisters is reflected in their relationship with their brothers, which is characterized by *faka'apa'apa* (respect) and *faka 'ehi'ehi* (avoidance).

Gender differences are also central to *anga fakatonga*. Ideally, females should stay home and do the indoor, "clean" work while males do the outside, "dirty" work and have more freedom of movement away from the home. There are also ideal standards of comportment, dress, and other aspects of appearance, the greatest emphasis being on demonstrating the modesty and dignity of females. Within families, physical punishment is frequently used in attempts to teach and enforce *anga fakatonga*, and, as I have argued elsewhere, this punishment has itself become incorporated into people's understanding of the Tongan way (Morton 1996).

Aspects of *anga fakatonga* such as these are used by Tongans as a means of measuring their own and others' degree of "Tonganess." Thus, 'Ana described herself as "not really Tongan," and her parents as not "totally Tongan Tongans," while others may call themselves "pure Tongans" or "real Tongans." One man commented that after visiting Tonga in 1990 he realized, "The Tongans here [in Melbourne] are more Tongan than the Tongans in Tonga!"

Anga fakatonga is a fluid, manipulable, yet powerful concept. While it is often represented as a determining influence, as something the individual cannot question, opposite representations are also common. One woman commented ironically that "it only suits Tongans when it suits them; what they want it to be. You can twist it around and just have the culture to suit you in what you want to do." A minister stated emphatically, "I will respect it [*anga fakatonga*] as far as it serves a purpose." Thus, to some extent individuals can make choices about which aspects of *anga fakatonga* they will keep and which they will modify or reject. Within families these choices are, by and large, made by adults, and the more closely those adults wish to adhere to *anga fakatonga* the greater the likelihood of children being expected to comply unquestioningly.

Another significant arena of conflict exists between parents. In each of the families I interviewed, one parent identifies, and is identified by other family members, as more "traditional" than the other, and this creates a constant tension that keeps the whole issue of cultural identity at a self-conscious level rather than being simply taken for granted. At times couples belonging to the Uniting Church have used the church-run debates and seminars as a forum for openly discussing their differences, as when a woman told a meeting that it was important to her that her children follow *anga fakatonga* and thus be unquestioningly obedient, but then her husband disagreed, saying he wanted to listen to his children's views and be more open with them.

Because *anga fakatonga* is such a broad concept, there is a "Tongan way" to do almost anything, from the simplest ordinary activities to the most elaborate ceremonial events. Thus, within each immigrant household, choices are continually made about the extent to which members will follow *anga fakatonga*. Some of the choices that cause particular concern include the extent to which physical punishment should be used; the extent of freedom to allow children, especially girls; whether to let girls cut their hair, shave their legs, pierce their ears, and do other "*pālangi* things"; whether to keep to the Tongan sexual division of labor with regard to household chores; and whether to allow children to play sport on Sunday, which in Tonga is by law a day of rest.

Respect (*faka'apa'apa*) is a value central to *anga fakatonga*, and its importance was stressed in all of the interviews I conducted. One man stated earnestly, "Respect! That's the heart; the *anga fakatonga* is coming from this!" Yet there are seemingly infinite variations in the definition and practice of respect. Some families insist on keeping the whole range of respect behavior, but most modify it, particularly in terms of relaxing avoidance between brothers and sisters. Still others argue that respect is just a matter of good manners and should not be seen as specifically Tongan. In some families children learn some Tongan respect behaviors, such as not touching their father's head or sharing his food and drink, but are not told it is a Tongan practice. One woman said she told her children, who had been born in Australia, that such things were just what they did in their family; she added: "I don't relate it back to Tonga." In some other families the children are told about the Tongan customs but are not expected to follow them.

Great variation is evident in the extent to which parents actively encourage their children to speak Tongan. Some parents, such as 'Ana's, discourage Tongan on the grounds that being successful in Australia will depend on good English-language skills. Parents who wish to bring up their children according to *anga fakatonga* are more likely to insist their children learn Tongan, such as the family with a rule that, within the boundaries of their property, only Tongan can be spoken. Children may also resist their parents' attempts to make them speak Tongan: despite the

Tongan-only rile, the five children in the family just mentioned frequently shut themselves in a bedroom to whisper together in English. Other children may simply choose to speak Tongan as little as possible: the father in another family, which instigated a Tongan-only rule for two days a week, laughed, "The good thing about it, it's a very quiet day!"

A great many variables affect the choices parents make about which aspects of *anga fakatonga* will be important in their households. Factors such as the length of stay in Australia, perceptions of the wider society, level of involvement with other Tongans, level of education, and personal histories are all important. Choices are not fixed, and a process of readjustment and transformation is constant. Everyday experiences, conflicts across the generations and between parents, and events such as the church-sponsored debates and seminars all contribute to this process. As indicated earlier, there is tremendous variation in families; adherence to *anga fakatonga* occurs in Tonga as well. Migration has an undeniable impact on families, but is not the only variable to take into account.

CONSTRUCTING CULTURAL IDENTITIES

What do Tongan children growing up in Australia make of their parents' attempts to follow the Tongan way? I asked Lupe, a woman in her early twenties from a "very Tongan" home, how she felt about her upbringing. She answered, "Although I sit back and I think 'Oh, I wish I wasn't Tongan' sometimes, and all these things that are expected of you; although I say that, I stick to them, so it does have an effect." I asked Lupe what were the most important things she had learned from her parents, and she replied, "I look at it and I think a lot of the ways that they taught me I'm going to do differently, so that's been really good. It's like, you experience a lot, and you learn from those experiences. And like, there's a lot of things I'd adapt like *faka'apa'apa* [respect] and things like that, but there's a lot of things I would let go of." It is significant that although she wants to adapt respect, she later identified it as the most important thing she has learned about being Tongan, *and* claimed it will be the most important thing she will teach her own children.

For parents, "adapting" a cultural value such as respect can be difficult, particularly when it potentially conflicts with other aspects of parenting they regard as important. Sita, a sixteen-year-old girl born in Australia into what she called a "traditional" Tongan family, identified strictness and the importance of respect as the key Tongan elements of her upbringing and said she planned to bring her own children up in the same way. Yet she also said she wanted to be like Australian parents, who she said "are more down to earth, they understand—I think they get along better with their kids, you know, that they can talk to each other like friends."

When I asked Sita if there were any aspects of *anga fakatonga* she might reject, she replied, "The bit about being afraid of the parents, and I'd like to be cool with my kids. Not as strict as Tongan parents now. They seem really old-fashioned."

Sita's ambivalence about what she sees as Tongan parenting is obvious. For Sita, choosing how to be a parent is intrinsically tied to her cultural identity, which at the time of our interview was somewhat confused, as will become apparent. The link between her ideas about parenting and her Tongan identity became clear when we were discussing *how anga fakatonga* is changing in some migrant families and I asked how she felt about that. She answered, "I don't think it's so good, because, I don't know, to me I think the Tongan culture's going to lose. It's not going to be there one day. I just think it's going to disappear sometime. That's what makes me want to bring my kids up the Tongan way."

To understand the way in which Tongan migrants such as Sita and Lupe are constructing their cultural identities, it is useful to see their identities as "framed" by both similarity and continuity and difference and rupture, with a dialogic relationship between these two states, as Stuart Hall has suggested for black Caribbean identities (1990, 226). It is fascinating to discover how each individual presents a slightly differently framed identity, varying in the extent of similarity and difference, continuity and rupture.

One of the most obvious forms of rupture occurs when, in the context of migration, an individual identifies with the new culture or is identified as doing so by others. For young children, the identification with the "other" culture, into which they are born or brought by their migrating parents, can be so complete that the discovery of their "difference" can be shocking. 'Ana described her moment of discovery at a school sports day:

> None of the kids I was with at school ever made it clear to me that I was brown. I never thought [about it] except one day, you know how you have those sports colors, and I was in the red group and one of the little boys in there said to me, "Oh, you're *brown*!" and I was like, I looked at it [looks at her arm with a shocked expression] and that was the first time, that was when I was about eight, I think. It never occurred to me that I was different. But now, looking at the photos, I *was* different. . . . We were the only brown kids in school, come to think of it.

Despite her "difference," 'Ana continues to identify more strongly with Australian culture and, as indicated by her comments about

Tongans with which I began this paper, she feels in many ways negative about Tongan culture. In Tonga, she said, "you're not actually doing what you want to do: you have to live by the culture, and by the society, everything . . . . I like Australia in that you can be your own person, whereas in Tonga you, I don't know, you can't be yourself really because everyone sort of dictates to you what you have to do, how you dress, how you're supposed to act, whereas here you can just be on the dole [unemployment benefit] and no one cares!" 'Ana's awareness of rupture coexists with a sense of continuity and similarity, because 'Ana believes that she has knowledge and "insider" status that give her an unquestionable ability to understand Tongans in ways that someone like myself, as a *pālangi*, cannot.

For some immigrant Tongans, the experience of rupture can occur when others question their identity. Kilisi, a tertiary student living in a large extended family who initially identified herself to me as "pure Tongan," went on to say, "I see myself as completely Tongan, but when I'm with Tongans I can pick out the Australian bits! I do things, and they think, 'Oh, she's not Tongan!' It really stands out. But I mean, it's nothing, that you're proud of, I'm not doing anything drastically wrong." Kilisi's identity is questioned most vigorously when she visits Tonga with members of her family. There, she says, other Tongans say: "Here come the *pālangis*." She added: "We're not *pālangis* you know. And sometimes you find that you don't fit in, because they pick you out as the *pālangi*. Even when you go out, there must be something there, because they say, 'Oh, she's from overseas' or something."

This kind of confusion is not uncommon, and while some handle it by adroitly shifting between identities as contexts alter, others find themselves rejecting the cultural identity others would ascribe to them. I even found that one young man rejected the very concept of cultural identity. Finau, whom I interviewed in Tonga in early 1996, commented:

Actually, sometimes I call myself Tongan, and not anybody . . . Sometimes people ask me where I'm from and I say, "Just from nowhere, I'm just a person. I'm just a person who has been brought up and raised up in a place which they call Tonga, or I've been raised up in New Zealand and they call that place New Zealand." Well, I'm a person who doesn't worry about being someone, being a person from that place, or being Tongan, or being American, or being European, or being a New Zealander, or being Australian. I just want to be a person—because I'm really sick of races and stuff like that.

Finau had spent his adolescence and early twenties living in New Zealand, America, and Jamaica, becoming involved with drugs and "gangs" (variously Tongan, Samoan and Mexican). Although many factors contributed to his desire to reject any cultural identity, one that he emphasized was his abhorrence of judgmental ethnocentrism, based on his own experiences and observations. He commented, "I really hate it: someone to say, 'Your people is this and this, they're really doing this right and really doing this wrong.'"

A RESURGENCE OF IDENTITY

Finau's wholesale rejection of cultural identity is unusual, but aptly illustrates the importance of acknowledging the subjective experience of identity. While others may continue to identify Finau as "Tongan," he can choose not to concur—unless perhaps he later chooses to for strategic or other reasons.

In contrast to Finau, Sita chooses to emphasize her Tongan identity, mainly because, she says, "it's different" and impresses her non-Tongan peers. As her older sister commented, these days "it's cool to be an Islander." Sita can do this easily, as she has grown up speaking Tongan and learning *anga fakatonga* within a large extended family in Melbourne and Sydney. For some of her Tongan friends it is not so easy: They do not speak Tongan and their knowledge of *anga fakatonga* is somewhat patchy, yet Sita says they yearn to be "real" Tongans.

I discussed this with an Australian youth worker involved with the Tongan population in Melbourne, who commented, "Of course some of the parents now, who've got little kids, think it's horrible that these kids [the teenagers] don't know the Tongan language, but of course they weren't in Australia twenty years ago when Australia was a very different society." To some extent it is true that the emphasis on "multiculturalism" in Australia has had a positive impact. However, other factors must be taken into account when explaining both the tendency of young parents nowadays to emphasize *anga fakatonga,* and the resurgence of interest in *anga fakatonga* among adolescents.

It is particularly important to see these developments in the context of events in Tonga, where rapid social change and the recent emergence of a pro-democracy movement have contributed to a widespread fear that *anga fakatonga* is weakening and may be lost (Morton 1996). While some embrace this change, others are responding with a reassertion of *anga fakatonga,* especially in relation to young people.

Some of the most ardent of those I call the "born-again Tongans"— the young people who have enthusiastically rediscovered their cultural identity—are those who were sent back to Tonga as rebellious youngsters in their early teens.[2] These adolescents, who have grown up in Australia, are sent to Tonga ostensibly to learn *anga fakatonga*, but actually to be disciplined (although in many respects these are much the same thing). When they return to Australia after a period of time, often several years, they identify very strongly as Tongans.

The Tongan churches in Australia have also played a role in the resurgence of interest in Tongan identity. Apart from the churches encouraging dialogue about *anga fakatonga*, it is mainly in church-related contexts that young people are given the opportunity to practice and display what De Vos called "emblematic ethnicity" (1990, 212); for example, wearing Tongan clothing to church, speaking in Tongan when giving presentations in church, and performing Tongan dances at church events.

These contexts also provide opportunities to be confronted by the issue of identity. A Tongan youth worker who accompanied members of a youth group to a National Christian Convention told me how they had insisted, prior to the conversation, that they would *not* be singing Tongan hymns, doing Tongan dances, or wearing Tongan clothes. Once there, however, they saw a large group of more "traditional" young Tongans from Sydney performing Tongan dances and immediately changed their minds. Since then they have been practicing their singing and dancing enthusiastically; as a second youth worker explained, "the difference was that they were doing it because they wanted to, whereas two or three years ago it was the parents telling them they had to do it." One of the young women in the youth group said, "Actually, that was one thing that was very important for me, as in identity: Tongan dancing . . . . And you know, it was just a dance and it was nothing really important but as the years came by I knew the importance of how to do it properly."

A renewed interest in ethnicity, including that occurring among the so-called white ethnics in North America, has been interpreted as a means of belonging and continuity (see, e.g., Cohen 1978, 401). A Tongan minister with whom I spoke provided a very similar analysis:

> What we have come to find is that culture can be a foundation of identity. I mean, there's always a saying that part of the problem with the Australians is that they don't have any particular culture! So everyone is looking for a culture to hang on to. And we have found it with our own children: when they were much younger everything Tongan is yucky. But as they grow up and you talk about dancing, they grab it. Dressing up for church—It's amazing! Our two girls went to Tonga two years ago; they came back, and every time now that go to church they dress up in Tongan [clothes]. In other words, they have found something they can claim as their own. And when the crisis comes, very interestingly enough, they stand themselves as Tongans, not Australians.

The appeal of asserting a Tongan identity seems to lie both in the flexible nature of *anga fakatonga* and in the subjective experience such identity provides. The children of the minister quoted can don their Tongan clothes for church, perform Tongan dances, and socialize with other Tongans, yet they can also attend university, aspire to professional careers, go to nightclubs, and otherwise participate in Australian society: they can successfully adopt multiple subject positions, or, in Hall's terms, they can negotiate continuity and rupture to form hybrid identities.

Because the identification involved is most crucially on this affective and symbolic level, it does not require an unquestioning acceptance of all aspects of "tradition" and "culture." Pita, an older Tongan man with children born and raised in Australia, said that he and his wife had explained aspects of *anga fakatonga*, even when they did not expect their children to follow them. "My wife has got a habit of explaining almost every single habit; why you do it. And I mean, the good thing about the young ones, they come up with their [own] reason. And some of [the Tongan ways] they didn't find any reason why you should do it; it's just for the sake of culture. Serves no purpose. So with these young ones, if they don't find any purpose in it they won't do it! Which is a great thing." Such statements help non-Tongans to comprehend the apparently paradoxical attitudes of Tongan immigrants like 'Ana, who have rebelled against *anga fakatonga* and rejected many of its values and practices in favor of a more individualistic, *pālangi* orientation and lifestyle, and yet retain a deeply emotional identification as Tongan.

"Born-again Tongans" and those who have always identified as Tongans also identify to varying extents as Polynesians and Pacific Islanders. In the past such identifications were imposed by outsiders, with diasporic Islanders lumped together for the purposes of gathering statistics, providing services, and so on. For young people today it is increasingly a matter of what Barbara Lal called "ethnicity by consent," where different ethnic groups merge and adopt a common identity in specific contexts (1983, 166). This process is facilitated by the overlapping of identification that can occur, as with the Tongan children who spent their early years in New Zealand, whose mother claims "they've got a real tie with a Maori background," and who prefer Maori dancing to Tongan dancing; the Tongan girl whose appearance allows her to sometimes pretend to be Samoan; and the Tongan youth group at a church convention who preferred the company of a group of Samoans who could not speak Samoan to that of a Tongan group that prided itself on its adherence to *anga fakatonga*. The Uniting Church is actively encouraging interactions between Islanders, and in 1994 held a seminar for Islander youth and their parents to discuss their common problems with settlement and within the family.

To some extent an identification as Islander is politically instrumental. A few Tongans in Melbourne have been involved in groups such as the Pacific Island Council of Victoria, but such activity has not been a major factor in the resurgence of cultural identity as has occurred in other migrant groups in Australia, notably the Italians and Greeks. Rather, young people's increasing identification as Polynesians and Islanders is part of the process of constructing cultural identity by experimenting with subject positions; it is a search for a satisfactory sense of self. Popular culture is contributing to these young people's positive identification with their Polynesian backgrounds, with sports stars such as Olympic boxer Paea Wolfgramm and soccer player Jonah Lomu, singing groups such as Kulcha, and of course, the movie *Once Were Warriors*.

If constructing a cultural identity is a question of "something to hang on to" and "something to claim as their own," as the minister suggested, the appeal of identifying as Pacific Islander may be explained. It offers an identification that is much broader and less specific that "Tongan" and incorporates a much larger peer group. It is also more easily adopted by those who are not fully versed in the language and culture of one or both of their parents. This was apparent when my own son saw the movie *Once Were Warriors*. By the age of fourteen he had spent years rejecting his Tongan identity, yet after seeing the movie he kept breaking into his version of a Maori *haka*, began wearing a carved bone pendant, put on his bedroom walls posters from the movie depicting young men with Maori facial tattoos, and was suddenly proud of being Polynesian.

Even for young people who are knowledgeable about *anga fakatonga* and who identify as Tongan, a broader identification as Islanders can be appealing, insofar as it greatly expands the scope of their affective and symbolic ties. This desire to emphasize sameness, at least in some contexts, stands in stark counterpoint to the current trend in theorizing that focuses on difference. Although at an analytical level it can be invaluable to address the intersecting elements of difference—ethnicity, class, gender, religion and so on—one can be left wondering just what any individual has in common with anyone else. By attending to the level of subjective experience one can recognize the crucial importance of sameness and identification as a fundamental element of sociality, which can exist in spite of, or even because of, difference.

One of the songs on the *Once Were Warriors* soundtrack, entitled "So Much Soul," makes my point, addressing the "children of Polynesia" and telling them that "Polynesian people have got their soul" and "unity is our only behavior" (Gifted and Brown 1994). A sense of belonging, togetherness, essential sameness—all the emotional, subjective aspects of cultural identity from which researchers have largely shied away—and are expressed in these lyrics. They also show how the complex cultural identity that can be forged in the context of migration and postcolonialism can overcome the false dichotomy of "traditional" and "modern." This is captured nicely in another line in the song that plays on the Polynesian value of respect: The "Polynesian children" are urged to give "respect to the soul community."

CONCLUSION

Despite the earnest debates in anthropology about the viability of the concept of "culture" (see Brightman 1995), it is certainly alive and well for the Tongans I have met in both Tonga and Australia. As exemplified in many of the quotes in this paper, they readily used terms such as culture, tradition, and identity in our interviews and conversations, most often in relation to the concept of *anga fakatonga*. As was shown in 'Ana's comments at the beginning of this paper, the essentialist notion that "the Tongan culture" exists as some kind of stable, bounded entity is readily accepted. This is confirmed in the way Tongans measure themselves and each other against the norm, as being more or less Tongan.

Yet 'Ana and other Tongans with whom I have discussed "culture" also acknowledge the characteristics more often identified in anthropology today: culture as strategic, constructed, fragmented, impoverished, contested, and so on. They hold both views of culture, invoking them according to context and, most importantly, incorporating both in the construction of their cultural identities. If anthropology has a lesson to learn from "the natives' point of view," it is that these two conceptions of culture are not mutually exclusive and, indeed, that they are essential characteristics of the same phenomenon. That people hold both views simultaneously makes the construction of cultural identities more confusing and complex than either modernist or postmodernist accounts would sometimes suggest.

NOTES

[1] Pseudonyms are used to protect the anonymity of Tongan migrants referred to in this paper.

[2] This is part of a wider practice of sending children between kin in Tonga and in host countries such as Australia (Cowling 1990, 200; James 1991, 17). This may involve several moves by the time a child reaches adolescence, with the intervals

between moves varying in length from months to years. This process, which I call repeat migration, means that in effect the child must repeat the settlement process with each move. James has suggested that "such children may not absorb Tongan values . . . . but rather will learn economic individualism and may cut themselves off from wider kinship ties" (17). Yet adults choosing to move children between kin claim to be motivated by notions of tradition and cultural identity, such as the need to retain kinship links and a desire for children to speak Tongan.

CHAPTER 9

Papalagi Redefined: Toward a New Zealand–Born Samoan Identity

Melani Anae

I AM—A Samoan . . . but not a Samoan
To my *'aiga*[1] in Samoa . . . I am a *"Palagi"*[2]
I AM—A New Zealander . . . but not a New Zealander
To New Zealanders . . . I am a "bloody coconut," at worst,
or a "Pacific Islander," at best
I AM—To my Samoan parents . . . their child.

Today cultures, identities, and communities, imagined or otherwise, are being examined as the processes of globalization erode national boundaries, integrating and connecting communities, organizations, and people in new space-time combinations. Although the concept of "identity" is not altogether new, issues of identity, ethnicity, ethnic groups, and the resurgence of nationalism are being vigorously debated in many fields of social theory, and in particular, anthropology.

There is undoubtedly today an overarching concern with anthropological theories of "ethnicity" and the "identity" of Third World peoples, as well as the "identity" of ethnic minorities entrenched in large Western nation states.

In some cases it involves a past defined by outsiders and used to forge an identity in the present, as in the Greek case.[3] In others it denies a past defined by outsiders, and uses a present cultural identity to forge a viable past, as in Hawai'i.[4] In many instances, national identities are being replaced by attachments to the local and particular, to tradition and roots, to national myths and imagined communities.

This paper is based on a close association with the Newton church community since birth, and fieldwork between 1992 and 1994. As research being carried out for my Ph.D. dissertation, Anthropology, University of Auckland, I am extremely grateful for the various funds and grants received over this period: a Ph.D. Graduate Scholarship 1992–95; grants from Auckland University Research Council and University of Auckland Research Fund; a Lottery Science grant; a grant from the Macmillan Brown Centre for Pacific Studies, Canterbury

In the case of Samoans born in New Zealand, it involves a denial of a present identity defined by "insiders" based on a partly-shared past to forge a viable identity in the present. It is about the construction of an identity, and is part of the "widening of the field of identities, and a proliferation of new identity-positions together with a degree of polarisation amongst and between them."[5]

A SAMOAN PERSISTENT IDENTITY SYSTEM AMONG THE ENGLISH-SPEAKING GROUP (ESG) OF NEWTON CHURCH (NEWTON PIC)

The ESG was set up in the early 1970s by Church leaders to meet the needs of N.Z.-born Pacific Island children whose first language was English, in order to fill the gap that formed for these young people after leaving Bible Class and to accommodate the few *palagi* members and spouses. Those graduates of Bible Class who did not want to be teachers or leaders and whose mother tongue was English just seemed to fall by the wayside.[6] The leaders of the church at that time, the Rev. Lye Challis[7] and the Rev. Leuatea Sio,[8] decided to form a body of English-speaking youth elders, which later became the ESG, to counter the problem of youth leaving the church. Others view its formation as the continuation of the assimilationist policies of some of the church leaders.[9]

Its formation coincided with the founding of the *'autalavou* or Samoan-speaking youth group. This was a move instigated by church leaders still smarting from the schism in 1969 when a rebel Samoan group, claiming that the Newton church was not "Samoan enough," broke away and formed the first N.Z.-based branch of the Congregational Christian Church Of Samoa, also known as the Ekalesia Fa'apotopotoga Kerisiano Samoa (EFKS).[10] It was hoped that the *'autalavou*, an institution borrowed directly from Samoa, would meet the needs of the Samoan-speaking and island-born members of the *ekalesia* (communicant members of the church community).

_____
University; and a Davidson-Te Rangi Hiroa Award. My 1998 Ph.D. dissertation was "Fofoa-i-vao-'ese: the identity journeys of NZ-born Samoans." I am indebted to my *'aiga*, members of my focus group: the ESG and the Newton church community. Also to my supervisors J. Huntsman, M. Meleisea, C. Macpherson, and colleagues S. Sua'ali'i-Sauni, E. Coxon, L. Foliaki, for your most helpful suggestions, and for being there. Special thanks goes to Rev. Leuatea Sio who started me on this journey with the question, "Why are our young people leaving the Church?" Any shortcomings are my own.

The composition of the ESG, which numbers approximately fifty members, is almost all N.Z.-born Samoan (there are a few *palagi* members and spouses, and one or two Cook Islanders/Niueans/Maori). Gender distribution is slightly more women than men, and ages range from twenty to sixty years old. Income ranges from student allowance levels of $70 per week to well over $1,000 per week. Occupations represented include university student, mechanic, homemaker, bank teller, doctor, dentist, lawyer, funeral director, travel agent, police constable, receptionist, teacher, childcare worker, administrator, and manager. Also in this sample group are six *matai*,[11] four N.Z.-born and two island-born.

Members and nominated elders' responsibilities cover the whole range of English-speaking and combined activities of the church, including administration of Sunday School and Bible Class (meaning that most members are or have been Sunday School and Bible Class teachers), outreach missionaries,[12] and participation in "combined areas" of church—session, choir, and services.

Fa'aSamoa Among Members of ESG

According to Shore, Samoan identity is embodied in their *aganu'u*,[13] their *fa'aSamoa*.[14] The *fa'aSamoa* is the ordering of a society of the highest kind, for it refers to the social order, the economic order, the historical order, and the moral order for Samoan people today. Indeed, the basis of Samoan identity is a passionate commitment to the *fa'aSamoa*, which is characterized by a unique relationship with the Christian God. As Samoa's motto acclaims, "Fa'avae i le Atua Samoa"—Samoa is founded on God.

Fa'aSamoa has an elusive quality, for although it undoubtedly exists, it derives ultimately from people's emotions and situations. Although the *fa'aSamoa* appears to be an enigma—there are many perceptions of what *fa'aSamoa* is and means, and one may rightly be concerned with the tension between the rhetoric and the reality of *fa'aSamoa*—every Samoan is very clear about what their perception of the *fa'aSamoa* is.

What is problematic is that time and space/geography produce variations of *fa'aSamoa* and Samoan ethnicity.[15] Within even three or fewer generations, significant differences have emerged between being a Samoan in New Zealand or California, as opposed to being a Samoan in Western Samoa. These differences include the ability (or inability) to speak Samoan and the degree of acculturation into Western cultures.

Consider the following perceptions of *fa'aSamoa* by some members of the ESG, firstly from a N.Z.-born *matai*:

When my father was alive, it was like none of us kids took advantage of the fact that he knew his *fa'aSamoa* inside out, and that he was the best teacher anyone could have, cause he just knew everything . . . we're sorry he didn't push us . . . to learn Samoan language and Samoan customs . . . I'd like my kids to know about the *fa'aSamoa* . . . I think up to a certain extent I'd push or force it upon them. But it's really woke me up . . . it's made me think, Hell I've really got to go to Samoa to find out about my *gafa*, the family tree, and just to see my uncles to get their blessings . . . .

From an island-born *matai*:

They [our parents] were brought up in the *fa'aSamoa* but they also looked at the Western ways and they adapted their lifestyles, just like we did when we came along in our generation . . . we picked up the stuff that was suitable for us so we still have the traditional *fa'aSamoa* upbringing but we were also exposed to the *fa'apalagi* . . . *fa'aSamoa* in New Zealand is just as valid . . . it's healthy cause culture does not stagnate, it has to move otherwise it would die . . . it's up to our young people coming in to be trustees of the legacy of their parents and grandparents to keep it going.

From a non-titled N.Z.-born:

[T]he *fa'aSamoa* here is an adaptation of the real *fa'aSamoa* back home. We grew up on this adaptation of the real *fa'aSamoa* back home . . . we HAD to be a success for our parents . . . to me it's something that's always developing, it had its roots in Samoa, but then it's come here . . . it's been adapted to the New Zealand situation . . . and Samoa is copying some of our ideas . . . Some opt out of the *fa'aSamoa* cause it's an expensive business.

'Aiga obligations are mainly to kin in New Zealand[16] and it is the parents who provide face-to-face contact with *'aiga* in Samoa. N.Z.-borns contribute indirectly by assisting parents with remittances and so forth. But in most of the accounts, perceptions of *fa'aSamoa* were profoundly characterized by giving, being proud of being Samoan, equating *fa'aSamoa* with Christianity and the Newton church (despite the tremendous stresses, strains, and negative aspects that accompany this identity), and the comparatively liberal attitudes of parents in enforcing the *fa'aSamoa* in New Zealand.

What makes *fa'aSamoa* persist for N.Z.-borns in the ESG in terms of the symbols used and in what social context are these symbols meaningful? Have the symbols changed? Are there new symbols?

Language: The Pressures to Speak English

English is the lingua franca for this group, therefore the combined service, combined session meetings, combined choir, Sunday School, and Bible Class are vehicles for the expression of English. Almost all N.Z.-borns in my focus group, although exposed to both Samoan and English in varying degrees during infancy, can speak only English.[17] One said,

> [A]nd the Headmaster said to my father, "Don't speak Samoan at home because it's going to hold your children back." So all of us were brought up speaking English, and sometimes my mum would speak broken English at home, but that's how we'd communicate . . . and the odd Samoan, like commands . . . so we were all brought up in English and we never learnt Samoan.

What is significant about this statement was the insistence that it was not by choice that they could not speak Samoan, but by circumstance. Those in the focus group who are fluent in both English and Samoan fall into two categories:

a. Those whose jobs or professions demanded that they should speak Samoan. Those in this category could not speak Samoan in their school-age years but ended up in jobs where the clientele consisted mainly of Pacific Islanders, namely Samoans.

b. Those whose parents insisted that only Samoan was to be spoken in the home, and those who were encouraged or made to join the ethnic-based Samoan organizations in the Newton PIC structure such as the 'autalavou (Samoan youth group), or the 'aufaipese (Samoan choir).

Samoan parents assumed that the priority for their children was to speak English during their involvement in the education system, and that on the completion of their education somehow the children would "know Samoan," with English taking second priority. This was not the case. Their knowledge of Samoan had been reduced to speaking a few commands, although most were fluent in "understanding" the Samoan language.

The stress and frustration at their inability to speak Samoan and the fact that most members expressed the desire to "pick it up" by either rigorous learning or going back to Samoa exhibits a strong desire to speak Samoan at some future stage. This desire serves to generate and maintain a sense of attachment to Samoan identity symbols even though the opposition of external pressures from New Zealand society has resulted in them speaking English only, with a smattering of Samoan.

Another important aspect is that the N.Z.-borns in my focus group all understand Samoan fluently. Many of those with children send their children to *'aoga Samoa* (Samoan language nest), and most single members expressed desires to send their children to *'aoga Samoa* when they indeed have their own children, regardless of the ethnicity of their spouses, to bring them up in the *fa'aSamoa*.

When asked what aspect of *fa'aSamoa* was more important, language, customs, or beliefs, 55 percent prioritized language. Of those, thirty-six percent were Samoan speakers and sixty-four percent were English speakers.

Those N.Z.-born Samoans who just opt out of the Pacific Island Church system never seem to go to other denominations, but merely have a "time out" period where they "do their own thing" or "get a life." My research shows that over fifty percent of ESG members have at some time or other had "time out" periods but have returned to church and their obligations, especially when they start having their own children and become more mature.[18]

The relatively small size of the ESG is an indication that many other N.Z.-born Samoan youth at Newton are actually joining the *'autalavou*. These N.Z.-born Samoans are opting to consolidate their *fa'aSamoa* in a more concrete way. Nevertheless, the ESG is a latently powerful group within the Newton church community.

These common threads—their experiences of New Zealand *fa'aSamoa*, being N.Z.-born Samoans within the Newton church, growing up together in the church, and being children/grandchildren of the first wave of Samoan migrants to New Zealand—bind the members of the ESG together into a cohesive, proactive unit, and they are fast becoming a formidable force within the Newton church structure.

But this force is, and will continue to be, tempered by the degree to which this group and its members identify with the *fa'aSamoa*. Educated and qualified though they may be in *palagi* terms, it is rather their service and participation in the *fa'aSamoa* embedded in the church structure that allows this power to be exerted. This power, previously unchallenged, was sorely tested by the recent restructuring proposals of the national body of the PIC.

INTRAGROUP DYNAMICS: THE OPPOSITIONAL PROCESS WITHIN THE NEWTON CHURCH

The persistence of the *fa'aSamoa* over successive attempts by the Germans to colonize Samoa between 1900 and 1914, and then New Zealand between 1914 and 1962,[19] is exemplified by opposition and the development of well-defined symbols of land, language, *matai* (chief), and *fa'alupega* (geneaology) systems, *'aiga* (family), and church. These, together with the concomitant spheres of participation through the Samoan language, the sharing of moral values and political organization mirrored in *tautua* (service to *matai*, church ministers, and *'aiga*), *feagaiga* (special relationship[20]), *fa'aaloalo* (respect), and reciprocity that distinguish Samoans from any other ethnic group, have served to maintain the persistent identity system for Samoan people in Samoa.

For island-born Samoans living in Samoa and New Zealand, the *fa'aSamoa* continues to meet their basic needs. Meleisea states that "[M]ost people who understand the system and the economic realities of Western Samoan society, agree that the majority of Samoans live by *fa'aSamoa* and prefer to retain its essential elements. The greatest threat lies in the . . . small though very powerful section of the community who could survive without *fa'aSamoa*"[21]

This is exactly the threat that N.Z.-borns in the ESG represent to many island-born Samoans and elders of the church—that is, the breakdown of the *fa'aSamoa*. Most of them are well-educated professionals, upwardly mobile, with incomes representative of middle-class New Zealanders, even though their parents and grandparents were laborers and factory workers. They have no need of *fa'aSamoa* to survive in New Zealand— indeed to many, it is a burden. Nevertheless the desire to be identitified as N.Z.-born Samoan, or Samoan instead of *papalagi* or New Zealander, is real, and it is interesting to look at why this is so.

Island-born Samoans believed that N.Z.-borns are becoming more monolingual, that is, prefer to speak English rather than Samoan; and monocultural, that is, prefer to follow a "kiwi" life-style. They also expressed the fear that N.Z.-borns have lost or are losing their Samoan "culture." These concerns are exemplified in the following quote from a current Samoan elder.

> I believe, because they're an educated group, because they're N.Z.-born, because they don't have a deep understanding of culture... and they don't understand church culture per se Pacific Island people... they will eventually destroy what we have. People (charismatic influence) have come in, and they've said that the *fa'aSamoa* stuff is corrupt... and our kids are taking the easy option... not to give money, and that's wrong because giving money is strength, it's tying us together... and the kids who are being saved are the ones whose parents are strong enough to say "You go to the Samoan service... the *'autalavou*, the *'aufaipese*, otherwise you get a hiding." [A]nd those kids are the strength of our Church, the ones who are not there are our weakness.[22]

Clearly then, island-born Samoans believe that to be a "good Samoan" one must speak Samoan, be obedient to elders, not be swayed by outside influences, and participate fully in affairs of the *'aiga* in New Zealand and in Samoa, as well as the church community. As part of the *ekalesia* (church community), the Samoan parents are members of the Samoan group as well as other church groups such as Samoan choir, *'autalavou* (youth group), and the *komiti tina* (women's committee). This means that as well as meeting personal *'aiga* obligations, N.Z.-borns of the ESG are expected to support their parents' groups in the church community, both physically and financially in all fundraising efforts, as well as their own ESG's commitments. Moreover, this participation is measured by the willingness and ability to give financially when called upon to do so.

While N.Z.-born Samoans are seen to be losing their "culture," what they have obviously not lost is their ability to actually "power" the *fa'aSamoa* in terms of the financial "giving" to meet *fa'aSamoa 'aiga* obligations, both in New Zealand and in Western Samoa. In practice, it is this aspect of Samoan culture that the church leaders are afraid that N.Z.-borns are losing. And it is this expectation that forces some N.Z.-borns to opt out of the church.

ESG Opposition to PIC Restructuring Proposals

Theoretically speaking, since 1969 the PIC has existed under the umbrella of the Presbyterian Church of Aotearoa New Zealand (PCANZ). In reality, the PIC, and Newton church in particular, has had quite a large measure of autonomy in the running and administration of its different parishes, in its very unique Pacific Island way. So much so that plans are afoot to restructure the PCANZ to accommodate the needs of this not "multicultural" church but Pacific Island Church. The new structure, touted as "PIC Synod," is a composite of current indigenous church structures, borrowed directly from Samoa, Cook Islands, Niue, and Tokelau, that would effectively give Pacific Islanders of the PIC freedom to express their faith fully in their own cultural terms.

What is interesting about this proposed structure of the Synod is that there is no accommodation for the ESG of Newton PIC. Although Newton is the only PIC that has such a group, its twenty years of involvement in church life and initiating outreach and community projects has firmly established its identity, with the appointment of ESG elders to Combined Session (the decision-making body of the church), the establishment of regular monthly youth services, and the election of ESG elders to Finance/Development Committees. All these have been consolidated in the work of the ESG and are reflected in the ministry of the ESG today. The ESG is quick to point out the inherent difficulties in such an undertaking:

[T]o disregard the needs of our N.Z.-born youth, to try and exist in a vacuum, cocooned from reality, would be a recipe for disaster. We are not in Samoa, Niue or the Cook Islands or Tokelau—we are in Aotearoa, and it will be foolish to think that a church structure borrowed directly from the islands (warts and all) will remain "traditional," or have the same effect in Aotearoa as it did in the Islands. Pacific Island institutions, and the concomitant problems/solutions associated with their continued existence, are contextual, and cannot be transplanted across time and space. As with the *fa'aSamoa, fakaNiue, fakaTokelau, peaKuki Airani*, which has been modified by our parents and grandparents . . . the proposed structure of the Pacific Island Church Synod must be creatively modified to suit Auckland, Aotearoa, November 1994, and hopefully for future generations.

Construction of N.Z.-born Samoan identity by ESG

In response to this restructuring, the ESG prepared a submission that in effect constructs their own N.Z.-born identity, in order to justify their inclusion in the proposed Synod as a sixth ethnic group,[23] in partnership with the Samoan, Niuean, Cook Island, Tokelauan, and Tuvaluan groups of the PIC.

Traditionally, the role of N.Z.-borns has been one of "bridging" the gap between the world of our Pacific Island parents and the new world of the *palagi*. As intermediaries between parents/*'aiga*/kin/communities and the state, we have grown up with two quite different types of world views and two quite different types of knowledge/power systems. Like our Pacific Island ancestors, we have taken freely from one to enhance the other, knowing that change was/is/forever will be inevitable, yet still confident that the cultural identities of our parents would remain intact throughout this process, buffered by the church/*'aiga*/kin institutional networks, which have remained staunchly in place. Our cultural identities as N.Z.-borns, however, have been questioned, undermined, and ignored, and have yet to weather the storm. We are part of our parents' and grandparents' worlds while living in a *palagi* world. As intermediaries we have become quite comfortable in this well-worn, rather schizophrenic role, sensitive to our parents' cultural and social needs in our home/family/church environments, yet aggressive and proactive at school/universities/work in the *palagi* world in order to survive the harsh reality of living in N.Z./Aotearoa. And all the while we have been continually meeting our social, cultural, and financial obligations to our *'aiga* and extended families, both here and in the Islands.[24]

Acknowledgement of the ESG would mean their formal inclusion in the new "PIC Synod" structure. If acknowledgement is not forthcoming, the PIC Church leaders would be in fact denying the existence of their own children/grandchildren within the PIC and, worse still, depriving them of a viable Pacific Island identity as N.Z.-borns.

This dilemma is not as sinister as it may sound. Many PIC leaders see this problem as uniquely Newton's. Being the mother church, its members represent first-, second-, and third-generation N.Z.-born Samoans. Other parishes have yet to experience this situation, but will have to face problems with their young people that Newton has already dealt with. Already at least two parishes are considering setting up an ESG.[25] It is also fast becoming a problem with the New Zealand-based branches of the Congregational Christian Church of Samoa.

The ESG submission has highlighted a "problem" that some PIC leaders were not even aware of, and preliminary meetings of the Special Committee for PIC Synod suggest that ESG proposals are being seriously considered. Nevertheless, the ESGs are consolidating by nominating new ESG elders and continuing their work for the church.

The implication of the construction of a N.Z.-born Samoan identity that the submission explicates is that N.Z.-borns see themselves as "bridges" or "intermediaries" between the world of their Samoan parents and grandparents, and the wider society. There is no identity crisis here. It is not that these N.Z.-borns are part of two worlds and are comfortable in neither, nor do they see themselves equally as Samoans and New Zealanders, as some scholars have observed,[26] rather, they see themselves more as Samoans in the role of guardians of their *'aiga* and the *fa'aSamoa* as they know it in New Zealand. And, in the same way, the ESG provides a bridge between disaffected youth and elders or traditional elements of the Newton church.

N.Z.-BORNS VERSUS "OTHERS"—IMAGES OF N.Z.-BORNS

The use of the term *"Papalagi"* in the title of my paper highlights the emphasis on cultural boundaries imposed by island-born Samoans on all "others," regardless of appearance and physical characteristics, and reflects an instance of opposition.

Originally the term *"papalagi"* meant "alien," "foreign," or "foreigner," and was used to describe Europeans or whites.[27] The Samoan gloss "skyburster" referred to the coming of the white man to Samoa's shores.[28]

Rolff gives a more extreme contemporary gloss of *palagi* as white people who are "untrustworthy," "anti-social," "socially insensitive," "uncaring," "lacking in love," "physically awkward," "unmusical," and "atheistic."[29] Over the last fifty years or so, however, it has become the term used by island-born Samoans to refer to Samoans born and raised beyond Samoa's shores.

Thus, although I consider myself a Samoan, my *'aiga* in Samoa often call me *"palagi."* When I asked people about this they explained that I spoke English, lived as white people do, and come from a country (New Zealand) unknown to them. Moreover, they explained that *palagi* was a term applied to a person who "does things differently to them" or a person who "does not help or participate in village activities." In this study it became apparent to me, firstly, that being called *palagi* expressed an attitude of indifference rather than of derision, and secondly, while it could be construed as having negative connotations, that it is merely an acknowledgement of difference—of birthplace and of socialization experiences. That is to say, it is not an affinitive denial of Samoan-ness.

This same experience has caused mixed reaction among members of my focus group. Reactions range from feelings of shame, guilt, and low self-esteem, to feelings of indifference, anger, amusement, and superiority. Undoubtedly, this phenomenon has caused N.Z.-borns to re-evaluate their identities and the *fa'aSamoa* in the New Zealand context.

The "new identity" that has emerged (among others) in the 1990s in New Zealand is grouped around the signifier "N.Z.-born," which in the New Zealand context provides a new focus of identity for the first, second, and third generations of Samoan communities living in New Zealand.[30] At the same time, however, it is important to note that this "N.Z.-born" identity is not a single, unified identity; it exists alongside a range of other differences that reflect lines of culture, gender, class, and religion.

What is important is that "N.Z.-born" not only is an example of the political character of new identities,[31] but also demonstrates how different Samoan migrant enclaves express their contemporary cross-national Samoan ethnicity in ways that are compatible with their various current lifestyles over time and in different localities.

Different groups of N.Z.-borns (whether they be church, sports, or community groups) take on the "N.Z.-born" identity. What they have in common is not that they are culturally, ethnically, linguistically, or even physically the same, but that they are seen and treated as "the same," that is, as non-white, non-island-born "others," by New Zealanders, recent island arrivals,[32] and island-born "elders."[33]

Hence, as my research reveals, N.Z.-borns, who in almost every case call New Zealand home and who do not want to live in Samoa, tend to identify themselves as N.Z.-born Samoans in the company of island-born Samoans; as Samoans in the company of non-Samoans; and as Pacific Islanders or Other on bureaucratic forms.

REFLECTIONS AND CONCLUSIONS

From the ESG perspective, members have retained the cultural, spiritual, and philosophical aspects of the *fa'aSamoa*, even though most do not regularly speak Samoan. They understand Samoan and speak Samoan when they can. They choose to be visibly identified as "Samoan": exhibiting *pe'a, malu,* and *taulima* (male and female body tattoos and arm tattoos); wearing modified *lavalava/tapa* shirts and dresses; wearing Samoan tortoise-shell rings, earrings, and bracelets; and wearing "Samoan" young women's hairstyles (long hair in a bun at the nape of the neck, or on top of the head). Some are also members of *'autalavou* and *'aufaipese*. They adhere to customs and traditions as expected by their parents and grandparents.

The fact that they are still part of the PIC and wish to remain so obviously means that they choose to be part of their *'aiga* and kin groups and concomitant *'aiga* and kin obligations, for the institution of the PIC church gives the N.Z.-born the most viable way to maintain a Pacific Island identity.[34]

It is also clear that the construction of a N.Z.-born Samoan identity by the ESG of Newton PIC attempts to deconstruct stereotypes of N.Z.-born Samoans as monolingual and monocultural, that is, as *papalagi*, or Samoans who are losing their culture.Those hegemonies were created by both *papalagi* (PCANZ) and island-born Samoans who are in positions of authority within the PIC church structure. These stereotypes enhance the superior political positions of the PCANZ (the *papalagi* faction) and their efforts to insist on a "multicultural" church, which would dilute the identity of the PIC in New Zealand.[35] They also bolster the elite status of traditional Samoan leaders and ministers, who stand to gain much more from the proposed structure of the PIC Synod, in "cultural" or traditional terms (in reality, economic benefits), from their much enhanced status.[36]

The irony of this all is that the stereotypes created by the wider New Zealand society, which are in line with assimilationist/integrative models and notions that culture (e.g., the *fa'aSamoa*) is static, are being perpetuated by island-born Samoans and elders. By reifying their knowledge and experience of the *fa'aSamoa*, they create conditions in which *fa'aSamoa* in New Zealand is said to be in a state of "decline." This in turn enables them to designate N.Z.-borns as *"palagi"* in some contexts.

At the same time, the ESG's construction of a N.Z.-born Samoan identity is one that cannot faithfully represent the ideology of each N.Z.-born

Samoan's individual identity within the ESG. It does, however, provide an opportunity for each N.Z.-born Samoan to develop his or her own concept of self in the interstice that divides children from parents, N.Z.-born from Samoan-born, and Samoan from *papalagi*, in all their processes of becoming.

Although many N.Z.-born Samoans are indeed experiencing an "identity crisis," research and media representations portray the downside of this crisis. They emphasize the Polynesian presence in gangs, among street kids, and in the prison system, while positive and creative Polynesian influences by groups in church communities and other organizations go largely unheeded.

Admittedly, the experiences of the N.Z.-borns in the ESG are unique to the Newton church. More research should provide different negotiations of identity in other contexts. However, as most Samoans in New Zealand are churchgoers, it may be the case that other N.Z.-borns in "younger" churches (especially the PIC and the Congregational Christian Church of Samoa) will reflect the experiences of Newton's ESG in years to come.[37]

The creative attempt by the ESG to redefine themselves describes identity formations that cut across and intersect natural frontiers and are composed of people not born in their "homelands" but who identify with them. They are a group that retains strong links with their parents' and grandparents' places of origin and their traditions—but they are without the illusion of returning to the past.[38] Their "new" identity is based upon a partly-shared history of their forebears and on the fifty-year history of the Newton church community. They have no mythical or legendary heroes but choose as role models their parents or founders and former leaders of the Newton church. Instead of abandoning traditional ethnic identities in the quest for socioeconomic and political equity, groups and communities are retaining them along the way, even when some of them have become upwardly mobile. The sense of their own individual and group identity has been forged in connection with their successive linkages with others as well as island-born Samoans. Conceptions of them by others, often stereotypes, have in turn affected their views of themselves and their roles in relation to other peoples. The collective identity symbols and their meanings mirror this cumulative historical experience.

Therefore, whether N.Z.-born Samoans are defined as *"palagi,"* "Pacific Islanders,"[39] or "bloody coconuts," this group of N.Z.-borns are confident knowing that they are children of their Samoan parents and of the Newton church—parents who have and are experiencing the *fa'aSamoa* and are continuing to enrich their lives with it.

The *'aiga*-based network of communication and chain migration from Western Samoa to New Zealand through an ongoing exchange of people, letters, money, and information serves to continuously reinforce and renew the *fa'aSamoa*. The phenomenon of the persistence of *fa'aSamoa* in New Zealand, the mainland United States, Hawai'i, and Australia is mainly explained in economic terms.[40] This same phenomenon is described in social structural terms by anthropologists as "The Western Samoan Kinship Bridge."[41] These views are supplemented by Spicer's concern with the emotional aspects of identity of peoples who exhibit a "persistent identity system." Spicer therefore offers another possible explanation as to why *fa'aSamoa* continues to exist in different cultural environments across time and space: through the mechanism of opposition. I have extended Spicer's concept of opposition to explain intra-group dynamics resulting in the construction of a N.Z.-born Samoan identity.[42]

My research has shown that the *fa'aSamoa* experienced and practiced by N.Z.-borns in the ESG reflects a Samoan persistent identity system and consists of well-defined symbols of homeland, language, church, and *'aiga*, as well as concomitant spheres of emotional and meaningful participation expressed by *tautua, fa'aaloalo, feagaiga,* and reciprocity in the context of the institution of Newton PIC.

I prefer Spicer's explanation for the persistence of identity, and his concept of opposition, because the conditions under which these systems survive are analyzable and can be empirically investigated in the narratives, stories, and experiences of people. More importantly, narratives that illuminate how N.Z.-borns themselves define and experience *fa'aSamoa* in New Zealand have been provided—narratives and stories that challenge dominant primordial and circumstantial constructions of Pacific Island identities.

For Samoan people, experiences of Christianity, colonialism, capitalism, and globalization, all instances of opposition, only serve to energize their persistent identity system as Samoans and will never confine them as "a people." They are merely Samoan people following the paths forged by their ancestors of the past and their *'aiga* in the present, and as such are continuing the voyage of their ancestors through time and space.[43]

NOTES

[1] *'Aiga*: family; extended family; descent group or kinship in all its dimensions.

[2] *Papalagi* (also *palagi*): sky-breaker (lit.); white man; European; foreigner; Samoan not born in Samoa in this context.

[3] J. Friedman, "The Past in the Future: History and the Politics of Identity," *American Anthropologist* 94, no. 4 (1992): 845.

[4] Ibid., 841–844.

Table 1 N.Z.-Born Samoan Population Statistics, 1936–1991

Year	Total Population	Inter-Censal Increase (percent)	Born in Samoa	Inter-Censal Increase (percent)	Born Out of Samoa	Inter-Censal Increase (percent)	Percent Born Out of Samoa
1936	362	—	279	—	83	—	22.9
1945	716	97.8	592	112.2	124	49.4	17.3
1951	n.a.	128.6	1,336	125.7	—	145.1	—
1956	3,740	128.6	2,995	124.2	745	145.1	19.9
1961	6,481	73.3	4,450	48.6	2,031	172.1	31.3
1966	8,663	33.7	7,447	67.3	1,216	–40.1	14.0
1971	22,198	156.2	12,354	65.9	9,844	709.5	44.4
1976	27,876	25.6	19,711	59.6	8,165	–17.0	29.3
1981	42,453	52.3	24,141	22.5	18,312	124.3	43.1
1986	66,254	56.0	33,864	40.3	32,390	76.9	48.9
1991	85,743	29.4	42,702	26.1	43,041	32.9	50.2

Source: New Zealand Censuses of Population. Table adapted from Macpherson 1991, 68.
* Estimate arrived at by assuming a constant rate of increase and calculating the square root of ([1956] ÷ [1945]) to determine the multiplication factor every five years; then ([factor] − 1) x 100% = percent increase every five years.

[5] Stuart Hall and Bram Gieben, eds., *Formations of Modernity* (Cambridge: Polity Press, in association with the Open University, 1992), 308.

[6] The usual "ideal" pattern was that one was baptized into the church; attended Sunday School; went to Bible Class; usually joined Youth Choir, Boys Brigade, or Girls Life Brigade; became a Bible Class leader or Sunday School teacher; joined their appropriate ethnic group on reaching adulthood; became a member of the ekalesia (communicant members of the church community); then became an elder, a lay preacher, or both!

[7] Robert Lye Challis (1903–1980) M.B.E, J.P., B.A., Dip. Soc. Sc. Born in London to parents of English working-class background. Left school at thirteen and worked in foundry. Ordained as LMS missionary in 1933 for Missionary service in the Cook Islands. Came to Auckland in 1943 to minister to Pacific Islanders then worshipping at Beresford Congregational Church. When Newton PIC established in 1943, he became the senior minister, assisted by the Rev Tariu Te'aia. He retired in 1973, after 40 years of ministry, and passed away in 1980. Fondly remembered by Newton PIC as "Papa Challis."

[8] Leuatea Iusitini, Sio. J. P. In 1994 received "Tuifau" Title from Western Samoa. Only three people outside Samoa have been awarded this title. Born in Sapanaua, Western Samoa, in 1925 to parents who were village ministers. Educated at Malifa, then Maluafou, Leulumoega. He migrated to New Zealand in 1950 for a better education. Although having ambitions to be a teacher, accepted the call in 1956 to become a minister, attended St. Johns Theological College, went to the university part-time. Was ordained as a minister in Newton PIC in 1957, the same year he was married. Became senior minister for Newton in 1973. Retired in 1993, after thirty-six years' ministry. Affectionately called "Uncle Bob" by ESG and young people of Newton (several versions exist as to how he came to be called this).

[9] U. Nokise, "History of the P.I.C.C.," and B. Duncan, "Christianity: Pacific Island Traditions," in *Religions of New Zealanders*, ed. P. Donovan (Palmerston North: Dunmore, 1990).

[10] Nokise, "History of the P.I.C.C."

[11] The titled head of an 'aiga, a chief.

[12] TROPICS is the ESG's discipleship training program. This missionary outreach commenced in 1987. After three months training, missionaries go on a field assignment overseas for a month. This program has the full support of the Newton PIC community.

[13] *Aganu'u*: action or conduct according to the customs of one's own country.

[14] B. Shore, *Sala'ilua: A Samoan Mystery* (New York: Columbia University Press: 1982), 222.

[15] E. Kallen, *The Western Samoan Kinship Bridge: A Study of Migration, Social Change and the New Ethnicity* (Leiden: E.J. Brill, 1982); D. Pitt and C. Macpherson, *Emerging Pluralism: the Samoan Community in New Zealand* (Auckland: Longman Paul, 1974).

¹⁶ Not sure whether this is because parents are still alive, or because of other reasons.

¹⁷ There are varying degrees of fluency in Samoan, from knowledge of commands only to a relative competency of sorts; none of the sample group knew no Samoan at all.

¹⁸ See also F. Taule'ale'ausumai, "The Word Made Flesh" (Pastoral Theology thesis, Faculty of Theology, University of Otago, Dunedin, 1990).

¹⁹ M. Meleisea, *The Making of Modern Samoa: Traditional Authority and Colonial Administration in the Modern History of Western Samoa* (Suva, Fiji: Institute of Pacific Studies of the University of the South Pacific, 1987).

²⁰ P. Schoeffel, "The Samoan Concept of Feagaiga and Its Transformation," in *Tonga and Samoa: Images of Gender and Polity*, ed. J. Huntsman (Macmillan Brown Centre for Pacific Studies, University of Canterbury, N.Z., 1995).

²¹ Meleisea, Making of Modern Samoa, 234.

²² Interview with Samoan elder.

²³ ESG Submission (1994), 7.

²⁴ A legitimate claim using De Vos's definition of an ethnic group being: "a self-perceived group of people who hold in common a set of traditions not shared by others with whom they are in contact. Such traditions typically include . . . religious beliefs and practices, language, a sense of historical continuity and common ancestry or place of origin" (De Vos and Romanucci-Ross, *Ethnic Identity*, 9).

²⁵ ESG Submission (1994), 2. I believe the young people at Mangere PIC want an ESG. I have also been told that the minister at Avondale Parish has to repeat the Samoan sermons in English for the benefit of N.Z.-borns in the congregation.

²⁶ Pitt and Macpherson, *Emerging Pluralism*.

²⁷ G. Pratt, *A Grammar and Dictionary of the Samoan Language, with English and Samoan vocabulary* (London: London Missionary Society, 1893).

²⁸ Albert Wendt, "Guardians and Wards: A Study of the Origins, Causes, and the First Two Years of the Mau in Western Samoa" (M. A. thesis, Victoria University, Wellington, 1965); M. Meleisea, *The Making of Modern Samoa: Traditional Authority and Colonial Administration in the Modern History of Western Samoa* (Suva, Fiji: Institute of Pacific Studies of the University of the South Pacific, 1987).

²⁹ K. Rolff, Ph.D. dissertation, University of California, Santa Barbara (1978), 126.

³⁰ Also first-, second-, and third-generation Chinese and other ethnic groups. The dearth of research on N.Z.-born Pacific Islanders, specifically the children and grandchildren of the first wave of Samoan migrants to New Zealand, highlights the need for concentrated research in this area; especially in the light of the demographic evidence that the Samoan population in New Zealand is the largest non-European, non-indigenous ethnic group in New Zealand, and that N.Z.-born Samoans make up more than 50 percent of the Samoan population (refer to the

1991 Census). Communities here include N.Z.-borns in church groups as well as N.Z.-borns in gangs and N.Z.-born street kids.

[31] How N.Z.-born Samoans identify themselves and the effect this has on the cultural continuation of the *fa'aSamoa* in New Zealand will have crucial relevance for all Samoan people, not only those in New Zealand, the United States, Canada, and Hawai'i. It will have a direct impact on the *'aiga* in Samoa, who depend on remittances sent from their "transnational corporations of kin" (Bertram and Watters 1985, 497–519) for their economic survival. See also F. Taule'ale'ausumai, "The Word Made Flesh" (Pastoral Theology thesis, Faculty of Theology, University of Otago, Dunedin, 1990) for new "N.Z.-born culture" within the religious context.

[32] This group is generally referred to by N.Z.-borns as "Freshies" or "FOBs," meaning "Fresh off the boat." In Samoa, this is countered by N.Z.-borns being referred to as a "BNZ," meaning "Bank of New Zealand" (which refers to their perceived higher economic status), as well as "born in New Zealand."

[33] Refers to island-born and -raised Samoans living in New Zealand in the context of Newton PIC, for example, island-born elders, elders of PIC, or ministers of PIC. I refer to this group as Samoan-New Zealanders (Samoans born and educated in Samoa), as opposed to New Zealand-Samoans whom I refer to as N.Z.-borns (those Samoans of full blood or mixed ancestry who were born in New Zealand and who identify themselves as Samoans, or who migrated at an early age (say five) and were thus educated in New Zealand).

[34] Pitt and Macpherson, *Emerging Pluralism*; Duncan, "Christianity: Pacific Island Traditions."

[35] Here I am referring to the White Presbyterian ministers and committees of the Presbyterian hierarchy (PCANZ) that have come into close contact with Newton PIC. Before the national merge with the PCANZ in 1967, the PIC was the largest Congregational church in New Zealand. Today, the PIC is the largest Presbyterian church in New Zealand, a fact which PCANZ cannot afford to overlook.

[36] This refers to a "ministers as *matai*" phenomenon and the *toea'ina* system. See T. T. Leilua, "Christian Baptism, a Sacrament of Unity" (B.D. thesis, Pacific Theological College, Suva, Fiji, 1988); T. Senara, "Samoan Religious Leadership: Tradition and Change" (M.A. thesis, Religious Studies, University of Otago, 1987).

[37] At the 1991 census there were 85,743 persons in New Zealand who belonged to the Samoan ethnic group. This figure represents more than half of the total Pacific Island population resident in New Zealand. Over fifty percent of those who belong to the Samoan ethnic group claim to be N.Z.-born Samoans (see Table 1 and C. Macpherson, "The Changing Contours of Samoan Ethnicity in New Zealand," in *Nga Take: Ethnic Relations and Racism in Aotearoa/New Zealand*, ed. P. Spoonley, D. Pearson, and C. Macpherson [Palmerston North: Dunmore, 1991], 68). Most Samoans are Presbyterians (i.e., PIC).

[38] Hall and Gieben, *Formations of Modernity.*

[39] As Albert Wendt, a well known "Pacific Islander," puts it: "Pacific Islanders exist only in New Zealand: I am called a Pacific Islander when I arrive at Auckland airport. Elsewhere I am Samoan."

[40] The MIRAB (migration, remittances, aid, bureuacracy) economy of some South Pacific Island states. This economic strategy is a successful, though fragile, phenomenon that depends on links maintained between *'aiga* in Samoa and abroad (see Bertram and Watters 1985).

[41] Kallen, *The Western Samoan Kinship Bridge.*

[42] E.H. Spicer, "Persistent Identity Systems," *Science* 174 (1971): 795–800.

[43] E. Hau'ofa, "Our Sea of Islands," in *A New Oceania: Rediscovering Our Sea of Islands* (School of Social and Economic Development, University of the South Pacific, Suva, Fiji, 1993), 16.

CHAPTER 10

"Fight Boys, 'til the Last . . . ":
Islandstyle Football and the
Remasculinization of Indigeneity in the
Militarized American Pacific Islands

Vicente M. Diaz

GAME FACE

Check out rock star Jon Bon Jovi wearing what Hawaiians call a *haku* lei on his head (Figure 10.1). Sharp, eh? Looking islander and all. Look closer: it's just a picture. And it's really an islander, a Micronesian from the Central Caroline Islands. Now *he's* got Bon Jovi's face on. The *haku* lei—called *mwaramwar* in Carolinian—is on his neck. And how the camera captures the leaves on his back just so is what gives Bon Jovi the islander look.

Look a third time, at the sleeves: The peculiarly Micronesian aesthetic of knotting the sleeves of t-shirts adds an additional signature of cultural ownership. Thanks to this effect, too, Bon Jovi now sports dreadlocks, a feature of globalization and localization that is found increasingly on young white *and* Pacific Island men (Mishra and Guy 1997).

I love this photograph as I love *mwaramwars*. The flowers and this photo seduce us with the sense and the sensibilities of the islands. Today,

For my athletic supporters: Thank you to Dr. Debbie Hippolite Wright and Rose Meno Ram for organizing and inviting me to the conference at which this paper was first presented; to Lawrence Cunningham for the use of his photo of the "Carolinian Bon Jovi" and for shooting my slides; to the families of John and Betty Kaniaupio, Billy and Millie Tai, George and Kenny Kaualoku, Mike Tomasiak, and the late David Kalama for sharing their stories and photo collections; to the Kaniaupio, Tomasiak, Harold Shiroma, and Felix Crisostomo families for sharing their home movies; to Angel Petrus and John Perez of UOG Learning for dubbing and projection assistance; to Yvette DeLisle and Eddie Siguenza for additional information and photos; to Tina and Gabriella who

FIGURE 10.1 "Carolinian
Bon Jovi." *Photo by Lawrence
Cunningham, at the Polowat-
Marianas Voyage 2000,
Tanapag, Saipan.*

when the islands are overrun with outsiders and concrete development
that destroy sources for flowers and leis, that in turn become commodi-
fied by parasitic and demeaning tourist practices in an age of globalization, the image gives the impression of cultural syncretism between the

---

cheer from the sidelines, and Nikki who rolls her eyes at this project. To
Hokulani Aikau, Doug Hartmann, and Fellows of the McArthur Fellow
Program, University of Minnesota, and Amy Kuuleialoha Stillman for feedback.
Earlier versions were presented at the "What is a Pacific Islander American?"
National Conference organized and hosted by Brigham Young University-Hawai'i
(Lai'e) campus, May 2000; and at the Micronesian Studies Seminar Series/Guam
Humanities Council Public Forum, University of Guam RFK Library, September
15, 2000. Funding for research and development of a script for an upcoming doc-
umentary was provided by the Guam Humanities Council, the Pacific Islanders
in Communication in Honolulu, and research support by the College of Arts and
Sciences and the Micronesian Area Research Center, University of Guam.

native Pacific and the west. It images islander agency and survival. Native cultural durability. The ability to negotiate consciously between things native and things foreign in ways that proclaim the native's presence by whatever means necessary.

But there is also something else intriguing if not troubling about this photo and its structuration of meaning. The longer I stare at Bon Jovi, or at my fellow Carolinian's back, the more uneasy I get with my initial impression of cultural syncretism. Where I would like to see islander agency through the white man's gaze, the white man's gaze remains nonetheless, perhaps all the more. Where I would like to turn the gaze inward, if not appropriate it, the way my Carolinian brother does, I'm also met with resistance from the material itself. For the material fact of Bon Jovi's presence on the islander's back, and the commodification of leis, and dread, point back once again to structures of power that are now given new form precisely through counter appropriations of them.

This essay presents histories, memories, and images about the Tamuning Eagles, a remarkably successful Guam youth football team that was founded by native Hawaiian men, and other non-Hawaiian men from Hawai'i, who had transplanted to Guam after World War II through work with the U.S. military. These materials are photographs, stills from 8mm home movies, newspaper clippings, and military and civilian government recreational records in local and national archives. They also include excerpts from taped interviews with former participants—coaches, players, cheerleaders, and parents—whose stories are typically filled with tremendous love and nostalgia. But the material also includes my own nostalgic and loving memories as a former Eagle, whose training in the sport gave me the means to attend college. Once in college, I was made aware of the history of American imperialism in the Pacific and the struggles of islander participation in it. University also showed me the promise and the pleasure of interdisciplinary and self-reflexive scholarship. And so, partly autobiographical, partly cultural/political economy, largely historical, exemplary of a native Pacific cultural studies (Diaz and Kauanui 2001), this project contributes to critical inquiry into the local/global interplay among race, gender, identity, and American empire. Recalling the tension found in the opening image, and with this material laid out before me, I ask, what, in considering the history of islandstyle football, is the face of American football as played by Pacific Islanders? What is the face of Pacific Islanders whose lives were deeply shaped by American football?

PRE-GAME WARM-UPS

The title phrase, "Fight Boys, 'til the Last," caps a fight song called *Black and Gold is Waving*. From 1970 (see Figure 10.2) to the late 1980s the song was sung faithfully and dutifully by thousands of Eagle boys (and a few female players), their coaches, cheerleaders, and parents.

Flying high and far, and thus giving a sense of an historical translocality, the Eagle dynasty launched a phenomenal record of 125 consecutive victories that spanned a decade and a half, reaching west from Guam to Japan, Okinawa, and the Philippines, and east to Honolulu, the west coast of the United States, and Las Vegas. In 1999, the Guam Raiders—heir apparent to the Eagle legacy—took the world title by defeating Russia in the World Youth Super Bowl in Orlando, Florida.

But the Tamuning Eagles' own (trans)local bid to achieve global notoriety failed when, in the mid-1980s, the Guinness Book of World Records organization refused the streak because it did not recognize the category "American youth football" despite the fact that it had dutifully accepted a 127-game winning streak by a Scottish youth soccer club (Jacala 1999).

Nationalism's sporting bias aside, I want to argue that the translocality described in the Eagles' remarkable winning streak extends deeper in history and reaches further in discursive and cultural space than local or regional fame. Indeed, the winning streak by this Guam youth football team can be understood in terms of an uneasy process of globalization, more specifically, a history of American imperialism and colonialism in

FIGURE 10.2   Team Photo, 1970 Tamuning Eagles, Tamuning, Guam. *Photo courtesy of Coach Billy Tai collection.*

the Pacific, especially as articulated through the social institution of sports in general, and football in particular.

This historical formation is also animated by local indigenous and other immigrant forces, a form of energy whose consequence is the re-articulation of American hegemony through an indefatigable process of *indigenous* re-articulation and reconfiguration. In that mutual but unequal process of historical structuration, the material and the conditions emerge to produce what I would call in places like the American colonized Pacific a "new multicultural local" that draws from a history of Asian and Pacific immigrant and transient labor. But I want to assert that this historical process of cultural reconstruction is also fundamentally gendered through western and indigenous, and displaced indigenous, patriarchal practices like militarism, football, self-rule or expression, and family-hood, all of which are featured prominently in the Eagle story. In this vein, let me begin with a photo of the uncanny.

This is me and a teammate, Mark Boddie, in Figure 10.3. It's uncanny, the homonym between his name and the critical injunction to trace how our *bodies* are *marked* by the interplay of gendered and racialized social practices and institutions like sports, the military, and the family.

Here's another set of "marked" bodies in Figure 10.4.

In football, humans engendered female get relegated to the sidelines, to cheer on and support their boys. Twenty years later, I interview

FIGURE 10.3   Me and Mark Boddie. *Courtesy of Billy Tai Family.*

Dannette, and another former cheerleader, Kuulei Tavares. Their memories are vivid. Danette recalls accompanying her brother to the field and wanting to play too, but "that wasn't appropriate." One day she is asked by Mrs. Lou Shiroma, wife of coach Hal Shiroma, to become a cheerleader, and she explains, "I'm telling you, that it was such a good feeling . . . I felt so important, because they were the team." Kuulei is even more direct: "It was exciting because there were lots of boys."

In their narratives one encounters in the practice of cheerleading sanctioned gender and heterosexuality through the manufacture of consent and pleasure by the girls, who now genuinely look back with tremendous nostalgia and sentiment. Indeed, in this re-presentation of Eagle stories, I turn to narratives that feature nostalgia and deep, heartfelt, fondness as the key attributes that have served to bond imperial, native, and other forms of hegemony.

FIGURE 10.4   Dannette Kaniaupio and cheerleaders.
Courtesy of John and Betty Kaniaupio.

STARTING LINEUP: HUI O HAWAI'I OF GUAM

As mentioned, the Eagles youth football team was founded and coached by Hawaiian and other "local" men from Hawai'i—Okinawans, Filipinos, Japanese, Chinese, Portuguese, and *Haole* (see Figure 10.5, 10.6, 10.7A, and 10.7B). These men were part of a big group of men and women who moved to Guam for employment with the U.S. military's massive rebuilding of Guam in the post-war, cold war years.

These men had played football at different levels in pre-war Hawai'i. In fact, football was an extremely popular sport among newly urbanized Hawaiian boys and young men, especially among the first and second generation Hawai'i-born and raised sons of Asian laborers. The sport of football in Hawai'i and in Guam, later, as I will detail shortly, was introduced by U.S. military personnel stationed in Honolulu at the end of the nineteenth century. The first match in the Pacific was played by sailors from the U.S.S. Charleston in Honolulu (Cisco 1999, 130), the same warship that, at the outbreak of the Spanish American War in 1898, had steamed into Guam's Apra Harbor to seize the island and end two centuries of Spanish colonial rule.

FIGURE 10.5   Under the watchful eye of head coach (late) David Kalama at the Paseo, 1971. *Courtesy of Kawika Kalama collection.*

FIGURE 10.6
Coaches. *Tai
collection.*

**FIGURE 10.7A,
FIGURE 10.7B**
Pre-Game
Warm-ups. Our
drills empha-
sized precision,
technique, disci-
pline, unifor-
mity, and
teamwork.
Reasons for our
success: they
melded our
coaches' modern
military training
and older
Hawaiian dis-
courses and
standards of
authority, disci-
pline, and per-
formance.
*Courtesy of John
and Betty
Kaniaupio
collection.*

As mentioned, football in the ensuing decades became an immensely popular sport in Hawai'i, featuring prep, college, and visiting professional teams.[1] Unique to Hawai'i were the famous local "barefoot" leagues, about which more will be said later. Football was also an important component of the pre-statehood process of demonstrating Hawai'i's assimilability into America. The fight song "Black and Gold" for example, is actually the school song and colors of the McKinley High School Tigers (Coach Kalama's alma mater), a school named for an American president who championed imperialism against anxious warnings that the social effects of empire—subject populations of aliens and the potential rise in their immigration—would have deleterious effects on the purity of the nation.

After World War II, many Hawaiians and other Hawai'i "locals" began to move to Guam to work for the military as civil service hires. Uprooted and rerouted, these men and women began to forge relations through "socials" and consciously sought to build a new *ohana* (family) for themselves in their new island home. By all accounts, nostalgic and otherwise, such socials featured an endless flow of alcohol and lots of *kanikapila* (making music) (Osorio and Young, 1997). In time, the transplanted *ohana* would itself grow new roots and offshoots.[2] A typical example, Coach Billie Tai and wife Millie Tai, both from Hawai'i, met and married on Guam and decided to raise their children there. Coach Tai explains:

> Even though we worked for the military most of us preferred to socialize amongst ourselves . . . Even if we didn't know each other in Hawai'i . . . on Guam, we all became one family, regardless whether you were Hawaiian, Japanese, Okinawan, Chinese, or what not. And so the kids grew up calling everybody 'uncle' and 'auntie.' (Tai 2000)

In 1966 the U.S. military in Guam organized for the first time youth football for its dependents. From the start the men from Hawai'i who had football experience, both in Hawai'i, and in the Guam military adult leagues, formed the first civilian team comprising their sons and their sons' local classmates and playmates. The decision to form a civilian team comprising "local" boys was a conscious one for these men who worked for the military but chose to live off-base. As it turned out, there was an old Seabees camp in the village of Tamuning that was decommissioned and was going to be razed, but the Hawaiian community successfully received permission to move into the old Quonset huts. This was why the Eagles, as the second and most successful of the civilian teams in the initially all-military league, hailed from Tamuning. Tamuning was one of the first civilian villages on Guam to urbanize after World War II, witnessing the rise of many little ethnic neighborhoods of post-war immigrant labor other than the already multiethnic 'ohana from Hawai'i. These included Filipinos, white stateside hires, Palauan blue-collar workers, and Chamorros displaced from their traditional villages and clans. To all, that former Seabee camp in Tamuning would come to be referred to as "the Hawaiian village." And places like Tamuning would lead Guam's postwar transformation in America's social, economic, and political image.

By the time we began to travel, it was only natural to also extend our gratitude and appreciation at home in a multilingual way, with Hawaiian serving as something of a lingua franca (see Figure 10.8).

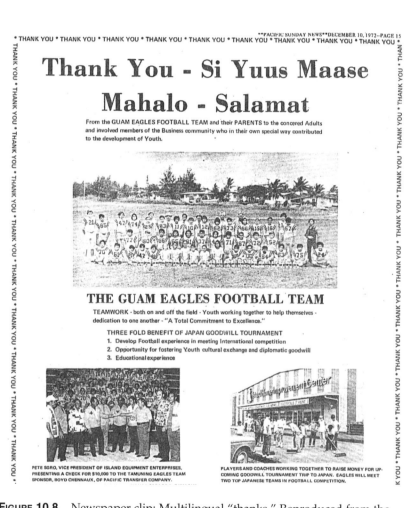

FIGURE 10.8   Newspaper clip: Multilingual "thanks." Reproduced from the *Pacific Sunday News*, December 10, 1972.

With aforementioned experience in Hawai'i's emergent multicultural and American milieu, men like head coach David Kalama and George Kaualoku continued to play ball when the U.S. Army and the newly created Air Force decided to organize tackle football for their Guam personnel in 1947.

Football's post-war history in Guam must be seen in the context of military interservice collegiality as the Army, Air Force, and Marines joined the Navy, which had sole and virtually tyrannical rule over the island before the war. Football was also organized to assist in relations between military and civil service personnel, like the folks from Hawaii, for stories of combat between the two are also epic among my informants.

The Eagle coaches first played with the all-*papolo* (all-Black) team by choice (see Figure 10.9). Alongside race as a marker of difference, of course, are gender, sexuality, stereotyping, and sexual objectification. A July 1947 Guam edition *Navy News* article on the inaugural season's jamboree contained the subheading, "Girls Galore," and the promise, " . . . one doesn't have to be a hidebound gridiron fan to appreciate the afternoon's fun. Anyone with an eye for beauty will feel right at home on Geiger Field on Saturday. Girls! Droves of Them! All of them football

FIGURE 10.9   Papolo Team, circa late 1940s. *Courtesy of Kawika Kalama.*

queens, and all of them mighty purty, too!" An accompanying photo of a
lineup of women had this excited caption: "These seven pretty bundles of
teenage beauty and mischief will reign over the football jamboree . . . next
Saturday."

Youth football, also organized by the military for its personnel in 1966,
only extended these organizational patterns. But I'm especially interested
in the role that displaced native Hawaiians and other multiethnic locals
from Hawai'i played in the introduction and development of "local" football on Guam. What does it mean that the quintessentially American
sport of football in Guam was mediated by a displaced Hawaiian island
sensibility in contract with the military? And that this particular configu-
ration itself owes to an even broader history of American imperialism
through militarism in the Pacific? To address these questions, we need to
first understand the interplay of sports and empire in Guam's history
under U.S. Naval rule from 1898 to the outbreak of war in 1941.

FIRST QUARTER: "NEW RECREATIONAL PRACTICES"

Unlike in Hawai'i, American football in Guam was a post-war phenomenon, although there were occasional games before the war despite complaints that "the weather [was] too warm for so vigorous a game"
(*Annual Report* 1919, 32). It was part of what Ron Stade (1998, 294) calls a
post-war "system of new recreational practices," and which I argue
remains an unexamined component of American hegemony in Guam.

Though football was organized in Guam only in the late 1940s, sports
in general was no bench-warmer in the colonial project since 1898, when
Guam was taken after the Spanish-American War. By the second decade
of naval rule, for example, the Navy had established a Guam Baseball
League—complete with a spring season and a mid-winter season—and
also introduced basketball, tennis, and volleyball to keep its personnel fit.
This was especially a concern in the tropics where, said one report,
"physical exercise was so necessary for Americans." The tropics were a
constant source of anxiety over the potential for physical, mental, moral,
and social degeneration. This local (or hemispheric) anxiety was also a
national concern by the end of the nineteenth century in the so-called
"health and fitness" drive analyzed by Harvey Green (1986). That drive
involved not only personal, but also collective (read "nationalist") concerns for upright civic and moral character through proper physical
maintenance. Not just the man, but the entire nation, was to be endowed
with masculine virility. But in American possessions like Guam, the anxiety also reflected an interest to uplift and discipline natives who were
typically characterized as degenerate and potentially troublesome. In

Guam, Naval Governor Capt. Henry Price reported to his superiors in Washington, D.C. that "calisthenics . . . have continued with beneficial results both from the point of view of health as well as on subordination" (*Annual Report* 1922, 2). For these and other reasons the Navy recognized the benefits of sports for the so-called "benevolent assimilation" of the natives. At the same time, a columnist for the *Guam Newsletter* observed in November, 1912, "the great interest of the people in baseball games . . . straight down to the smallest, scampering *patgon* child." He continued, "It will surprise most Americans to see how thoroughly the Chamorro people have learned the game and . . . to see how well some of them play it. There is plenty of material among the Chamorros to form two cracker-jack native teams that would make things very interesting for any aggregation the Marines . . . can get together."

Less than a year later, in their first year of existence, an all-native team (called the Carabaos) beat an officers' team (called "The Allies," aka, "The Great White Hopes") for the championship of the mid-winter league. In his 1918 report, the governor writes: "athletics flourish in Guam . . . mainly baseball . . . some of the natives are excellent players . . . and excel in base stealing" (32). Let us henceforth view this excellence in "base stealing" as an historical metaphor for native appropriation of imperial practices built on the appropriation of native land and bodies.

Organized sports and daily calisthenics quickly became key vehicles to modernize (meaning "Americanize") the Chamorros, although again one must keep in mind the enthusiasm and interest, indeed the Chamorro talent, for appropriating things like stealing bases. Still, the military recruited sports to advance the bases. For example, sports were enlisted for teaching English, understood as the best way to civilize the native. A 1924 article in the *Guam Recorder*, "English in the Schools of Guam," observed "organized athletics (to be) one of the best forces to cause children to speak English spontaneously . . . ", and "as the best medium for inculcating a sense of fair play . . . honesty and truthfulness." This was in the context of military rule in Guam. In the context of football's own history, we see stunning analogs.

SECOND QUARTER: HISTORICIZING FOOTBALL

Derived from rugby and soccer in the 1880s, football began and flourished as the sport of good ol' college boys from elite East Coast Ivy League schools. In his book *Reading Football*, Michael Oriard argues that the rise and spread of football's popularity was made possible through the emergence and circulation of a powerful popular press. In particular, Oriard argues that football benefited from the newly developed conventions and formulas of sensationalized storytelling and illustrations characteristic of journalism toward the end of the nineteenth century and the beginning of the twentieth century. Football, he argues, had to be narrativized and given story form for it to spread the way it did, and the rise of news as big business helped that happen. Readership could not be assumed, it had to be constructed, and herein lies what Oriard calls football's "cultural narratives" that drew from multiple sources and trafficked in prevailing notions of racial (Anglo-Saxon) and gender (male) superiority and (hetero) sexual normality as models for a progressive America (1993).

Though it drew from multiple sources, football was not only on the receiving end of troubled and troubling narratives of race, class, gender, and sexuality. As a good example of physical fitness and rigorous activity for men, football was also an active participant in the construction and maintenance of such ideas, and of ideas of what the nation should be. Of these ideas, I want to dwell specifically on shifting notions of manhood and masculinity, and the alliances with militarism.

As a particularly good example and form of physical fitness and rigor for men (Kett 1977; Green 1986), football not only helped establish manhood, it helped usher in a new "masculinity," according to Gail Bederman (1995). In contrast to earlier ideals of manhood as exemplified in a self-restraining, prim and proper gentleman, this new masculinity emphasized savage-like toughness and ruggedness and was a response to social and political challenges facing the nation and the status quo toward the end of the nineteenth century. In his social history of adolescence in America, Kett links prevailing ideas about manhood as the developmental endpoint of growth from infancy and infantility, but now writ large as the story of the nation's natural position as new leader of the civilized world. It appears that what's really at stake in the discourse about infantility and adolescence is maturity, especially manhood.

Bederman fine-tunes the argument to chart the emergence of a new civilized nation with a new civilizing mission led by a new masculinity built by the end of the nineteenth century in opposition to new challenges to the established order. With Bederman and others (see Oriard 1993) we can identify at least four interrelated sources of anxiety that prompted the need to refashion both manhood and civilization into a new masculinity for men and a new virility for the nation. These were as follows: (1) the new immigrant, typically figured as effeminate; (2) the new woman, figured as manly; (3) social and physical "softness" resulting from modern technologies and modes of production that might not require much exertion; and (4) a rapidly disappearing frontier. Football, as well as other rigorous sports like boxing, was shaped by and helped to engender this nationalized, racialized, sexualized economy.

Given the intertextuality between football and narratives of racial and gendered superiority that drove the national project, it comes as no surprise that one finds an equally historical and culturally productive teamwork between football and that other interesting bastion of masculinity, the military. Indeed militarism and football would develop into good teammates, whether in the project of shaping bodies into boys and girls, boys into men, girls into women, children into adults, or savages into citizens.[3]

Historically, for example, the impetus for establishing youth football programs gained its biggest boost after World War II with the return of GIs to the homefront. Not only was there an unprecedented explosion in the number of young boys in need of guidance and fashioning, there was also a new economy of leisure that went with a new consolidation of the domestic space. Nuclear families were now living in new suburbs and new restless energies, both young and older, needed to be spent properly. In narrative, design, and technique, football would develop in step with militarism in such a way that we might label this particular (post-war) formation of American hegemony _militant gridiron_. Militant gridiron is the kind of football that the comedian George Carlin once referred to as "twentieth-century New World Order Paramilitary Power Struggle." In football today one encounters, as part of the "offensive strategy," "aerial assaults" like "bombs," "bullets," and "shotguns" from quarterbacks referred to as "field generals," who might also lead a powerful "ground attack." The action takes place "in the trenches" against a defensive unit that might engage in a "blitz," which is short, of course, for the German word "Blitzkrieg."

HALFTIME: TAKING STOCK

Permit me to dwell on two rituals in Guam's translocal history of militant gridiron that highlight the theme of cultural reconsolidation through Guam's post-war development.

In Guam, the biannual change of command at Andersen Air Force base was ritualized by a "hand-off." A photo appearing in the _Guam Daily News_ on October 7, 1966, indicates it as a tradition already. I don't know if this ceremony is still practiced today, because by the early 1970s the military had begun to discontinue its sponsorship of organized football. By the mid 1970s, the Government of Guam's recreation departments would take the helm. "GovGuam," as it is called affectionately and otherwise, was created by the U.S. Congress in 1950 to grant limited home rule to the Chamorros, and to serve as civilian successor to the U.S. Naval Government. Its creation and evolution would also coincide with, and be shaped by, the emergence of a dynamic post-war Asian economy into which Guam would be plunged via the emergence of a visitor industry catering primarily to the Japanese market. Anyway, in another uncanny anticipation of things to come, in the next day's issue of the *Guam Daily News*, following the appearance of this photograph, the headline read "Elective Governorship Bill Signed." Though GovGuam was created in 1950, the governor of the island had still been appointed by the President of the United States, which was to change in the first local gubernatorial elections in 1970. The headline in effect describes another kind of political hand-off, another change of command: from military to civilian self-rule, but with an infrastructure established to suit America's strategic interests in the Pacific. These entangled rituals and their bustling environment lead me directly to one particular Eagle handoff that stands out vividly in my memory.

In the pre-game ceremonies of the 1971 season, which launched our unbeaten streak, our first popularly-elected governor, Carlos G. Camacho, tossed a football to our own leader, quarterback Ricky Soriano, a Filipino from Tamuning. In an inversion of the earlier chronology of photos and headlines, that toss by Governor Camacho was followed by one from Admiral Paul Pugh, Commander of the Naval Forces of the Marianas, to his counterpart, the *Haole* quarterback of the Naval Station Raiders.

I want to suggest that the ritual game-opening toss by the island's two most powerful men to their respective youth counterparts, the miniature field generals of the island's top two youth teams, was deeply symbolic of more than military-civilian relations through sports. It symbolized local patriarchal rites of passage under the tutelage of football: Balls were passed from fathers to sons. That particular opening ceremony itself represented a change of command, not just from one officer to another, but from father to son following the successful mentorship between Navy father and native son as if to convey the idea that the native son is finally ready to branch out on his own. Indeed, by 1970, the neocolonial (or post-colonial) mythology describes Guam's coming of age, marking equality between America and Guam, bonded now by the gesture of their leaders passing their balls to the next generation. In football parlance: a pass complete, a first down; colonial rule advances through post-colonial replication. In my interview with Eagle families, one gets, not surprisingly, a confirmation of the organization of identities, roles, and relations along clearly defined gendered lines. This was certainly true of the value of the organization in the upkeep of the nuclear family. I asked Auntie Millie, Coach Tai's wife, what life was like as an Eagle wife and mother:

MILLIE TAI (MT): "I participated with the other moms, preparing food after the games, washing uniforms . . . Billie was out of the house many months, taking the boys to practice, to the games, but I didn't resent it because that's what our boys needed, and I was very happy they were getting that."

V. DIAZ (VD): "Getting what? What did they get out of this?"

MT: "Well, I think the father was giving the boys a lot of time, which the other fathers weren't giving to their boys . . . "

BILLIE TAI (interrupts): "I never had that father and son relationship . . . My father was not like that . . . I missed quite a bit of that type of life, and I wanted to make sure that my sons got that . . . "

Here, the narrative of fatherly love and attention—necessary for the boys' proper growth and the family's well-being—is traced back to their absence in a father's own troubled childhood in pre-war Hawai'i. Elsewhere, Mrs. Tai refers to her husband's upbringing as "savage," meaning "disorderly and undisciplined." Coach Tai confirms this description: As a little boy, he had already learned how to deal poker, blackjack, and Monte. In Guam, for the determined Tais, the cycle of family disorder and undiscipline would be broken and football would play a privileged role therein.

In the interplay between gender, football, and family (hinting back to social ills of native urban drift in post-overthrow, prewar Honolulu), this narrative also transports us to the space occupied by Hawaiians and their families in the historical development—the generation—of local football in Guam. This interplay, too, is represented in additional layers surrounding that opening toss in 1971: In 1971 our formidable foes from Naval Station, the Raiders, were in fact sponsored by local businessman Kurt Moylan. But Moylan was no ordinary businessman; he was a businessman from Hawai'i who had also become a politician, and in fact, in 1971 was also Governor Camacho's right-hand man as Guam's first elected lieutenant. governor. In 1971, even though the league was sponsored by the Navy, the Navy's top youth team itself was sponsored by a Hawaiian businessman. Indeed, in Guam's post-war boom, Military, Federal, GovGuam, and Japanese outlay began to attract Honolulu-based capital (such as E.E. Black Construction, Hawaiian Rock, and Kaiser Development, just to name a few contractors). Hawaiians' interest and roles in Guam's development must be acknowledged, and a Hawaiian's role as Guam's first elected lieutenant governor comes directly from that lineage. How's that for Hawaiian complicity in local "base stealing" in the post-war years?

THIRD QUARTER: *IMUA* (FORWARD!)

For those of us who learned football under the men from Hawai'i, playing the American game of football was also fundamentally mediated by a Hawaiian style and sensibility that sought to maintain itself through its transplantation. There was a particular cultural and social signature to the football that we learned, one that piggybacked on, and in the process altered, the cultural meanings of the modern American sport.

What this means is that in Guam, militant gridiron was also animated by a displaced indigenous Hawaiian sensibility, coupled with a displaced multicultural local sensibility from Hawai'i. These "Hawaiian" sensibilities and customs included their own unique forms or traditions of recreation, militarism, including their own kinds of indigenous and hybridized masculinities, that rework and get reworked by militant gridiron. Let me outline in broad terms their "moves."

Lets begin with the multicultural, multiethnic, Hawai'i "local" style that was displaced in Guam. This style featured the reconstituted *ohana* (family) we encountered earlier, which in the context of football featured men who were active in what I had earlier called post-overthrow, post-plantation, pre-statehood multicultural recreational practices like barefoot football in Hawai'i (see Figure 10.10).

FIGURE 10.10   Barefoot football.

Hawai'i barefoot football was a local style of football, multi-"racial" and multi-"cultural" through and through in Honolulu and the rural outskirts. It was also a key player in the emergence of a new, early twentieth-century, multiracial society, through the participation of first- and second- generation immigrant workers. As such, Hawai'i barefoot football also participated alongside the post-overthrow and pre-World War II discourse of Hawaii's acculturation and therefore its readiness for (post-war) statehood.

Barefoot football was also an athletic analog to the emergence of "pidgin" as the local lingua franca, a hybrid Hawaiian-immigrant language that united plantation laborers of the day and that is now celebrated as a "local kine" language. "Barefoot kine" football also had the reputation of being more "rugged" (read a new island masculinity here) than the town players, more "down-home" than those who by the 1920s and 1930s were already playing visiting stateside college and even professional teams. But as in Guam (later), football in Hawai'i also owes its roots to American imperialism and the presence of the military and less directly to what Oriard calls the "lords of east coast," Ivy League schools, or to the emergence of the popular press and its football hype. These origins and their context, including the structure, the practices, and the symbols—what Oriard refers to as football's "cultural narratives"—must be understood as being in productive tension with the particular ways that Hawaiians and other settled migrants in Hawai'i played the game, how they made it theirs. Yet, the military's role, and American imperialism through the determinations of the military, also cannot so easily be dismissed or discarded despite the local processes of cultural customization and appropriation.

Though we need to consider the multicultural elements of modern football, we also need to distinguish the non-indigenous "multiethnic local" from a distinct (but not necessarily "pure") indigenous Hawaiian cultural sensibility. Indigenous Hawaiian traditions also include their own gendered assumptions and orders—their own brands of masculinity and femininity—that continued to manifest themselves through the ways that our coaches/uncles taught us the sport.

Deeply interlaced in our routine drills, which shaped our minds and bodies, were icons of a longstanding Hawaiian warrior tradition that stressed as much training, preparation, and discipline as anything that the U.S. military or football architects could create. This is captured in the word *"Imua!"* which every rookie had to learn quickly in preseason training. We yelled it when we were going to hit or get hit. We yelled it during calisthenics when we hit the ground, or when Coach Tai punched our stomachs during leg-lifts. We yelled it before and after the games, and during games, coming out of the huddle. In fact, the term means "forward" or "onward," with connotations of perseverance, and its association with athletics comes from the song "Imua Kamehameha," which is the Kamehameha Schools' fight song to rally the schools' mascot, the Warriors. The Kamehameha Schools are a private, remarkably well-endowed school system reserved for students of Hawaiian blood. It was created and endowed by crown resources in the nineteenth century as an alternative to the Punahou schools, which were founded by missionary and other *Haole* interests in Hawai'i. Eagle head coach David Kalama attended the Kamehameha Schools before transferring to McKinley in his senior year. (According to his son, Kawika, "Pop transferred before the school had the chance to kick him out").

In deeper context, "Imua!" is understood to have been the battle cry of King Kamehameha I as he urged his warriors forward in his lineage's epic conquest of the archipelago in the 18th century. In light of the warrior history behind the term and the term's circulation in Guam youth football ranks, we need to ask just how much of what we picked up in the football fields was Hawaiian in origin, and how much was of modern American militarism? And to what extent does it make a difference?

FOURTH QUARTER: KANIKAPILA/MUSIC MAKING

As a way to address these questions, I suggest we look to what Hawaiians call *kanikapila* (making music) to help us begin to understand what is native and what is not, and for me, to especially delineate the complexity and the blurring between the two. There is a contemporary pop song in Hawai'i, popular in Guam too, that goes: "In the islands, we do it islandstyle/from the mountains to ocean/from the valley to the leeward side."

In the song, reference to island style invokes food, music, and relations. Elsewhere, the lyrics link the practice with cultural antiquity: "*Kanikapila* in the Old Hawaiian Way."

Indeed, post-game and post-practice *kanikapila*, featuring tunes like the aforementioned (pilfered) "Black and Gold is Waving," Hawaiian favorites like "Paupau Pilikia" ("Troubles are over"), or heavily nostalgic and highly popular songs like "Tiny Bubbles" and "Pearly Shells," were important elements of the Tamuning Eagle football reality (see Figure 10.11). Undoubtedly these were a continuation from *kanikapila* in the earlier days of the *'ohana*'s transplantation and growth in the immediate post-war days.

Then, and later, *kanikapila*, assisted by alcohol, helped these guys return to their islands figuratively, when they couldn't physically. Through music they kept distant locales, families, and sounds of the islands alive. Through song they brought the islands to wherever they went, including to other islands. In time, they carried *kanikapila* to the Hawaiian village in Tamuning. If football shaped and encroached upon the domestic sphere, the *Ohana* took *kanikapila* to the football field, and by extension, to us.

So sing we did. And I want to ask, just what kind of football is this, that included singing all the time? It's not exactly the image one expects from tough, rugged football players! I recall one of our opponents teasing us that we were like a choir, a glee club. If so, it was also a glee club that seriously "kicked butt" on the field. And then prided itself in being good sportsmen and being gentlemanly and inviting the losers to eat potluck with us afterwards. Here recall Bederman's critique of a new masculinity, of which football and militarism and American imperialism were a part (1995). Now consider this new masculinity at play in the islands but orchestrated through older island traditions of music-making and merriment.

This masculinity-in-softness, or softness in masculinity, is detectable in the fuller story behind the battle cry "Imua!" from the Kamehameha legacy. When sung in its entirety, and when understood historically and in cultural context, the song reveals a distinct island style, a Hawaiian style and masculinity. Shortly before he died, I had the opportunity to interview Coach George Kaualoku. During the interview, despite a cancerous throat, Uncle George insisted on singing the old songs, including the melodic "Imua Kamehameha." Unless we can swing a Compact Disk to accompany this text, you will have to take my word (or anybody else's word who has heard Uncle George sing) that despite the cancer, or perhaps even more so with it, the song, and his rendering of it constitutes what Hawaiians call *nahe nahe* (sweet). May I also suggest that our winning legacy was sweet, not simply because we won all the time, but also because we sang sweet songs? Could that be what made us good football players? Of course, all that is sweet can also be bitter.

The song, "Imua Kamehameha," was composed by Charles E. King, a Hawaiian composer, scholar, and distributor identified by George Kanahele as "the Dean of Hawaiian Music" (Kanahele 1979, 214). King was the godson of Queen Emma, and a student of the deposed monarch, Queen Liliuokalani (and a member of the first graduating class of Kamehameha in 1891). Through his training, discipline, and performance under the "Royal Composers," King developed a deep knowledge of Hawaiian language, lore, and customs. According to Kanahele, King was "fascinated" by and knew well the texts and the meanings of the old *meles* or chants, which both inspired him and provided him with the materiality for his own compositions (like "Imua Kamehameha"). But King was

also a "keen student" of contemporary music, who was especially interested in "the metamorphosis" of ancient chants into melodic chants. This
put him at odds with an industry and a time when Hawaiian music was
gaining wild popularity in the United States and around the world. King
challenged the so-called *Hapa Haole* or "half *Haole*" music that was
parading as Hawaiian in the airwaves, imploring the industry to stop
"murdering" Hawaiian music, to adhere to its structure and content. For
Hawaiian to be Hawaiian, he argued, its traditional tempo had to be
honored (not jazzed up), and its lyrics and its content—especially the
place names—had to be kept in Hawaiian. He also insisted that its
melodic quality had to be *nahe nahe*, sweet. We can presume, I think, that
King thought that "Imua Kamehameha" retained these rules and was,
thus, an extension of the old *meles,* which also captured something of the
authenticity and spirit of Kamehameha the First's heroic conquest of the
archipelago.

But what of the other songs that we used to sing before and after practices and games, and throughout our travels? Songs like "Pearly Shells"
or "Tiny Bubbles," which most people would recognize as *Hapa Haole*, or
maybe full-on *Haole* songs for the complete absence of Hawaiian words
and places, as well as their various recording styles? Following King, we
might see these as quintessential examples of *Haole* appropriation to the
point of completely murdering Hawaiian. In this view, the lyrics of
"Pearly Shells" are especially telling:

Pearly Shells from the Ocean
Shining in the sun, covering the shores
When I see them, my heart tells me that I love you
More than all those little pearly shells.

Here, there are no Hawaiian words, and/or places. The kind of shells,
the aspect of the ocean, the exact beach or shoreline, are now entirely
generic. How meaningless, how un-Hawaiian is that? Or what kind of
meaning, what kind of Hawai'i is that? Recorded by Hawaiian enter-
tainer Don Ho, the song usually conjures up Waikiki beach as the place
strewn with white lovers. This might be seen as a colonial metonym for
what Hawai'i is supposed to be all about: paradise and romance for the
westerner or tourist.

Worst yet, some of you might recall that the tune for a while was itself
appropriated by none other than C&H Sugar, co-participant in the overthrow. Shall we sing along?

C&H (C&H) Pure Cane Sugar (Pure Cane Sugar)
From Hawai'i (from Hawai'i) shining in the sun . . .

And yet, as it turns out, there is in the melodic quality to Pearly Shells an older tradition of sweetness, of *nahe nahe*, older than any kind of energy that twentieth century sugar barons can muster. (This traffic in sweetness tempts the observation that *nahe nahe* can be viewed as an alternative form of fuel—a particularly Hawaiian customization—to energize critical academic work and play). For, according to Elizabeth Tatar (Kanahele 1979), "Pearly Shells" is an adaptation of a nineteenth-century popular song called "Pupu A'o Ewa," which was first sung as a *himeni*, or a Christianized version of a Hawaiian mele (or is it a Hawaiianized version of a Christian hymn?). Interestingly, Tatar points out that the song has also been classified as a "men's song," a "barber shop song," a "hula," and even once, a *"Hapa Haole"* song. King himself called it a *himeni*. Whatever it is (or was), Tatar asserts that "Pupu A'o Ewa" is

> one of the few Hawaiian songs that have been successfully adapted into English . . . And, after a century, it remains an excellent example of a Hawaiian song which clearly stemmed from the himeni, integrated some old Hawaiian musical devices, and finally lent itself admirably to the popular musical demands of modern times. (Tatar 1979, 319)

If I am following Tatar correctly, "Pearly Shells," through partial retention of the melodic structure, is the product of the successful and admirable modernization of Hawaiian music. I doubt if many Oiwi or Kanaka Maole—indigenous Hawaiians—participating in the contemporary revival of traditional Hawaiian practices and knowledge would view "Pearly Shells" as a traditional Hawaiian song. I'm certainly not arguing that case.

I do want to assert, however, that for me and other Eagles, under the directorship of our coaches, Pearly Shells was a *nahe nahe* song that, in the translocal context of Hawaiian diaspora, might even be viewed as a quintessentially Hawaiian tune for its ability to help *Imua* Hawaiians forward in new geographic and discursive shores. If, through the generic words in the song, there wasn't a conjuring of old places and sweethearts for these Hawaiian men in the diaspora then, the song sung today certainly does invoke much *aloha* or love for those men, and those particular days when we were winners.

POST-GAME TALK: SWEET VICTORY?

At the same time, it is imperative to check nostalgia's tendency to sweeten the sour. Especially to not disavow what's problematic about hybridized masculinities that underwrite the winning ways. Let's eavesdrop on a talkstory session with my former teammate, Kenny Boy (KB), coach Kaualoku's son, as he recalls the consequences of trying to follow Pop's footsteps:

> KB: Playing for dad was hard, eh?, 'cause I would take no crap from nobody . . . and if I slammed somebody too hard, I would get it from dad too. But I learned a lot . . . and I wish a lot of kids out there could have his knowledge, of the sport . . . 'cause everything he taught was how he played, and he played rough.
>
> I used to come out and help the kids after I graduated, help coach . . . In fact I was the only coach to get voted out by the families (laughter). I was too rough (laughter).
>
> VD: What happened?
>
> KB: I used to hit the kids like he used to hit us. I used to shove them . . . not beat 'em up, but I used to shove them, hit them hard. I tried to teach them the way he taught us. As time went by, the parents wouldn't accept it, they thought I was too rough. Dad came up and said, eh, you cannot coach no more. I said why? He said, you too rough, I said, dad, I only doing what you taught us (father and son laugh heartily).

As it would turn out, the son learns only too well; the family quickly regulates this brand of roughness the way the sport of football and the modern state through its military regulates violence. But now, recalled from a distance, there is humor, albeit laced with an edge. That edge erupts when I ask Kenny Boy's dad, Coach Kaualoku (or Uncle George), what were his fondest memories of the Eagle days in Guam. His answer: "Just drink beer (laughs). That's the only memory I get . . . morning to nighttime (laughs), drink beer." Son Kenny is laughing even harder. He seizes the narrative and goes to town, as if with vengeance:

> KB: "Drinking beer. (hah hah) That's his memories (hah hah). Drinking beer and coaching football . . . at the same time (hah hah hah). Coolers full. Never come home til the coolers empty . . . Yup, spent many nights sleeping in the back of the truck, 'let's go dad' (laughter). One by one the moms would be coming . . .
>
> VD: Did that happen a lot?
>
> KB: Yup, all the time . . . already dark, moms are coming, you know their cars . . . kids are playing, dads are drinking . . . school night . . . was like that *every* night (laughter).

In the recollection, beer mixes freely with football; kids not at home doing homework; moms gotta go get 'em. *Now* they can laugh; then, the abuse, and the irresponsibility, certainly could not have been funny to the wives, teachers, and families. But now, the memories are hilarious. Coach/uncle George breaks into another story: One time, toward the tail end of the legacy, a *papolo* whose son was on the team arrived late to a game already underway. The kids were out on the field, but there were no coaches on the sidelines. They were instead *already* behind the bleachers, at the pickup trucks, drinking and singing. The *papolo*, recalls Uncle George, comes over and is confused and amazed: Who is coaching the kids, he asks? Nobody, they reply, the kids coaching themselves! The *papolo*/father busts a laugh, grabs a beer, and exclaims, "you guys allllright!"

For son Kenny—he's heard this story many times—this was the beginning of the end of the Eagle legacy. The organization got too big, too powerful, too "political," he explains finally, "Got modernized" was how he preferred to see it. In time, the original coaches began to pull away, gradually to be replaced by a new generation of younger coaches. As the island grew, so did the league, along with the number of age brackets for which to field Eagle teams for the dizzying numbers of local kids coming out to play for the Eagles. In time, the organization got too big, too unwieldy. For Kenny Boy, it deviated from its purer origins. "Got modernized," he says, establishing closure both to the session and the narrative.

But I'm not satisfied. I laugh with them, but am also nervous about the edge with which the memories are recalled. An edge that betrays a legacy in the Eagles very different from the fun and games. Very different from the nostalgia and romanticization that structure the memories of the winning legacy. But what I don't know is whether this is modernity or if it is indigeneity playing modernity. Whose, or which masculinity orchestrates these tunes?

IN THE SHOWERS

In my interviews, I asked former teammates, cheerleaders, and coaches what, if anything, was the winning legacy all about. For most, the responses were precisely the themes and images presented here: discipline, training, conditioning, family support. Order in the family.

Me, I began with the following conviction: The legacy is that we beat the other at his own game. Now, immersed in the historic and mnemonic materiality of those years, I'm less sure just who is the "we" and just who we "beat." Despite, or perhaps because of, the tremendous nostalgia surrounding the memories of that history. Consider the memories of Kuulei, one of the cheerleaders we met at the beginning of this essay. For Kuulei, the most important thing about the Eagles is the *aloha* that we shared after the practices and games, when our coaches/uncles gathered us together and spoke words of wisdom about playing hard, playing together, playing clean, and having fun. Of eating and singing and dancing afterward. Like Kuulei, my strongest memories are also of the *aloha* that the Eagle *Ohana* gave me that I have for them in return. That, and the rarest experience that colonized islanders can ever have: knowing what it means to be a winner at the colonizer's own game. No wonder there is so much nostalgia, like the sweet-smelling *mwaramwars* that adorn island heads graced by icons of Americanized globality.

NOTES

[1] For a critical consideration of the National Football League's annual playing of its Pro Bowl in troubled Hawaiian terrain, see Hanlon n.d.

[2] See Kauanui 1998 for a critical treatment of Hawaiian diasporic subjectivity in relation to "on-island" Hawaiian political and cultural identities. See in particular her re-articulation of the term *"ohana"* for describing transplanted Hawaiian identities in foreign soil.

[3] For a history of sports and the military, see Wakefield 1997.

CHAPTER 11

The Dynamics of Aloha

George H. S. Kanahele

FACT OR FICTION?

It is hard to think of another word that over so many decades has aroused more public attention, sometimes even controversy, among both Hawaiians and non-Hawaiians than aloha. Opinions of all shades and fervor, ranging from the ridiculous to the exalted, have been expressed on the subject. These include such notions as *aloha* is: "undefinable," "sheer nonsense," "a monumental hoax," "the summum bonum of life," "Hawai'i's social cement," "unique to Hawai'i," "the power of God," "a priceless style of human interaction." These conflicting views mask what seems to be a constant "search for the elusive Spirit of Aloha" that more often than not is discussed in the newspapers, especially in the letters to the editors. All the while the question is asked, "Is aloha dead?" and always the answer is either yes, maybe, or no.

What intrigues us is not the predictable cynicism that crops up in those pages, but the serious and sincere efforts made by many reasonable, dedicated citizens of the community, from all racial backgrounds, to foster, support, idealize, and even institutionalize aloha. Local government leaders, for example, consistently make solemn pronouncements about the need to preserve and enhance the Spirit of Aloha. We are constantly reminded that Hawai'i is officially called the Aloha State. The Hawai'i Chamber of Commerce makes annual Aloha Spirit Awards to employees in the islands who offer exemplary service to customers. A University of Hawai'i professor and futurist has proposed that new citizens take an "aloha-ness" test rather than a loyalty test. An organization led by Hawaiians, with help from the tourist industry to be sure, has presented the annual Aloha Week Festival for many years. The list goes on and on,

---

This essay was previously published in *Kū Kanaka: Stand Tall: A Search for Hawaiian Values,* by George H. S. Kanahele (Honolulu: University of Hawai'i Press, 1986), 467–494.

showing the pervasive influence of the term in much of the contemporary life of Hawai'i. Indeed, aloha has become so thoroughly identified with all the people of Hawai'i that for all intents and purposes it is common property. Even the millions of tourists seem to end up "owning" a piece of it by the time they leave the islands, wanting to return.

Yet Hawaiians still have a strong proprietary interest in the word. Many feel that somehow aloha is unique to them, their personal gift, because of what Hawaiians have been able to bring to it over the centuries. While it may have its counterparts in other places in the world— as in so-called Southern hospitality or in Maori *aroha*—Hawaiians think that their version is one of a kind, the only one in the world. Not a few Hawaiians believe that, when they utter the word, they have put their *mana* into it, and, therefore, that if they chose to do so, they could also withdraw their *mana* and make the term powerless. One Hawaiian leader has said that Hawaiians have given too much aloha for their own good, and that now is the time to give it "an honorable funeral." Others, however, feel that no one can ever give enough and that aloha is the Hawaiians' greatest gift to the world.

THE TRADITIONAL CONTEXT

As with so many other things from our past, the etymology of "aloha" is shrouded in mystery. Its origin goes back to the very beginnings of the Polynesian people in Kahiki, the homeland, and beyond, for the root word is found in all Polynesian languages, and always with essentially the same meaning. Whether it be spelled and pronounced *aroha* in Maori, *alofa* in Samoan, *aroha* in Tahitian, or *alōfa* in Tongan, each variant contains the elements of love, compassion, sympathy, or kindness. Since Hawaiian is related to all Polynesian languages, we find a possible clue in the culture of the Maori. Joan Metge, the Maori scholar, suggests that originally *aroha* may have meant "love for kin." While she does not offer any etymological evidence for the opinion, it makes good sense, because of our understanding of the natural affinity that human beings have for their offspring and our knowledge of kinship structure in Polynesia.

Without detailing the fabric of traditional kinship, let us point out some of the ways in which aloha functioned or was expressed as part of an integrated value system. To begin with, the most natural and "first expression" of aloha, as [Mary Kawena] Pūku'i (Pūku'i, Haertig, and Lee 1979) wrote, was between parent and child. The parent-child relationship began at conception, because Hawaiians believed that "the child's nature and character were influenced by the behaviour of the parents while the baby was in the womb. If mother and father were busily occupied with work the child would be industrious and hardworking. So likewise with psychic attributes." Thus if the parents showed love and kindness, these attributes would be reflected in the character of the child. On the other hand, if they showed jealousy and peevishness, then the child's disposition would reflect these traits. Many other attendant rules governed diet, prayers, types of work the mother could participate in, and so on, all of which were prescribed and followed in order to ensure the "perfect" child.

The great care that was taken to guard the child's development during gestation was sanctified by the _'aha'aina māwaewae_ feast celebrated within twenty-four hours after the birth of the firstborn son. Actually it was less a feast than a sacrament of consecration of the child to Lono, for "its safeguarding and welfare." Pūku'i (Handy and Pūku'i 1972) pointed out that Lono symbolized the family's and the child's priorities as "subsistence, livelihood, peace and plenty." The ritual of the feast served to clear the way in the life ahead by setting the child's "feet (_wāewae_) in the way (_ma_) of the spiritual flow or channels ('_au_) of his responsible elders."

The _'aha'aina palala_ was held a year later, honoring the child's first birthday. It was not a sacramental ritual like the _mawaewae_. We are told that "the _pālala_ expressed the _aloha_ of all the relatives and friends, and in the case of an _ali'i_, of all the people for the first-born newly arrived. This aloha was expressed in the form of gifts to the child, and in the composition of chants (_mele_) which were performed with dances (_hula_)." Pūku'i added that the modern "baby _lū'au_," as a carryover of the _pālala_, "retains little of the spirit of aloha." She criticized the modern version because relatives and friends are expected to put cash contributions in the big calabash, prominently located near the entrance to the feasting place. In contrast, the _pālala_ was a feast of goodwill, not of obligation, which, if Pūku'i is right, made this one of the few "pure gifts" of aloha in traditional Hawai'i.

But all of this outpouring of aloha for the newborn _hiapo_ and his first-year feast was offset by the unloving custom of infanticide. Pūku'i (Handy and Pūku'i 1972) explained this practice. "Hawaiians loved children; as soon as a woman mentioned the fact that she did not want the child in her womb, relatives and neighbours would beg for it and no matter how large a family there was always room for one more. Infanticide was practised so that there might be no low-born person to claim blood relationship to the chiefs." Worse things have been done in the interest of preserving genetic purity and artificial barriers of class, but at least infanticide was not a common practice in ancient Hawai'i.

During the earliest years of childhood, the bonds of motherly affection are closest, as the child is wrapped in aloha. Good parents avoid manipulating love as a means of influencing the child, just as they do not use the punishment of withdrawal, the so-called silent treatment. They give, instead, an outgoing and steady flow of kindness, gentleness, warmth, and love for the child. Hawaiians, as do all natural parents, knew what psychologists and physicians tell us today: When babies are deprived of love, as it is manifested in all its forms, they are as liable to get sick from the psychic deprivation as they are from exposure to germs or to an improper diet.

This dependency, however, does not last for long, because by age four the child is released from its mother's side to join the *'ohana*, the family circle of siblings and other kin. While the child is still the object of close affection and care, he is taught how to adapt to people who are more self-reliant and self-sufficient. From then on, the "hard" values, as opposed to "soft" ones, come into play.

The principles and practices of fostering and adoption tell a lot about the role of aloha in such matters. The Hawaiian attitude is expressed in the saying, *"Ka lei hā'ule 'ole, he keiki"* (A lei that is never cast aside is one's child). Indeed, no child was ever cast aside and not cared for. Hawaiians have no expression comparable to the American notion that "every barrel must have one bad apple," at least as it might apply to a child. All babies are loved. Pūku'i (Handy and Pūku'i 1972) described how the relationship between an adopting parent and a child develops: "The relationship comes about as a result of mutual affection and agreement, at first tacit, then unobtrusively discussed, between the child and the older person . . . . This is a relationship involving love, respect and courtesy." The adopted, or *hanai*, child, was aptly referred to as *"He 'ohā pili wale"* (a young taro that attaches itself to an older corm). As "young taro" they were meant to flourish in a system designed to ensure that every child would have a place as a member of a family, never as what we call a "ward of the state." In such an environment of constant sharing and mutual support, child abuse was unheard of. We are told that any parent who neglected a child was bound to be the object of public scorn.

If the family offers a natural channel of aloha in the child-parent relationship, it offers the same between husband and wife. The ideal relationship is conveyed in the saying: *"Ke aloha pili pa'a o ke kāne me ka wahine"* (the lasting love of man and woman). The sense of everlasting aloha is captured in the phrase *pili pa'a*—where *pili* means to cleave to or cling to, and *pa'a* means firmly, permanently. Hawaiians have no equivalent to the American expression, "a clinging vine," referring to a woman who holds onto a man tightly, desperately, all but helplessly. In the traditional arrangement, the man is *pili kua* (standing back of his mate), the protector, while the woman is *pili alo,* the protected one "standing in front" of her husband. Pūku'i touchingly described the ideal couple.

> I can tell you about this kind of love. About people who really loved. About healthy persons who when their mates got leprosy went with them to Kalaupapa. They lived out their lives together there. They were ordinary couples who farmed their land together, nursed each other when they were sick, prepared the mate for burial when he died. They were my own *kūpuna.* The elders in my own *'ohana* who mated *noho pū,* without contract or ceremony. And when the new laws came, they said, "We don't need a paper marriage. We have always loved each other. We always will." They knew about "till death do us part," but not because of *kauoha,* a command or law. Because of what they truly felt.

The picture of a healthy husband following his leprous wife to Kalaupapa is not less poignant than that of a wife following her husband into battle, feeding him, nursing his wounds, and sometimes, in a close and desperate conflict, fighting beside him. Not uncommonly, wives accompanied their menfolk on the battlefield. Such was the fate of Manono, who fought until she fell lifeless on the body of her husband, Kekuaokalani, slain in the battle of Kuamo'o in 1819.

Aloha in the marriage relationship meant fidelity, not only for strengthening the marital bond but also for preserving the stability of the family. Anything less than fidelity was *"he nohona huikau, noho aku noho mai"* (a life of confusion, living this way and that). In a society whose socioeconomic and political existence depended on family order, it is clear why faithfulness and mutual trust and respect were esteemed values governing the conduct of husband and wife. Despite the "flirtations" of some women who boarded foreign ships, and the caricatures of "adulterous" behavior written by scandal-mongering missionaries, promiscuity was never condoned, even among unmarried men and women. The thrust of Hawaiian society was aimed at tightening, not loosening, the bonds of marital and familial loyalty.

In a larger sense, *aloha pili pa'a* can be applied to the relationships among all kinfolk, extending back to a family's remotest origins. This sense of bonding is conveyed again and again in the genealogical preoccupation of Hawaiians: *"E kolo ana nō ke ewe i ke ewe"* (Kinfolk seek the society of other kinfolk and love them because of their common ancestors) (Handy and Pūku'i 1972). *Aloha 'ohana* was not limited to the living, but extended to past members, ancestors, and ancestor-gods as well. This attention appears not to have been a merely passive display, but rather an active demonstration of emotion, charged by periodic remembrances of family events through prayers, dances, chants, feasts, and other mnemonic devices. Furthermore, we must keep in mind that Hawaiians believed that this aloha was constantly reciprocated by spiritual ancestors. Thus, "clinging" to one's ancestors was motivated by both duty and an expectation of *kōkua* from extraterrestrial levels. In this, Hawaiian culture was similar to Japanese and Chinese culture, to name just two.

If Hawaiians esteemed aloha, no doubt they did so partly because they understood what we might call its "transforming power." That is best expressed in the saying, *"Aloha mai nō, aloha aku: 'o ka huhu ka mea e ola 'ole ai"* (When love is given, love should be returned; anger is the thing that gives no life). In other words, love begets love; anger ends in anger. The same thought is expressed in another saying: *"Ua ola loko i ke aloha"* (Love gives life within), a recognition that aloha is vital to one's mental, emotional, and physical well-being. A similar idea appears in the statement, *"He kēhau ho'oma'ema'e ke aloha,"* which compares love to "cleansing dew." Like cleansing dew, the cleansing power of aloha can soothe and even eliminate the pain and hurt one may be suffering from. As for anger and its destructive effects, practical wisdom is offered in the saying: *"Nau ke ku'i, lohi ka lima"* (When one grinds the teeth, the hand slows). This means that anger can so upset a person's ability to function normally that it slows his work, reducing his productivity and efficiency. (All these wise sayings are taken from Handy and Pūku'i 1972.)

Modern psychologists have collected sufficient evidence from observations and experiments to demonstrate conclusively this "transforming power" of love. In short, according to analysts both *haole* and Hawaiian, aloha had its own charge of *mana*, for which the *'ohana*, or kinship system, was an ideal transmitting agent. But did that *mana* extend from the family into the general society as well?

BEYOND THE 'OHANA

It is good—and easier—to share aloha with one's kinfolk, for "blood is always thicker than water." The real test of love comes outside the family circle, where genealogical and genetic ties are absent and one has to make links with comparative strangers. To what extent did aloha for each other permeate the general populace in Hawaiian society? After so long a time the question cannot be answered with statistics. But one indication of what might have happened is the way in which Hawaiians perceived friendship.

A good friend was prized and praised; a bad friend, condemned. The true friend was "a nest of fragrance" *(he pūnana na ke onaona),* an analogy that heightens the importance of the friend because fragrance, particularly that of plants, invariably was associated with divinity. On the other hand, the false friend was nothing more than a hypocrite: *"he hamo hulu puna mawaho"* (a brushing on the outside with whitewash) (Handy and Pūku'i 1972). Hawaiians were warned about the fellow with the "friendly face outside, hardness inside," or the fair-weather friend who seeks your company when you are prospering, but forgets you when poverty and misfortune strike you.

At least four different terms denote the several kinds of friends: *hoa, makamaka, aikāne,* and *hoa aloha,* each denoting more or less a different degree of friendship. *Hoa* is the generic term found in all Polynesian languages. *Aikāne,* as in *pili aikāne,* refers to a comradely relationship between males, as compared with *pili hoa aloha,* which refers to a devoted friendship. That the word Hawaiians of old used for expressing the most intimate form of friendship incorporates aloha is no coincidence.

Makamaka is defined as "an intimate friend with whom one is on terms of receiving and giving freely." It has a peculiar tie with the role of the host. If a total stranger were to be welcomed into a home and treated well there, his host or hostess would be referred to as a *makamaka*. According to Pūku'i (Handy and Pūku'i 1972) it connotes a more intimate relationship than that which is implied in the English idea of a host. It means a "more or less permanent obligation in the matter of exchange in friendship and hospitality. A bond of aloha has been accepted, and by acceptance becomes enduring if cherished. *Ho'omakamaka* means to make friends by extending hospitality."

In this connection, the Hawaiians' measure of aloha is best illustrated in their attitude toward a stranger. Few statements can express it better than the proverb "Love is the host in strange lands" (*'O ke aloha ke kuleana o kāhi malihini*) (Pūku'i 1983). That is to say, for the stranger the proper welcome is one expressed with aloha. Although it should be reciprocated, it is noteworthy that the initiative for showing aloha is always the host's, or in the larger societal sense, the resident *kama'aina's*. To quote Pūku'i (Handy and Pūku'i 1972) again, "In old Hawai'i, every passerby was greeted and offered food whether he was an acquaintance or a total stranger." The approaching person would be greeted by a calling out, or *heahea:* "*Hē mai! Mai! Mai!*" (Come hither, come!). The host or hostess did not first run a security check on the person to determine whether he or she would be worth inviting in. The invitation was offered spontaneously, out of aloha, for to offer it grudgingly or ambivalently would have robbed it of any pleasure or sense. Of course this kind of openness did expose the host to the risk of being taken advantage of, but probably that was so unlikely that the Hawaiian of old did not seriously think about it. In any case, the risk was certainly well worth taking because of the satisfaction he would get out of the spontaneous giving. Besides, the greeting made good psychological sense, for trying to pretend hospitality is always an unrewarding and frustrating experience.

The relationship between aloha and *ho'okipa* is clear: Hospitality flows from an outpouring of aloha first, not the other way around. As someone said recently, "For *ho'okipa* to work smoothly, it must be generously lubricated by aloha."

Heretofore, we have talked primarily about aloha as it is expressed among and between commoners. But the picture changes when we look at the exchange of aloha between commoners and *ali'i*. The inequalities in that relationship involve a whole set of values, in which aloha is only one and certainly not the most important. Fear, awe, respect, loyalty, obedience, and similar values would better characterize such a relationship. To be sure, some *ali'i* were venerated, if not beloved, by the *maka'āinana* because of their outstanding leadership and exemplary conduct. Such were chiefs Kakūheihewa of O'ahu, Manokalanipō of Kaua'i, Liloa and his son 'Umi of Hawai'i, among others. As Kepelino remembered, "The chiefs of Hawai'i were taught to be humble, kind, sympathetic, openhearted." But, if Malo is right, "only a small portion of the kings and chiefs ruled with kindness; the large majority simply lorded it over the people." The result was that the "people generally lived in chronic fear and apprehension of the chiefs." And, he added, "On account of the rascality (*kolohe*) of some of the chiefs to the common people, warlike contests frequently broke out between certain chiefs and the people, and many of the former were killed in battle by the commoners. The people made war against bad kings in old times."

Admittedly, this is an oversimplification of a very complex relationship, but, in general, the values associated with the commoner-nobility relationship in a society as rigidly stratified as Hawai'i's would tend to be less concerned with aloha. The social distance created by their sanctity removed the chiefs from the chance to share with commoners in the spontaneous giving of affection, sympathy, compassion, and kindness. Malo's description of the relationship is, perhaps, less an indictment of the chiefs than a statement of hard facts.

COMPETING VALUES

One of the first questions we asked concerned the extent to which aloha might have been a central value in traditional Hawaiian society. Some modern Hawaiians believe that it was the most important of all ancient Hawaiian values. For example, the Reverend Akaika Akana, for many years pastor of Kawaiaha'o Church until his death in 1932, stated, "Aloha, the very kernel of the Hawaiian ethics, the very core of the Hawaiian life, unsurpassed by anything of modern ethics, was the dominating law which regulated the domestic and civil conduct of old Hawai'i." Unfortunately, neither he nor others who believe that idea have provided satisfactory support for it based on historical data and observations. Instead, they seem to have reasoned that, since modern Hawaiians are so well known for their aloha spirit, then they must have inherited it from their *kūpuna* who, therefore, must have considered it very important. Perhaps, too, Pastor Akana spoke in such favorable terms about aloha because of his ministerial emphasis upon Christian love. Probably this is a fair comment to make about the opinions of most people today, who try to explain behavior in old Hawai'i in terms of their own modern ideas, prejudices, and experiences.

We do not doubt that aloha was an important value in the traditional culture of our *kūpuna*. We have presented as good a case as any so far in support of this position. But when we look at the total value system as it related to religious, economic, technological, philosophical, aesthetic, or political behavior, and examine the varied attitudes, motives, standards, emotions, and other factors that shaped the thoughts and actions of Hawaiians of old, we see many values at work, each sharing center stage, so to speak, depending on the situation, timing, actors involved, and the "script," as it were. Aloha is only one of those values, among many, although an important one. In the parent-child relationship, it is of central importance, although other values were at work, too. In cases of greeting and welcoming guests or strangers, clearly hospitality and generosity were the primary considerations, but aloha also was involved. On the other hand, when a man was called up for corvée labor or to fight in a war, loyalty and obedience (or fear), not aloha, might have been sufficient reason for him to respond to the summons. In other words, we discover changing sets of shifting values that appear on and off the stage of life when they are called for—always varying because they depend on the needs of the moment.

We could probably make an equally good case, or an even stronger one, for several values other than aloha as being central to Hawaiian society before 1778. For example, loyalty, or *kūpa'a*, unswerving allegiance to a chief or a family, was a central value. Pūku'i (Pūku'i, Haertig, and Lee 1972, 1979) herself said as much when she defined the *'ohana* concept: "It is a sense of unity, shared involvement and shared responsibility. It is mutual interdependence and mutual help. It is emotional support, given and received. It is solidarity and cohesiveness. It is love—*often;* it is loyalty—*always* [italics added]." Loyalty to the *'ohana's* ideals, goals, and leaders is the moral constant, while aloha comes and goes.

It is important to recognize Pūku'i's perception of the *'ohana* as being a self-reliant, self-sufficient working group, for this is why the "sense of unity . . . solidarity and cohesiveness" were indispensable. The *'ohana's* survival and well-being depended on its organizational integrity. We have seen already how, as a self-sufficient economic unit, the *'ohana* had to function in a fairly rational way, that is, with a division of labor and specialization among the workers, and with leadership and management provided by the *haku*. Among the values of honest work, industry, cooperation, efficiency, and so on that must be associated with achieving the economic goals of the *'ohana*, loyalty must be paramount. The *'ohana* economic system worked best when its members put aside personal desires or ambitions for the common good of the group, agreeing to abide by the group's collective will as that was declared by its leaders. Loyalty, obedience, unity, pulling together—these are the important "cluster" values that must have appealed to the pragmatic Hawaiians.

Loyalty also served as a dominant value in the political relationship between *ali'i* and *maka'āinana*. It is relatively easier and more realistic for chiefs to obtain allegiance and obedience rather than aloha from their subjects. One can be loyal without having much aloha, but one cannot have aloha and be disloyal at the same time. That is analogous to being respected, but not necessarily liked. Probably a relationship such as that may have been the general rule for most *ali'i* and their *maka'āinana*.

The simultaneous operation of competing values, as opposed to aloha alone as the central value, is the only realistic view for us to take. Otherwise trying to explain all historical events in terms of only one point of reference puts too great a strain upon belief. For example, how can we account for a society that took aloha as the "dominating law" for regulating its "domestic and civil conduct," and yet spent much of its time and resources in waging war? Reverend Akana would have found this contradiction difficult to explain away, just as Christian ministers and theologians have always had to wrestle with the same problem when soldiers of Christian nations, which profess the Gospel of Love, go into battle shooting at Christian enemies for very unloving causes. But when we recognize that Hawaiians were motivated by powerful motives or values other than aloha, such as loyalty to their chiefs (who in their turn were motivated by prestige, power, and territoriality), then we can deal better with apparent contradictions in our history.

At this point we need to dispose of the mistaken interpretation of aloha as the Hawaiian way with confrontation. Francine du Plessis Gray, in her book *Hawai'i: The Sugar-Coated Fortress* (1972) wrote, "The Aloha Spirit, from the start, has been the Hawaiian's way of tolerating rather than fighting strangers, his way of avoiding direct confrontation." This statement (which, unfortunately, has been much quoted) is a flawed understanding of aloha as well as of all the other Hawaiian values. We have seen that *ho'okipa* is hardly a negative or passive way of meeting the stranger. On the contrary, it is a very affirmative approach, requiring spontaneity, openness, and aloha on the part of a host or hostess, and allows no room for merely tolerating a stranger. The idea of tolerating is entirely contradictory to both the spirit and practice of these values. Furthermore, to suggest that Hawaiians avoided direct confrontation out of fear or some false notion of aloha is to ignore the whole set of operative values that Hawaiians respected, such as aggressiveness, courage, dignity, honor, competitiveness, and rivalry. Among a people to whom the warrior was a heroic figure, and the craftsman was an honored neighbor, no man worth his *mana* would have run away from a meeting of any kind, not even from an outright challenge. The principles of reciprocity and personal honor would have upheld his virtue and made him behave as an honorable man.

In any event, the biases of outsiders (or of ourselves) should not detract from the importance that Hawaiians gave to aloha in their traditional system of values. Even though the values operating at any one time or place may have shifted, according to the many factors calling them forth, the value of aloha was an important one, never far from the consciousness—or the conscience—or the people.

MARRIAGE WITH THE GOSPEL OF LOVE

No one can fully understand the dynamics of aloha today without tracing its evolution through the period of Christianity after it was introduced in 1820. That the meaning of aloha underwent some change is a reasonable assumption, although measuring the change with much precision is difficult. Less difficult is noting changes in the objects receiving aloha—God, humankind, Christ, one's enemies, the Gospel—and some of the effects of these changes on the attitudes of Hawaiians toward themselves and the new world to which they were being introduced. We must believe that the value we feel or perceive as aloha today is the product of evolution, even the child of the marriage of an ancient, traditional Polynesian concept with its Christian counterpart.

For Christianity, founded as it is on the Gospel of Love, aloha probably was as good a word as the missionaries could find to express their central ideal of love. Aloha means precisely the same thing in all the Polynesian languages scattered across the Pacific. Some people think that Hawaiians have greater empathy than most other people do. That stronger empathy, we believe, comes from a traditional mind-set that is more finely attuned to the feelings of others.

The Christian philosophy of love, with its concept of agape, added a new dimension to aloha. In Hawaiian thought, aloha already connoted a higher sense of abstract or spiritual love, but with agape it was heightened to include the purest form of love as that was proved by God's love for humankind, selfless and boundless. It also transformed aloha into a form of giving that was identical with unadulterated altruism. This, in effect, cancelled out the old idea of altruism. Agape superimposed upon aloha meant that aloha became a higher form of giving, without expectation of receiving anything in return. This has been so widely accepted by modern Hawaiians that almost every Hawaiian will tell you today that, of course, this has always been the meaning of aloha.

The superlative importance of aloha probably began when Hawaiians came around to believing the Christian message that *"Aloha ke akua"* (God is love). Before 1778 Hawaiians had not equated aloha with any one of their many *akua*. So when the new, almighty, all-knowing, omnipresent, supreme Jehovah replaced the discredited and powerless gods of old, aloha was in effect apotheosized, and, in the process, was elevated above all other values. One of the casualties of this process was the relationship with the *'aumākua* (ancestral spirits), which was the only loving relationship that Hawaiians had established with their deities.

Christianity added another dimension to aloha with the idea of "love of humankind," irrespective of a person's title, genealogy, class, sex, or *mana*. Theologically, the idea was based on the precept that all people are the children of God. Just as God loves all, so ought we to love all human beings, for we are all of equal worth in his sight. The teaching sowed the seed for egalitarianism and democracy which by 1840 had been partly translated into the first constitution of the Hawaiian kingdom. Equality among commoners was not an alien idea to the *maka'āinana*, for whom *'ohana* values such as *kōkua* and *laulima* tended to encourage it. But it was most definitely a revolutionary concept as far as the *ali'i* were concerned, and whether they ever fully accepted it, even after constitutional and democratic reforms were introduced, is questionable. Eventually, as modern Hawaiian society evolved into a "classless" society American-style, the traditional elitism was replaced by egalitarianism.

The encounter between aloha and the Gospel of Love produced the inevitable synthesis of a traditional Hawaiian and a foreign set of values. By and large, the elements from both sources were compatible. On the one hand, the agape-love of Christianity gave aloha an impersonal and altruistic dimension that it did not have before, and, on the other hand, took away aloha's strong emphasis on reciprocity. Agape-love also provided aloha with a theological and philosophical frame of reference that it could not have had before. One of the more significant results of this marriage is the way in which aloha has gradually assumed a position as the ranking value in Hawaiian culture, both traditional and neotraditional.

"ALOHA . . . PURE GOLD OR TINSEL-COVERED COMMERCIALISM?"

One of the signs of our times is the willingness to suspect that nothing is safe from being commercialized. In the minds of many people that is certainly what has happened to aloha. The commercialization of aloha goes back more than a century, when Hawaiian monarchs still ruled. The *Hawaiian Kingdom Statistical and Commercial Directory and Tourist Guide of 1880-81* reported that different commercial articles were being sold with the word aloha shown on them. Those articles included gift or souvenir items meant for Hawai'i's early tourists, who started coming in the 1860s. In 1880 King Kalakaua was still on the throne, and we may assume that— if he was consulted—he saw nothing wrong either in the use of aloha for commercial products or in the promotion of tourism in the islands.

Interestingly, the most famous product of aloha for the time was Queen Lili'uokalani's composition "Aloha 'Oe," which she published in 1885 in Boston and which was a best-seller for many years. Another musical product that carried the name aloha was the instrument that the Aloha 'Ukulele Company produced in the 1920s. By this time, we should note, Hawaiian music was the most commercialized part of Hawaiian culture, as Hawaiian troubadours and dancers had been performing all over the world on regular circuits, selling their music with their aloha. The best known of the many products was the "Aloha Shirt," patented in 1936, and practically the symbol of Hawaiian-style living. The style was very popular with local people, including Hawaiians, and in time became an item that every tourist wanted to wear or to take home as a remembrance of his venture into exotic Hawai'i.

During all those decades no public outcry rose up, of the kind often heard today against the commercialization of aloha. This is not to say that some Hawaiians and others may not have been offended by the business, but none of the great Hawaiian traditionalists of the time, such as George Mossman, spoke against the exploitation of aloha by businessmen. In *Shoal of Time*, [Gavan] Daws wrote:

> The Hawai'i Visitors Bureau, trying to establish just what was so attractive about the islands, concluded that the word "aloha" was crucial. It was a Hawaiian word, and it could be used as an affectionate greeting, or as an expression of good will or love. It went together with a kiss on the cheek and the gift of a lei, a flower garland. It captivated tourists descending

from the skies, grateful for safe passage but still faintly stunned and disoriented after hours of high-speed travel westward in pursuit of the sun. If the tourist industry could really dispense good will, or even a convincing imitation (a plastic lei?), the value of aloha as a business commodity would be incalculable. (Daws 1974)

A larger issue than just aloha is at stake. Aloha is the "point guard," so to speak, for Hawaiian culture as a whole. And the commercialization of the culture is really the heart of the matter. But commercialization in this context means more than profiteering; in fact, in the public mind it is almost indistinguishable from such terms as "prostituting" or "corrupting" the culture. What all this refers to is anything—an act, a word, a picture, a gesture, an object, or an attitude—that desecrates, insults, violates, or destroys what Hawaiians believe to be vital and sacred in their history, environment, beliefs, and themselves. Thus, the merchandising of the lei greeting that involves a young man (or a girl) placing a lei, not always a plastic one, around the neck of an arriving tourist, with a perfunctory kiss thrown in, is insulting to Hawaiians because it turns a traditionally warm and personal gesture of respect into a mechanical, impersonal, and false business transaction. It turns what is supposed to be a moment of social celebration into a cash proposition, truly a reversal of ends and means. Similarly, the marketing of an '*ōkolehao* bottle cast in the shape of a helmeted *ali'i* wearing a feather cloak is to Hawaiians an insult, because it demeans the cherished symbols and values of the sacred chiefs. Not all Hawaiians will agree on these or other examples, for they have not yet considered such standards and measures that might be taken to control commercialization. But the point is clear: the abuse of aloha is only a part of the much larger phenomenon of cheapening Hawai'i.

THE POLITICIZATION OF *ALOHA*

If aloha has been commercialized, it has also been politicized by both Hawaiians and non-Hawaiians alike.

Much more significant is the use of aloha in the term *aloha 'āina* by the Protect Kaho'olawe 'Ohana movement. Not since the turn of the century, when Hawaiian activist John Wise and others used the name for a publishing company and a newspaper as part of their political movement, has the phrase been employed with so much calculation and impact. It means love of the land, or the country, and therefore can be synonymous with patriotism. Very few ideas can generate more political interest than loving and protecting the *'āina* in Hawai'i.

In its early years (that is, during the mid-1970s), the organization's name was the Protect Kahoʻolawe Aloha ʻĀina Movement. In their collection of remembrances about Kahoʻolawe, Walter Ritte and Richard Sawyer, both of whom were arrested for trespassing when they made unauthorized landings on the island, wrote that one of their goals was ensuring "through Aloha ʻĀina, the proper use of Hawaiʻi's natural resources" and instilling the value of Aloha ʻĀina. In order to achieve these goals, they said, they intended to educate the public to "the relevance of aloha to the entire world. By beginning at home with *Aloha ʻĀina*—one aspect of aloha—we can better understand the concept of aloha as a universal value." Politically speaking, *aloha ʻāina* meant the preservation of as many traditional rights as possible that were connected with the land, including access to trails, historic sites, beaches, and so on, either through or on private properties; the inalienability of certain lands; and the restoration to Hawaiians of the primary use of lands ceded to the federal government.

Although the supporters of the movement may not see it as a political organization, their objectives, legal obstacles, remedies, even opponents, are essentially political. Neither their cause nor their tactics have endeared them to everybody, whether Hawaiian or non-Hawaiian, but they have taken hold of a dramatic issue that has afforded them more media exposure than any other movements have received. Consequently, they have managed to disseminate their message widely, reaching the mainland and many foreign countries. Their members have grown in number and influence.

The politicization of aloha in this instance has drawn little or no criticism from anyone, and no charges of "corrupting" or "prostituting" the culture. On the contrary, the movement has received widespread public approbation because of its concern for the land and the values it represents.

Hawaiians today still regard aloha as highly important, in comparison with other Hawaiian values. When participants were asked to evaluate the relative importance of twenty Hawaiian values, *aloha* was ranked number one.

EVERYBODY'S PROPERTY

Once at a public discussion on the "Aloha Spirit," an Oriental minister who evidently had lost patience with Hawaiians who kept insisting that aloha was unique to them, shouted, "Aloha or love is universal. The Hawaiians don't have a lock on it." He probably spoke for other non-Hawaiians who dislike the proprietary way in which Hawaiians hold on to aloha as if they owned it. On the other hand, some people don't care if the Hawaiians do "own" it, but simply want to share in it. As Gene Hunter, a former *Honolulu Advertiser* reporter wrote, "We have the Hawaiians to thank for it. They have given of it, as they have given away so much. But it is not exclusive to the Hawaiians. It can be shared by all" (October 21, 1970).

All of us must recognize that for a long while, a strong communal claim has been made among Hawai'i's people, either to "owning" or sharing the Aloha Spirit. The evidence is all around us. It has been appropriated and institutionalized as the unofficial name of the state by legislative decree. It's been worked into our everyday speech and thought. And it's been commercialized in every direction. Whether we like this or not, aloha has been lifted above its Hawaiian origins, to become as much public property as air and sunshine. Aloha is everybody's prerogative—and should be everybody's gift.

CHAPTER 12

A Compromise Identity: Tongan Americans in the United States

'Inoke F. Funaki and Lupe M. Funaki

Tonga has become a diasporic society over the last few decades. Although many insist on centering the Tongan society in the archipelago that constitutes the Kingdom of Tonga, the outside world has taken interest in all actions, structures, and events, both in the islands and in Tongan communities spread around the world. These Tongan overseas communities are principally in New Zealand, on the Australian East Coast, and in the United States, specifically in Hawai'i, California, Utah, Arizona, and Texas. The increasingly diasporic nature of the Tongan society creates new identities as well as modifies existing identities. This paper discusses the elements of the traditional Tongan cultural identity and suggests the need for appropriate and practical adaptations considered fit for the union of the *anga fakatonga* (Tongan way) and the *anga fakapalangi* (American way), in the United States. Thus, the notion of a "compromise identity."

Some Pacific islanders express concern that the term "compromise" might convey a message that the Tongan cultural identity may be short-changed. Therefore, they suggest that a more suitable substitute might be "a navigated identity" or "a negotiated identity." They assert that the idea of a "negotiated identity" portrays the islander as having the will and ability to determine the appropriate adaptations to be made so as to minimize the discomfort caused by the perceived discrepancy between the expectations of the *anga fakatonga* and the realities of the *anga fakapalangi*.

According to Marcus (1977, 222), Tonga developed a "compromise culture," an "early, stable complex of institutions, ideas, and practices, which integrated Tongan culture with a version of European culture," during the period of the first three Tupou monarchs [1875, 1893, 1918]. Throughout Polynesia at this time, "older institutions and customs were censored, reorganized, and retraditionalized (Marcus 1989, 197). Furthermore, Morton (1996, 22) wrote the following:

The strands of Tongan and European (and Fijian and Samoan) have been interwoven to such an extent that they cannot be disentangled. Of all the factors contributing to the historical transformation of *anga fakatonga,* the Tongans' adoption, and adaptation, of Christianity has wrought the deepest and most pervasive changes—so much so that the categories of tradition and Christianity are now inseparable in the minds of many Tongans.

Consider this plausible scenario.[1] There was a man from a small village on the eastern side of Tongatapu, the main island of the Tonga group, who drove a Lincoln Continental, the only one in the Kingdom of Tonga. He had eight children, and all of them lived in the United States. Most of them worked as gardeners/landscapers. His wife had a stroke and was permanently hospitalized in the United States. He lived alone in the village, and he had no land.

He regarded himself a happy man. He was considered fortunate by villagers because his children sent him money and many other good things, and came often to visit. But consider the precariousness of his situation. If all his children in the United States had lost contact with him, then his life would be considered tragic, and people would pity him. Yet, if all his children had stayed in Tonga and lived with him in the village, people would also feel sorry for him.

There was only one certain avenue to the good life in Tonga under the conditions of land shortage, availability of few jobs, and limited economic opportunities. It was a paradox of sorts: He must have a family in a foreign country, but with Tongan ways of thinking; members of his family must go to America, but stay "Tongan" in their heart. "Staying Tongan" means maintaining one's identity as a Tongan. More important, it also means behaving, thinking, and feeling in a Tongan manner: what Tongans call *anga fakatonga,* the Tongan way.

This case may be considered by many as quite extreme and atypical. It does, however, indicate the necessity for Tongans, especially Tongan immigrants, to make adaptations and accommodations so as to receive the benefits of both worlds: the *anga fakatonga* and the *anga fakapalangi.*

Several years ago Kelepi 'Ofahengaue,[2] an expert on Tongan culture from the village of Talafo'ou, Tongatapu, was asked what he considers the identifying elements of the Tongan culture of his generation. He explained what he referred to as the *Faa'i Kavei Koula* (Four Golden Strands of Tongan Culture): (1) *Faka'apa'apa,* especially to God and people with authority; (2) *Feveitoka'i'aki,* especially among relatives first and then others; (3) *Fetokoni'aki,* beginning with relatives and extending outward to everyone; and (4) *Lotu,* especially how one demonstrates sincere worship and true spirituality.

Faka'apa'apa is to do homage or obeisance; to show deference or respect or courtesy. *Feveitoka'i'aki,* being closely related to *faka'apa'apa,* connotes the idea of respecting one another's feelings, being scrupulous. *Fetokoni'aki* refers to helping one another or sharing. And *Lotu* generally indicates a person's regard for things pertaining to religion, worship, and spirituality.

Morton (1996) noted in her study of Tongans in Tonga that the socialization of children places great emphasis on the attainment of three salient cultural values: *'ofa* (love), *faka'apa'apa* (respect), and *talangofua* (obedience). In a survey she conducted of 230 teenagers, she asked the question, "What do you think were the most important things you were taught as a child?" Their answers, like those of the adults she spoke with, emphasized the three central values of *'ofa, faka'apa'apa,* and *talangofua.* Hence, she reaffirmed that:

> Religion also centers on these values, which are seen as traditional values that have been strengthened by Christianity. They are explicitly defined by many Tongans as **intrinsic to their cultural identity,** and in the context of rapid socio-cultural change they have become especially significant symbols of that identity and are increasingly perceived as under threat. (Morton 1996)

This paper proposes a cultural identity prototype called the *"Faa'i Kavei Koula,"* a hybrid of the models identified by 'Ofahengaue and Morton (1996). Specifically, in this model the human values being emphasized through socialization as the elements of Tongan cultural identity are: (1) *Faka'apa'apa;* (2) *Anga'ofa;* (3) *Mateaki,* especially in carrying out one's duties; and (4) *Lotu.* In this model, *faka'apa'apa* and *lotu* are used as defined previously above. Additionally, *faka'apa'apa* represents related dimensions such as *talangofua* (obedience) and *'apasia* (reverence). *Anga'ofa* embraces sharing, helping, and kindness, which include related concepts such as *fetokoni'aki, feveitoka'i'aki, fetoka'i'aki, tauhi vaha'a,* and *'ofa.* Finally, *mateaki* connotes loyalty and devotion, especially in the way one fulfills his or her *fatongia* (obligations).

The dimensions of the *Faa'i Kavei Koula* prototype described in the preceding paragraph appear to be in harmony with the concept of civility, considered by some experts as the aim of higher civilization. Hinckley wrote in *Standing for Something:*

> Civility is the root of the word Civilization. It carries with it the essence of courtesy, politeness, and consideration of others . . . . All of the education and accomplishments in the world will not count for much unless they are accompanied by marks of gentility, of respect for others, of going the extra mile. (2000, 53)

Thus, a Tongan is considered to be *poto*,[3] to be clever and skillful, if he or she understands and acts according to the protocol requirements of the *Faa'i Kavei Koula*, which is *anga fakatonga*. If, however, he is found to be lacking in propriety, then he is labeled as *vale*.[4] In this way, there is a great deal of pressure in the socialization process of children and adults, too, for compliance and conformity, in order to appear *poto* instead of *vale*. Note, however, that this entire process of socialization basically emphasizes affective and social (personality) development, rather than cognitive and intellectual growth. Therefore, traditionally for Tongans, the acquisition of *poto* through this socialization was considered ultimate, and hence the pursuit of intellectual development through formal education was looked upon as unnecessary and not so significant. It is not surprising, therefore, to note that Tongans would experience difficulties and great challenges in their effort to acculturate to the majority host culture, the American way, especially in their experiences in the academic domain.

A COMPROMISE: ADAPTATIONS AND ACCOMMODATIONS

As noted above, the cultural values of *faka'apa'apa, anga'ofa, mateaki,* and *lotu* compose the *anga fakatonga (Faa'i Kavei Koula)*, which when practiced in its true form of Tongan traditional socialization, tends to promote rigidity, conformity, passivity, and non-critical thinking. These are to be expected in a society that is highly collectivistic, as is the case with Tonga. Additionally, the parenting style of most Tongan families is authoritarian. In this style of child-rearing, the parents' word is law, not to be questioned, and misconduct brings strict punishment. Furthermore, parent-child communication is low (Berger 2001, 287). Thus, when Tongan parents demand strict obedience and generosity of their children in the United States, they appear very autocratic, as too controlling and domineering.

A look at the *fa'a samoa* (Samoan way), as experienced by Samoans in New Zealand, would reveal mixed experiences similar to those of Tongans in the United States regarding the *anga fakatonga*. Among these Samoans in New Zealand, the most positive evaluations of *fa'a samoa* were formed by those living in households in which Samoan was the operating culture, in which the household was organized around Samoan principles, and which were heavily involved in kin-based activities (Schoeffel and Meleisea 1994).

Accordingly, the promotion of Samoan culture in these households was based on the emphasis by parents of the moral superiority of elements of the culture:

The *fa'a samoa* is a loving culture. You know in the *fa'a samoa* everyone is looked after. There are no people who are excluded or who are left to fend for themselves like in *Palagi* culture . . . (Macpherson 1995, 14)

Secondly, mixed evaluations of *fa'a samoa* were formed by young adults in households where Samoan was one of several operating cultures. The *fa'a samoa* was seen to be context-specific. It was one of several cultures that operated and competed for attention. In these households Samoan parents and other adults were committed to parts of Samoan culture but were openly critical of others.

Accordingly, in these households, the *fa'a samoa* was not presented as the best or only way of comprehending the world. Parents would portray the Samoan culture as being "better" or more "useful" in some respects and "worse" or less "useful" in others:

Samoan culture is good. Even if you having nothing you still have your family and as long as you have the family you will always have a place to stay and food to eat. But you have to understand that because of the culture nobody will ever get very far. (Macpherson 1995, 15)

On other occasions, Samoan parents would argue that behavior was neither right nor wrong, but rather more or less appropriate in various situations. Thus, they say:

Behavior 'x' is alright for Europeans because it's part of their custom. But don't ever do that in the presence of Samoans or you will make us ashamed because it is very bad in Samoan custom. Samoans will think your family doesn't have any manners. You should know that sort of behavior is okay to me because I am Samoan and I believe it is right. But don't do it around *palagi* because they will think you don't know their ways and that you are ignorant. (Macpherson 1995, 15)

Finally, the negative evaluations of *fa'a samoa* were formed by young adults in a group of households in which Samoan culture was either excluded or deliberately marginalized. It was represented as something of limited utility that would prevent Samoan young adults from acquiring useful or more relevant knowledge.

Therefore, parents who based their decisions solely on utility would argue that because their children's future is in New Zealand, there is no use in their being familiar with the values and institutions of Samoa. Thus, they say:

Samoan is no use. You're not going to stay in Samoa and besides all your friends are *palagi*. They can't understand Samoan. If you want a good job

Samoan is no use. Where are the books written in Samoan? The teachers can't speak Samoan. (Macpherson 1995, 16)

On the other hand, those parents whose decision is based on the supposed "inferiority" of Samoan culture would argue that Samoan culture has little to offer. In these households, parents were either explicitly or implicitly critical of the *fa'a samoa*. They say:

The *fa'a samoa* is the pathway to poverty and trouble. Look around and see what you get from following the custom. Look at all those lawyers who get a title and then steal from clients to pay for all the *fa'a samoa*. They end up in jail . . . and they're supposed to be smart, but the *fa'a samoa* can bring even them down. Look at the trouble that people get into following the *fa'a samoa*. That's the problem with *fa'a samoa*. People are too proud. They fight over this, fight over that. They fight over insignificant things like a little word which they should just ignore. (Macpherson 1995, 17)

From the scenarios of positive, mixed, and negative evaluations of *fa'a samoa* by Samoans being raised in New Zealand, one can quickly assess the similarities of their experiences with those of Tongans in the United States. If *anga fakatonga* (Tongan way) is substituted for *fa'a samoa* (Samoan way) wherever it occurs in the above scenarios, the meaning and context of every statement or scenario would remain unchanged. The Tongan would evaluate the *anga fakatonga* exactly the same way a Samoan would evaluate the *fa'a samoa*.

For the Tongans in the United States, three compromises to the traditional cultural identity are suggested for consideration. The first regards the concept of time. For Tongans, as is true of most Pacific islanders, time is a commodity that is always plentiful and can even wait for the villager, who is never in a hurry. Tonga is known as "Where Time Begins" because of the International Dateline. And Tongans everywhere, including those in the United States, are proud to let others know of that fact. The truth, however, is that Tonga might be more aptly described as the place "where time stands still." Life in Tonga and of Tongans abroad is as unchanged, uncomplicated, and leisurely as one is apt to find in the remotest of places on earth. What is probably most troubling is the fact that the way time is conceptualized by Tongans usually leads to a Tongan way of life that is often characterized as "easygoing": Whatever does not get done today can be done tomorrow. As a result, the Tongans, especially the ones in the United States, will have difficulties in directly associating the concept of time with advance preparation, opportunities for growth and development, and wealth.

The second compromise regards traditional commitments to family and society, especially the practice of sending remittances to family mem-

bers back in Tonga. According to *anga fakatonga,* this act marks true generosity and being very kind. But in the United States, Australia, and New
Zealand, this practice has perpetuated a hand-to-mouth-existence for
many Tongan families, who may be financially and socially worse off
than any other minority group in their neighborhood.

Dr. Tukuitonga (1999), Director of Pacific Health Research Centre at
the University of Auckland, New Zealand, reported that unemployment
among Pacific people is high. In 1997, 17 percent of the Pacific islanders
were unemployed compared with 9.5 percent of European New
Zealanders. In 1981, 80 percent of Pacific islanders earned less than
$20,000 per year compared with 64 percent for other New Zealanders.
These statistics were for a community of Pacific islanders in New Zealand
that consisted of Samoans (51 percent), Cook Islanders (22 percent),
Tongans (14 percent), Niueans (9 percent), Fijians, and Tokelauans. As a
result, Pacific island families were financially and socially worse off than
any other ethnic groups in Manukau City, New Zealand. This also led to
other, related problems such as overcrowding and poor quality housing.
In 1996, more than 26 percent of Pacific households had more than seven
people living in one dwelling compared with 4.6 percent for non-Pacific
islanders. All this suggests that the traditional custom of sending remittances to family members in Tonga should be viewed with greater objec-
tivity and good judgment.

Finally, the third suggestion concerns the parenting style of most
Tongan families. They need to consider being more authoritative rather
than being too authoritarian. Authoritative parenting is a style of child
rearing in which the parents set limits and provide guidance but are willing to listen to the child's ideas and make compromises. Authoritarian
parenting, the style most common among Tongan families, requires high
standards for proper behavior and punishes misconduct strictly and
severely, with low parent-child communication (Berger 2001). Often
times, the authoritarian child-rearing practice leads to child abuse, especially physical abuse, as well as spouse (wife) abuse in many Tongan families in Tonga as well as in the United States. Related to these unfortunate
consequences are the side effects of various forms of aggression such as
physical punishment, which is allowed by most authoritarian families
(284).

Therefore, Tongans in the USA would be well-advised to adopt a compromise identity, which is equivalent to having a mixed evaluation (refer
also to scenarios of *fa'a samoa*) of the *anga fakatonga.* This compromise is
what social scientists refer to as cultural pluralism. Here, everyone is governed according to laws established by the macro-culture, and everyone
must follow certain customs as are necessary for harmonious living in

one society. At the same time, members of the various ethnic groups (micro-cultures) are encouraged to retain their traditions (i.e., language, religion, artistic expressions, etc) if they wish to do so. Such situations would open windows of opportunity wherein Tongans, the minority, benefit from the richness of the host culture, while at the same time they can make some small cultural contribution of the *anga fakatonga*, especially those dimensions worthy of retention and passing on as a cultural heritage.

NOTES

[1] This is an adaptation from the works of an unknown author with the title *Tradition.* Retrieved November 6, 2000, from the World Wide Web: http://jan.ucc. nau.edu/~small/tradfp.html

[2] The conversation with Kelepi 'Ofahengaue took place in May 1994 in the residence of his younger brother Moana 'Ofahengaue at Hauula, Hawaii. Kelepi is considered by many on Tongatapu, especially on the eastern part of the island, as a "keeper of Tongan traditions" because of his many years of service as the Pule Fakavahe (mayor) of his district, which gave him unlimited opportunities to carry out functions of the *anga fakatonga* for the King and nobility.

[3] The idea of *poto* among Tongans is based on the notion that children are naturally naughty and mischievous. Therefore, the main aim of socialization is for them to become *poto:* clever, socially competent, and capable, especially with regards to the characteristics of *faka'apa'apa* and *anga'ofa.*

[4] The concept of *vale,* being foolish, ignorant, unskilled, or incompetent, is the opposite of *poto.* Again, one's inability to show or disregard of proper manners in social situations, with respect to *faka'apa'apa* and *anga'ofa,* would certainly warrant a label of *vale,* until he demonstrates otherwise.

PART FOUR
Gender and Sexuality

Women of the Pacific Islands, especially of Tahiti, have been made into stereotyped exotic, erotic objects in the minds of many Europeans and Americans, and of some Pacific Islanders, too. At the same time, many island women have suffered from Western-inspired preferences that have not recognized the beauty in their large frames. In "Colonialism's Daughters," Karina Kahananui Green examines this paradox. She finds its roots in the history of specific encounters between European and American men and island women in the eighteenth and nineteenth centuries.

Haunani-Kay Trask ponders the difficult choice of loyalties presented to women of color generally and Pacific Island women specifically, between solidarity with other islanders irrespective of gender and sisterhood with other women irrespective of race. In "Pacific Island Women and White Feminism" she critiques the colonial quality of White feminism in the islands, and sides with her fellow Pacific Islanders.

Carolina Robertson takes on a very different issue—the special role accorded to certain individuals who express sexual ambiguity in island societies—in "The Māhū of Hawai'i."

CHAPTER 13

Colonialism's Daughters: Eighteenth- and Nineteenth-Century Western Perceptions of Hawaiian Women

Karina Kahananui Green

While catching an *auana* (modern) hula review in Waikiki, the observer is presented with a stunning image. Female dancers appear in full-length *holukus,* which are Victorian-inspired gowns that modestly cover the young women from chin to ankle. Long locks of hair are swept up into elegant coifs. Fresh flowers shower the dancers' hair, necks, and wrists. These young women are visions of dignity.

However, the actions and sounds that accompany the dancers quickly shatter this image. Ukuleles string out music more appropriate for a striptease than an *auana* hula. Hips wiggle voluptuously while inviting eyes wink on cue; all too often, song lyrics express themselves suggestively. Take, for example, the ever-popular "E Ku'u Hot Cha Cha":

> Oh, my hot cha cha baby
> How do you like it, hot cha cha
> His wooing tease hot cha cha
> That makes my hot cha cha tremble so

How can appearance and manners be in such conflict? Many would dismiss such a scene as merely an example of the tourism industry's willingness to sell tickets with sex. However, this statement does not explain the ambiguity behind the modesty of appearance that accompanies the teasing words and gestures. In addition, this interpretation does not address the fact that this ambiguous, teasing representation of the Hawaiian woman took over two centuries in the making, predating tourism's influence by more than a century.

There are several factors that have contributed to these conflicting images of the Hawaiian women. One important factor is the series of White images of the Hawaiian woman during their first century of contact.

Western explorers arrived on Hawaiian shores in the late eighteenth century. Their first impressions of Hawaiian women were as aggressive, sexual, and maternal beings. However, the nineteenth century ushered in several new waves of incoming Westerners. Missionaries, merchants, whalers, and artists added new layers of perceptions to the explorers' already contradictory foundation. By the beginning of the twentieth century, the qualities attributed to Hawaiian women, as well as the attributes that they should attain, were varied and conflicted.

Although many influences helped to create the imagery of the Hawaiian woman in the eighteenth and nineteenth centuries, I will concentrate on the two most important: the explorers and the missionaries. First I will examine the Western temperament at the time of exploration, and how earlier perceptions of Tahitian women affected the explorers' attitudes toward Hawaiian women.

In the second part of the chapter I deal with the missionaries' arrival in the nineteenth century and the subsequent revisions of Western ideas about Hawaiian women's attributes and aspirations. It is also important to review how Hawaiian royalty, the people most affected by these perceptions due to their constant contact with Westerners, dealt with these perceptions. From this analysis I hope to arrive at a better understanding of the Hawaiian woman's present-day dilemma, in which imagery has become a powerful shaper of human relations.

THE WESTERN TEMPERAMENT

Even before the Western world and Polynesia met, many Europeans were passionate about the discovery of a primitive people who represented a return to a more simple, natural lifestyle. Sir Thomas More's utopian ideals may have peaked in popularity by the seventeenth century, but his vision of an earthly paradise continued to inspire philosophers into the eighteenth century. Discovery and expansion in the New World had also brought about a new cult of exoticism, which stressed that a rational non-Westerner could help correct the corruptions of Western civilization through example. All that was missing were living specimens to apply these two principles in action.

The French philosopher Jean-Jacques Rousseau, rejecting polite society and civilization while favoring rural solitude, used literary hero Robinson Crusoe as his model for the ideal human existence.[1] Crusoe helped to illustrate for Rousseau that humans, in their natural state and away from civilization, could live a life of self-reliance and peace. Rousseau's sentiments strengthened the argument that Western society could benefit from the example of primitive societies.

The eighteenth century was full of lively debates between the champions of Western society and the new generation of philosophers like Rousseau. There was a new, liberal consciousness in the European philosophical community that not only leveled Western civilization and its achievements, but simultaneously lifted up the image of certain primitive cultures in their natural state. However, if European intellectuals were willing to give their ethnic brothers a chance at honorary equality, what role did they accord to women, either Western or non-Western?

Unfortunately, according to Rousseau, a woman's role in eighteenth-century European society was rather limited. In his "Discourse Upon the Origin and Foundation of the Inequality among Mankind," he states that man in a state of nature never desires anything beyond satisfaction of his physical wants, and that "he knows no goods but food, a female, and rest."[2] He later describes how women also contribute to men's lives in terms of the physical and moral aspects of love. Rousseau first explains that physical love is the desire that unites the two sexes; he approves of physical love, but not of the strictures and demands of moral love.

Therefore, one role that women played in life was as random receivers of sexual conquests. Secondly, in the tradition of Adam and Eve, women played the part of temptresses and femme fatales. These comments on women suggest that, in the view of Rousseau and similar thinkers, women were out to undermine men's potential, both in civilization and in the state of nature. Women, according to this line of thinking, limited men's freedom and achievement by refusing to be content with physical love and ensnaring them in the commitments of moral love.

If Rousseau and some eighteenth-century European men distrusted women and wanted a new arrangement of the relations between the sexes, some women did as well. Lady Mary Chuleigh's poem, "To the Ladies," helps illustrate the dissatisfaction of women with the duties of female life. Like Rousseau, she rejects marriage, but from a woman's point of view:

> . . . Then shun, oh! shun that wretched state,
> And all the fawning flatterers hate.
> Value yourselves, and men despise:
> You must be proud, if you'll be wise.[3]

It was into this environment that concepts of an ideal female counterpart in a state of nature were introduced. This ideal woman would possess all the qualities that the Western woman allegedly lacked in motivation, action, and appearance. Her appearance would not be dictated by society's corrupting influence. She would be a willing participant in physical love, yet not expect moral love in return, with its commitments, jealousies, and possessiveness. Most importantly, she would never get in the way of natural man's need for independence and isolation.

This was the background of ideas about women and men against which, towards the close of the 1760s, England and France commissioned explorations to the South Seas. The leaders of these explorations quickly became national heroes. Their images, as men who lived independent lives unrestricted by civilization, made them living approximations of Robinson Crusoe in the public mind. Perhaps it was only natural that these men, Europe's newest celebrities, would claim to have found in the South Seas the "natural woman" of European yearning.

FIRST IMPRESSION: TAHITIAN WOMEN

The blue eye half hid,
Says from under its lid,
I love, and I am yours if you love.
The black eye may say
Come and worship my ray
By adoring perhaps you may win me.

—anonymous[4]

When *H. M. S. Dolphin* discovered Tahiti in June 1767, one of the first comments made by ship's master Robertson in his journal was about Tahiti's young girls. He wrote of the "many fine young girls of different colours, some was light coper collour of a mullato and some almost if not altogether white—this new sight attract our men's fance a good dale." Later, while visiting a coastal village, Robertson commented further that their looks were "as fair and had good features as the generality of the women in England" and that no Englishman "would [have] thought them of another country."[5]

Soon after the *Dolphin's* departure, Frenchman Louis-Antoine Bougainville and his crew arrived in Tahiti and reported similar descriptions of the Tahitian women. He found that "there complexions are, of course, much fairer than of the men, their features are very delicate." While Bougainville found their faces "handsome," he felt that what distinguished them was the "beauty of their bodies, of which the contour has not been disfigured by a torture of a fifteen year duration."[6] The explorers in general were pleasantly surprised by the fair to golden complexions, soft features, and lean builds of Tahitian women, which they saw as similar to Western standards of female beauty.

However, the most outstanding perception attributed to Tahitian women was their alleged mix of innocence and sexuality. During their first interaction with the Tahitians on their ship, Bougainville and his four hundred young French sailors were welcomed in a unique way. Bougainville described that, although he tried to keep the Tahitians off his ship and content in their numerous canoes, one young girl managed to jump onto the main deck. Once she had secured her position, she "carelessly" dropped her clothing and stood naked in front of the young men in a seemingly unconscious stance. Bougainville concluded that the Tahitian woman "suffers no constraint . . . everything invites her to follow the inclination of her heart, or the instinct of her sensuality." In addition, he believed that in Tahiti, "a gentle indolence falls to the share of the women; and the endeavours to please, are their most serious occupation."[7]

Robertson's impressions were less romantic in style, but still conveyed the same imagery of sexual willingness. While Robertson's crew tried to barter their nails for food and water on their fourth day in Tahiti, Robertson mentions that several Tahitian men noticed his crew "feasting their eyes" on several attractive young girls. The Tahitian men consequently motioned the crew over to pick out their favorite girl in exchange for a nail. Although Robertson noticed that the girls were "a little afraid" by the situation, the young girls "soon after turned better acquainted." This incident was the beginning of a very active sex-for-nail barter that resulted in the loss of the ship's complete nail supply as well as many nails missing from the actual ship.[8] This incident helped create the simultaneous images of Tahitian girls as innocent and also sexually awakening.

When Robertson met with the Queen of Tahiti and her court, he wrote that one woman in particular "moved closs by me and felt my legs and thighs." When the woman then "lookt at my hairy breast, this madde the lady call out with surprise 'Oh. Oh.'" Once again, the interpretation of this situation was that of a budding Tahitian female sexuality being awakened by Western men.[9]

Captain James Cook's voyages to Tahiti produced lively tales of Tahitian women as well. When one crew member tried to desert right before the ship's departure, the hunting party found him "lying down between two women with his hair stuck full of flowers" and dressed in Tahitian attire. His explanation was that the older of the two women had propositioned him. However, she "was not so selfish or jealous" to limit his attentions to her but "suffered a young woman for whom he had expressed a desire to his Love with her and between these two" he was found and carried off to the ship. Consequently, the deserter was put in irons; before being released he received two dozen lashes.[10]

The early explorers' experiences generated many self-gratifying commentaries. David Samwell, the surgeon's mate on Cook's third voyage, remarked smugly on the Englishmen's ability to satisfy the young Tahitian girls' sexual curiosities. Samwell wrote of how the "beautiful Nymphs of Otaheite" were rejected sexually by the earlier Spanish explorers, which "appeared very strange to these blooming girls." When the Tahitian women told the English crew about the Spanish abstaining from sex, Samwell added that "we gave them every consolation in our power . . . blind sinners that we are."[11]

Several other journals concluded that the Tahitian women were sexually admirable. Clerke noted that chastity was by no means "the reigning Virtue of these Isles, the good lasses readily contribute their share to our entertainment, and render'd our Bill of Fare compleat." Anderson was not only impressed by the women's sexual openness, but also by the lack in Tahiti of the negative aspects associated with open love in Europe. He commented that in Tahiti the "gentle empire which Love has planted amongst them is so far from loosening that it cements the bands of Society." He thought that the sexes seemed to live in "the most perfect harmony undisturb'd by jealousy on either side," and found it ever more admirable that the women were free of jealousy because "that almost universal passion seems to be quite a stranger amongst the female part" in Tahiti.[12]

Even though the *H. M. S. Dolphin* was stationed in Tahiti for only a month and Bougainville's stay lasted only eighteen days, the stories they brought back to Europe of South Seas women were full of powerful imagery. Cook's later voyages and the numerous tales that followed only cemented the vision of the Tahitian woman as an eager person with girlish charm. Although she was defined by her sexuality, it was more on the level of a sensually awakening teenager, rather than on an adult level. This mix of innocence and sin made for a woman-child who was eager, yet safe; it was sexuality wrapped up in a cuddly, reassuring demeanor. As a result, it seemed that the West had found an ideal mate for its "man in the state of nature." She was free of society's conventions, jealousies of moral love, and sexual repression.

Although the Tahitian woman of stereotype fascinated European men and she received rave reviews as a sex receptacle, she did not benefit in any way. Her sea nymph image overrode any real encounter with her person. She was a lifeless stereotype, a mere male fantasy. The effects that this image would have on Hawai'i and its women would prove to be even more powerful.

FIRST IMPRESSIONS OF HAWAIIAN WOMEN

Europe perceived the Tahitian woman as the refreshingly sexual renegade of the female gender. In reality, these perceptions made her the most dutiful of patriarchy's daughters. Although she was sensual, it was in a way that neither threatened nor intimidated males; it was sexuality along with submission.

If the Tahitian girl was the good daughter of European expansionism, her Hawaiian sister was the problem child of the family. Where the Tahitian girl was fair, fine featured, and of slight build, the Hawaiian woman was darker, broader, and more comfortable in flesh. Where the Tahitians' allegedly unconscious sexuality resembled a pubescent youth just realizing her power on the opposite sex, the Hawaiian woman's sexuality possessed a mature decisiveness. Where the Tahitian girl was seen as disinclined to work, the Hawaiian woman was quite active in her work and play.

The Hawaiian woman, in contrast to the Tahitian girl of White male fantasy, was not the European stereotype. Her appearance alone decided this. When Captain Cook's crew moved north to Hawai'i, they ventured evaluations of Hawaiian women's physical qualities that were less than glowing. William Anderson, the surgeon of the third voyage, commented that the "general figure of the women is too masculine to pretend to beauty," while their bodies were "stout" and "broad." James King, second lieutenant of the crew, wrote that the Hawaiian women were darker than the Tahitians, "tawny . . . and mean looking people." Cook, in a more objective vein, commented on what he regarded as an odd hairstyle, long in the front and short in back. Captain Clerke of the *Discovery* concluded that this fashion gave Hawaiian women a "strange, savage appearance." Clerke further commented on the Hawaiian women's "masculine" appearance, which "by no means [is] to be compared with the Otaheite Damsels." Samwell's assessment was less harsh: He found Hawaiian women to be very clean, "have good teeth, and perfectly void of any disagreeable smell." But even Samwell ultimately concluded that the Hawaiian women were "not so fair as the Girls of Otaheite."[13]

Because the Western explorers were apparently not as sexually attracted to the Hawaiian woman, she was rejected as a candidate for the role of female sex object occupied by the Tahitian woman. At the same time, however, this rejection liberated the Hawaiian woman from being confined to a certain set of qualities as had been her Tahitian sister. Rather than being limited to the image of a sexually eager teenager, she put more flesh into the Polynesian woman in both the physical and the mental sense. Where the Tahitian girl was an empty image of the projected fantasies of European men, the Hawaiian woman was a flesh and blood woman.

The explorers' descriptions of sexual activity with Hawaiians were not as detailed as those with Tahitians, but some did exist. Samwell wrote, for example, "This afternoon we had a great number of Girls on board," and on another occasion he noted that some Hawaiian women "stay on board two or three days while we cruize off and on the Island."[14]

That women were a common sight on shipboard was emphasized when a Hawaiian chief forbade any Hawaiians to go onto a ship upon the arrival of another chief. Samwell commented that "This interdiction, which they call Taboo, was so strictly observed that we had no girls on board of us to day." Samwell also noted that the ships' men were pulling so many nails from the inside of the ship to pay for the Hawaiian women's services, a strict watch was needed over the crew or else "we should have the ships pulled to pieces at this place."[15]

Sexual contact between Hawaiian women and these Western men was obviously frequent. However, where the Tahitian girls were described in Venus-like allusions, Hawaiian women were ascribed no such romantic interpretation. When describing Tahitians, Clerke stated that "Chastity is by no means the reigning Virtue . . . the good lasses readily contributed their share to our entertainment, and render'd our bill of fare compleat." Yet, when commenting on the exact same behavior of the Hawaiians, Clerke remarked that they were "profligate to a most shameful degree in the indulgence of their lust and passions."[16]

Why were the Tahitian girls celebrated for their sexual favors, while the Hawaiian women were looked down upon for theirs? Clerke's two statements help provide an answer. While the Tahitians were described as being preoccupied with the satisfaction of their partners, the Hawaiians were described as being preoccupied with their own satisfaction. This was a more mature and demanding sense of sexuality than the Westerners had found in the playful Tahitian model.

The Hawaiian women's attitudes had brought danger back into sex. The European female brought danger into sex by allegedly attempting to turn physical love into commitment. The Tahitian experience had alleviated this sense of danger by its appearance of physical love without obligation. However, Hawaiian women brought back this danger in a new, intimidating way. By putting their satisfaction as first priority, they gained control over the situation in ways that the European model and the Tahitian model had never attempted. By paying attention to their own sexuality, Hawaiian women claimed equality and, as a result, they paid little attention to the stroking of Western male egos.

When George Vancouver landed in Hawai'i, he wrote of the difference in receptions he and his men received in Tahiti and Hawai'i. In Tahiti, he noticed that the women tried to please them as well as they could. However, when arriving in Hawai'i, the crew was treated with "distant civility" and indifference.[17]

Another visitor to Hawai'i noticed a disregard for Western importance on the part of Hawaiian women. A Lieutenant Mortimer wrote that in many instances he "observed we were made the objects of their ridicule; and if they were witnesses of any action of ours on board of ship that appeared to them ludicrous or absurd, they never failed to take notice of it on the stage with considerable embellishments." In one instance, Mortimer observed a fellow crewman who was "smitten" with a native girl and propositioned her. However, when he got her back to the ship, he eventually found out that the girl was a boy. Mortimer commented that the Hawaiian men and women enjoyed "this mistake so much, that they followed us to the beach with shouts and repeated peals of laughter."[18]

Hawaiian women did not hold back their thoughts on sensitive matters. During his third and final voyage, Cook restricted his crew for a time from having any relations with the Hawaiians. When many "young women" came to the ship in a canoe and made "many lascivious motions and gestures" to indicate their intentions, the crew's refusal was not taken well. When they were refused admission to the ship, the young women "scolded us very smartly" in a harsh manner.[19]

This sexual confidence was exhibited by Hawaiian women of various ages. In contrast, older Tahitian women were not seen as sexual objects. For example, on Cook's first voyage, Joseph Banks commented on the Tahitian queen: "She appeared to be forty . . . .She might have been handsome when young, but now few or no traces of it were left."[20] So the Tahitian woman of European stereotype had a limited shelf life. On the contrary, Hawaiian women expressed their sexual vitality into maturity.

Once, a part of Cook's crew attended a Hawaiian performance where "an elderly woman" who was dressed magnificently in feather leis and *kupe'es* (wrist and ankle bracelets) performed a solo dance. While younger girls watched from the sidelines, "The dancer threw her arms about and put her body into various postures . . . . She continued dancing about a quarter of an hour and we thought it much superior to any dances we had seen."[21] On another occasion, the men in a particular Hawaiian village were preparing for war when a huge group of women gathered and performed a dance that "bespoke of joy and licentiousness." While most of the dancers were younger women who disrobed at various times throughout the performance, there was "in particular a woman advanc'd in years who stood in front and might properly be called the . . . prompter of the rest." As the leader, this older woman "dancd with uncommon vigour and effrontery, as if to raise in the spectators the most libidinous desires and incite her pupils to emulation in such wanton exercise." Age did not handicap Hawaiian women or their confidence.[22]

The most important aspect, however, of the Hawaiian woman's character was the fact that her strength and power were not limited to her sexuality. Her strength was conveyed through authority as well. Female chiefs took care of relations with the Westerners much of the time. One chief in particular, named Naheana, demanded the most respect. Described as "exceeding fat and unwieldy and of some consequence among the people," Naheana strengthened relations between Cook's crew and the island's chiefs. Her attire—a great quantity of red and white striped cloth wrapped around her waist, arm bracelets made of enormous boar's tusks, a thick bunch of human hair wrapped around her neck, a fly flap under one arm, and a cock under the other emphasized her demand for respect.[23]

The power of the Hawaiian woman extended to more direct action, as well. Earlier, I noted that Bougainville described the inclinations of Tahitian women thus: "[A] gentle indolence falls to the share of the women; and the endeavors to please are their most serious occupation." This statement, however inaccurate it may have been, suggested that the Tahitian women were disinclined to work and were only serious about pleasing the Western explorers' sexual fantasies. However, because Hawaiian women were perceived as being "masculine," explorers described the Hawaiian women as often being in the middle of the action.

Westerners described how the wives of warriors often accompanied their husbands to battle, and were sometimes killed. These wives often stayed in the rear, carrying such necessities as water, poi, and dried fish for when their men were thirsty or hungry. However, the main reason for their presence was to back up their husbands if they were wounded or killed in battle. They then picked up the husbands' clubs and continued to fight.[24]

Assertive behavior was not limited to warfare. Cook's crew was exposed to female boxing matches while they were trading goods. Anderson wrote how several pairs of women "box'd with the true spirit of female acrimony, one of the first sending off her antagonist with a bloody nose."[25]

Surfing was another sport that Hawaiian women enjoyed. Samwell marveled at the nonchalant style in which young boys and girls would enter dangerous waters to ride the waves:

Sometimes they fail in trying to get before the surf, as it requires great dexterity and address, and after struggling awhile in such a tremendous wave that we should have judged it impossible for any human being to live in it, they rise on the other side laughing and shaking their locks.

The Western onlookers commented that the Hawaiians' chief amusements "presented nothing but horror and destruction" to them. In addition, they watched in amazement when "young boys and girls of nine or ten years of age [were] playing amid such tempestuous waves that the hardiest of our seamen would have trembled to face."[26]

In addition to active participation in battle and dangerous sports, Hawaiian women had important everyday responsibilities. King noted that male and female laborers in Hawai'i were "properly divided" with the women doing an equal amount of work. The women were responsible for the manufacturing of cloth for common wear, mats for sleeping and battle, and ornamental dresses. In addition, they nursed their children and helped with cultivating the land, as well as food gathering and preparation. The Hawaiian women's work was of good quality: Clerke expounded upon the quality of women's craftsmanship, saying that their clothing had "a pleasing appearance, and I think . . . altogether very ingenious and pretty.[27]

Because Hawaiian women were not burdened with the role of sex goddess that had already been assigned to the Tahitian women, they were open to fuller description with the many faces of womanhood. Where the explorers saw Tahitian women only as perpetual teenagers, they could see Hawaiian women in broader roles usually reserved for older women, such as loyal wife and mother. Hawaiian women who followed their husbands to war displayed this loyalty, which the Western observers appreciated, however out of character they may have thought it for a Western woman.

Overall, while the Tahitian woman's lifestyle was censored in order to keep her sexual image intact, perceptions of the Hawaiian woman were less constricted. The short period of contact with the Tahitians resulted in limited interaction with the people and a lot more freedom for explorers to create their own fantasy images. The product of these fantasies was a strange mixture of exaggerated attributes of femininity. This ideal of primitive, sensual womanhood made a nice complement to Western ideals of primitive masculinity. The Tahitian model was petite, fair skinned, and inclined to "gentle indolence," in stark contrast to masculinity's supposed brawny, darker, industrious nature. Also, the explorers dehumanized Tahitian women to the point that they were seen to exist only for men's pleasure. Although European, romantic sentiments wanted an alternative model of femininity to the Western woman, their celebration of the Tahitian model illustrated that in fact they did not want to stray too far from their Western standard. The explorers' perception of Tahitian women was in actuality very similar to the standard held up for Western women, with the very important exception that, while European women demanded the commitment of moral love, the Tahitian woman was supposed to embrace, even to embody, free love.

In contrast to the Tahitian contact, the explorers were stationed in Hawai'i for longer stretches. Captain Cook's crew, for instance, stayed in Hawai'i for over ten weeks.[28] These longer stays resulted in more exposure to the people and less fanciful interpretations of the islanders. This second Polynesian model was less simplistic. Hawaiian women's actions and attitudes were less easy to categorize because their qualities did not correspond as readily to Western ideas of femininity. Unlike the Tahitian and Western female models that saw women as background to man's way of life, Hawaiian women invaded Western territory. Hawaiian women's actions were interpreted by explorers as more masculine than feminine. By questioning the explorers' sexual potency, Hawaiian women lacked the very quality that Western men were searching for and thought they had found in Tahitian women: sexual reassurance. Moreover, through their partnerships in battle with their husbands, boxing matches, surfing, and sexual assertiveness at all ages, Hawaiian women were described in a more powerful, allegedly masculine fashion. Testaments to their loyalty in motherhood and marriage made Western definitions for Hawaiian women even more complex. The blurred line between gender roles puzzled explorers.

GENDER ROLES AND AMBIGUITY

Some Western commentators were amused by the ambiguity. Samwell concluded that Hawaiian women had "tempers in their dispositions, but are truly good natured, social, friendly and humane, possessing much livelyness and a constant flow of good humour." In addition, he pointed out that they were "brought up from their youth in the most unbounded liberty both of words and actions." Overall, Samwell felt that the Hawaiian women and their "lively" ways "deserve every thing that can be said in their praise."[29]

Other explorers were simply surprised by the extent of assertion. While watching a particular boxing match, King commented that

the old observation is true that in enmity a woman is a more implacable adversary than a man. . . . I am rather inclind to think their passion for speedy and universal conquest was the reason of our heroines engaging with such irresistible fury, as the shame of being conquer'd seemd to affect them more than the severity of the blows.[30]

This exhibition astonished King due to the women's ability to react to competition as fiercely as the men. Other commentators were merely repulsed by the supposedly masculine behavior of the women. Clerke wrote that Hawaiian women "equal any people in lewdness" and that there was sex "in daily practice amongst them" without "reproach or shame."[31]

Although the Westerners could not agree on how to interpret the Hawaiian woman's feminine and masculine behavior, these various commentaries helped to give her life in the eyes of Europeans. They could see her as more fully human than her Tahitian sister. As lover, mother, and fighter, the Hawaiian woman embodied a multidimensional, earthly female figure that defied stereotyping. She was seen as a woman who was not limited by her gender, sexuality, or age. She was able to take on "masculine" tasks while still retaining her femininity. She was able to express her sexuality without having to hide behind a mask of innocence or coquettishness. Finally, her age did not define what position she should assume, whether it be lover, wife, or mother. The Hawaiian woman in the eighteenth century was described by her own terms.

MISSIONARY PERCEPTIONS OF HAWAIIAN WOMEN

When British and American missionaries arrived on Hawaiian shores in 1820, they saw Hawai'i as more than just a new place to Christianize. It was for them a crusade against ignorance and lack of true faith, and against the favorable images that had been distributed by some European observers of non-Christian Hawai'i.

The descriptions and conclusions that many explorers brought home from the South Seas disturbed members of organized Christian churches greatly. John Ledyard's journal contained an entry that seemed to undermine their view of God's and society's roles in the making of man. During a tour of a Hawaiian village in 1779, Ledyard came upon a hut that was inhabited by a man whose "wife and daughter [were] the emblem of innocent and uninstructed honor." In addition, while surveying the Hawaiian landscape, Ledyard commented that "nature had bestowed her with graces with her usual negligent sublimity." These interpretations of Hawai'i and her people suggested that, in Ledyard's eyes at least, society of the sort favored by Europeans was not needed to create a good citizen, and that nature, not God, was the instigator of

Hawai'i's beauty. Such sentiments gnawed at Christians' missionary hearts.[32]

Other commentators were less subtle in their admiration of Hawaiians. Sydney Parkinson wrote that "ambition, and love of luxurious banquets, and other superfluities," were not known in Polynesia. He also believed that, since they worried less about the future and concentrated on the present, Polynesians were able to enjoy themselves more than Europeans, and thus they led happier lives. Parkinson pointed out as well that, because Polynesians were "unaccustomed to indulgences in clothing and diet, which Europeans have carried to an extreme," they were healthier and more "robust." He felt that the Polynesians resembled "what the ancient Britons were before their civilization," and that Polynesian virtues demonstrated that civilization and religion were not required for a successful society.

Samwell, like others, questioned whether "civilized" Europeans were in fact superior to the "savages" they encountered in Hawai'i. Other European writers, influenced by the explorations, delighted in the idea of human salvation through impulse and nature rather than through civilization and Christianity. One anonymous poet, drawing heavily on perceptions of Tahitian sexuality, fantasized about the love practices of Polynesian women:

Lo here, whence frozen chastity retires,
Love finds an alter for his fiercest fires;
The throbbing virgin loses every fear,
Venus alone absolves her frailties here . . .
O spread the empire, love, from shore to shore,
Till wedlock cease, and jealousy's no more
Let sniveling wives and sermons to be chaste
And rail against all of the Ladies of taste.[33]

Other European writings influenced by the explorations were less obsessive about Polynesian sexuality and paid more attention to the implications of European contact. An anonymous poem attempted to enter the mind of the Tahitian man Omai as he was taken to England by early explorers on their return home. Writing back to the Tahitian queen, Omai had much to observe and little good to say about British manners and morals, which he contrasted sharply to his memories of the simple pleasures of Tahitian life.[34]

As some European writers began to question the virtues of European civilization and Christianity, missionaries of various Protestant backgrounds began to arrive in Hawai'i early in the nineteenth century. Not only were these missions supposed to save people, but they were meant to show the world that, contrary to the explorers' favorable reports, the Hawaiian islands were in a state of confusion, disease, and religious error. William Ellis, a missionary from England who arrived in Hawai'i in 1823, believed that Captain Cook had made "faithful transcripts of the first impressions" of Hawaiian life; but he stressed that Cook's favorable impressions of Hawaiians must be constrained by the understanding that Cook's "acquaintance with the people was superficial, and the state of the society which they witnessed was different from what generally existed." The Hawaiians had put on a special show for Cook, thought Ellis. By virtue of longer time in the islands, Ellis thought he and other missionaries knew the Hawaiian people much better.[35]

The missionaries' motivations for coming to Hawai'i ranged from the dutiful to the dishonorable. Ellis, for one, was ambivalent. He said his goals were to "enlighten the minds of Hawaiians, convince them of the absurdity in idolatry while presenting them with their true God and Savior and to promote better faith, lives, worship." Just a few pages later, however, he included an entry on "Commercial Advantages of Hawaii" that speculated on possible markets for sugar cane and coffee.[36]

Many of the missionaries, of course, were more sincerely Christian in their motivations. Sarah Joiner Lyman, an American missionary, expressed how she simply wanted to help Hawaiians learn of Christianity and a civilized way of life. With the conflation of race, religion, country, and grooming habits so common in the Victorian era, she further stated that "though their skins are dark, they are just as good by nature as those who go to the sabbath school so neatly drest in our beloved country."[37] The object for Hiram Bingham and his mission to come to Hawai'i "was to honor God by making known his will, and to benefit those heathen tribes, by making them acquainted with the way of life."[38] Before many of the missionaries had actually come to Hawai'i, their general belief was that Hawaiians were undoubtedly nominated for salvation. The missionaries believed that, through example and teaching, they would steer the Hawaiians into Christianity and Western lifestyles. What the missionaries saw as Hawaiian savagery they believed to be a matter of inadequate nurture more than perverse nature.

They soon came to question this view when they actually met their first flesh-and-blood Hawaiians. Before coming to Hawai'i, Lyman thought that Hawaiians were as virtuous in their state of nature as Westerners, but on contact she changed her mind: "[U]ntil I began to visit among the people, I had not correct ideas of their condition . . . awful stupidity prevails among the people . . . .Like brutes they live, like brutes they die." Soon she questioned both their susceptibility to salvation and her ability to save them.[39]

When Hiram Bingham first sailed into Hawaiian waters on March 3, 1820, Hawaiians surrounded the boat to barter goods with the new arrivals—surely a casual encounter, but the people's bodies, their clothing, and their demeanor shocked Bingham: "[T]he appearance of destitution, degradation, and barbarism, among the chattering almost naked savages, whose heads and feet, and much of their sunburnt swarthy skins, were bare, was appalling." He told how many members of his party "with gushing tears, turned away from the spectacle." Others with "firmer nerve" continued to look on, exclaiming their emerging doubts: "Can these be human beings! How dark and comfortless their state of mind and heart! How imminent the danger to the immortal soul, shrouded in this dark pagan gloom! Can such beings be civilized? Can such beings be Christianized?"[40]

C. S. Stewart, an American missionary who brought his party in 1823, saw the Hawaiians as "naked figures" with "wild expressions." He saw the people before him as "half-man, half-beast," and questioned "Can they be men? Can they be women? Do they not form a link in creation connecting man with the brute?"[41]

This missionary image was drastically different from what had gone before. Just fifty years earlier, explorers were touting Hawaiians as the healthy, vivacious people that Westerners had once been before the negative effects of society had set in. Now the missionaries saw Hawaiians as a step or two lower than Europeans on the ladder of evolution.

The "savage" appearance of Hawaiian women, which Stewart mistook for masculinity, was commented on frequently by the missionaries. While the flesh of the Hawaiian women was seen as the result of gluttony, their dark complexion was seen as an indication of lower intelligence. C. S. Stewart judged that the Hawaiian women, especially the royalty, were "excessively corpulent" and that they reached their size because their "only care is 'to eat, and to drink, and to be merry.'" Stewart looked down on such an attitude because he thought it illustrated a lack of control. Stewart also wrote that Hawaiian women in general were "tall . . . masculine . . . dark mulatto," with wild hair and features "too broad and flat for beauty."[42] Hiram Bingham noted the darkness of complexion and hinted at a relationship between pigment and intelligence. One Sunday, a Hawaiian woman brought her two children along to Bingham's sermon. He commented later that the young girls were "shy, but bright looking little daughters (less tinged with copper and olive than their fellows)."[43] Such descriptions of Hawaiian women as masculine, overweight, broad featured, and "tinged" with color conjured up images of persons with indeterminate gender identity, assertiveness, and undefined bodily proportions. In the eyes of the missionaries, the Hawaiian women seemed unable to control themselves sexually or physically, and perhaps mentally.

This lack of boundaries extended into missionaries' perceptions of Hawaiian women's actions and behaviors as well. The missionaries thought there were not enough divisions between male and female spheres, even though the Hawaiians did practice the *kapu* system, in which certain actions were limited to one sex and prohibited to the other.[44] It is true that, during recreation, the sexes interacted freely at all ages, with few activities being designated "feminine" or "masculine."

Bingham commented on such an episode that seemed inappropriate to him. While looking for the governor of Hawai'i, he came upon the beach where hundreds of "almost naked men, women, and children, from the highest to the lowest rank, including the king and his mother" were playing in the water. Watching the sexes mingling freely as they swam, surfed, danced, and ran "like sheep," Bingham remarked that these activities "exhibit the appaling darkness of the land, which we had come to enlighten." The problem for Bingham was that the scene not only showed a lack of hierarchy between commoners and royalty, but also the absence of restrictions for women in hearty activity.[45]

Sarah Lyman also looked down on these enjoyments. She wrote that "It is astonishing how the natives pervert every kind of amusement," noting that "all ages of all sexes" engage in swinging from tree vines and see-sawing. She thought that in pursuing such amusements together, the "natives" constantly "exposed [themselves] to danger"; these games were "the occasion of much iniquity," by which she meant immorality. She also witnessed men and women of all ages surfing together. She said that "it is too much practised" and that it was a "source of much iniquity, in as much as it leads to intercourse with the sexes without discrimination." While she apparently meant sexual intercourse, she did not elaborate on how surfing contributed to sexual activity. Nonetheless she was firm in her belief that gender-mixed amusements contributed greatly to the degradation of the Hawaiian people.[46]

The missionaries thought that much of the problem was the inappropriate blending of gender roles—Hawaiian women did not practice the distinct sphere of feminine domestic duties that the Victorian missionaries thought they ought, nor did they cultivate what the Europeans and Americans regarded as a feminine appearance.[47] Therefore, according to the missionaries, what the Hawaiian women needed was to be inculcated with a sphere of femininity, as a way of establishing social order and appropriate behavioral boundaries. To this end, the female missionary was the perfect model of Victorian femininity.

The missionary literature presented missionary wives as foils of their male partners in terms of their essential natures and their duties. Bingham said that the male missionaries were of "firmer nerve," while the females were more inclined to "gushing tears" when facing conflict.[48] The Westerners believed that women, by their very nature, were susceptible to meekness, passivity, and support.

Juliette Cooke, a Honolulu missionary wife, commented on Mrs. Castle, also a missionary wife and her admired role model: "one of the loveliest women, mild, meek, and humble, yet firm where duty was concerned."[49] Sarah Lyman also praised passivity as a treasured trait, lauding her daughter for enduring a slow, untimely death "so peacefully and meekly."[50] The general self-image that the Western missionary women in Hawai'i projected was of being the weaker sex, as per the dictates of Victorian culture.

Though they pictured themselves as weak, in fact the missionary wives took on many responsibilities, mainly limited to the approved domestic sphere: home and motherhood. In domestic chores, missionary women were supposed to be energetic, thorough, and enthusiastic. The chores were often onerous. Juliette Cooke wrote in her journal that "the sewing for a family comes heavily upon a mother"; she alone was responsible for fashioning the pants, shirts, dresses, and bonnets worn by all her family. She confided to her journal that these duties, together with her ill health, were quite a burden. Yet her public face was resolutely cheerful. She wrote her sister-in-law in 1839, "You wish me to tell you if I was pleased with my housekeeping . . . .I like it very much . . . .True, a mother has many cares, but they are sweet cares" that should not be shrugged off onto any others.[51]

Missionaries, male and female, contrasted these virtuous missionary women against the women of Hawai'i, whom they saw as both indolent and ill-served by their husbands. Bingham asserted that the "domestic condition of the women, and the heathen influences employed that are forming the character of the rising generation, demand our sympathetic regard." He laid the fault largely at the door of the "pagan" and "heathenistic" husbands who "failed at producing much domestic happiness as her share." Stewart echoed those sentiments, but also pictured Hawaiian women as ever "lounging in listless inactivity."[52] Though the missionaries showed some sympathy for Hawaiian women, they nonetheless charged them with inactivity.

How the missionaries reached the conclusion that Hawaiian women were not nurturing or hardworking is unclear. In addition to preparing food for their families, Hawaiian women, both common and royal, gathered food and fished as well. Queen Kalakua's daughter, Princess

Kalakua, once stopped a boat full of foreigners for an hour because she wanted to fish on the rocks for lunch. Ellis and Bingham both commented on the good order and industriousness of Hawaiian villagers, men and women, and their agricultural and fishing enterprises.[53]

In addition to food preparation and helping with some cultivating duties, Hawaiian women were also responsible for their families' clothing. This duty included the making of *tapa* cloth, in which bark was stripped from tree sticks and then laboriously pounded for hours until it reached a soft, supple texture. Tapa making was a duty of both royal women and commoners.[54]

Hawaiian women also spent much of their time on child rearing; it made for strong mother-child bonds. Once, when young King Liho Liho arrived home after a month away from his mother, Stewart described their reunion as "quite affecting; I have never witnessed an exhibition of natural affection, where the feelings were apparently more lively and sincere": Liho Liho knelt before his mother, placing a hand on each cheek, and kissed her twice. According to Stewart, while the mother gazed tearfully at her son, "the queen's heart seemed to float in her eyes, and every feature told a mother's joy." Stewart also found that Hawaiian mothers were able to be strict when that was called for. On a visit to a village on the Big Island, he witnessed an elder mother expressing her anger at her son's public display of drunkenness. The mother lifted her hand, pointed to her son, and exclaimed, *"Pupuka! Pupuka!"* (Shameful! Shameful!) The mother spanked the boy and dragged him home. Stewart described this woman as a "pious Christian mother" in "countenance" and "manner" because of her firm actions. Hawaiian mothers were on the one hand engaged and affectionate with their children, and on the other firm disciplinarians. Motherly care and affection were also extended beyond blood kin to others. For example, two elderly Hawaiian women frequently came to massage the oft-ill Sarah Lyman, and greatly eased her suffering.[55]

Thus it is clear that Hawaiian women did in fact have a feminine sphere where they spent their energies productively for their families and community. Why, then, did the missionaries persist in describing them as domestically and femininely challenged? One reason might be that the missionaries were less concerned by what the Hawaiian women did than by how they did it. Juliette Cooke once complained that, although the "natives" were "willing to do anything," they did it "in native fashion." By this she meant not only that they performed tasks using Hawaiian materials and techniques. She was also complaining about their attitude.[56]

Key qualities of Western womanly ideals were self-sacrifice and meekness, and in these the missionary women were expert. Bingham related the story of an occasion when a Hawaiian "woman of rank" called on a missionary wife to make her a dress. The missionary "readily granted" this first request, and did not demur when two more dresses were requested. Upon the fourth request, the missionary began to hesitate. She told the Hawaiian woman she was of "feeble health," responsible for her household chores, tending to her family and sewing for several people. When the "rude giantess" continued to insist, the missionary relented and made the fourth dress. Bingham concluded that "our female helpers, in midst of infirmities and family care," showed "the spirit of self denial for the sake of another's good" and put "their interest in the well-being of the natives" above themselves.[57]

Other missionary women put themselves last in similar, uncomplaining fashion and showed other varieties of sacrifice and self-discipline. Sarah Lyman wrote in her journal of how she missed her mother's cooking, then abruptly ended the entry with these words: "But our food ought to occupy few of our thoughts. I think it very sinful to spend much time or strength in preparing it, or to allow ourselves to partake largely when set before us." Lyman chided herself for having "indulged the habit of laying in bed a half an hour or more after the sun rose." She was "convinced" that no one should lie in bed after dawn, and promised herself to "reform" the bad habit, ending the entry with "I pray that I may be enabled to persevere." Juliette Cooke portrayed herself in letters as meek and uncomplaining. She acknowledged that "my own health has been poor," and described in detail how she was "frail, frail," given to "palpitation of the heart, dyspepsia, and some other local infirmities." Yet she was quick to assert that household chores and child rearing were "bliss" for her.[58]

To the cynic, these women's descriptions of pain or desire coupled with self-denial and an assertion of happiness would suggest martyrish posturing, even passive-aggression. However, such an interpretation does not do justice to the women's sincerity. These women's journals and letters describe a conflict between their wishes and needs on the one hand, and their responsibilities on the other. Every time—from the responsibilities of motherhood to the impulse to control one's eating for the greater good—feminine duty prevailed. Such a recourse to duty enabled them to give order and structure to their lives in a foreign, seemingly loose environment.

Thus, missionary women defined for themselves a distinct sphere of femininity. The women looked smaller and slighter than their men, and they kept their diets small to ensure this appearance. They worked hard in household duties, child bearing and rearing, and acts of service. They performed all these tasks in a meek and self-sacrificing manner.

Hawaiian women performed a similar set of womanly tasks, but they did other things as well, such as fish and raise crops; and they did all these things with a style that contrasted strongly to the meek ideal of Western womanhood.

From the start, the missionaries were shocked by the Hawaiian women's lack of meekness. They surfed, see-sawed, and swung freely. Stewart recalled that when his party first approached Queen Ka'ahumanu about learning to read and write, she dismissed them again and again from her presence with a "powerful and haughty" attitude (she was, after all, the queen). Bingham also visited her and tried to gain her favor, and was put off by her "dark, commanding eye, deliberate enunciation, air of superiority and heathen queen-like hauteur." Lounging on a mat with "naked feet and toes extended in diverging lines towards the different sides of the room," Ka'ahumanu showed "her stiffness towards the missionaries, to whom her little finger, instead of her right hand, had been extended."[59]

Royals were not the only women to show assertive or even aggressive behavior toward male missionaries. During a tour of Maui, Bingham was confronted by a woman who claimed to be a priestess of Pele, goddess of the volcano on the Big Island. The priestess had traveled to Maui to proclaim that Pele was offended by the missionaries' disregard for her power. Bingham described the priestess as "marching with haughty step" attended by her two daughters, and as having "long, dishevelled hair, and countenance of wild, with spears in her hands." Her speech attracted a huge crowd of Hawaiian supporters.

Here was a Hawaiian woman who offended the Western missionaries by her demeanor. Far from the meek, passive, subservient woman who was the Western ideal, here was a powerful, assertive woman. Although they were offended initially, the missionaries soon figured out how to turn the gender situation to their advantage. They made allies of the most powerful women in Hawai'i; these alliances proved to be an important tool in their mission to Christianize the Hawaiian population.

The strongest ally was Queen Ka'ahumanu, widow of Kamehameha I. As the wife of the late king, her influence over the islands was great, but she desired even more prominence for herself and her heirs. Bingham remarked that she aimed for "equal privilege with men." Her alliance with the missionaries strengthened Ka'ahumanu's political position in the islands. Although her interest in Christianity was real, her interest in positioning herself and her posterity was strong as well. Bingham noted her "degree of suavity and skill for managing the minds of others" and reckoned she would make a key contribution to the success of the Christian mission.[60]

Ka'ahumanu soon converted to Christianity, and by 1825 she was helping lead the female worship service alongside missionary women. At these weekly meetings, several hundred Hawaiian women would listen to scriptures, sing hymns, pray, and then be asked at the end to convert if they had not already done so. With Ka'ahumanu at the forefront of the new Christian movement they won massive conversions among the Hawaiians, and Ka'ahumanu's influence was increased. Her power—both in the church and in state affairs, where she often dominated her son, King Liho Liho—was not limited to O'ahu, but soon extended to the other islands as well. She issued orders prohibiting secular labor on the sabbath and encouraging Hawaiians to take advantage of Christian religious teaching. If other Hawaiians failed to obey, she was quick to reprimand them and compel obedience, from people up to and including Wahinepio, the governess of Maui.[61]

Hawai'i's most affluent and influential women had their power enhanced by the Christian movement. By becoming leaders in the Christian faith they were able to achieve new levels of influence. However, their alliance with the Western missionaries came with a price, which was paid by succeeding generations of Hawaiian women.

THE EFFECTS OF WESTERN PERCEPTIONS

Because Hawaiian women were characterized by both the explorers and the missionaries as assertive and strong, the example of Ka'ahumanu might seem to illustrate the fact that Hawaiian women in general had retained their character. However, this conclusion could not be farther from the truth. Hints of what was to come were evident from the first contacts between missionaries and Hawaiians. While Stewart thought most native women to be savage beyond repair, he did find one Hawaiian woman whom he described as extraordinary and admirable: a poor, elderly, blind woman named Pua, who "manifested a childlike simplicity and meekness of heart—no one appeared more uniformly humble, devout, pure, and upright." Bingham similarly took heart in his perception of the first Hawaiian woman who "took the vows of Christian marriage, [and] proved herself to be an obedient, meek wife, where little of these qualities had been known among her countrywomen."[62]

Soon, these qualities of obedience and meekness were attributed to such outspoken leaders as Ka'ahumanu. Stewart commented that, before her Christian conversion, she had an "aggressive" disposition, but that upon becoming a Christian she had "perfectly corrected" her behavior.[63] The very assertiveness in Ka'ahumanu that had made her a crucial influence in large numbers of conversions was being "corrected" in order for her to fit into the Western sphere of womanhood.

Not only were Western beliefs altering Hawaiian values of womanhood, they were causing self-hatred among Hawaiian women as well. Queen Kapiolani announced on her death bed that "I have followed the customs of Hawaii in the time of the dark hearts . . . .I have renounced my ancient customs in full." The very color of their skin was a reminder to Hawaiians of their "dark" ways; a renunciation of their culture was a way to redeem this fundamental flaw. Although Ellis had previously characterized Kepuolani as "savage," her deathbed rejection of her culture redeemed her in his eyes.[64]

Many commoners and chiefs followed the path of Kapiolani, dismissing their cultural wisdom as backward. Stewart crowed that "the more enlightened chiefs and people have made great sport of the credulity of others who are not converted, calling them *'ca poe naau po,'* the dark hearted party." Stewart was especially pleased that even Kapiolani came to look down on the "great ignorance of her people of Hawaii; for they are *'Nui roa naau po'*—very dark minded."[65]

Newly converted Hawaiians ridiculed a variety of native cultural practices. Traveling on the road one day, Stewart came upon a crowd gathered to taunt some women for making *tapa* cloth, a native material. The group was yelling out such words as *"'ino, pupuka debelo'*—wicked, foolish, devilish." Soon, anything related to Hawaiian culture was seen as backward and dangerous by many Hawaiian converts.[66]

Both sexes in Hawai'i suffered during this period, either as targets of converts' contempt or as self-contemptuous for their native ways. However, Hawai'i's royal women were perhaps in the most difficult position, because of their close contact with the missionaries. Like the men, they were expected to renounce their Hawaiian culture and embrace Western ideals, including conversion to Christianity. But for females there was an intergenerational legacy to be paid: Although Hawaiian women were assertive leaders of the Christian movement in the 1820s, subsequent generations learned only that women must be meek. With the deaths of Ka'ahumanu and the other members of the first wave of Hawaiian Christian women leaders, the lessons in Hawaiian womanhood were silenced. Instead, royal youth received strict instruction in the duties of Western womanhood, for example, at the royal boarding school run by Juliette Cooke.

Although Cooke was a caring teacher to her pupils, they learned at her school to value Western womanly ideals and to denigrate their own cultural inheritance. These young Hawaiian girls agonized over their inability to fit into the Western ideal of feminine appearance. Stewart commented that, at the school, "the females do not look so well or so much at ease in their European dresses . . . . I am told [they] have talked of eating less so that their persons may be more delicate, and their clothes sit better."[67] As they partook of Christianity to fit their souls to the Western model, dieting was a way to alter their bodies to fit the ideal image of Western womanhood.

Skin color and facial features were a problem as well. While a young girl, Liliuokalani (later the queen) wrote that her royal cousin Bernice Pauahi was "one of the most beautiful girls [she] ever saw" because of her light complexion and fine features. These were the gifts, in Liliuokalani's estimation, that brought Bernice a husband in her eighteenth year. Liliuokalani thought that she, on the other hand, lacked real physical beauty and so had to emphasize gifts of learning.[68]

This new generation of female Hawaiian royals was extremely self-conscious about their Hawaiian looks. They were not comfortable with the dark skin color, broad features, and Rubenesque bodies in which their mothers and grandmothers had been so much at home. Their very physical manifestation was a rude and constant reminder that, no matter how Westernized of manner they might be, they would always be seen first and foremost as a Hawaiian squaw.

By the end of the nineteenth century, Hawaiian royal women were going in two different directions, in response to their appearance. Like their Hawaiian foremothers, the women who were Hawaiian in appearance could not embody the Western ideal. Just as the earlier Hawaiian women were rejected in favor of the more subservient, reassuring Tahitian women, late in the century Hawaiian-looking women were dismissed as backward. Ironically, however, this very rejection liberated some Hawaiian-looking royal women from the constraints of idealization.

The most celebrated woman who took this path with a vengeance was Princess Ruth of the Big Island. Weighing in at over 440 pounds and topping six feet, Princess Ruth's very appearance made her a presence to be reckoned with. Her broad features were accentuated by a nose that had been flattened even more by surgery for an infection. To complement her stature, listeners said that Princess Ruth's voice sounded like a "distant rumble of thunder."[69]

The U.S. minister to Hawai'i dismissed Princess Ruth as a "woman of no intelligence or ability." However, his assumption probably came from a swift evaluation of her appearance and manners. In addition to her great size and stature, her disregard for Westerners in general was expressed through a refusal to speak English and a rejection of the Christian faith. Instead, she spoke Hawaiian fluently and focused her attentions toward traditional Hawaiian views of religion and spirituality. Many Westerners were unable to discern the indignation in these choices, and instead took them as signs she was backward and stupid.[70]

Yet Ruth was far from stupid. As the governess of the Big Island and the granddaughter of Kamehameha I, she possessed more land and wealth than all but a few Hawaiians. She was a sharp, savvy business-woman. For example, on one occasion she "sold" her claim to half the Crown lands in the kingdom to sugar mogul Max Spreckels for $10,000, knowing full well that the claim was void on a technicality and Spreckels would be unable to take possession. Spreckels sued Princess Ruth but was unsuccessful, and the media had a field day at his humiliation. She was not only powerful but calculating as well.[71]

FIGURE 13.1 "Mama Nui," Kaiulani's god-mother, Princess Ruth Keelikolani. She was a half sister to Kings Kamehameha IV and V. From *Princess Kaiulani*, by Kristin Zambucka (Honolulu: Mana, 1982).

Ruth's independence and assertive nature were encouraging signs that the character of her ancestors was still alive. Yet Ruth endured many humiliations and cruelties on account of her appearance. One indication that the cruelty got to her was the fact that she was particular about how she dressed and how her hair was done, right down to corset and Victorian ringlets, despite the fact that she did not approximate the Western ideal (see Figure 13.1). Ruth may have extended traditional Hawaiian female power into her own age, but even she was not completely immune to Western ideals. Because of her robust appearance, she was dismissed as stupid by the ever-more-powerful Westerners, and she spent her last years in seclusion.[72]

The other path taken by Hawaiian women was reserved for those who physically embodied the Western ideal of womanhood. The woman most celebrated for this accomplishment was Princess Kaiʻulani. As a half-English, half-Hawaiian woman, she had a compelling ability to appear Westernized. Kaiʻulani was celebrated around the world as a Christianized, lighter-skinned, sicklier, and younger model of Hawaiian womanhood.[73]

While the young princess was away at boarding school in England, the Hawaiian monarchy was overthrown. Kaiʻulani quickly went to America to plead to Congress for the restoration of the monarchy. After her address, the American newspapers wrote nothing about her speech, but a great deal about her good looks. One Washington, D.C., newspaper exclaimed that she was "the very flower—an exotic—of civilization . . . . She is tall, of willowy slenderness, erect and graceful, with a small pale face, full red lips, soft expression, dark eyes, and a good nose." Another newspaper commented: "Her accent says London; her figure says New York; her heart says Hawaiian. She is beautiful."[74]

Because of the constant attention since childhood to the way she looked, Kaiʻulani was obsessed with keeping her weight down. In one letter to a friend, she complained that she was frustrated to be gaining modest amounts of weight; she offered the explanation that "I don't want to be fat, it is so vulgar, you know." Her preoccupation with her weight and beauty were manifested in her fancy for attracting the opposite sex. Kaiʻulani wrote to a friend while in England that "I feel so naughty and I have such a nice flirtation on pour le moment." She later explained that she and her two friends are "about the three biggest flirts you could find, so we simply have a lovely time."[75]

Kaiʻulani was not unaware, however, of the implications of her light-hearted playing and obsession with beauty. When she wrote to her aunt Liliuokalani in hope of stopping an arranged marriage to a Japanese prince, she hinted at knowledge of the confinement and limitations of the

FIGURE 13.2 After Princess Kai'ulani's death in March 1899, the Advertiser wrote of her: "Everyone admired her attitude. They could not do otherwise. Her dignity, her pathetic resignation, her silent sorrow appealed to all. The natives loved her for her quiet, steadfast sympathy with their woe, her uncomplaining endurance of her own. The whites admired her for her stately reserve, her queenly display of all necessary courtesy while holding herself aloof from undue intimacy. It was impossible not to love her . . . " From *Princess Kaiulani*, by Kristin Zambucka (Honolulu: Mana, 1982).

life that lay before her: "I feel it would be wrong if I married a man I did not love. I should be perfectly unhappy and we should not agree and instead of being an example to the married women of today, I should become merely a woman of fashion and most likely a flirt."[76]

Kai'ulani and Ruth illustrate the dilemma faced by Hawaiian women after a century of contact with Westerners. What was once a group of happily ample, assertive, and multidimensional women was now a divided group of unhappy people who had to decide between independence and beauty. Although Ruth was able to assert her power, she was unable to be taken seriously because of her imposing looks. Although Kai'ulani was praised for her beauty, that beauty was the very trait that imprisoned her.

She was unable to be anything more than an exotic flower and a novelty for the West.

Like Tahitian women in the era of exploration, Kai'ulani and Hawaiian women of her appearance were asked to give up a measure of their humanity in order to be looked upon with desire from the perspective of Western males. The Western perception of both Kai'ulani and the Tahitian stereotype was a mix of sexuality and innocence, but not an integrated person of intellect and action. In both cases, the exoticized, eroticized female was condemned to an existence as an escapist fantasy for Western males.

This faint image of a Polynesian woman, as an "exotic flower" of civilization, was appealing to Westerners because she was merely a decoration that could go along with her homeland's landscape. Amid the palm trees and crashing surf lay this unintimidating nymph who existed to serve and to be marveled at by civilized folk. This "good" Hawaiian daughter, this exotic flower, would find a place on the colonialist shelf alongside Pocahontas and Madame Butterfly, as the brown-yet-attractive and obedient daughter of Western expansionism.

Because beauty brought such confinement to Kai'ulani and Hawaiian women like her, as to Tahitian women in stereotype, it might seem easy to choose independence over beauty. However, Princess Ruth illustrates the fact that true independence from Western influence was impossible by the latter part of the nineteenth century. Though she maintained her independence in action, she was psychologically dependent nonetheless.

In the eighteenth century, when the explorers came to Hawai'i, they did not have much influence over the Hawaiians because they had no power over them. As a result, Hawaiian women of that time were unaffected by the explorers' lack of attraction to them.

However, by the time of Ruth and Kai'ulani, Western domination was nearly complete in economic, religious, and social terms. Though Ruth spoke Hawaiian and clung to Hawaiian ways, she was nonetheless influenced by Western attitudes. She was troubled by the fact that she did not fit the West's view of beauty, and so was unable to completely appreciate her independence.

A century of contact had changed the model Hawaiian woman from a mother, lover, and even warrior to a whisper of a woman, a delicate, exotic flower who died of consumption like Kai'ulani at age twenty-two. With Hawaiian womanhood split into two polar opposites by the end of the nineteenth century, the beautiful and meek were deemed the winners, and the more native-looking and assertive were accounted losers. However, the beautiful and meek, like the Tahitian nymphs before them, did not win much except a decorative place on the shelf. They were dehumanized and reduced to cardboard figures.

As the losers, the earlier Hawaiian women and the Ruth prototype were stripped of honor and beauty. However, they managed to salvage more of their character and independence. Expressing themselves strongly and taking charge of their lives, they retained their full humanity and expressed the essence of Hawaiian womanhood: the celebration of their motherhood, leadership, initiative, and sexuality.

It is these two contrasting images—of the strong, assertive Hawaiian woman and the Tahitian temptress, of Ruth and Kai'ulani—that lie at the root of the split presentations of Hawaiian womanhood one encounters in Waikiki today.

NOTES

[1] Brian Fagan, *Clash of Cultures* (New York: W. H. Freeman, 1984), 92.

[2] Jacob Neuman, ed., *French and English Philosophers* (New York: Collier, 1910).

[3] Roger Lonsdale, ed., *Eighteenth Century Verse* (Oxford: Oxford University Press, 1984), 36.

[4] T. F. Thieselton, *Folklore of Women* (Williamstown, Mass.: Dorner House Publications, 1975), 58.

[5] George Robertson, *The Discovery of Tahiti: A Journal of the Second Voyage of H. M. S. Dolphin Round the World Under the Command of Captain Wallis, R.N., in the years 1766, 1767, and 1768*, ed. Hugh Carrington (London: Hakluyt Society, 1948), 148, 215.

[6] Comte Louis-Antoine de Bougainville, *A Voyage Round the World*, trans. Johann Reinhold Forster (London: Royal Academy, 1772), 250–251.

[7] Ibid., 257, 256.

[8] Robertson, *Discovery of Tahiti*, 166, 208.

[9] Ibid., 213.

[10] J. C. Beaglehole, ed., *Voyage of the Resolution and Discovery, 1776-1780* (Cambridge: Cambridge University Press, 1967), excerpt from Samwell's Journal, 1075.

[11] Ibid., 1149.

[12] Ibid., 1309, 946.

[13] Beaglehole, *Voyage of the Resolution and Discovery*, Anderson's Journal, 1366; King's Journal, 611; Cook's Journal, 280; Clerke's Journal, 1320; Samwell's Journal, 1180.

[14] Ibid., Samwell's Journal, 1157.

[15] Ibid., Samwell's Journal, 1166, 1164.

[16] Ibid., Clerke's Journal 1308, 596.

[17] George Vancouver, *Voyage of Discovery to the North Pacific Ocean and Round the World*, ed. John Vancouver (New York: Da Capo Press, 1967), 166, 169. Reprint of the original London 1798 edition.

[18] George Mortimer, *Observations and remarks made during a voyage to the Islands of Teneriffe, Amsterdam, Maria's Island near Van Diemen's Land, Otaheite, Sandwich Islands, Owhyhee, the Fox Islands on the north west coast of America, Tinian, and from thence to Canton in the brig Mercury commanded by John Henry Cox* (New York: Da Capo Press, 1975), 29, 47.

[19] Beaglehole, *Voyage of the Resolution and Discovery*, 1151. This happened on more than one occasion.

[20] Sir Joseph Banks and Sir Joseph Dalton Hooker, *Journal of the Right Hon. Sir Joseph Banks: During Captain Cook's First Voyage in the H. M. S. Endeavour in 1768–71 to Terra del Fuego, Otahite, New Zealand, Australia, the Dutch East Indies, etc.* (New York: Macmillan, 1896), 84.

[21] Beaglehole, *Voyage of the Resolution and Discovery*, 1167–1168.

[22] Ibid., Anderson's Journal, 977–978.

[23] Ibid., Samwell's Journal, 1160.

[24] William Ellis, *A Narrative of a Tour Through Hawaii, or Owhyhee* (Honolulu: Hawaiian Gazette, 1917), 93–94.

[25] Beaglehole, *Voyage of the Resolution and Discovery*, 963.

[26] Ibid., Samwell's Journal, 1165.

[27] Ibid., King's Journal, 625; Clerke's Journal, 1321.

[28] R. T. Gould, *Captain Cook* (London: Gerald Duckworth & Co., 1978), xc. First published 1935.

[29] Beaglehole, *Voyage of the Resolution and Discovery*, Samwell's Journal, 1181.

[30] Ibid., King's Journal, 963.

[31] Ibid., Clerke's Journal, 596.

[32] John Ledyard, *John Ledyard's Journal of Captain Cook's Last Voyage*, ed. James Munford (Corvallis: Oregon State University Press, 1963), 120.

[33] John Courtenay [pseud.], *A Poetical Epistle, Moral and Philosophical, From an Officer at Otaheite. To Lady Gr**v*n*r* (London: T. Evans, 1775), in Fuller Collection, Bishop Museum Library, Honolulu.

[34] [Anonymous], *An Historic Epistle, From Omai to the Queen of Otaheite: Being His Remarks on the English Nation* (London: T. Evans, 1775), in Fuller Collection, Bishop Museum Library, Honolulu.

[35] Ellis, *Narrative of a Tour Through Hawaii*, 17–18.

[36] Ibid., 26, 34.

[37] Sarah Joiner Lyman, *The Lymans of Hilo* (Hilo: Lyman House Memorial Museum, 1979), 29.

[38] Hiram Bingham, *A Residence of Twenty-One Years in the Sandwich Islands* (New York: Sherman Converse, 1848), 67.

[39] Lyman, *Lymans of Hilo*, 45.

[40] Bingham, *Residence of Twenty-One Years*, 81.

[41] C. S. Stewart, *Journal of a residence in the Sandwich Islands during the years 1823, 1824, and 1825* (Honolulu: University of Hawai`i Press, 1970), 88.

[42] Ibid., 133, 94.

[43] Bingham, *Residence of Twenty-One Years*,107.

[44] Ellis, *Narrative of a Tour Through Hawaii*, 294.

[45] Bingham, *Residence of Twenty-One Years*, 86.

[46] Lyman, *Lymans of Hilo*, 110, 63–64.

[47] Ibid., 34.

[48] Bingham, *Residence of Twenty-One Years*, 61.

[49] Amos Starr Cooke and Juliette Montague Cooke, *Amos Starr Cooke and Juliette Montague Cooke: Their Autobiography Gleaned From Their Journals and Letters*, ed. Mary Richards (Honolulu: Daughters of Hawai`i, 1987), 221. Reprint of 1941 edition.

[50] Lyman, *Lymans of Hilo*, 136.

[51] Cooke, *Autobiography*, 122–123, 225, 178.

[52] Bingham, *Residence of Twenty-One Years*, 53; Stewart, *Journal*, 93.

[53] Ellis, *Narrative of a Tour Through Hawaii*, 57, 210; Bingham, *Residence of Twenty-One Years*, 115.

[54] Ellis, *Narrative of a Tour Through Hawaii*, 82.

[55] Stewart, *Journal*, 194–195; Lyman, *Lymans of Hilo*, 91.

[56] Cooke, *Autobiography*, 123.

[57] Bingham, *Residence of Twenty-One Years*, 109.

[58] Lyman, *Lymans of Hilo*, 58, 91; Cooke, *Autobiography*, 179.

[59] Stewart, *Journal*, 164; Bingham, *Residence of Twenty-One Years*, 164, 79.

[60] Bingham, *Residence of Twenty-One Years*, 79.

[61] Ibid., 226.

[62] Stewart, *Journal*, 248; Bingham, *Residence of Twenty-One Years*, 167.

[63] Stewart, *Journal*, 165.

[64] Bingham, *Residence of Twenty-One Years*, 183; Ellis, *Narrative of a Tour Through Hawaii*, 63.

[65] Stewart, *Journal*, 253, 261.

[66] Ibid., 264.

[67] Ibid., 135–137.

[68] Liliuokalani, *Hawaii's Story by Hawaii's Queen* (Rutland, Vt.: Charles E. Tuttle, 1978), 26. Reprint of 1898 edition.

[69] Michelle Bodner, *Princess Ruth* (Honolulu: University of Hawai`i Press, 1982), 102.

[70] Ibid., 36, 126.

[71] Ibid., 54.

72 Ibid., 77, 44.
73 Kristin Zambucka, *Princess Kaiulani* (Honolulu: Mana, 1982), 12.
74 Ibid., 104.
75 Ibid., 97, 95.
76 Ibid., 88.

CHAPTER 14

Pacific Island Women and White Feminism

Haunani-Kay Trask

Pacific Island women, like Hawaiian women, seek a collective self-determination. That is to say, we want to achieve sovereignty through and with our own people, not separated from them as individuals or as splintered groups. Such individualism and separation promise only more confusion and more alienation, the very maladies which so afflict industrial peoples.

Our culture of sharing with the larger family group mitigates against the development of those self-centered and self-motivated values required of capitalism. Hawaiians hold other cultural values more dear: affection, generosity, traditional group activities like fishing and dancing, and, perhaps most telling of all, gathering together to share work, play, grief, and love. Tragically, we are imprisoned in a dominant culture that values and rewards unceasing work, accumulation of things, and calculation of every dollar, every child, even of every smile.

Therefore, self-determination for us means self-determination within our own cultural definitions and though our own cultural ways. Being Hawaiian-hyphen-Americans is not our life's purpose. We are not immigrants seeking a better life. The best life Hawaiians ever enjoyed existed long ago, before the coming of white people to our land. For Native people, forced assimilation and acculturation are nothing less than racism and, in extreme cases, genocide. Sovereignty, for us, promises the institutional and psychological opposite of racism. Sovereignty is the assertion that _what we are_—culturally, emotionally, and physically—is _what we prefer to be._

Secondly, our efforts at collective self-determination mean that we find solidarity with our own people, including our own men, more likely, indeed preferable, to solidarity with white people, including feminists. Struggle with our men occurs laterally, across and within our movement.

This essay was originally published in _From a Native Daughter,_ by Haunani-Kay Trask (Monroe, Me.: Common Courage Press, 1993), 263–276.

254   **Haunani-Kay Trask**

It does not occur vertically between the white women's movement and indigenous women on one side and white men and Hawaiian men on the other side.

We have more in common, both in struggle and in controversy, with our men and with each other as indigenous women than we do with white people, called *haole* in Hawaiian. This is only to make the familiar point that culture is a larger reality than "women's rights."

It is imperative to understand that for us, *haole* Americans are the interlopers in Hawai'i, whether they happen to be feminists or Marxists or capitalists or California New Agers. In their presence, we feel vast differences in heritage and in values. Between Hawaiians and the *haole*, the cultural lines are drawn deep and fast across two hundred years of history. At this point in our struggle, race and culture are stronger forces than sex and gender. We will make common cause with our own people, and with other Native peoples, before we make common cause with non-Natives in our lands.

I have arrived at this political strategy after years of failed alliances with *haole*, including *haole* feminists. In Hawai'i, as in so many parts of the island Pacific, *haole* feminists have steadfastly refused to support our efforts to regain our lands, to protect our civil rights, and to achieve self- government. They have defined what is "feminist" as that which relates to women, and only to women: for example, reproductive rights, women's health problems, employment, and educational concerns.

But to most Native people, women's concerns are part of the greater concern for our *lahui*, our nation. For example, we see our lack of control over our bodies as a result of colonialism. Therefore, poor Hawaiian health is directly traceable to Americanization of our country, including loss of our lands where we once grew healthful Native food. High breast cancer rates for our women are similarly related to our forced assimilation into the junk-food, supermarket, American diet. In specific cases like these, our problems—such as high infant mortality, oppressive working conditions, and low wages—relate to our loss of self-government and the subsequent loss of control over our lives.

But *haole* feminists don't see the causal connection between our life conditions and our status as colonized people. Their failure of vision is a result of their privilege as white Americans. In Hawai'i, they see the oppression of women but they refuse to see the oppression of Hawaiian women as a product of colonialism. To grasp the nature of our oppression requires an understanding that *haole*—feminists and Marxists included—are part of the colonial forces. In fact, *haole* in Hawai'i benefit from American colonialism here just as French people in Tahiti benefit from

French control and the domination of French culture in Tahiti. *The very existence of colonials in the colonies is an indication of their privilege.* Of course, this truth is usually met with strong resistance since, to most Americans, the United States is not a predatory country: It has no colonies. By birth and ideology, the United States is "democratic." Translated: The United States was not created out of stolen Native land, but was constituted by a Christian god or by history, or both, and thus "belongs" to Americans. Through unconscious extension, then, Hawai'i is just another part of the United States and, like the rest of the Americas, is without a history of conquest, of Native dispossession, suffering, and disenfranchisement. Thus, Americans in Hawai'i, including *haole* feminists, assert their ignorance of where they live, where Hawai'i is (i.e., in Polynesia and not off the coast of California), and how they themselves contribute to our oppression.

It is a brief step from this kind of arrogance to the unquestioned belief that *haole*-defined feminist concerns are the same for all women in Hawai'i, indigenous and foreign alike. Predictably, then, *haole* feminists assume we as Native women agree with their identification of what constitutes feminism. Worse, we must see our own concerns—such as land and sovereignty—as clearly secondary to so-called "women's issues."

But why is land, our mother, not a woman's issue? The answer, almost too obviously, is that Hawaiian land—this land that all of us in Hawai'i enjoy— is *not* the mother of *haole* feminists, since *haole* are *not* born of this land. Thus do history (and genealogy) separate our politics—and our analysis.

For other Natives, this chasm between white and Native is familiar; it is the very core of the colonial struggle. *Haole* who are feminist or Marxist continue to display an appalling imperialism grounded in a fundamental, unquestioned racism that views Native history, culture, and ways of life as inferior to white Western history, culture, and ways of life. This attitude of assumed superiority is like the air white people breathe: an envelope of security that is crucial to their survival. Patronizing in their life stance toward Native peoples in general, *haole* come to Hawai'i swathed in their own colonial assumptions. Given this, it is not surprising that our indigenous movement for land and self-government has few *haole* supporters. After all, what concerns white women of the ruling culture is rarely the same as what concerns Native women in colonized cultures.

Donna Awatere, Maori nationalist, argues as follows:

> The first loyalty of white women is always to the White Culture and the White Way. This is true as much for those who define themselves as

feminists as for any other white woman. This loyalty is seen in their rejection of the sovereignty of Maori people and in their acceptance of the imposition of the British culture on the Maori. This is to be expected as the oppressor avoids confronting the role they play in oppressing others. White feminists do this by defining "feminism" for this country [New Zealand] and by using their white power, status and privilege to ensure that their definition of "feminism" supersedes that of Maori women."[1]

In Hawai'i, the arrogance Awatere insightfully describes causes the failure of many coalitions (and potential coalitions). Since *haole* insist we follow their lead, many of our women, including myself, choose not to work in such a racist context. We set our own agendas, namely, the goal of nationhood on an independent land base. *Haole* who want coalitions with us must first come to an understanding of their place as beneficiaries of our dispossession and their obligation to support our drive for sovereignty. They must first educate themselves about our colonial history and the benefits they have received—and continue to receive—as a result of that history. Only then can *haole* actually help our struggle.

The divergent path of most Native movements in the Pacific away from *haole* issues confirms the truth of this analysis. In my political experience, self-determination for the Hawaiian people has never been a central goal for *haole,* whether they identify with feminism, Marxism, or some other ideology. Even those *haole* who theoretically support Native self-determination don't lend their organizing skills, money, or time to our struggle. As in life, so in politics: Actions speak more clearly than words.

This does not mean *haole,* including feminists, have no role to play in our larger struggle for self-determination. Their place is to support our efforts publicly, to form anti-racist groups that address our people's oppression through institutional channels, and to speak in our defense when we are attacked by white people.

This last function is crucial. Native people should never answer arrogant *haole* who charge us with racism because we want to re-establish a separate land base and a separate government. It is the duty of sympathetic whites to address their own racist people. Those *haole* who accept this role are more than welcome but the time has long passed when we will adopt somebody else's political model for our struggle, including our path toward nationhood.

THE HAWAIIAN EXAMPLE

Imagine our lives. We are 20 percent of a population overwhelmingly Asian and white. This means we are strangers in our own land. The economic, social, and political institutions, language, land tenure, transport, and communication systems that presently dominate Hawai'i are all of American origin. Indeed, Hawai'i's ownership by the United States has been an American assumption for so long that Americans are shocked to learn we Native nationalists view the United States as a *foreign* country illegally and immorally occupying our lands. Of course, these feelings are not unlike those that other Native peoples—such as Palestinians and Northern Irish—express toward non-Natives who occupy their lands. Few Americans know or care that Hawai'i was invaded by the American military in 1893, our legally formed government was overthrown, and our islands were forcibly annexed to the United States in 1898 against the wishes of the Hawaiian people. Since then, our ancestral lands have been continuously occupied by a foreign country and its military.

Now, we are trying desperately to preserve and transmit what is left of our language, our dance, and our religion. We are fighting on every island to stop resort development, missile-launching facilities, and the paving over of entire valleys with wealthy homes for the world's rich. We are protesting the biggest presence of the American military anywhere in the world. In the meantime, our people fill up the prisons and unemployment lists, or give up Hawai'i altogether for life as the wandering dispossessed.

There is a fearful, crazy quality to our lives. At one and the same time, we teach traditional dance to our children, only to watch it degraded into tourist exotica; we stop one hotel only to learn that the land in dispute is zoned for another hotel a few years down the road; we assert our religion, asking the American courts to protect our volcano god, Pele, from development, only to learn the government has plans to drill massive geothermal wells deep into her breast. We practice our religion by opening the Makahiki season—a period of four months in honor of the fertility god, Lono—on an island so devastated by American military bombing it resembles a desert.

While all this goes on, we are surrounded, everywhere, by millions of tourists, nearly seven million by 1993, or thirty tourists for every Hawaiian. This inundation translates into daily horror: As we go to a *heiau* (temple) to worship, there are tourists making noise, leaving rubbish on the sacred stones, clicking cameras. Our beaches, once open and free to everyone, are now shoulder to shoulder with tourists demanding the shoreline for themselves. Crime has soared as a direct result of a tourist economy; our lands are scarred with hotels, curio shops, golf courses, marinas, fast-food outlets, gas stations, and freeways. And finally, in a personally humiliating way, our women, including myself, are "Native artifacts," besieged by tourists constantly preying upon us and our culture.[2]

This is the horror of the third stage of colonialism, in which a culture has been so thoroughly penetrated by commercialism that Native people become exotic ornaments for the First World. Beyond the problems of tourism and cultural degradation, the whole question of territorial control in Hawai'i is further evidence of the complexity and depth of our colonization. The myths of democracy and Americanization as beneficial to Native Hawaiians have meant a Native population in the thrall of America. Decolonization must then shift from a primary focus on the mind of the colonized to a dual focus on re-invigoration of the Native culture, with its protective land ethic and accompanying spiritual ethic, and an emphasis on political analysis of the colonial situation.

Since the modern Hawaiian Movement began in 1970, land struggles have seemed, to many Hawaiians, a separate issue from cultural revival. Part of the reason for this is simply that those being evicted from lands or occupying military lands in protest of their use were not the same people striving to teach our ancient dance, create language immersion schools for children, or save historic sites from demolition. This distance actually reflects another problem, namely, the necessity for an evolution from cultural pride as Native Hawaiians to political resistance as Native nationalists. The first state is a precursor to the second. But the current problem for us Native nationalists is how to move our people from pride to resistance.

It is not simply that resistance increases the emotional and economic risks of an already burdened group but that the layers of colonization are so deep, the number of Hawaiians so small, and the opposing forces so overwhelming. We also have to contend with a public image that is far from sympathetic. Still, after more than twenty years of struggles the lessons are clear. Cultural revitalization without national consciousness sidetracks decolonization and maintains a large distance between cultural people and political people.

The dangers of such distance among our ranks are many. Tourism, like capitalism in general, thrives on anything that can increase profits. More authentic cultural rituals are easy prey to commodification, especially when so many of the Native people are already under the thumb of tourism as workers.

Secondly, the American myth of pluralism approves of ethnic diversity as long as it remains apolitical. In other words, traditional *hula*, Hawaiian language schools, and Hawaiian religion do not threaten American ideological hegemony unless they are attached to a Hawaiian national consciousness rather than an American national consciousness.

Thirdly, land struggles without a governmental base are not national struggles and are, therefore, played out within the parameters of civil rights actions. The issue of indigenous claims is stillborn. Meanwhile, Marxists, white feminists, and liberals agitate against Native national consciousness by arguing that it is exclusionary; it is unfair (in the sense of anti-democratic); it is racist; and it is strategically unwise since, as the *haole* tell me daily, "You need all the help you can get."

In reality, the attitude of most Marxists and socialists is the same as that of white feminists and liberals on many issues. Few members of these groups are willing to question their presence on our lands or to learn our history, especially the periods that involve the illegal and immoral actions of the American government. They all assume a similarity among the cultures of Native peoples everywhere, a similarity that conveniently excuses these foreigners from educating themselves about the particular place where they are living, including the Native people who have been dispossessed by foreigners to make way for foreigners. Marxists see class, not culture; white feminists see women, not people; and liberals see only individuals and individualism. None of these groups understand Native nations, despite the presence of over three hundred in the United States; and all of these groups unthinkingly assume white culture as the unquestioned context within which political change will occur. When we Native nationalists bring up Hawaiian culture and its inseparability from our people and our place, we are criticized for being romantic by the Marxists, for being racist by the liberals, and for being trapped in the patriotism of Western-style patriarchal nationalism by the feminists.

To my mind, what all these positions have in common is the belief that culture is irrelevant; not white culture, just Native culture. Such disregard for our culture in our own land recalls missionary imperialism in Hawai'i in the nineteenth century. Then, Hawaiians were bombarded by white people who fervently believed that Hawaiian culture was an impediment to the salvation of the soul. Today, Marxists believe Hawaiian culture is an impediment to evolution and revolution; liberals believe it is an impediment to full civil rights; and white feminists believe it is an impediment to women's liberation. The similarities with missionaries are striking.[3]

The main problem for our Movement now is the lack of connection between cultural and political actions. I see this as a strategy question more than a theoretical problem, and I don't think it is insurmountable given that in the last few years cultural leaders have begun saying publicly that they are nationalists. At the same time, political people have begun to see cultural revival as more central to psychological decolonization than they once believed. Apparently, the simple passage of time has allowed all of us in the Movement to understand how culture and politics work together in strengthening our people's identification as a *people*. The depth of this identification is often a measure of the level of decolonization. Put bluntly, the more Hawaiians identify as Hawaiians, the less they are able to live with their identity as Americans and thus, with American ownership of their birthright, Hawai'i.

Indeed, the whole area of decolonizing the mind is very delicate. Language, for example, is a critical decolonizer. Thinking in Hawaiian means, at the least, thinking in the language of the land and the culture. Even without political analysis, Hawaiians who are familiar with their Native tongue are already thinking about things Hawaiian. They are more receptive to a Native nationalist argument because the language explains our commonalities as a people, that is, as a nation.[4]

The same thing can be said for Hawaiians who know their history. Understanding the wisdom of the Hawaiian way on the land, and the rapid destruction of this way by the West, also makes for more receptivity to the choice of Native control and Native governance, that is, to the choice of Native nationalism.

Still, decolonization works in stages, and every place is unique in this respect. Hawai'i's uniqueness is as the most colonized place in the Pacific. We have the most to fight against—for example, military saturation—and we are a minority in our own land. Unlike the Maori, our islands are not territorially independent from the original colonial power. Unlike the Samoans, we do not control our islands, the bulk of which are held by the State of Hawai'i, the federal government, and a dozen or so major multinational corporations. Unlike the Tahitians, the vast majority of our people do not speak their Native language. And our trust lands (like American Indian reservations, but without recognition of our nationhood) are controlled by the state and federal governments, which lease our lands to non-Natives.[5]

On an ideological level, we are more integrated into popular culture, especially television and film, than other Pacific Islanders. Popular culture alone is a tremendously powerful agent of colonization. Decolonizing young minds addicted to television and worse seems impossible without an alternative. This is where Hawaiian culture plays a significant role. It instills pride; it takes young minds away from colonizing situations by providing physical and intellectual alternatives; and it opens up mental space for political analysis, otherwise they develop separately and culture becomes an apolitical refuge from the colonial world. The potential for resistance is thus lost at the point of divergence, something Marxists fail to see because they are blind to the significance of culture in decolonization. In the end, of course, decolonization is a long, generational process that can terminate at any plateau without bearing the fruit of Native national consciousness. Our only recourse is eternal vigilance, and the recruitment of young Hawaiians into the nationalist movement.

Self-determination for Pacific Islander women is expressed within the parameters of colonialism, as part of the broader economic and political context of their unique island histories. Thus, what Pacific Island women contribute to their particular struggle for independence depends primarily on their cultural heritage and their colonial histories rather than on feminist movements in the colonial nations. In the end, what Pacific Island women do will be different because the Pacific islands are not the First World, nor are Pacific Island women First World women.

NOTES

[1] Donna Awatere, *Maori Sovereignty* (Auckland, N.Z.: Broadsheet, 1984), 42.

[2] For a discussion of Hawai'i state policy on the rapid expansion of the tourist industry and its crucial influence on in-migration and population growth, see Nordyke 1989, p. 134–172. For a statistical picture of the kinds of tourists who visit Hawai'i and how much they spend, see the Bank of Hawaii's annual economic report. The 1990 report notes that 4.3 million tourists originated in the United States while 2.4 million originated in foreign countries (Bank of Hawaii 1990). The Japanese, who comprise about 1.3 million visitors annually, spend nearly 4.5 times what U.S. visitors spend. This explains why so many signs in major resort areas are written in Japanese as well as in English, and why so much propaganda in Hawai'i is focused on welcoming Japanese tourists. For examples of the socioeconomic and environmental problems resulting from corporate tourism, see *Hawai'i Business,* April 1985; Matsuoka and Kelly 1988; and Stannard 1986.

[3] For a lengthy exploration of the distance between Marxism and Marxist analysis and Native American analysis, see Churchill 1983.

[4] For a thoughtful work on the link between the use of Native languages and decolonization, see Thiongo 1986.

[5] See "Faces of the Nation" (1988), a video produced by Nā Maka o Ka 'Āina for Ka Lāhui Hawai'i, a Native Hawaiian initiative for self-governance. The video explains the historical theft of Hawaiian sovereignty and the contemporary push for Native nationhood. Available from the Center for Hawaiian Studies, University of Hawai'i, or at www.namaka.com.

CHAPTER 15

The Māhū of Hawai'i

Carolina E. Robertson

When the lights dimmed in the Waikiki Shell on September 21, 1987, an audience of thousands rose to its feet to cheer the memory of *kumu hula* (master
teacher) Darrell Lupenui. Hawaiians filled the lawn of Honolulu's outdoor
concert arena in a tribute to one of the great creative forces in the Hawaiian
renaissance movement. I was aware that we also were mourning the death of
a prominent and respected *māhū*—a person of mixed gender who had found
sanctuary in the domain of Laka, god/goddess of the ancient hula.

    Māhū from the full continuum of gender variation and from every
island of Hawai'i participated in Lupenui's memorial concert, both as
members of the audience and as chanters and dancers. Some of them
wore dog-tooth necklaces and silk tunics. Others sported jeans, T-shirts,
and stacks of flower leis that they gave away to friends and family in one
of the oldest gestures of *aloha*. *Māhū* with children along translated some
of the dance gestures and Hawaiian words for them.

    Like the great musician they were honoring, these *māhū* embody an
ancient Polynesian principle of spiritual duality and integration. The
outer presentation of the *māhū* is usually female, even when the person is
biologically male. In *Women of Polynesia,* Tui Terence Barrow describes the
māhū as an "intermediate sex":

> Sex is to the Polynesians a very down-to-earth thing which need not be too
> much thought about and is certainly not repressed. Sometimes Mother
> Nature cannot make up her mind whether to make a man or a woman,
> even in Polynesia, so she mixes up a little of the male with some of the
> female element. In Polynesia transvestites in whom the male and female
> are not clearly differentiated, either at the physical or psychic level are
> called the *māhū* who, although physically speaking more men than
> women, prefer to dress and act as women.[1]

This essay was previously published in *Feminist Studies* 15, no. 2 (1989): 312–322.

Transvestism is but one aspect of the *māhū* phenomenon, which defies reduction to any of the notions of gender familiar to us in the West.[2] I have, for example, met several women who were raised as boys by their parents or grandparents. Mary Kawena Pūku'i has also documented cases in which girls were raised as boys to keep them free of sexual liaisons with men.[3] In earlier days, these girls would have been considered *kapu* (taboo), and they would have been chosen for some special task, possibly associated with healing or with the performance of sacred *hula*. Several elderly men have told me that, after begetting many sons and no daughters, their parents decided to raise their youngest boy as a girl. In this way they sought to provide additional labor for women's tasks and insure a creative presence that otherwise might not have emerged in the imbalance of a homocentric household. This practice seems to date back to ancient times.

Pūku'i notes an account by David Malo of a hermaphrodite, or physically bisexual person, born during the time of Pa'ao, an important high priest and religious revisionist of ancient Hawai'i. La'a-kapu, wife of a ruling chief of the island of Hawai'i, gave birth to a child of indeterminate sex, whom she named Ka-uhola-nui-a-māhū.[4] This name could be interpreted on many levels, as is the case with all Hawaiian words. One possible translation would be "the great unfolding of the *māhū*." *Uhola* means the kind of unfolding associated with receptivity, or the opening of the mind. This interpretation is consistent with another version of the origins of the *māhū*. "The hermaphrodites—also referred to as *māhū*—said to have landed at Waikiki were respected men, talented priests of healing and the *hula*. Whether this is history or legend, it reflects attitudes of approval and admiration. Hawaiians always knew we had in us something feminine and masculine."[5]

The *māhū* population today embraces an astounding variety of individuals. It can designate women who dress and work as men, men who dress and work as women, women or men who dress and act so as to obscure their biological classification, women who will only associate with other women, men who dress "festively," men who undergo hormone treatments and/or eventually change their sex surgically, true hermaphrodites, and women and men who might, in English, call themselves "gay." Any of these people may choose to procreate or to raise children through the traditional adoption arrangement known as *hanai*. In fact, parents sometimes put their children in the care of *māhū*, for mixed gender individuals are recognized as special, compassionate, and creative.

Because the *māhū* embody the synthesis of the female/male principle in Hawaiian culture and cosmology, they have been intimately associated with the Hawaiian renaissance movement and the revival of the ancient *hula* tradition. As noted earlier, the deity Laka oversees the *hula* and is perceived by some practitioners as female and by others as a deity of mixed gender. Although men danced in the *hula* of ancient times, missionaries taught that dancing was unseemly and especially inappropriate for true males. Consequently, this tradition was handed down primarily through women and *māhū* and, until the Hawaiian cultural renaissance of the 1970s, was associated with femaleness. However, dancers who trained under some of the great teachers of this century—Henry Pa, Edith Kanaka'ole, Ma'ika Aiu Lake—see the *hula* as an androgynous tradition. "Gender," as we might see it in the dance, is determined by the spiritual and aesthetic identity of the dancer. Thus, the same chant danced by a *wahine* (woman) would flow through her own energy; danced by a *kāne* (man) it would carry his own stamp; and danced by a *māhū* it would fuse *wahine* and *kāne*, probably favoring the female side because of the emphasis on fluidity and grace. Female *māhū* presenting themselves as men are the only segment of this population which has not been active in the world of *hula* performance.

Drawings and etchings made of *hula* dancers by eighteenth-century Europeans often portray the dancer as androgynous.

Through a sequence of unrelated historical circumstances, the subtly defined gender identification of Hawai'i's precontact women and men underwent radical transformations. After the 1819 death of Kamehameha I, who was responsible for the unification of the Hawaiian islands, his widow, the powerful Queen Ka'ahumanu, abolished the old *kapu* system that was so repressive to women and commoners, championing the right of women to communicate directly with the gods. In 1820, exactly one year after Ka'ahumanu had most of the old male temples destroyed, Calvinist missionaries arrived on Hawaiian shores, bringing their own laws and *kapu* system. By the mid-nineteenth century, the missionaries had successfully imposed a "breast *kapu*" and had further undermined *hula* dancing by discouraging anyone from participating. Calvinist notions of propriety established the "overdressed" style. In the course of the nineteenth century, then, *hula* was at the same time feminized and largely pushed underground because its spiritual or "pagan" content was censored by the missionaries.

Although male dancers today often shed their Victorian layers and dance in the bare-chested *pa'u* of old Hawai'i, women continue to observe the breast *kapu* of their invaders, replacing the "overdressing" of the missionary age with the *mu'u mu'u*.

Some of the sacred *hula* chants and dances, especially the *mele ma'i*, which represent and encourage procreation, have been handed down in a "*hula* underground." Most of the practitioners in this arena have been women and *māhū*. Family chants and hula gestures are often transmitted from grandmother to granddaughter or through prominent *māhū* in a lineage of dancers. Many *māhū* have a special link to the past that is manifested even in their physical presence. Many of those *māhū* whose presentation of self defies gender classification are characterized by a corpulence that harks back to times of old, when massiveness in both women and men was equated with high status. Marshall Sahlins reminds us that in old Hawai'i the aesthetic of the *māhū* physique was rooted in the royal visage:

> The ideal beauty of the chief is counterpart of his or her ideal potency. The high chief is 'divine,' as we should say ourselves: huge, fattened, skin lightened by protection from the sun, body glistening with perfumed oil, bedecked in the dazzling feather cape that is the treasure of his kingdom. And why not generate a kingdom on such a fundament? Existing only in the eye of the beholder, beauty is necessarily a social relationship . . . in Hawaii, beauty is placed as it were at the center of society, as a main principle of its organization."[6]

Chiefess Nomahanna stood six feet and two inches tall and measured about forty-five inches around the waist. Royal women were often fattened through a combination of forced feeding and *lomi-lomi* (massage), for their girth was directly related to their status and power. According to Barrow, Tahitian chiefesses were often sent to "fat farms" where they could increase their size, rest, and socialize while protected from the harsh sun.

Many contemporary Hawaiians who follow the older ways through spiritual healing, ritual leadership, and *hula* retain the aesthetic of precontact Hawai'i. John Ka'imikaua, who worked closely with Darrell Lupenui, has been one of the leaders of the Hawaiian spirituality movement.

Most *māhū* of great size are involved in the hula tradition as *kumu:* teachers, drummers, and chanters. Their girth, with weight often exceeding 500 pounds, is part of their beauty and *mana* or spiritual power. These androgynous individuals stand in the community as a metaphor for the balance of female and male throughout Creation.

Sadly, corpulence presents many dangers in the modern, urban context of Hawai'i. Darrell Lupenui, who in his thirty-six years of life influenced all his peers and many of his elders, was brought to his death by the kidney and heart complications occasioned by the seven hundred pounds he carried as both a gift and a burden. His life dramatized the complexities and the richness of the *māhū* role in Polynesian cultures.

Today, the ancient war temples lie in ruins, replaced by Pearl Harbor and the missiles of Kaho'olawe. Yet many Hawaiians continue to bring gifts of flowers and food to the gods that linger in ancient sacred sites. The guardianship of Mo'okini *luakini,* one of the few restored temples on the island of Hawai'i, has passed to a woman, Auntie Leimomi Mo'okini Lum.[7] On the northern coast of Kaua'i, *hula* devotees leave offerings on the altar of Laka. During the year, *hula* schools make their pilgrimage to this *heiau* to dedicate new students to the patron deity of the dance. These rituals come alive in the ever-changing web of gender and spirituality, bearing witness to the belief systems that have allowed the *māhū* to survive and flourish in the creative context of performance.

NOTES

[1] Tui Terrence Barrow, *Women of Polynesia* (Wellington, N.Z.: Seven Seas, 1967), 76.

[2] The reader might note a certain linguistic awkwardness in the present article and the sources quoted. This reflects the limitations of our English vocabulary in a discussion of gender variation and the linguistic necessity of assigning a polarized female or male identity to every person. In Hawaiian, by contrast, there are not female/male adjectives or articles, and proper names are also androgynous. In speaking of female or male gods, Hawaiians emphasize the integration and balance of both energies. The notion of gendered polarity or opposition is foreign to their thinking.

[3] Mary Kawena Pūku'i, E. W. Haertig, and Catherine Lee, *Nānā I Ke Kumu* (*Look to the Source*), v. 2 (Honolulu: Hui Hānai, 1972), 113.

[4] Ibid., 108-109.

[5] Ibid., 110.

[6] Marshall Sahlins, *Islands of History* (Chicago: University of Chicago Press, 1985), 17.

[7] "Auntie" and "Uncle" are terms of respect. Many male *māhū hula* teachers, especially on the more traditional island of Moloka'i, are addressed as "Auntie."

PART FIVE
Social Problems and Responses

Part Five turns to consideration of social problems, social services, and healthcare needs of Pacific Islander Americans. In "Family Dynamics Among Pacific Islander Americans," a team of scholars headed by Diana Fitisemanu presents analysis based on interviews with Fijian, I-kiribati, Tongan, and Samoan family members in Hawai'i. They describe the various meanings of family among Pacific Islander Americans, the structure of power in their families, and the ways that caring is expressed. They offer a controversial interpretation of the place of physical discipline in islander families: They suggest that corporal punishment among Pacific Islander Americans is experienced primarily as a form of caring, not of abuse, as it is often construed by other sorts of people in American society.

In "Historical and Cultural Aspects of Native Hawaiian Health," Kekuni Blaisdell describes the traditional culture of healthcare among Hawaiians and the impact of European and American concepts and practices to the detriment of Hawaiian health. He then calls for a return to ancient ways.

E. Victoria Shook gives "An Introduction to the Practice of Ho'oponopono," a communally based mode of conflict resolution among Hawaiians. She places it in the context of fundamental Hawaiian values and community structures, and suggests it can be used fruitfully to solve a wide variety of social conflicts among Hawaiians. Debbie Hippolite Wright builds on such a perspective in "Pacific Islander Modes for Dealing with Sexual Abuse." She notes a high incidence of sexual abuse and related behaviors among Maori in New Zealand. After detailing the patterns in such abuse, she describes the Koru model of healing based on traditional Maori values and communal resources.

CHAPTER 16

Family Dynamics among Pacific Islander Americans

Diana Fitisemanu, Karina Kahananui Green, David Hall,
Debbie Hippolite Wright, Brucetta McKenzie, Dorri Nautu,
and Paul Spickard

A television news program not long ago showed images of a Samoan family in California. A neighbor saw large numbers of people entering the family's home, heard a "great deal of noise," and called the police, saying something suspicious was going on next door. Police arrived on the scene, surrounded the house, and confronted the Samoan family. With a police helicopter beating the air overhead, the officers frisked men and women, young and old. It was never clear to observers what they were looking for, but gradually it became clear to the police what they had found.

They had found a birthday party. The Samoan household's baby was one year old, and, since they were loving and respectful people, they had invited all the members of their extended family to come share in the auspicious occasion. The joyous event included singing and dancing, which triggered the neighbor's complaint. The police were embarrassed by their mistake. The party-goers were bewildered and intimidated at the treatment they had received.

Pacific Islander American families are not much understood by non-Pacific Islanders. It may be partly because they are not much studied. This is a first foray into that large, almost uncharted territory: the family among Pacific Islander Americans. It was undertaken by the Pacific Islander Americans Research Project, a student-faculty research unit sponsored by the Institute for Polynesian Studies and the Division of Social Sciences at Brigham Young University-Hawai'i. The interviewers comprised four women and a man, all Pacific Islanders and all students at BYU-Hawai'i.

This essay was previously published in *Social Process in Hawai'i* 36 (1994): 26–40.

They interviewed forty-one people in fall 1992 and winter 1993, all Pacific Islanders in their twenties and thirties, and all students at BYU-Hawai'i. Twenty of the interviewed people were men, twenty-one were women. Sixteen were Tongan, seven Fijian, five I-kiribati, and thirteen Samoan. All spoke about their families of origin—the households in which they grew up, generally in their countries of origin although sometimes in the United States.

The four Pacific Island peoples represented by the interviewees— Samoans, I-kiribati, Fijians, and Tongans—come from widely separated parts of the Pacific. Physically they do not resemble each other: Samoans and Tongans are Polynesians, I-kiribati are Micronesians, and Fijians are Melanesians. Linguistically and in most aspects of culture they are quite distinct. Yet with respect to family structure and dynamics, the people interviewed in this study exhibited remarkable similarities. Except as noted, their families' attributes were similar enough that it was decided to describe them together in this article.

THE MEANING OF "FAMILY"

The people interviewed had two definitions of "family." One, which they frequently offered when they were asked to respond to the English term, had to do with what many people would understand as the nuclear family: father, mother, and children, all living under one roof. A Tongan man said, "I think of my own family: my brothers, sisters, my parents, my home." Intertwined with that definition, however, was the imperative of respect. The man went on: "When I hear the word family, I think of respect and unity . . . . In Tonga we are very family-oriented and everyone is, it's a part of our culture that we respect our parents truly."

When the interviewers asked people the word for "family" in their native tongue, each had a quick response. For some Tongans, it was *famili*, a term borrowed from English. But most of them also recognized *kainga*, which also included, as one said, "The extended family and cousins, uncles, aunts, grandma, granddad." The Samoan word, *aiga*, is linguistically related to *kainga*, and carries the idea of going back five generations and including all collateral kin under an umbrella that large. The Fijian word for this extended family is *matavuvale*. In Kiribati, it is *te utu*.

Both these conceptions of family operated in the minds and lives of the Pacific Islanders interviewed. Most people had associations with the word "family" that had to do with the larger entity. A male Tongan defined his close family as "My cousins, my grandparents, my family, even down to second cousins. Anyone who is related . . . cousins, uncles, and grandparents . . . . My uncles and aunties are like mothers and fathers. My cousins are just like brothers." Sometimes the idea of the extended family conjured up associations that were warm and social. "A lot of kids, happy, togetherness with the family, big feast," said one woman. "Love, picnics, beach . . . . To go out and do the work together, have fun together," said a man.

Frequently the people interviewed spoke of the sense of belonging and joy felt when all the extended family gathered to mark a significant milestone, such as the baby's first birthday party described at the beginning of this paper. Other occasions included births, deaths, weddings, graduations, and coming-of-age-ceremonies. All branches of the family chipped in to pay for such occasions. One Tongan man said, "When there's a family occasion such as a funeral or birthdays or any party . . . everyone is helped out, even if . . . you are already married and have your own family, you still come and support and help pay for all expenses." One person spoke of getting together with her extended family at Christmas and holidays for about three weeks at a time, to have fun together.

In other instances, people associated the extended family with more formal occasions that had to do with decisions affecting the whole group. One person said, "Our tribe will come together and discuss about . . . money given by the government . . . . If there is a disagreement . . . it is brought to our grandfathers . . . [who] would be listening . . . and then solve the problem."

Frequently, though individuals understood and valued this large family ideal, in practical fact most of their lives were organized around their nuclear families. Although they spoke of their families as extended entities and recalled large family occasions with fondness, almost every time they were asked about actual decision-making, discipline, and expressions of love, they zeroed in on the nuclear family as the unit of action. Frequently they would say, "My father . . . " or "My sister . . . " Seldom did they speak about aunts or cousins unless prodded by the interviewer.

It seems clear that Pacific Islanders value both the extended and the nuclear family. A commitment of loyalty, obligation, and support to both groups is crucial to the Pacific Islander American way of family.

THE STRUCTURE OF POWER

The respondents were unanimous in describing male-dominated families. Fathers made the final decisions on all significant issues. A Kiribati woman said, "The father is the head of the family . . . . He's the boss. Even though my Mom disagrees, she has to go along." A Fijian said, "Usually my Dad made the important decisions. He may let us think about the decision, but usually he is the one who decides." The mother frequently was accorded some input, often taking the role of intermediary to express the opinions of other family members before the father did the final deciding. A Tongan woman said, "My Dad makes all the decisions . . . . [M]y Mom . . . suggests softly and then my Dad will say yes or no." A Tongan man said, "My Dad is the head of the family, he makes the decisions. But Mum also has a say in making decisions . . . . [She] suggests, but it all comes down to the father."

Out of respect, the children obey. Sometimes obedience means a serious change in their life plans. One Tongan woman recalled, "When I finished high school I didn't want to go on my mission [a Mormon custom, involving two years' service abroad for a man, a year and a half for a woman]. Then my father forced me to go on a mission, so I had to go and I didn't have any decision in the matter. My father made the decision for me to go."

With respect to the question of the relative importance of the extended and nuclear families, it is perhaps worthy of note that almost all of the examples that the respondents gave of such decision-making took place within the nuclear family. A few spoke of times when aunties or uncles broke into nuclear family decision-making. But in the vast majority of cases, the parents, and specifically the father, made decisions. They were not referred to some larger extended family council or clan leader.

Sometimes older siblings, brothers in particular, felt themselves deputized to take on the decision-making role. One Tongan said, "I'm considered one of the older ones in the family, so I can tell the younger cousins or brothers what to do. [When] the father's not around, the mother [makes the decisions. If] the mother's not around, the next oldest." Another said, "I'm their teacher. I look after the younger ones."

EXPRESSION OF CARING

To a person, the people interviewed described their families as loving ones where a great deal of caring was expressed. But they said that caring was seldom expressed in words. A Samoan man said, "There's not such thing as 'I love you,' or 'I feel for you.' There's none of them. It's expressed through Christmas and birthday presents. There is no verbal expression. I couldn't even say 'I love you Dad' or 'I love you Mom.'" A Samoan woman said of her parents, "They didn't really express it in words . . . . My Mom took care of me." She told how her father would show his love for his children by walking them over a mile to school.

"When we were afraid Dad would walk with us until it got light . . . then he would walk all they way home and start working in the plantation."

An I-kiribati man said, "We don't hug or say it but . . . I show my love for my mother by obeying her words." Many described obedience to and respect for elders as way of showing love. A Tongan said love meant "Respect for the elderly people. Do not question the authority that they have. Whenever they need help, help them out . . . . My grandfather, always have to carry for him heavy stuff. You know, he can carry it, but he's older. So . . . I carry it for him." People talked about sharing of food as an important way of showing love. Members of the extended family would drop by, especially on Sundays after church, and would automatically receive the best food which the household was able to provide.

So the love that exists in abundance in these families was expressed not in words but in deeds, gestures, and behaviors. Pacific Islander men displayed their love by looking out for the welfare of their female family members. By contrast, women tended to demonstrate care and concern by doing manual tasks of a nurturing kind. This can be seen in the testimony of a man who lives in the same college community as his two sisters. As for familial caring, he said:

> That's a real important role. Especially since my sisters are here we really care for each other and they really care for me. I check on them sometimes to see how they are doing. If I meet them at the dances or at the movies I make sure they come home and I leave or go out on a date with someone. Same relationship how they care for me. Like if I'm going to the temple or something they ask me if my white shirt is clean, and I bring it over to them and they wash it or something, or if it's all right with me I just tell them that I'm okay.

Other males reported similar surveillance and chaperoning activities. No one seems to have felt a need to chaperone the men.

Many of these same respondents had no difficulty expressing their love for family members to the interviewers, but they could not articulate themselves directly to their families.

DISCIPLINE

One of the ways that the parents of the Pacific Islander respondents expressed their caring was by disciplining their children. Discipline among Pacific Islanders is intimately connected with caring, and also with respect. The word "respect" appears over and over in the transcripts if the interviews, perhaps more frequently than any other word. Some Tongans used the word *"faka'apa'apa,"* which evokes an elaborate system of duty, honor, obligation, and security that stands as the rock of stability at the base of Tongan society (Tuifua 1992). One young man said *"Famili . . .* in Tongan . . . means the relationship we have in a very respectful way . . . . [W]hen I hear the word *famili,* it creates that sense of respect." It is in context of the value which Pacific Islanders place on caring and respect that one must understand the issue of discipline.

From the perspective of middle-class, White Americans, Pacific Islander disciplinary practices seem harsh. Almost always, in the families of the people interviewed, discipline involved forthright physical punishment. Dubanoski and Snyder (1980) go so far as to label such practices as "child abuse." They may not be right.

Almost always, it was the fathers who did the heavy hitting, and boys especially were their targets. One recalled, "We got hit. By a stick or a broom or something . . . . One time . . . I got hit. I was so upset at my Dad's sister. She came and stole something at home, and I was very young and I swore at her . . . 'cause I was so mad, and my Dad heard. He came and he hit me and I still have a lot of scars all over my body because he was so mad." Another man recalled an occasion when "I didn't tell my Dad where I was going to go. So I walked in the house and he threw a big punch. A big punch!" That would not happen now, however, in this person's estimate: "Now that I'm tall and bigger and much stronger, my Dad doesn't hit me anymore. You've taken his punishment in a good way, so now you just talk."

Girls also got hit, but not so often and not so hard. Mothers were more likely to scold or to reason with children than to hit, although sometimes they, too, got physical. One woman remembered that, "Usually in our family when we do something . . . [our mother would] always come and sit me out, and tell me to sit down, and then she tell me not to do this because—and then she would explain it and everything. But sometimes she would pinch." Only a few of the respondents reported being slapped by aunts or uncles. Sometimes the delegation of leadership to the oldest member of the younger generation meant that an older brother or sister felt empowered to slap a younger sibling, but that was very rare.

The people who were interviewed had a somewhat different understanding of this physical punishment than some non-Pacific Islanders might suppose. They spoke in positive terms of the corporal punishment they had experienced. A Tongan man said he would discipline his children "just how I was punished, because I like it that way, 'cause right now I don't regret anything that my parents did to me. I think that's how they show their love to me." In all four ethnic groups, the children expressed this same idea, that physical punishment was one way they knew their parents cared for them. A student from Kiribati said the father's beatings "showed his love for us, because if they didn't do that we would be really naughty." A Samoan woman said that "If somebody were to ask if I was abused when I was a child I would say no." A Samoan man said, "I think I learned more being disciplined—being hit, rather than not being hit. I think I learned more from my father through discipline. If it wasn't for him, I wouldn't be here today." A Tongan said that physical punishment "made me do what I am supposed to be doing." A woman told how her father had insisted her brother go spend two years on a Mormon mission, and had beaten the younger man up when he refused to go. During the missionary period, the young man wrote and thanked his father for beating him into going, and he did not change the story once the mission had ended.

Some observers may contend that this sort of positive statement about physical punishment simply reflects the psychological dependency of an abused person upon her or his abuser. But it may be equally valid, given the ubiquity of the practice of physical punishment throughout the Pacific areas under study, to take these statements at closer to face value. If the people involved do not experience physical punishment as tyranny and abuse—if, to the contrary, they see the punishment as centrally important to the development of their own positive character qualities and to the maintenance of family stability—by what right may someone with another theory of childrearing impose a negative value judgment? (cf. Gray and Cosgrove 1985)

The literature on child abuse suggests that physical punishment may be more dangerous when it is negatively sanctioned (Dubanoski and Snyder 1980). Conversely, it may be less dangerous in the Pacific Islander American instance, where it is viewed as a natural and positive way to raise one's children. Also, if physical discipline is a usual method rather than a desperate last resort, it is less likely to be abusive (Parke and Collmer 1975). Similarly, if physical discipline is swiftly and unselfconsciously administered, it is unlikely to result in serious injury (Korbin 1987a, 1987b).

A Tongan woman summed up the Pacific Islander American view of physical discipline. Back home, she said, "My Mom gave me the stick." When she came to the United States she was surprised to learn that, "Over here parents are not supposed to hit your kids . . . . That's how you teach your children . . . . If you don't hit them they will not learn anything." Physical discipline in these Pacific Islander families was one prime way by which parents showed the depth of their caring. Children showed their caring in return by obedience, by respecting the elderly, by taking care of their siblings, and by not answering back.

CULTURAL CHANGE

Each of the people at the time of the interview was living in Hawai'i, thousands of miles from her or his homeland and native culture. Nearly all were also physically remote from their families, extended and nuclear, though some had a few local relatives. Moreover, their countries of origin were undergoing dramatic changes under the impact of global market forces and the swirling movements of goods, people, and culture across and around the Pacific. It is inevitable that these particular individuals should have expressed personal feelings at some variance with what they perceived to be traditional family imperatives in their native cultures.

Many people when interviewed said they would not do exactly as their parents had done. This was especially true in the matter of discipline. Even though they valued the punishment they had received, they said they would exercise a lighter hand on their own children. One woman quoted above as approving of the way she was raised, said nonetheless, "I think whenever my parents see anything wrong they would just hit you without letting you explain your point. So what I want to do is let them [my children] explain first." Several respondents echoed these sentiments. They would not completely eschew corporal punishment, but they wished to inject an element of dialogue before leaping into discipline. Another said he would let his children have a bigger say than he had in making decisions about their own lives: "I would let them choose for themselves. I would just explain everything to them and let them choose." Most of the respondents were not quite so liberal: They would discuss issues with their children, they said, but not allow them total freedom to make their own choices.

Both these desired changes—talking with children before punishing them and discussing options before making decisions—will depend on establishing new patterns of verbal communication. Not only were all the people interviewed better at showing love than speaking love, they felt themselves tongue-tied before their parents in most situations. One Tongan man described a case that applied to others as well: "Even though we have something in mind to say . . . it's very rude to talk back to our parents, even if we feel they are not right. And [if] there is something in our hearts that we need to express to them, we cannot say until, I don't know, you just cannot say anything back."

One of the factors one would like to tease out is the impact of religion on moving the people interviewed for this study away from traditional family dynamics. All are members of a faith, Mormonism, that is highly bound up with White, middle-class, American culture. As one put it, "The Mormon belief is that you give up your culture and you take on

Mormon culture." In practical fact, since some of the respondents came from nuclear families that were Mormon with extended families that were not, their Mormonism drew them out of the extended family network. Then, too, certain Mormon practices are built around the nuclear family. Some spoke of having family home evening, a weekly togetherness time practiced by most Mormon families. Some spoke of family councils—another Mormon device—where they tried to air grievances and work out differences.

The person whose family showed the most evidence of these Mormon influences was a Tongan male whose parents had since accepted a calling as a bishop—the equivalent of a pastor or priest in Protestant or Catholic circles. The young man described his family's situation: "My Dad used to discipline us [physically, but] ever since my Dad got the calling for church . . . he does away with the Tongan whack!, belt stuff. He gets on a one-to-one basis and we just talk and clear it off . . . . So instead of taking me into the room and belting me he just talked to me really good and made me feel so bad that I started crying. By my Mum she got really mad, so got the thing and started to beat on me, but my Dad just talked to her and my Mum tried to convince him to hit me, but he didn't." Because of the influence of the church, this family seems to have made a cultural transition in its way of relating.

Yet this family was unique among those interviewed for this study, in the degree to which it had adopted a foreign model of family communication. Because this is not a longitudinal study, it is not clear at this point exactly how much culture change actually has taken place in these families, or will take place in the future. Nor is it clear what part of any culture change can be laid at the door of Mormonism, and how much ought to be attributed to more general causes.

SUMMING UP

From these interviews, it is possible to construct a fuller picture of the roles and behavior patterns that characterize Pacific Islander Americans than has existed up until now. For example, the respondents have given a picture of family structure where much of what is most important is organized around the nuclear family, yet the collateral family takes over at key points. The wider kin network is emotionally important to the individual and is there for ceremonies and celebrations, as well as for major decision making. In some instances, extended family members are accorded positions much like those of parents and siblings, although most daily functioning happens within the nuclear family.

There is a strict hierarchy of power and authority in Pacific Islander American families, with parents taking primacy over children, men over women, older siblings over younger siblings. A great deal of caring is expressed in these families, but it is seldom expressed verbally. Together with caring, respect is the highest value in the Pacific Islander American family system.

One of the forms through which caring and respect are mediated is physical discipline. This takes the form of hitting and slapping. It generates obedience, and, in the minds of the informants, is a good thing—indeed, a necessary tool for character development.

Nonetheless, one can see the acids of Euroamerican culture eating away at more traditional Pacific Islander customs. Many informants expressed a desire to tone down the hitting and increase verbal communication in the next generation. The trend seems to be toward emphasizing the attributes of the nuclear family. The degree to which this trend is affected by the respondents' Mormonism and the degree to which they are more generalized social phenomena are unclear and await further research. Surely, both factors are at work.

CHAPTER 17

Historical and Cultural Aspects of Native Hawaiian Health

Kekuni Blaisdell

PRE-WESTERN HEALTH STATUS

Cook's Journals of 1778 described the native men and women as "above middle size, strong, muscular, well made of a dark copper colour [who] walk gracefully, run nimbly and are capable o great fatigue" (Beaglehole 1967). The women "have handsome faces . . . are very well made . . . very clean, have good teeth and are perfectly void of any disagreeable smell."

Because of their long geographic isolation of more than 500 years, the *kanaka* of old were free of the epidemic, contagious pestilences which were the scourge of the continents (Bushnell 1966; Blaisdell 1983; Stannard 1988). However, they did have some focal infections, including a low frequency of dental caries, as observed in skeletal remains (Snow 1974; Chappell 1927).

Metabolic disorders, such as gout, degenerative and rheumatoid arthritis, are also evident in pre-contact human bones, so that other soft-tissue maladies, such as diabetes and atherosclerosis, so prevalent among modern *kānaka*, probably also occurred to some extent among those at risk, such as high-fat and high-salt consuming, sedentary and corpulent *ali'i* (Blaisdell 1983). Trauma was probably the most common of ailments. Poisoning was rare (Blaisdell 1985). "Kava debauchery" among some *ali'i* was mild and the only form of "drug abuse" (Beaglehole 1967; Blaisdell 1983). The few documented instances of mental illness contrast with Cook's account of the natives as "social, friendly, hospitable, humane . . . possessing much liveliness . . . blessed with frank and cheerful disposition." Some congenital defects were known, the best documented being

This essay is an abridged version of the one published in *Social Process in Hawai'i* 32, no. 1 (1989): 1–21. In this essay Kanaka Maori people are referred to as "Hawaiian," "Native Hawaiian," and "native Hawaiian." We have learned that these terms have colonial and racist origins. (Blaisdell, 2002) clubfoot, which persists in highest frequency among modern Hawaiians compared to the other ethnic groups in Hawai'i (Chung et al. 1969).

HEALTH PRACTICES

The traditional native diet of the *maka'āinana* (eyes, watchers, caretakers of the land) was superior to the usual modern Western fare for it was high in fiber and starch, low in saturated fat and sugar, and ample in protein, minerals and vitamins (Miller 1974; Dirige and Hughes 1985). Personal hygiene was fastidious, with bathing two to three times daily, and with careful individual disposal of body wastes (Bushnell 1966). The *kapu* maintained strict public sanitation and environmental protection. This accounted for unknowing control of potentially harmful microorganisms. Vigorous physical fitness in recreation, such as surfing, and in work, such as tilling taro fields, and constructing stone retaining walls for fishponds, contributed to lithe, muscular bodies (Beaglehole 1967; Dirige and Hughes 1985).

Wellness represented adequate personal *mana*. Illness resulted from loss of *mana* due to lack of *pono* with oneself with oneself, others, including spiritual forces, violation of a *kapu*, or external infliction from *'ānai* (curse) or *'anā'anā* (ill will from another, not synonymous with western sorcery) (Malo 1951; Handy, Pūku'i, and Livermore 1934; Pūku'i, Haertig, and Lee 1972, 1979; Kamakau 1964). Once illness had occurred, diagnosis was a matter of determining the mechanism of loss of *mana* and *pono*. Treatment was directed at restoring the lost *mana* and *pono*. As a start, the patient himself, especially if he were a *maka'ainana*, assessed and managed his illness, having been trained since childhood in self-reliance (Handy, Pūku'i, and Livermore 1934; Pūku'i, Haertig, and Lee 1972, 1979). If he did not recover, he would likely seek the care of an experienced *kūpuna lapa'au* (elder healer). Only if this failed, and he could "pay" the appropriate professional "fee," such as a hog, would he seek the care of a *kahuna lapa'au* (physician priest) at the *heiau ho'ōla* (healing temple) (Malo 1951; Kamakau 1964). Medical practices included:

> Integrated psycho-spiritual methods of prayer, drama, revelation, suggestion, extrasensory perception, faith-healing, sorcery and group therapy (Malo 1951; Pūku'i, Haertig, and Lee 1972, 1979; Kamakau 1964; Blaisdell 1983).
>
> Physical methods, such as careful observation, palpation, body-molding, massage, manipulation, clyster-enema, hydro-thermo-heliotherapy, and fracture setting (Handy, Pūku'i, and Livermore 1934; Pūku'i, Haertig, and Lee 1972, 1979; Blaisdell 1983; Snow 1974).

Pharmaceutics as part of rituals with symbolism, empirical effective use of numerous medicinal plants, such as the mild narcotic *'awa*, cathartics *kukui* and *koali*, antidiarrheal *pia*, poultices with *pōpolo* and *noni*, and the mineral *alae* (Handy, Pūku'i, and Livermore 1934; Blaisdell 1983).

Surgery with incision of abscess, prepuce subincision and minor resections with sharp bamboo, bone or shell, and amputation with basalt adze (Pūku'i, Haertig, and Lee 1972, 1979; Blaisdell 1983; Snow 1974).

This highly-refined, holistic and preventive health system, harmoniously integrated in their social fabric with nature about them, and their spiritual realm was to receive a devastating blow from contact with the West.

WESTERN CONTACT

The fatal impact of foreigners beginning in 1778 on these most isolated of islanders initiated five main, interrelated factors accounting for the grim status of *kānaka maoli* in their homeland today (Blaisdell 1987). First, was rapid depopulation from about 800,000 hardy natives at the time of Cook's landing, to a nadir of 40,000 at the time of the *haole* overthrow of the Hawaiian monarchy. This represents a 96 percent decline—a holocaust by any definition (Stannard 1988).

Initially this decimation was mainly from introduced gonorrhea, syphilis, probably tuberculosis, and perhaps viral hepatitis, by Cook's crewmen (Stannard 1988; Blaisdell 1983). There followed infectious diarrheas, measles, influenza, pertussis, pneumonia, mumps and recurring epidemics, such as four major smallpox outbreaks, and later leprosy, plague, scarlet fever, diphtheria and rheumatic fever (U.S. Congress 1988; Blaisdell 1983). These were infections for which the natives lacked immunity from over 500 years of isolation from the rest of the Pacific and the world.

By 1893, the 40,000 Native Hawaiians were also outnumbered by 50,000 foreigners. The trend was to worsen, so that only 20 percent of current residents of Hawai'i are *kānaka maoli*. With the beginning slow upturn in the Native Hawaiian population in the early 1900s, due to a rise in the birth rate, in spite of high infant mortality, there has been a progressive decline in their biological Hawaiianness. The current *kānaka maoli* outmarriage rate of 60 percent means the present figure of 8,000 pure Hawaiians will decline to less than 1,000, and that those with less than 50 percent Hawaiian will rise to greater than 70 percent with entry into the twenty-first century (Miike 1976).

Second, is foreign exploitation. This began at the time of Cook with the replacement of the traditional island subsistence-sharing economy by the for-profit barter and later money economy. Firearms, sandalwood lumbering, whaling, cattle-ranching, foreign military threats, and later sugar-growing brought foreign economic and political control of the ruling *ali'i*, who were too easily swindled by greedy Western merchants (Agard 1982; Trask 1983).

Western (not Hawaiian) legalized theft of native lands started with the *haole*-designed Māhele of 1848 which created private ownership of land (Kelly 1980; Kame'eleihiwa 1986; Trask 1983). The Kuleana Act of 1850 that followed resulted in less than 1 percent of the land being awarded to less than 20 percent of eligible *maka'āinana* (Kelly 1980; Kame'eleihiwa 1986). The *'āina* was no longer a sacred trust for all and the future, but rather, a commodity to serve immediate individual material ends. Loss of land and access rights by natives led to disruption of *'ohana* and their alienation from the planging, fishing and gathering ecosystems of the traditional *ahupua'a* (Kelly 1980; Handy, Handy, and Pūku'i 1972; Kame'eleihiwa 1986; Trask 1983).

These pressures were mixed with suppression of native religion, language, art, dance, music, the lunar calendar, education and health care, by Calvinist missionaries after their arrival in 1820, through their influence on the reigning monarchs, and later by their assuming key positions in the government (Kelly 1988; Kimura 1983; Tagupa 1981). Dismantling of the *'ohana* and *kahuna* on-the-job learning systems and their replacement by de-Hawaiianizing Western classroom methods did not train natives for leadership, but for subservience to *haole* rule (Trask 1983; Kelly 1988). American imperialism culminated in 1893 with the U.S. armed invasion of the independent kingdom of Hawai'i, and toppling of the native constitutional government by white businessmen with the aid of the U.S. minister (Blount 1893). Exploitation continued after the establishment of the Territory of Hawai'i, and continues today under statehood by a non-Hawaiian establishment of the government, the military, and multinational corporations (Trask 1983, 1985).

Third, is cultural conflict. Its pain was immediately felt by the *kanaka maoli* who encountered the Cook expedition. For who could deny the greater *mana* of fire weapons, metal instruments, large sailing ships, the wheel, leather and clothing textiles, books-read-and-writing, and freedom from the punishment of *kapu* violations?

In 1819, despairing because the *kapu* were no longer effective, the Hawaiian leaders themselves formally abolished these official sacred laws which also governed personal hygiene and public sanitation. Gross pollution of person, home, land and water followed (Blaisdell 1983). Cultural conflict was also evident in the eagerness with which many *ali'i* pursued material luxury by exploitation of *maka'āinana* labor in sandalwood and other trade (Trask 1983).

Collaboration with foreigners on their terms invariably results in conflicting values. Even today, every Native Hawaiian knows and feels the struggle within himself. Traditional values call for group affiliation, sharing with others, caring for nature, working together within the *'ohana* system for common goals, and respect for the inherent value of everything in the Hawaiian cosmos. In contrast, the necessity for survival in the dominant Western world fosters individual competitive assertion for personal power, materialism, degradation and commercialization of native culture, language and religion, with waste and destruction of the *'āina* and other natural resources (Blaisdell 1987; Trask 1985). The constant pressure by the dominant Western society on Native Hawaiians to assimilate into the anti-Hawaiian Western mode always carries the guilt of betrayal to the ways of native ancestors.

Accentuating the pain of every Native Hawaiian is the increasing use, and therefore misuse and abuse, of the term "Hawaiian" to refer to what is clearly *not* Hawaiian and sometimes even anti-Hawaiian. This failure of non-Hawaiians to respect the distinctive identity of Hawaiians as *the* aboriginal people of Hawai'i in Hawai'i with special rights is humiliating.

The clash of cultural values described above has resulted in loss of Hawaiian identity, self-worthiness and self-confidence, and for many despair and loss of willingness to live in a no-longer meaningful society, with resulting self-destructive behavior (Blaisdell 1983, 1987; Marsella et al. 1985; Andrade 1988).

Fourth, is adoption of harmful foreign ways. Besides the vexing non-Hawaiian attitudes described above, *kānaka maoli* have too eagerly embraced unwholesome Western lifestyles. In modern times, a salient example is misnutrition by consumption of excessive saturated fat, sugar, and salt, as in ready-made commercially processed food importations promoted by profit-oriented non-Hawaiian corporations. Such highly-advertised products contribute to the wide prevalence of heart disease, hypertension, diabetes, obesity and cancer in Native Hawaiians, as well as others of course (Dirige and Hughes 1985; Aluli and O'Connor 1988).

Displaced and dispossessed, few Native Hawaiians now have the opportunity and accessibility to live off the land and sea as in earlier times (Trask 1985). Western self-destructive habits also include consumption of tobacco, alcohol, and harmful illicit substances (Blaisdell 1983, 1987; Marsella 1985; Andrade 1988). Economic and social assimilation pressures contribute to urban crowding, fast-lane automobiling, reckless recreation, lack of physical fitness, increasing dependence on government welfare, and ill-coping with stress (Blaisdell 1987; Marsella 1985; Andrade 1988).

Fifth, is neglect, insensitivity and sometimes, malice. The dominant Western society has been generally indifferent to the plight of Native Hawaiians and often hostile toward their culture and practices. Since the early 1800s, Christian missionaries have regularly denounced, rather than recognized, the now largely underground traditional healing methods (Pūkuʻi, Haertig, and Lee 1972; Blaisdell 1983; Kelly 1988).

In 1859, because the natives were considered to be a dying race, the Queen's Hospital was chartered by the government of the Kingdom "for treatment of indigent sick and disabled Hawaiians," supported by a hospital tax and private subscriptions (Greer 1969). In 1909, eleven years after U.S. annexation, a minority of the all-white hospital corporation secretly deleted the terms "indigent" and "Hawaiians" from the hospital charter, and ended government responsibility for the hospital. No longer was there free medical care for needy and sick natives (Houston 1950).

Growing resentment in Hawaiian communities in 1921 led the U.S. Congress to set aside 200,000 acres of U.S. occupied Hawaiian Kingdom land for social and economic "rehabilitation" of native Hawaiian homesteaders defined as "any descendant of not less than one-half part of the blood of the peoples inhabiting the Hawaiian Islands previous to 1778." The program failed because mostly third-class raw lands were assigned without suitable infrastructure, and financing for housing was inadequate. Most of the usable lands were commercially leased to *non*-Hawaiian firms for income because no government funds were provided for administration of the program. In addition, many of the most suitable lands were transferred for other colonial government purposes without payment of rent (Trask 1982).

Vital statistics by the Americanized Hawaiʻi government since 1900 have persistently demonstrated Native Hawaiians to have the worst health profile in the islands, with the shortest life-expectancy, highest mortality rates, and greatest rates for most chronic diseases (Blaisdell 1983, 1987). These deplorable health indices have been regularly ignored until the recent resurgence of Hawaiian activism. Even as late as November 1985, when the Native Hawaiian Health Needs Study was unveiled at a public conference, top administrators in the Hawaiʻi State Department of Health faced with the obvious question, "What is your department doing about this?" replied: "Our department is color blind. If Hawaiians choose not to use our services, the fault is not ours." Fortunately since 1987, the new director of the Department of Health has reversed the position of his department toward Native Hawaiians. He has established an all-Hawaiian member Native Hawaiian Health Task Force and created a new Office of Hawaiian Health to improve his department's services to Native Hawaiians in their homeland (E Ola Mau 1986-88).

A Turning Point

In the 1960s, rural Native Hawaiian communities, already economically exploited, were besieged by rapid encroachment on remaining agricultural lands. Retaining remnants of the traditional lifestyle of taro-farming, fishing, canoe-building and voyaging, reverence for nature, Hawaiian language, music, and hula, fostered by a supportive land base, Hawaiians in these communities began to proliferate. These included Protect Kaho'olawe 'Ohana (PKO), which led a protest against U.S. Navy bombing of the island of Kaho'olawe. Kona, Sand Island, Mokauea Island, Waimanalo, Kahana, Wai'anae, Nanakuli, Hana and East Moloka'i became sites of protest over evictions of Native Hawaiians to make way for non-Hawaiian *malihini* (newcomers).

Formal land base claims by Native Hawaiians began to take several forms: reparations for the 1893 U.S. armed invasion and taking of Hawaiian nationhood; legal claim to ceded Hawaiian Homelands and other trust lands abused by the State and Federal governments and by large Hawaiian private trust estates; and U.N. recognition of aboriginal land rights. In the 1970s, Native Hawaiian political organizations began to proliferate. Native Hawaiians began to learn what had been suppressed in their school curricula. Restlessness mounted in Hawaiian communities. Native Hawaiian health organizations were undertaking health programs in their own Hawaiian communities. Kanaka Maoli activism resulted in the 1988 U.S. Congress Native Hawaiian Health Initiative. In 1992, this modest Federal mandate established five Native Hawaiian Health Care Systems providing outreach health promotion, disease prevention and traditional healing services. However, the February 2000 U.S. Supreme Court Rice Decision subsequently threatened all Kanaka Maoli-only programs. To protect these programs, Kanaka Maoli are currently urged to accept the subordinate status of a U.S. indigenous people, with a puppet government under the State of Hawai'i and the Department of Interior. This will mean relinquishing all claims to Kanaka Maoli lands and independent nationhood.

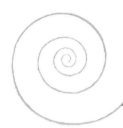

CHAPTER 18

An Introduction to the
Practice of Ho'oponopono

E. Victoria Shook

A rich body of knowledge about the physical, emotional, and spiritual well-being of an individual in relationship to family, community, and environment has existed in the Hawaiian culture for centuries. One of the specific practices is a complex system for maintaining harmonious relationships and resolving conflict within the extended family; this system is called *ho'oponopono*, which means "setting to right." Within the last ten years this concept has become popularized and a number of individuals, mostly within social service programs, have attempted to use this traditional family concept and practice. The purpose of this study is to illustrate how some individuals on the island of Oahu have adapted *ho'oponopono* for use in their social service agencies or private consultation and counseling practices.

It is likely that many variations exist in the description and practice of *ho'oponopono*. The description that has received the most widespread acknowledgment is that given by Mary Kawena Pūku'i, a respected *kumu* (teacher) of Hawaiian culture (Pūku'i, Haertig, and Lee 1972).

THE CULTURAL CONTEXT FOR HO'OPONOPONO

In a multicultural society like Hawai'i, there has been confusion over how to establish ethnic and cultural boundaries. How can "Hawaiian" be defined for this study? In 1983 the number of pure Hawaiians was estimated to be quite low at 8,291. The number of part-Hawaiians was much higher at 174,579, which totals approximately 19 percent of the state's population.[1] Numerous problems exist in determining the prime cultural

---

This essay was previously published in *Ho'oponopono* (Honolulu: East-West Center, 1985).

affiliation of individuals with mixed ancestry, and there is disagreement among agencies in Hawai'i on how ethnicity should be determined.

Much of the traditional Hawaiian culture has been left behind and cannot be considered a defining feature of contemporary Hawaiian identity. These remnants from the past include a hierarchical social organization, traditional land-use patterns, and the material culture of precontact Hawai'i, which has been relegated largely to museum exhibits. Knowledge of traditional folk medicine, which seems to be held primarily by the elder members of the community, is another measure of Hawaiian identification (Howard 1974). Today, the elders' knowledge and skills are being supplanted by Western ones as exposure to American ideas and practices becomes widespread. The use of the Hawaiian language as a vehicle for transmitting culture from one generation to the next has diminished greatly. It is estimated that only approximately 2,000 native Hawaiian speakers remain, and these individuals are more than 60 years old.[2]

What then is left? Despite the dramatic loss of the social organization of the *ali'i* (chief) system, the language, the land, and many cultural traditions, there seems to be a recognizable pattern of social interaction identified as Hawaiian or perhaps more accurately as Hawaiian-American. Perhaps the feature of cultural identity that is most central to my study is the continued preference by Hawaiians of employing a social interaction style that stresses interpersonal harmony and avoidance of overt conflict.

If we examine both the meaning of the Hawaiian family and the beliefs and practices that constitute a system of social order, we can see how this complementary emphasis on maintaining harmony and avoiding conflict operates. Once this foundation is laid, *ho'oponopono* as a conflict resolution method begins to rest securely.

FAMILY AND SOCIALIZATION

The extended family in Hawaiian culture is the center of life. The word for family, *'ohana*, is derived from the words *'oha*, for taro, and *na*, the designation for plural. The taro plant is linked with myths about the origin of people, as well as being the staple food. The meaning of *'ohana*, therefore, takes on metaphorical significance. Pūku'i stated, "members of the *'ohana*, like taro shoots, are all from the root."

Children have an important role in the family and are desired by most adults. *Hānai*, or adoption, is a frequent practice. In a study of a Hawaiian Homelands community on the leeward coast of Oahu, Gallimore, Boggs, and Jordan (1974) reported that 30 percent of the families had children other than their own living in the house. The authors listed two common reasons given by informants for taking a child in a *hānai* relationship: (1) A woman is unable to bear a child, or (2) a woman with older children desires an infant. Infants are generally indulged and are often the focus of attention in the family. Because of this value and the practice of *hānai*, high rates of illegitimacy are not an overbearing cause for concern in the Hawaiian community. Once children are brought into the world, they are to be cared for and loved (Young 1980).

As an infant becomes a toddler, a shift in attention occurs. The child is no longer indulged and is expected to begin assuming family responsibilities. Older siblings are involved in caring for the younger children. Thus the child-rearing process fosters interdependence and increased opportunity to exercise adult-type roles by working and contributing to the family's economic and social welfare.

The family's structure is characterized by what might be called a benevolent authoritarianism. Elders, the *kūpuna*, are respected for their wisdom and experience and are often the teachers of the children.

Children learn household tasks through observation and experience. They learn to be unobtrusive since to do otherwise is to risk rebuff and punishment. They may seek help and approval from adults, but in a subtle manner that is not intrusive. Rewards and punishments in the family are often meted out to a group rather than to an individual. This fosters one of the two primary strategies used by children to get along in the family: sibling cooperation. The other strategy is conflict avoidance with adults.

All these socialization practices underscore a predominant value pattern of affiliation. This value is expressed often in the Hawaiian language with words such as *laulima* (cooperation) and *kokua* (help), words that reinforce the idea of cooperation and interdependence. Generosity, hospitality, sharing, and reciprocity are also valued. These values have application to many areas of endeavor, including work. For example, *ukupau* is still used by some businesses in Hawai'i. The word refers to the practice of people helping one another with their work tasks so that they can finish early and commence with fun and relaxation. This contrasts with the predominant American work pattern of adhering to a strict time clock system and requiring workers to be on the job for a specified period of time regardless of task completion. Another example illustrating these Hawaiian values is the work involved in a party, or *lū'au*. Preparation of the many varieties and large quantities of food for a *lū'au* requires that many people contribute time, money, and skill. With the spirit of *laulima*, however, this cooperative work has its own reward in the pleasant social interaction and accomplishment of what otherwise might be a formidable task.

The successful maturation of a person in the Hawaiian culture thus requires that an individual cultivate an accurate ability to perceive and attend to other people's needs, often without being asked. These are attitudes and behaviors that help cement the relationships of the *'ohana* and the community.

Social Order

A philosophical look at Hawaiian concepts unearths a profound belief in a universe that operates on principles of harmonious relationships. "The Hawaiian of old realized that it was necessary that these forces be kept in 'harmony' and that they were all in some way interrelated" (Mossman and Wahilani 1975). Evidence of the importance of this triad of relationships can be seen in the social values and beliefs that affect the selection of practices used to maintain social order.

First, spiritual concerns pervade much of Hawaiian interaction and ceremony. The recent popularity of traditional forms of *hula* has brought back a strong spiritual element to dance. Blessings of work endeavors, social gatherings, and opening and closing ceremonies are commonplace. Christian values coexist with a deep respect for the ancient gods (Paglinawan 1980; Mossman and Wahilani 1975).

The love of nature is also apparent in the popular phrase *aloha 'āina* (love of the land). There has been a resurgence of Makahiki festivals in recent years. These yearly celebrations, traditionally held in the fall, were a time for sports and religious activities and were a tribute to Lono, the Hawaiian god of agriculture. Today's festivities usually combine the spiritual tribute with an opportunity to build community strength and conduct community fundraising activities. Another example of the eminence of land can be found in the focus of an activist group called the 'Ohana. The group is dedicated to the protection of an uninhabited island, Kaho'olawe, used as a bombing target by the U.S. military. Members and supporters of the 'Ohana maintain that Kaho'olawe has significant historical and spiritual value and should be treated with due respect.

Perhaps the importance of harmony in relationships can best be summed up by the attributes of the word *aloha*. This often-used Hawaiian word expresses love and also is a greeting and a farewell. More subtly, it suggests the highly valued character traits of generosity, friendliness, patience, and productivity. The spirit of *aloha* carries with it an understanding that the ability to soothe and prevent conflicts, shame, and other disruptive occurrences is important, and that if the harmony has been disrupted, one should have the courage to ask for and give forgiveness.

A fascinating study of how some of these facets of Hawaiian philosophy manifest themselves in the ideology and behavior of contemporary Hawaiians was done by Ito (1978, 1982). Her anthropological study of urban Hawaiian women elaborated on a concept she termed "retributive comeback." She suggested that the women studied believed that negative sanctions, such as illness or misfortune, would befall them or their kin if they acted, felt, or thought in a negative way toward another person. Negative relationships with others created entanglements called *hihia*. In order to ameliorate this negative state of affairs, the individuals were required to restore balance and harmony through self-scrutiny, admitting their wrongdoing, asking forgiveness, then changing one's behavior or enlisting the help of a spiritual ally such as the Christian God or a family *'aumākua* (ancestor god). This is an example of how the belief in the interrelatedness of kin, ancestors, and the natural world manifests itself. The belief in retribution, with its remedy of self-scrutiny, confession, and forgiveness, is strikingly similar to the underlying beliefs and overt practices in *ho'oponopono*. Perhaps the presence of the "symbolic conscious," as Ito calls it, in contemporary Hawaiians is one thing that makes *ho'oponopono* a timely and functional remedy for Hawaiians today.

The Reemergence of Ho'oponopono

Although variations of *ho'oponopono* had been in existence before the Europeans came to Hawaii, the practice had fallen from popular use quite dramatically by the mid-1900s. Those elements of the process that were influenced by Hawaiian religious practices and beliefs were most subject to abandonment. Some of the remaining modifications of *ho'oponopono* retained the essential purpose of problem solving but were greatly simplified. One such practice that incorporated Christian values was opening the Bible and pointing to a passage that might give insight and guidance to a troubled individual or group. *Ho'oponopono* could also mean getting together with family members to talk out problems or to seek forgiveness for a transgression.

In 1963, a young social worker who worked at the Queen Liliuokalani Children's Center (QLCC) was given a case involving a seriously delinquent boy and his mother.[3] Previously this case had been handled by seven agencies. It was a difficult case because it involved cultural issues that earlier case workers had been unable to understand and resolve. Keola Espiritu (pseudonym), the young social worker, had been given the case by the QLCC director because of Keola's interest in Hawaiiana.

While uncovering the details of the problem, Keola learned that the mother attributed the cause of the boy's problems to a curse that had affected him since his birth. The curse was the result of a promise the woman had made to her dying mother—a promise that later had been broken. The woman had promised never to marry a divorced person and eventually had done so.

The repercussions of this broken promise were realized shortly after her son's birth. When the baby was born, he was unnaturally still, not crying or moving. The mother fasted (*ho'okeai*) in order to divine the nature of the problem. During the fast she had an insight that linked the baby's lack of movement to her broken promise. After her realization the baby began to respond more normally. Some years later the father died, leaving his wife and son alone. The son had gotten into trouble as an adolescent and by the time the case was at QLCC, Keola reported that he thought the boy was "flirting with death," because of two serious encounters with the police. In one incident the boy pulled an unloaded .45-caliber pistol on a police officer; in another he challenged fifteen officers to a karate duel.

The case presented quite a dilemma for the social worker who, although raised in rural Oahu with strong Hawaiian traditions, had received professional training with a Western cultural orientation. When Keola shared this concern with his supervisor he was given permission to contact Mary Kawena Pūku'i (also called Tūtū, an affectionate and respectful name for an older person that loosely means "grandma" or "grandpa"). He approached Tūtū Pūku'i and requested her assistance so that the agency could learn how to help this and other Hawaiian families "the Hawaiian way."

Tūtū consented; she, a psychiatrist, a psychologist, and several social workers began meeting on a weekly basis as the "Culture Committee." The process that Keola and the others used to articulate the cultural concepts was not a didactic one. Instead, case material was brought to the committee, then Tūtū would "talk story" about related beliefs and practices. The sessions were taped for reference. Keola and others explored the concepts that were pertinent to his case; these included *'ohana, ho'okeai, ho'ohiki* (promises), the consequences of breaking promises, and the methods for resolving problems. The subject of *ho'oponopono* came to light when the group discussed traditional remedies for family problems.

Tūtū talked about a form of *ho'oponopono* that she had used all her life and that had been used by her family in Ka'u, Hawai'i. It was an understanding of *ho'oponopono* based on practical experience. It was Pūku'i's method that Keola used with the woman and her son to help them understand and resolve their problems, untangling the mixture of Hawaiian and Christian beliefs that had confounded the issues. The intervention resulted in a positive outcome. According to Keola, the boy was able to finish high school and "make it in society."

The excitement generated by the possibility of similar beneficial out-comes in other cases, as well as the amount of learning that was taking place as a result of the weekly meetings, kept the group going for seven years. The QLCC staff realized that sensitizing workers to cultural beliefs and practices should be a primary goal of their work, particularly since QLCC was an agency serving the Hawaiian community. In a related pro-ject, some years after the committee began, QLCC tested the practice of *ho'oponopono* in the social work setting.

A DESCRIPTION

Ho'oponopono is a method for restoring harmony that was traditionally used within the extended family. According to Pūku'i, it literally means "setting to right . . . to restore and maintain good relationships among family, and family and supernatural powers" (Pūku'i, Haertig, and Lee 1972, 60). The metaphor of a tangled net has been used to illustrate how problems within a family affect not only persons directly involved but also other family members. The family is a complex net of relationships, and any disturbance in one part of the net will pull other parts. This metaphor reinforces the Hawaiian philosophy of the interrelatedness of all things.

The family conference was traditionally led by a senior family member or, if necessary, by a respected outsider such as a *kahuna lapa'au* (healer). The problem-solving process is a complex and potentially lengthy one that includes prayer, statement of the problem, discussion, confession of wrongdoing, restitution when necessary, forgiveness, and release. An outline of the conditions and steps of *ho'oponopono* follows.

Ho'oponopono is opened with *pule,* which is prayer conducted to ask God and/or the *'aumākua* for assistance and blessing in the problem-solving endeavor. *Pule* is usually led by the senior person conducting the session. Reliance on spiritual assistance heightens and strengthens the emotional commitment of the participants. Prayer lays the foundation of sincerity and truthfulness, necessary conditions to be maintained throughout the process.

In the beginning phase there is a period of identifying the general prob-lem, known as *kūkulu kumuhana.* (This term has two additional meanings that are a part of *ho'oponopono. Kūkulu kumuhana* is the pooling of strengths for a shared purpose, such as solving the family's problem. It also refers to the leader's effort to reach out to a person who is resisting the *ho'oponopono* process to enable the person to participate fully.) During this initial phase the procedures for the whole problem-solving sequence are also outlined in order to reacquaint all participants with them.

Once the proper climate is set, the leader focuses on the specific problem. The *hala*, or transgression, is stated. *Hala* also implies that the perpetrator and the person wronged are bound together in a relationship of negative entanglement called *hihia*.

Because of the nature of *hihia*, most problems have many dimensions. The initial hurt is often followed by other reactions, further misunderstandings, and so forth until a complex knot of difficulties has evolved. It is the leader's responsibility to choose one of the problems and work it out with the family through the process of *mahiki*, or discussion. With one part resolved, the group can uncover and resolve successive layers of trouble one layer at a time until the family relationships are again free and clear.

The discussion of the problem is led and channeled by the leader. This intermediary function keeps individuals from directly confronting one another, a situation that could lead to further emotional outburst and misunderstanding. Traditionally, the Hawaiians felt that allowing emotional expressions to escalate discouraged problem resolution. Each participant who has been affected by the problem in some way—directly or indirectly—is asked to share his or her feelings, or *mana'o*. The emphasis is on self-scrutiny, and when participants share they are encouraged to do so honestly, openly, and in a way that avoids blame and recrimination. If in the course of discussion tempers begin to flare, the leader may declare *ho'omalu*, a cooling-off period of silence. This enables the family to reflect once again on the purpose of the process and to bring their aroused emotions under control.

When the discussion is complete, the *mihi* takes place. This is the sincere confession of wrongdoing and the seeking of forgiveness. It is expected that forgiveness be given whenever asked.[4] If restitution is necessary then the terms of it are arranged and agreed upon.

Closely related to *mihi* is *kala*, or a loosening of the negative entanglements. Both the person who has confessed and the person who has forgiven are expected to *kala* the problem. This mutual release is an essential part of the process and true *ho'oponopono* is not complete without it. The *kala* indicates that the conflicts and hurts have been released and are *oki* (cut off).

The *pani* is the closing phase and may include a summary of what has taken place and, importantly, a reaffirmation of the family's strengths and enduring bonds. The problem that has been worked out is declared closed, never to be brought up again. If other layers of the problem need to be worked out, the final *pani* is postponed. Sometimes *ho'oponopono* may take many sessions. Each session has a *pani* about what has been resolved and includes a closing prayer, *pule ho'opau*. After the session the family and leader traditionally share a snack or meal to which all have contributed. This demonstrates the commitment and bond of all who participated and provides a familiar means to move from the formal problem-solving setting to normal daily routines.

In summary, *ho'oponopono* is a highly structured process with four distinct phases: an opening phase that includes the prayer and a statement of the problem; a discussion phase in which all members involved share their thoughts and feelings in a calm manner and listen to all the others as they speak; a resolution phase that enables the exchange of confession, forgiveness, and release; and a closing phase to summarize what has transpired and to give spiritual and individual thanks for sincere participation.

NOTES

[1] Taken from the *State of Hawaii Data Book, 1983*, Table 17, p. 40.

[2] Taken from *Native Hawaiian Culture: Language*, by Larry Kimura, p. 191 in *Native Hawaiian Study Commission Report*, Vol. 1, 1983.

[3] See "Ho'oponopono: A Way to Set Things Right," *Honolulu Sunday Star-Bulletin and Advertiser*, July 18, 1971, p. B-8.

[4] Pūku'i, Haertig, and Lee (1972, 74) report that retribution from the *'aunākua* would befall an individual who did not forgive when asked.

CHAPTER 19

Pacific Islander Modes for Dealing with Sexual Abuse

Debbie Hippolite Wright, Ngati-Koata, Ngati-Kuia, Raukawa, Te Ati-Awa

My Dad did so much damage to us kids. He abused every one of us even the boys, and now we really can't stand him because of what he did. Each one of us has had problems. . . . I think our problems are because of the sexual abuse. . . . All of us have been divorced. . . . Worse, my sister tried to kill herself. I think we're all pretty messed up. I think it was because of the abuse.

This common scenario reflects the devastating aftermath of childhood sexual abuse on the lives of victims. It depicts some of the repercussions sexual abuse commonly has on the entire family. In this young woman's situation her father's behavior not only jolted her and her siblings' lives, but also the lives of their respective families. From her perspective, the sexual abuse had a ripple effect that spanned three generations, undermining the very constructs of her individual personhood and diminishing family bonds.

This chapter will elucidate core dynamics that exist in the lives of many Maori women and draw comparisons to similarities with other Pacific Island women who are survivors of childhood sexual abuse. It suggests a definition of sexual abuse compatible with Maori and Pacific Island women, and describes two culturally competent paradigms of healing and moving beyond simply surviving to thriving.

I have seen devastation occur in the lives of my clients in my work as therapist in the area of child sexual assault or sexual abuse. However, I have also observed the natural network available to and drawn upon by Pacific Island women survivors of sex abuse. The following vignette typifies several dimensions that exist in the lives of many Maori women and other Pacific Island women. It subtly reveals the attachment between female relatives, roles of women, and a natural network available for survivors of sexual abuse. Additionally, it affirms the need to understand inter-generational dynamics of familial abuse and the implications for healing the survivor, the family, the extended family, the tribe, and the village or broader community.

> One time there were a lot of us [female relatives] together peeling potatoes and carrots and getting the vegetables ready for the *hangi* [underground oven]. My uncle had just been convicted of sexual abuse of a child, someone who wasn't related to us. . . . But he has abused or tried to abuse almost every girl cousin I know. . . . Sad aye. Anyway it was on everyone's mind and then someone quietly mentioned she had been sexually abused too. . . . And you know it was funny, not funny hah hah but funny that everyone except for one of us said she had been sexually abused by one of our relatives. . . . There was about 10 of us there. The oldest was a woman who must have been in her 70's. . . . The youngest would have been in her twenties maybe. . . . But I found out later that a couple of my nieces and nephews who are now teenagers were also abused by some of their older cousins. . . . The horrible thing is that we're all related. . . . How can we ever get our *mana* [position, power, prestige] back as Maori if we are doing this shit to each other.

It is my belief that when Maori and Pacific Island women recognize and come to terms with the pervasive and insidious effects of their childhood abuse they are better able to heal. They are in a position to empower themselves and the immediate and extended family by avoiding the cyclical patterns of abuse often found in families where abuse takes place.

PREVALENCE OF SEXUAL ABUSE

It is difficult to grasp the full extent of sexual abuse because of the secretive nature of the problem, definitional difficulties, and the methodological variations of research (McGregor and Dutton, 1991). According to Peters, Wyatt, and Findelhor (1986), outcomes of prevalence studies depend on the extent of the questions posed to research participants. They contend that the studies specifying the act, the relationship to the perpetrator, and age discrepancy between the perpetrator and victim reveal higher prevalence rates. In many Maori and Pacific Island cultures the more explicit questions may not result in greater prevalence rates because for many Pacific cultures some subjects like sex are *tapu* (restricted, sacred) and not generally talked about in trans-generational or cross-gender situations. Additionally, Maori and Pacific Islanders are suspicious about participating in research projects perceived as conducted by Pakeha (people of European descent) in a Pakeha way.

There has been an increasing momentum in acknowledging, reporting, and researching childhood sexual abuse in New Zealand, particularly since the early 1980s. Researchers focusing on the prevalence of intra-familial sexual abuse in Christchurch, a predominantly Pakeha city, found that one in eight women (or 13 percent) experienced intra-familial sexual abuse (Bushnell, Wells, and Oakley-Browne 1992). In a later study that had broader research parameters, Anderson et al. (1993) found that 32 percent of the participants from the general population were abused before age 16. That same year a women's health survey conducted by Martin et al. (1993) indicated that a little over one-third (36.2 percent) of respondents reported experiencing some form of sexual abuse. Approximately 12 percent reported childhood sexual abuse before age 16. Having said this, the prevalence of childhood sexual abuse in New Zealand and other parts of the Pacific continues to be somewhat of an enigma because it is extremely difficult to calculate accurately. There is also a noticeable lack of information about Maori and Pacific Islanders regarding sexual abuse in general.

DEFINITIONS OF SEXUAL ABUSE

An overwhelming agreement has emerged among researchers and law-makers in Western countries that sexual intercourse between a child and an adult is abusive. However, beyond that, there are vast definitional variations of childhood sexual abuse with very little likelihood of developing a universal definition.

Definitions vary from country to country, from culture to culture, and even from one social agency to another (Bachmann, Moeleer, and Bennett 1988; Wong 1987; Goodyear-Smith 1993). European and American definitions are generally grouped according to: (a) the age of those involved, (b) what acts are deemed "harmful," (c) cultural perceptions of sexual behavior, and (d) the social and moral climate that exists at a given time within a society.

I propose a different orientation based on Maori and Pacific Island values. Instead of defining sexual abuse by familial relationship, age difference between the perpetrator and the victim, existence of violence, coercion, or frequency of incidents, a unique Maori definition of sexual abuse based on cultural values is defined as the trampling of a person's *mana* or personal power and identity by others' sexual comments or behaviors. This definition is grounded in the Maori value of relationships, which Maori view as important and sacred engagements. The Maori proverb *"he aha te mea nui, he tangata, he tangata, he tangata"* (What is the greatest thing of all, its people? Its people, its people) reflects the central importance of relationships. There are many cultural rituals, practices, and motifs that set out the tenets for developing healthy relationships; not adhering to these tenets would indicate an inappropriate relationship of some kind. For example, sexual comments or behaviors that demean a person's *wairua* (spirit) or *hinengaro* (intellect and emotions), or that denigrate the *tinana* (body) rob an individual of *mana* (power, prestige) and are therefore abusive.

MODELS OF TREATMENT FOR SEXUAL ABUSE

There are two forms of treatment for sexual abuse prominent in current Western literature: individual counseling and group therapy. Interestingly, both models focus on the survivor completing a series of steps to alleviate suffering. They also advocate the first two steps in the healing process as firstly, developing an ongoing trusting relationship between therapist and survivor, and secondly, the disclosure of abuse to the therapist or group (Walker 1988; Josephson and Fong-Beyette 1987).

For some women, having the opportunity to recall and retell their stories within a supportive therapeutic environment is enough for them to feel a significant change (Herman and Hirschman 1981). A competent, professional therapist can provide this safe, supportive environment, whereby a cathartic release can take place (Meiselman 1978). Regardless of the mode of treatment, it is imperative that the therapist recognize that no two survivors are the same. Each woman has her own set of experiences and her own set of problems.

Through the course of individual counseling the therapist helps the survivor to view her abuse from an adult perspective. This process offers the survivor an opportunity to appraise the abuse in a more realistic light, rather than from an outdated perspective locked in time. However, the process may also heighten the victim's sense of loss over aspects in her life that cannot be regained (Blake-White and Kline 1985; Walker 1988). The therapist also assists the survivor to learn appropriate ways to release her anger and rage bottled up since the childhood abuse. Many survivors fear the intensity of their rage and may have either suppressed these feelings or acted them out inappropriately (Herman and Hirschman 1981).

There are two major advantages of group therapy: the ability to reduce feelings of isolation and the opportunity to provide modeling for relationships with clear and explicit boundaries. These are two common characteristics most often experienced by individuals from incestuous families (Herman and Schatzow 1984; Alexander, Neimeyer, and Follette 1991; Goodman and Nowak-Scibelli 1985). A group approach is also very conducive to Maori and Pacific Islander victims because of the collective nature of Pacific cultures.

> You learn a lot from other people's stories. There was a Maori incest victim that I knew with very similar experiences, similar states, situations, and events. She was about two years ahead of me [in her healing]. I learned a lot from her but I was also teaching somebody else who was just starting her healing process. So I learned to look ahead of me and I learned to look behind me. (Anonymous survivor, July 1994)

The three types of groups most often used in the treatment of sexual abuse are: (a) short-term time-limited groups, (b) open-ended long-term groups, and (c) self-help groups. Short-term groups are usually comprised of five to eight members with either one or two therapists leading the group. Groups usually meet for a period between eight and twelve weeks (Alexander, Neimeyer, and Follette 1991). The strength of this format is the ability to explore a wide variety of topics and painful issues such as shame and isolation. New schema for dealing with old problems are also considered.

Long-term open-ended groups are also advantageous for survivors. First, there is ample time to develop issues in depth. Long-term groups are also beneficial in that they have experienced group members who help new members by modeling advanced stages of healing (Blake-White and Kline 1985). Self-help groups encourage members to develop a collective plan of action that benefits each member of the group. Developing a collective plan for healing fosters members' sense of empowerment and control over an important aspect of their lives (Herman and Hirschman 1981).

Unfortunately for Maori and Pacific Islanders, many Western methods of healing focus almost exclusively on the survivor. These methods are steeped in a medical model of treatment. The common belief is that the therapist possesses the ingredient or remedy to heal or restore health and well-being to the survivor. By contrast, in Maori and Pacific Island cultures healing comes about by employing strategies and methods that help all concerned. All systems affected by the abuse, including the victim, the perpetrator, and their families, work simultaneously towards resolution and healing. These indigenous models reflect a holistic approach to healing.

Hoʻoponopono

Hoʻoponopono (to set right) is a process of conflict resolution and healing for Kanaka Maoli (Native Hawaiians). Like the Maori and other
Pacific Island families, the Hawaiian *ʻohana* (family) is the center of all
relationships. It is in the extended family that the process of making
amends and putting things right takes place.

There are five ground rules that set the stage for *Hoʻoponopono*: (a) Each
individual in the *ʻohana* must commit to be part of the problem-solving
process. (b) All communications that are part of *hoʻoponopono* are shared
in an atmosphere of *ʻoia io* (the essence of truth). (c) The *ʻohana* must share
a sense of *aloha* for one another or be committed to reinstating the spirit
of *aloha*. (d) Everything that is said in a *hoʻoponopono* is kept confidential.
(e) The *haku* (mediator) must be commonly agreed upon and perceived as
impartial (Pūkuʻi, Haertig, and Lee 1972, 1979).

The initial step of *Hoʻoponopono* is *Pule* (prayer). Offering *pule* is
intended to evoke a spirit of understanding, wisdom, sincerity, and openness to the problem at hand. *Pule* also enhances participants' consciousness that the work done through *hoʻoponopono* is *kapu* (sacred).

The next phase is *kukulu kumuhana* (a pooling of *mana*): a combining
of spiritual, emotional, and physical strength directed toward a positive goal. This takes place as the facilitator reaches out to individuals
who may be hurt and hostile. The *haku* (mediator) or facilitator helps
the group to deal with barriers of resistance and assists them in using
their energy in a positive way through *hoʻoponopono*. Once participants
pool their energies, a clear identification of the problem can be established.

The third phase is *Mahiki* (discussion), the core of a *hoʻoponopono*, the
time of uncovering the emotions, actions, and motivations behind the
problem (Pūkuʻi, Haertig, and Lee 1972). All family members direct their
comments through the *haku* to reduce the possibility of confrontation.
Anger and emotions are viewed as valuable in *hoʻoponopono*, but are not
allowed to run unchecked and misdirected.

The fourth phase is *Hoʻomalu* (silent period), a period of thought and
reflection, a time for easing pressure and tension. Family members are
encouraged to regroup and think about what has transpired in the session. This phase could last from a few minutes to a few days.

The fifth phase is *Mihi* (forgiveness), a time of coming together. Family
members no longer talk through the mediator but rather confess and seek
forgiveness with each other. Forgiveness is sought and given for each
specific problem, and if restitution needs to be made, the terms of the
restitution are settled upon.

The next phase is *Kala* (unbinding), the releasing and letting go of the conflicts and hurt. It is a mutual release of the conflict. In extreme cases when all other options for resolution have failed, there is an option called *Mo ka piko* (severing the umbilical cord). If an individual who refuses to engage in the healing process shows no remorse or desire to put things right, the offender may be asked to sever all ties with the *'ohana* permanently.

The last phase involves a closing prayer or pule *ho'opau* and the sharing of food to close the *ho'oponopono*. The prayer and food acknowledges the spiritual and physical dimensions of the *ho'oponopono* healing process (Shook 1995; Pūku'i, Haertig, and Lee 1972, 1979; Paglinawan, 1972).

There are no empirical outcomes of *ho'oponopono* to date as its use in the contemporary therapeutic context is new. Practitioners are also reticent to impose quantitative methods of data collecting on this culturally sanctioned and validated approach. However, families and practitioners alike who have participated in the process of *ho'oponopono* describe it as very conducive and effective with Hawaiian families.

Koru Model of Healing

This section offers a culturally appropriate model of healing developed by utilizing information gathered from Maori women abused as children, Maori counselors, and incorporating *tikanga* Maori (values, customs, rules), as well as my own experience as a therapist. The Koru model (Figure 19.1) is applicable to healing for Maori because it encompasses key elements within the Maori world-view. For example, each stage has spiritual, interpersonal, physical, and emotional components. I have chosen to characterize each phase of the healing process with a Maori value, although in reality these values are interwoven at all phases of the model.

The Koru motif was chosen to depict the process and stages of healing because the *koru* or unfolding fern symbolizes growth, development and potential. The young *koru* grows surrounded and protected from the elements by larger and stronger ferns. Similarly, in order for abuse survivors to receive optimum benefits from the stages of healing it is crucial that they are supported and nurtured by others. Ultimately, in the final stage of healing, when survivors are strong enough, they are then able to become actively involved in contributing to the supportive environment for another's healing.

Healing must begin at the center of an individual's being, which is typified by *aroha* for oneself and others. The process of developing *aroha* generally begins within the context of a small support system such as a family, therapist, trusted partner, or friend.

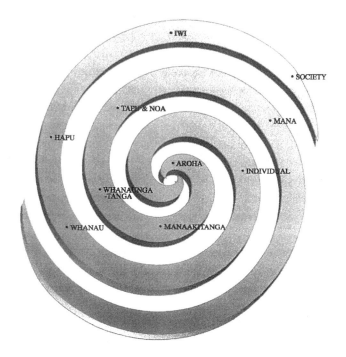

FIGURE 19.1   Koru model.

Stage One: Aroha (love)

The initial phase of healing for victims of abuse is reinstating *aroha* for oneself and others. Sexual abuse victims question their worth, their ability to love and be loved. The majority of the women I interviewed described low self-esteem and self-loathing. One woman said, "I started therapy with an amazing woman . . . . I came out of there feeling like I had all this confidence, wisdom, survivor strategies, and healing strategies."

Another woman said,

> You can't imagine how lonely and isolated I felt carrying around that awful secret. I thought I was the only one that felt the way I did, and the only one that experienced what I did. I know that was naíve, but it's true I believed that my pain and anger was unique. It wasn't until I mustered up enough courage to start talking with friends about what happened to me that I realized they were telling me similar stories out of their own experiences. Sharing with other women about what happened liberated me. I discovered I wasn't alone.

Eating disorders also pointed to self-hate. However, some obese women lacked the self-recrimination evident in other populations. Obesity was not a weapon to inflict further self-criticism, because for Maori, food has important cultural significance; it represents nurturing, care, abundance, and belonging. This is evident in the following comment: "I'm not worried about my size. I don't think I'm big because of the abuse. My whole family is big boned, we love to eat."

Participants described at least four elements that helped them maintain a positive self-concept. They were relationships with God, with spiritual or deceased beings, a valued family or tribal *taonga* (such as a carved object), and significant others. The *Aroha* stage of healing helps survivors construct a positive self-concept by supporting and educating them and adding to their consciousness about themselves in relationship to abuse issues. As victims learn to love themselves, they will ultimately learn to love and trust others.

Stage Two: Manaakitanga *(caring)*

The next phase of healing is identifying and developing support systems that can provide sustained emotional, spiritual, and physical safety for the survivor. This type of support may come from a combination of relatives, friends, therapists, or other survivors. One survivor said that because her home where the sexual abuse took place "was so chaotic" she became "a super achiever in school—I did well, and participated in everything that was going on including sports." As a child this woman found a vital support network from her school friends and teachers until she was mature enough to seek assistance explicitly dealing with sexual abuse.

Supporters model *manaki* (caring) in various ways, such as providing non-judgmental feedback or "reality checks" for victims who are still developing their own sense of self. They may challenge the survivors' ineffective or inappropriate ways of dealing with their pain and suffering while offering encouragement to continue with their healing. Supporters may also become surrogate *whanau* (family) to survivors, providing physical and emotional assistance until they can disclose their abuse to family.

An example of *manaakitanga* is the help given in women's support groups. Women reported feeling accepted by members of such groups. They were seen as "normal" rather than "weird." Although they did not condone members' outrageous behaviors, group members shared an intimate understanding of the reasons for the behavior.

Deceased loved ones were another resource, providing participants with *manaaki*. During incidents of abuse, participants received comfort and strength from spiritual beings. None of the women perceived their out-of-body experiences as pathological, problematic, or frightening. Each felt that hearing and seeing *tupuna* (ancestors) was helpful to their survival and ultimate healing. Maori language and *tikanga* (customs) provide a framework for validating the spiritual experiences of Maori survivors who believe beings from the spiritual world can and do intercede on their behalf.

Stage Three: Whanaungatanga *(maintaining contact with relations)*

The third phase is characterized by *whanaungatanga*. During this phase the client is seen as moving beyond victimization to confront the abuser and, if necessary, establish appropriate boundaries within the family. Initiating acceptable relationships with family members requires survivors and their families to confront family of origin matters, particularly areas that may have contributed to the sexual abuse. This could be, for example, a family belief system supportive of coercive sexual behaviors, poor parental skills, and other forms of abuse and neglect.

Intervention during this phase includes preparing and supporting the client and family during *whanau* (family) meetings where the sexual abuse is disclosed, confrontation of the abuser takes place, and other pertinent issues are addressed. Therapeutic configurations could include the survivor paired with parents, siblings, grandparents, aunts and uncles, or all concerned. Since the abuse described in this project was overwhelmingly perpetrated within extended families, improvement in any of the systems involved will aid the survivor's healing.

Stage Four: Tapu *and* Noa *(restricted & non-restricted)*

The fourth phase of healing is characterized by the values *tapu* and *noa* [restricted and free from restriction]. In *tikanga* Maori, *tapu* and *noa* are methods of setting appropriate boundaries. Work in this phase focuses on understanding and developing healthy interpersonal relationships with emphasis placed on establishing clear boundaries particularly within the extended family and tribe. Depending on the specific situation, it may be appropriate and important for the survivor and her *whanau* to seek "*Marae* Justice" or *marae* healing. It is a traditional process of seeking condemnation of the perpetrator's misconduct by bringing the abuse to light in a traditional forum. During *marae* justice a representative for the survivor describes the abuse, then the perpetrator has a chance to state his piece and then ask for forgiveness from the victim and her family (who may also be his relatives). Members of their extended families then collectively design punishment, restitution, and recommendations for the perpetrator's healing. The balance between *tapu* and *noa*, or restricted and non-restricted sacred and non-sacred aspects of relationships within a tribe, affirms a continuation of Maori values.

Stage Five: Mana *(power, authority)*

Integrating the woman's new sense of worth and belonging characterizes the final phase of this model. Progressing through the previous healing stages is a validation of *mana wahine* (women's power).

When Maori women have regained a sense of their own *mana*, their healing includes helping others. Help can consist of volunteering at prevention programs, crisis lines, women's shelters, or supporting a friend or relative. A suggestion from one survivor to others was "if you can tell your story then tell it. Something that you may have experienced may help the next one. It was other people's stories that help me with my *hikoi* (journey)."

On a broader scale *wahine* (women) can also influence change in organizations, communities, and society. They can take steps to stop the sexualization of children, the treatment of women as sex objects, and the abuse of power through sex. For example, *wahine* may encourage religious organizations to publicize their stance on sexual abuse and advise their devotees about counseling available in their community. Religious leaders would benefit those they serve by receiving specific training about assessment and early intervention of sexual abuse.

Institutions of higher learning must attract Maori and Pacific Islander students to various human service professions. Well-trained Maori and Pacific Islander public health workers, community psychologists, and social workers will add preventive measures in communities. Funds need to be appropriated to develop and accredit indigenous counseling programs.

Open and frank discussions should take place within Maori and Pacific Islander communities to deal with several crucial issues concerning sexual abuse. Some of these issues include culturally appropriate methods of prevention and healing, research methodology, training sex abuse counselors, and cultural censure for infractions.

The women in this project felt compelled to herald a warning to society about the pain and suffering that comes from childhood sexual abuse. Helping others in this way was an important step for them to move from being survivors to living full healthy lives. "Commitment to making the world a better, safer place for women and children has helped many survivors become thrivers" (Dinsmore 1991, 46).

Pacific Islander Modes for Dealing with Sexual Abuse

The two Pacific Island modes for dealing with sexual abuse offered here are grounded within Pacific Island cultural frameworks. The approaches are both holistic and naturalistic in origin. There are common elements that are evident in both the *Ho'oponopono* and *Koru* models that are important to emphasize. The first commonality is recognizing the fundamental importance of healing the individual within the family context. Often the perpetrator of the offense is an extended family member. Pacific models attempt to make things *pono* or right for the victim and her family (including deceased ancestors), as well as for the perpetrator and his family (including deceased ancestors).

The second commonality between the two models offered here is their incorporation of spiritual, social, emotional, and physical aspects of resolution and healing. The spiritual dimension of healing does not connote religious affiliation, but rather the recognition of a spiritual reality validated by Pacific peoples.

Third, Maori and Pacific Islanders have a natural female support network commonly referred to as *Mana Wahine* (women power, prestige, position). If *Mana Wahine* is tapped into, the network of women relatives, friends, and others can offer a wealth of support and guidance, particularly from those who have experienced similar situations.

Fourth, in the Pacific way the victim and her family may work in concert with the family of the perpetrator to come up with a collective stance on restitution and punishment for wrongs committed. Finally, reaching out or contributing to another's healing journey is an important part of healing oneself.

PART SIX
Hawaiian Nationalism

In the last third of the twentieth century and into the twenty-first, the lands of the Pacific have witnessed an upsurge of nationalism. From the Cook Islands to the Federated States of Micronesia, island peoples have achieved various forms of independence from outside colonizing powers. Three large island groups—Guam, Hawai'i, and Aotearoa—remain in the hands of the colonizers. They are also the homes of many islanders who have moved there from other parts of the Pacific. Nationalist movements are under way in all three places, and they affect not just the native peoples of those places (Chamorros, Hawaiians, and Maori) but also the other islanders who live in those places. The issues of political self-determination and cultural sovereignty are integral parts of the experience of Pacific Island peoples, in the United States and in other outposts of the diaspora.

Michael Kioni Dudley and Keoni Kealoha Agard recite "A History of Dispossession," by which American expatriates overthrew the Hawaiian Kingdom and set the stage for those islands to be annexed by the United States. Such an understanding of the history of colonial usurpation is essential to comprehending recent movements for national and cultural sovereignty.

In "Ho'omana," Jay Hartwell ushers us into the movement that grew up in Hawai'i from the 1970s. In a lyrical description of ceremonies taking place on the island of Kao'olawe, he shows us modern Hawaiians reviving (some would say re-inventing) ancient religious practices and using them to strengthen the sovereignty movement.

Davianna Pomaika'i McGregor writes of "Recognizing Native Hawaiians: A Quest for Sovereignty." In an essay that rings with passion even as it is built on a scholarly foundation, she describes the need for and history of the Hawaiian sovereignty movement. She then lays out the various forms that political action might take and the strategies pursued by various groups working for sovereignty for the Hawaiian people. Finally, she establishes a set of issues to be decided in order to reassert Hawaiian national integrity.

CHAPTER 20

A History of Dispossession

Michael Kioni Dudley and Keoni Kealoha Agard

When the white man first appeared in Hawai'i, there were about a million Hawaiians living in the islands, at best counts.[1] The lands were lush and verdant, the seas filled with fish. Life was good. The people were healthy, vigorous, and happy.

Hawaiians were people of the land. Chiefs frequently worked the land along with commoners. Kamehameha I, for instance, loved the hard work of raising *kalo* (taro), and could often be found in his *kalo lo'i* through the entire working day—from dawn until the heat of the day and then again from later afternoon until dark.

From ancient days the *ali'i nui*—the ruling high chief or king—had charge of the lands. It would be incorrect to say the lands belonged to him but, supported by his special nurturing role in relation to surrounding nature, he controlled the lands and had total say over them. The chiefs under him who held land did so at his pleasure, and their lands returned to the *ali'i nui* at their deaths. Private ownership of land was unknown.

Since islands are roughly circular, the traditional land divisions in Hawai'i resemble the slices of a pie. The *ahupua'a*, the subdivisions of a district, can be pictured as thin slices of the pie. The narrow end of the *ahupua'a* is at a central or inland mountain top, and it broadens out as it progresses towards the shore and out into sea. Each *ahupua'a* was for the most part self-sufficient, producing everything needed by the people living within its boundaries. People did not live in villages: Their homes were scattered over the area of the *ahupua'a*. Hawaiians had no money and did not barter. But those who fished in the sea needed to fill out their diet with the crops that others raised in the uplands, and the uplanders needed fish. Society was based on generosity and communal concern. Fishermen gave freely, and farmers gave freely. And all flourished. A

This essay was previously published in *A Call for Hawaiian Sovereignty* (Waipahu, Hawai'i: Nā Kāne O Ka Malo Press, 1990), 1–46.

konohiki, or overseer, assured that a constant flow of products moved through the *ahupua'a,* meeting everybody's needs.

When Captain Cook arrived in the islands, the Hawaiians, whose gods were thought to appear in human form, mistook him for a god. Fascinating stories have come down telling how Hawaiians thought the clothes Cook wore were different-colored layers of his skin, how the shiny buttons on his coat were thought to be flashing lights from within him, and how, because of his pipe, the "god" was thought to exude smoke, just as did the goddess of the volcano, Pele. Cook was only in the islands for a few days in 1776 before a storm forced him away. When he returned a year later, word of his arrival had spread through all the islands, even those hundreds of miles distant. The venereal disease brought by his men had also spread just as broadly, and with the disease its accompanying suffering, insanity, and death.[2] The destruction of the Hawaiian had begun.

Traders introduced bartering and introduced money. And the Hawaiian chiefs made tragic mistakes in learning their use. The sandalwood trade is one example. Within one generation Hawai'i was almost completely stripped of its sandalwood forests and, for the most part, all that the Hawaiians had to show for their loss were great debts to the traders. Worse, great numbers of people were brought off the lands and away from the sandalwood trade—the first serious tear in the fabric of traditional society and in the flow of food and services in the *ahupua'a.*

Hawaiian chiefs imitated the Westerners. They had so many "different" things, and the new, "different" things were thought of as better. Traditional ways came to be viewed as "not as good as Western ways." And what lay in the way of "becoming Western" had to go. Kamehameha I held on during his lifetime, but at his death in 1819 the powerful chiefess Ka'ahumanu effected the laying aside of traditional societal laws (the *kapu* system) and the religion that supported it.

Traditionally the *ali'i nui* controlled land tenure in Hawai'i. When white people came to the islands, they were occasionally awarded land to live on. But the traditional meaning of "give you lands" included the perhaps unexpressed proviso, "which you will hold at my pleasure."

While private ownership was a foreign concept to Hawaiians, it was a necessary part, indeed the basis, of Western economic activity.

Almost from the time of their arrival, the missionaries exerted some influence over the kings. As relations within the outside world became more complex in the late 1830s and 1840s, King Kamehameha III began to look for people to assist the kingdom who were educated in the Western ways. He found a number of missionaries willing to take positions in government. Other capable white newcomers also joined, taking some of the government's most powerful positions. By the end of 1844 there were fourteen white men in government service. All three of the most important members of the king's cabinet were white.[3]

To a man, the whites in government were convinced that the capitalistic economic system was necessary and good for Hawai'i. They had known nothing else. They argued that if a man had a piece of property that he could call his own, he would work hard to make something of himself. Private ownership would transform the Hawaiian society into a hardworking, industrious, and prosperous nation. The whites seemed incapable of realizing that Hawaiians in general could not think in a capitalistic way. The Hawaiians had experienced only the *ahupua'a* life. Generosity and free giving were the very basis of the economic system at work in the *ahupua'a:* One *gave away* all this surplus. That way everybody was provided for. Capitalism demanded that one keep his surplus, that he deny it to others. Hawaiians could not understand why anyone would want to do that. Wealth was the accumulation of things of value which others wanted, and this made no sense to the Hawaiians. What the Hawaiians desperately needed in the 1840s was for the government to reestablish and fortify the *ahupua'a* system.[4]

The famed Hawaiian intellectual and author David Malo and others said this. In 1845 they collected thousands of names of native Hawaiians on Maui and on the island of Hawai'i petitioning the king to get rid of the white men (*haoles*) in government and to take a stand against private ownership. Their cries fell on unheeding ears. The *haoles* would be kept in their powerful government positions "because they were needed," as the king said.[5]

It must be noted that some of these advisors were truly dedicated to the king and in every move tried to do what was best for the kingdom. They were misguided. They hoped to get Hawaiian natives out of urban slums and back onto the land by creating a class of landed commoners who would work small, personally owned farms. Yet, through their miscalculation of the Hawaiians' ability to deal with private ownership, these advisors indeed were the direct cause of the Hawaiians losing their lands to the white foreigner.

As the 1840s progressed, Kamehameha III succumbed increasingly to the advice of the whites in his Cabinet. By the latter part of the decade, *haole* advisors had in fact completely taken over government decision making.[6] Then, using the experience of the temporary British takeover in 1843 as an example of something that could easily happen again, they scared an unwilling king and his chiefs into establishing private property.[7]

THE *MAHELE*

In 1848 Hawaiian lands were divided up. This "division" of lands is called the *mahele*. Originally the idea was to divide the land three ways: one-third each for the king, the chiefs, and the commoners.[8] As it turned out, the chiefs were given about one and a half million acres. Some land was also set aside for the Fort. The king kept about a million acres—the "crown lands" as they were later called. Most of the rest, roughly another one and a half million acres, was set aside as "government lands."[9]

According to the original plan, in 1850, two years after the land division took place, native Hawaiian commoners who had lived on a piece of property for the previous ten years would be allowed to make a claim to between one and two acres of land surrounding their homes. These were called *kuleana* claims. Since these claims would take place two years after the original division, the *kuleana* lands claimed would be portions taken from the chiefs' lands, the crown lands, or the government lands.

Additionally, portions of the "government lands" were also set aside for sale to native commoners who did not qualify for *kuleana* and land claims.[10] *Kuleana* holders who wished to increase the size of their lands would also be able to do so by purchasing additional, inexpensive property from among the "government lands."[11]

The "crown lands" and the "government lands" have become very important to the Hawaiian people today. Native Hawaiians claim that both belong exclusively to them and to no one else, and they want them returned to form part of the land base for the Hawaiian nation.

In regard to "government lands," part of the present claim centers around the questions of precisely whom the "government lands" were set aside to benefit, and who—according to the intent of the *mahele* itself—was allowed to buy them.

One purpose of the "government lands" was to provide income to run the government. Money would come from selling or leasing the lands. But from the beginning of *mahele* discussion among the chiefs, there had been clear statements that land would not go to non-Hawaiians. They were to be sold to native Hawaiian commoners for fifty cents an acre.[12]

Non-Hawaiians were not considered as possible purchasers. In 1847, a year before the final division in the *mahele*, small portions of land were *awarded* (not sold) to non-Hawaiian individuals, both in and out of the government, who either had previously held them "at the pleasure of the king" or who merited some reward at that time.[13] Those were the only non-Hawaiians who had, or were expected to have, any serious claim to land in the islands. The "government lands," then, were set aside for purchase by native Hawaiian people alone.

By comparison with roughly 100,000 native Hawaiian citizens in 1848, the fifteen hundred or so resident non-Hawaiians were a tiny minority. And the number of that tiny minority who had become naturalized citizens was so insignificant that they possibly never entered into Kamehameha III's consideration as also "to be benefited by the government lands."

Further, since most non-Hawaiians had become naturalized citizens in order to marry native Hawaiians, they were Hawaiian family members anyway. Their descendants would all have Hawaiian blood. There was thus little reason to think of them as "separate" and "individuated" non-Hawaiian beneficiaries of the government.

Additionally, there is strong reason to believe that Kamehameha III purposely avoided any reference to non-Hawaiians when he stated whom he intended to benefit from all aspects of the *mahele*. Throughout this period, native Hawaiians in the neighbor islands were petitioning and demonstrating against both the *haoles* in government and the possibility of Hawaiian land being sold to non-Hawaiians. In response to the protesters, Kamehameha III constantly reiterated that the *haole* presence in government was only transitory, and that they would remain only until Hawaiians could be trained to run the government. He was clearly committed to the idea that Hawai'i would be a Hawaiian nation—owned by Hawaiians and run by Hawaiians for the benefit of Hawaiians. There is every reason to believe, then, that the King's specific intent was to include only native Hawaiians among those who would have lands and benefit from the government.[14]

When native Hawaiians, then, argue that at the time that the *mahele* was signed into law, the "government lands" were set aside for them and them alone, the evidence supports their claim. They alone could buy the land. They alone were the intended benefactors of the *mahele*. "Government lands"—and the rest of the islands—were set aside so that native Hawaiians might dwell upon them and establish themselves forever.

Despite the good intentions of the king, the *mahele* was one of the greatest disasters ever suffered by the Hawaiian people. It effectively handed over to white people, citizens and foreigners alike, ownership and control of the land. Kamehameha III was not the intellectual, strong-willed, charismatic leader the times demanded. Shortly after signing the *mahele* in 1848, he began to drink heavily again. From May 1849, he began to neglect his Privy Council meetings. All of the modern changes, all of the pressures were too much for the king. He simply gave up. The dominant, white members of the Privy Council then ran the government.[15]

In 1850 the commoners were to be allowed to claim *kuleana* lands and to purchase "government lands." But almost a month before the lands were opened to them, the Legislature confirmed the decision of the *haole*-dominated Privy Council allowing all residents, even foreigners, unrestricted rights to buy and sell lands.[16] Under *haole* supervision, the "government lands" so carefully set aside "forever" for his commoners by a loving king, were competed for: cash-poor commoners unaware of the meaning of land-title versus shrewd *haoles*, some backed with almost unlimited wealth—just as Malo and the other petitioners had predicted.

The commoners hardly even entered the contest. Their life experiences had taught them to work the land under the direction of someone who would make sure they were provided for. Under the new system, they might have their own land to farm, but how would they get their crops to a market? And once there, how would they know how to bargain for a price? The *mahele* was doomed to failure because there was no marketing structure outside of the port towns to support private enterprise. The whole concept was too foreign and too complicated for the commoner. Uneducated, unaccustomed to leadership, he could not organize the marketing structure himself, and there was no one to do it for him. He wanted to return to life in the *ahupua'a* where he provided one commodity to the flow of goods while others to whom he was related and whom he loved provided him with clothes and fish and pigs and *taro* and potatoes and all the other things he needed in life.[17]

The chiefs, in a different way, were also having their problems with capitalism. They were frequently inept at handling money and were almost always in debt. After the *mahele,* although they did not have money, they did have land. They passed the law in 1850 which allowed non-Hawaiian aliens to purchase property because they wanted to be able to sell their lands to pay existing debts and to buy more things. From then on, the chiefs were always in need of more and more money, and were forced to sell off more and more of their land.

By the end of 1850, the same year the law was passed allowing purchase of lands by anyone, thousands of acres had been sold to whites. Within two more years, the acreage sold would be in the hundreds of thousands. Before the monarchy came to an end forty years later, most of the chiefs' lands and vast parts of the crown lands and government lands had been sold to whites.[18]

The American Board of Foreign Missions cut off support for the American missionaries in the islands during the same year that land first became available. The missionaries then petitioned the Privy Council, controlled at that time by whites, for land. Their petitions were made during the same months that the native Hawaiian commoners were securing title to the *kuleanas* they had claimed. In contrast to the small *kuleanas* being granted to Hawaiian commoners—many between one and two acres—the white missionaries were granted 560 acres each at a nominal cost. The missionaries, now cut off from support by the American board, turned to business.[20]

SUGAR: THE WHITE TAKEOVER CONTINUES

During the forty years between 1850 and 1890, the missionaries and their children, and other shrewd newcomers, put their future in sugar. They continued buying up lands from the chiefs, and they also bought and leased thousands of additional acres of the "government lands."

Business more and more became "the important thing" in the islands. But it was the white man's business: They owned the property. Sugar plantations grew large and powerful. The whole island economy came to depend on sugar. Whites imported Chinese, Japanese, and Portuguese to work in their fields, eventually bringing in sixty-one thousand immigrants.[20] With the new Asian immigrant population now so large, *haoles* who were landed or otherwise influential were a tiny part of the population indeed. But, given their position, they thought of themselves as masters of the uneducated, uncultured farm laborers. They also saw it as their place to completely dominate the Hawaiians. These were their islands. And the islands and all of the people in them existed for them and for the pursuit of their wealth.[21]

In 1876 Hawai'i made a treaty of reciprocity with the United States which allowed Hawaiian sugar to be sold to America without paying import taxes. Reciprocity treaties could expire, however, and the first one did in 1883. The *haole* sugar growers in Hawai'i wanted a more permanent relationship that would guarantee exporting their sugar to the United States tax free. Annexation as a Territory of the United States would guarantee it. Many in the white community were American citizens who would never have Hawaiian citizenship. Most of the other whites held at least dual citizenship with the United States. Thus, the greatest majority were predisposed for Annexation.

In 1887, sugar interests were in trouble. It had been four years since the expiration of the first reciprocity treaty. The old treaty was being renewed on a year to year basis. The United States had not agreed to a new one. The United States would not budge on a new treaty unless the exclusive right to use Pearl Harbor as a naval station was included. They wanted King Kalākaua to sign their new constitution—which since that time has been referred to as the "Bayonet Constitution." It effectively stripped the king of most of his power. The House of Nobles, for instance, would be elected instead of appointed, and new voting requirements were so strin-gent and so carefully written that elections would be controlled by the white community. People the whites wanted would fill the House of Nobles. The House of Nobles would control the Cabinet. The Cabinet, according to the Constitution, would control the King. And the *haole* would have control of the kingdom.

After elections were held, when he no longer controlled the Legislature or the Cabinet, King Kalākaua, following the Constitutional requirement that he comply with the decisions of his Cabinet, signed the new reciprocity treaty giving America exclusive use of Pearl Harbor. For as long as the treaty would remain in force, that right would continue. The date was November 29, 1887.

It soon became obvious that the new reciprocity treaty was only a ploy to get Pearl Harbor. In 1891, less than four years after ratifying the treaty, Congress passed the McKinley Act allowing all the sugar of the world to enter the United States free of import duty. The United States had Pearl Harbor, but Hawaiian sugar no longer had any advantage over other for-eign sugar. This crippled the Hawaiian sugar industry and within a year caused major depression in the islands.[22]

King Kalākaua died in 1891. His sister Lili'uokalani, succeeded him. Within two years, her reign was toppled by the white business commu-nity and the American Minister with the support of American armed forces. The financial depression precipitated an overthrow. The planters and the business community were suffering great losses and the depres-sion was getting worse each month. If Queen Lili'uokalani could be deposed and the islands annexed to the United States, sugar could be back "in the money" and the economy could rebound. For while the McKinley Act let all foreign sugar into the United States free of duty, it also provided a domestic price support of two cents per pound.[23]

The *haole* community at this time comprised about 15 percent of the population. A small number in that *haole* community owned most of the land and ran most of the business. They needed to secure their posses-sions and their place of power against any possible confiscation by the larger population. Native Hawaiians wanted control of their government back. And they wanted their country back. Many in the white community supported the Hawaiian goals. The small clique in power was convinced that as long as a native Hawaiian monarch ruled, there was the possibil-ity that they might lose everything they had. They were looking for some pretext to take over the government and annex the islands to the United States for their own security. The independent nation of the native Hawaiian people would be sacrificed to insure the economic advantage of a group primarily composed of children of the American missionaries who had come to save the Hawaiian people.

Quite soon after her accession to the throne, Queen Lili'uokalani received a petition signed by two-thirds of the citizens—mostly Native Hawaiians—imploring her to do away with the Bayonet Constitution and to return the powers of government to the native Hawaiian citizens.[24]

In 1892, anticipating that the Queen would do away with the Bayonet Constitution—an act they could use as justification for her overthrow—members of the white community formed the Annexation Club. Unknown to the queen, Lorrin Thurston, one of the founders of the club, left for America where the Secretary of State and the Secretary of the Navy (speaking for President Harrison) gave Thurston encouraging words about Annexation should the overthrow take place.

When Thurston returned, he and the others in the Annexation Club waited for the chance for revolution. They met repeatedly with the American Minister plenipotentiary for Hawai'i, John L. Stevens. He plotted with them for the overthrow.[25]

On January 14, 1893, Queen Lili'uokalani told her cabinet of her intention to adopt her newly finished Constitution. She was encouraged to wait for a few days by members of the cabinet who immediately took the news to the Annexation Club. A "Committee of Safety" was formed, composed of twelve members from the Annexation Club and one outsider. On the Committee, there were five Americans, six Hawaiian citizens by birth or naturalization (who also held dual citizenship from America), one Englishman, and one German. They resolved to proclaim a provisional government. "The queen herself, they said, had committed a revolutionary act when she proposed to alter the constitution, and this justified the 'intelligent part of the community' taking things into their own hands."[26]

Hearing that was happening the Queen published word that she was formally laying aside her own constitution and committing herself to abide by the Bayonet Constitution. She also sent announcement of this formal declaration to all of the foreign ministers in Hawai'i, including the American minister. Now there was no justification for the overthrow. But the Committee of Safety was not about to let that stop them.[27]

Details of what happened in those few days are best told in the words of the President of the United States, Grover Cleveland.

Message of President Grover Cleveland to the Congress

The 16th of January. Under the auspices of the Committee of Safety, a mass meeting of citizens was held to protest against the Queen's alleged illegal and unlawful proceedings and purposes. Even at this meeting the Committee of Safety continued to disguise their real purpose and contented themselves with procuring the passage of a resolution denouncing the Queen and empowering the committee to devise ways and means "to secure the permanent maintenance of law and order and the protection of life, liberty, and property in Hawaii."

The committee, unwilling to take further steps without cooperation of the United States Minister, addressed him a note representing that the public safety was menaced and that lives and property were in danger, and concluded as follows: "We are unable to protect ourselves without aid, and therefore pray for the protection of the United States forces." Between four and five o'clock in the afternoon, a detachment of marines from the United States steamer Boston, with two pieces of artillery, landed in Honolulu. The men, upwards of 160 in all, were supplied with double cartridge belts filled with ammunition and with haversacks and canteens, and were accompanied by a hospital corps with stretchers and medical supplies. This military demonstration upon the soil of Honolulu was of itself an act of war, unless made either with the consent of the Government of Hawaii or for the *bona fide* purpose of protecting the imperiled lives and property of citizens of the United States. But there is no pretense of any such consent on the part of the Government of the Queen, which at the time was undisputed and was both the *de facto* and the *de jure* government.

Thus it appears that Hawaii was taken possession of by the United States without the consent or wish of the government of the islands, or of anybody else so far as shown, except the United States Minister.

They met the next morning, Tuesday, the 17th, perfected the plan of temporary government, and fixed upon its principal officers, ten of whom were drawn from the thirteen members of the Committee of Safety. Between one and two o'clock, by squads and by different routes to avoid notice, and having first taken the precaution of ascertaining whether there was any one there to oppose them, they proceeded to the Government building to proclaim the new government. No sign of opposition was manifest, and thereupon an American citizen began to read the proclamation from the steps of the Government building almost entirely without auditors.

The provisional government thus proclaimed "to exist until terms of union with the United States had been negotiated and agreed upon." The United States minister, pursuant to prior agreement, recognized this government within an hour after the reading of the proclamation, and before five o'clock, in answer to an inquiry on behalf of the Queen and her cabinet, announced that he had done so.

Some hours after the recognition of the provisional government by the United States Minister, the palace, the barracks, and the police station, with all the military resources of the country, were delivered up by the Queen, upon the representation made to her that her cause would thereafter be reviewed at Washington, and while protesting that she surrendered to the superior force of the United States, whose Minister had caused United States troops to be landed at Honolulu and declared that he would support the provisional government, and that she yielded her authority to prevent collision of armed forces and loss of life and only until such time as the United States, upon the facts being presented to it, should undo the action of its representative and reinstate her in the authority she claimed as the constitutional sovereign of the Hawaiian Islands.

I believe that a candid and thorough examination of the facts will force the conviction that the provisional government owes its existence to an armed invasion by the United States. Fair minded people with the evidence before them will hardly claim that the Hawaiian Government was overthrown by the people of the islands or that the provisional government had ever existed with their consent. I do not understand that any member of this government claims that the people would uphold it by their suffrages if they were allowed to vote on the question.

The law Government of Hawaii was overthrown without the drawing of a sword or the firing of a shot by a process every step of which, it may safely be asserted, is directly traceable to and dependent for its success upon the agency of the United States acting through its diplomatic and naval representatives.

But for the notorious predilections of the United States Minister for annexation, the Committee of Safety, which should be called the Committee of Annexation, would have never existed.

But for the landing of the United States forces upon false pretexts respecting the danger of life and property the committee would never have exposed themselves to the pains and penalties of treason by undertaking the subversion of the Queen's Government.

But for the presence of the United States forces in the immediate vicinity and in position to afford all needed protection and support, the committee would not have proclaimed the provisional government from the steps of the Government building.

And finally, but for the lawless occupation of Honolulu under false pretexts by the United States forces, and but for Minister Steven's recognition of the provisional government when the United States forces were its sole support and constituted its only military strength, the Queen and her Government would never have yielded to the provisional government, even for a time and for the sole purpose of submitting her case to the enlightened justice of the United States.

By an act of war committed with the participation of a diplomatic representative of the United States and without authority of Congress, the Government of a feeble but friendly and confiding people had been overthrown. A substantial wrong has thus been done which a due regard for our national character as well as the rights of the injured people required we should endeavor to repair.

She surrendered not to the provisional government, but to the United States. She surrendered not absolutely and permanently, but temporarily and conditionally until such time as the facts could be considered by the United States.

NOTES

[1] David E. Stannard, *Before the Horror: The Population of Hawai'i on the Eve of Western Contact* (Honolulu: University of Hawai'i Press, 1988).

[2] Gavan Daws, *Shoal of Time: A History of the Hawaiian Islands* (Honolulu: University of Hawai'i Press, 1974): 9.

[3] Daws, *Shoal of Time,* 108.

[4] We are indebted to Lilikalā Dorton for the reasoning behind why the *mahele* was such a disaster: Native Hawaiians were unable to embrace it and make it work because (1) capitalism was diametrically opposed to all they had ever learned (The society economy of the *ahupua'a* was based on generous giving. Capitalism is based on conserving, saving for one's self.) and (2) because the *ahupua'a* society satisfied all of their needs, natives did not know how to go about marketing their produce. She cites a passage in *The Works of the People of Old* (Samuel Kamakau, tr. by Mary Kawena Pūku'i, ed. by Dorothy Barrere, Honolulu: Bishop Museum Press, 1976, pp. 122–123) where Kamakau tells that "peddling" was a practice despised by the ancestors. A peddler was held in extreme contempt.

Dorton's doctoral dissertation, "Land and the Promise of Capitalism: A Dilemma for the Hawaiian Chiefs of the 1848 Mahele," is one of the first modern historical works written from the Hawaiian point of view. It was submitted to the History Department of the University of Hawai'i in December 1986, and is available at Hamilton Library, University of Hawai'i. Since publishing this work, Dorton has reassumed the surname of her Hawaiian ancestors and is presently known as Lilikalā Kame'eleihiwa.

[5] Daws, *Shoal of Time,* 109, 125; Dorton, "Land and the Promise of Capitalism," 238–252.

⁶ Armstrong Letters, Armstrong to Chapman, Sept. 18, 1844. Cited in Ralph S. Kuykendall, *The Hawaiian Kingdom,* 3 vols. (Honolulu: University of Hawai'i Press, 1938–1957): vol. 1, p. 238.

⁷ Kuykendall, *Hawaiian Kingdom,* 1:291; also Daws, *Shoal of Time,* 125.

⁸ Wylie to Judd (No. 10) November 19, 1849, in Report of Secretary of War, 1855, Appendix pp. 7–8. Cited in Kuykendall, *Hawaiian Kingdom,* 1:291.

⁹ Donald D. Kilolani Mitchell, *Resource Units in Hawaiian Culture* (Honolulu: Kamehameha Schools, 1982); Kuykendall, *Hawaiian Kingdom,* 1:294.

¹⁰ Act of 11 July 1851, [1851] Hawai'i Laws 52–53. We take this quote from Dorton, "Land and the Promise of Capitalism," 316. She takes it from Neil M. Levy, "Native Hawaiian Land Rights," California Law Review, 63.4 (1975): 857. See also Kuykendall, *Hawaiian Kingdom,* 1:291, for variation.

¹¹ Dorton, "Land and the Promise of Capitalism," 316.

¹² Act of 11 July 1851, as in note 10 above.

¹³ Dorton, "Land and the Promise of Capitalism," 265.

¹⁴ Daws, *Shoal of Time,* 109.

¹⁵ Dorton, "Land and the Promise of Capitalism," 332.

¹⁶ Mitchell, *Resource Units in Hawaiian Culture,* 263. See also Dorton, "Land and the Promise of Capitalism," 265.

¹⁷ That this was the case is clear from a letter in The Polynesian, January 5, 1850, quoted in Kuykendall, *Hawaiian Kingdom,* 1:92.

¹⁸ Mitchell, *Resource Units in Hawaiian Culture,* 264, taking figures from *Hawai'i Pono* by Lawrence H. Fuchs (New York: Harcourt, Brace and World, 1961): 61.

¹⁹ Dorton, "Land and the Promise of Capitalism," 321, citing Jean Hobbs, *Hawai'i: A Pageant of the Soil* (Stanford, Calif.: Stanford University Press, 1935):157–177, and Amos Starr Cooke, *The Chiefs' Children's School* (Honolulu: Honolulu Star-Bulletin, 1937): 349–350.

²⁰ A. A. Smyser, "Annexation Caused Tears of Joy-and Sadness," *Honolulu Star-Bulletin,* Aug. 9, 1988.

²¹ Daws, *Shoal of Time,* 241 and passim.

²² Daws, *Shoal of Time,* 265, 268.

²³ Daws, *Shoal of Time,* 266–267.

²⁴ Lili'uokalani, *Hawai'i's Story by Hawai'i's Queen* (Boston: Lee and Shepard, 1898): 230–231.

²⁵ Pōkā Laenui (Hayden Burgess), *A Thief in Judgement of Itself,* ms. available at 84-794-D Farrington Hwy., Wai'anae, HI 96792, p. 8.

²⁶ Daws, *Shoal of Time,* 272.

²⁷ See President's Message following.

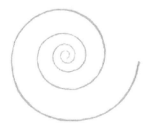

CHAPTER 21

Ho'omana

Jay Hartwell

The journey to the island of Kaho'olawe begins seven miles across 'Alalākeiki Channel at a small cove on the island of Maui. In the predawn darkness, a dozen men and women stand on the beach and hold hands in a circle beside their outrigger canoes. Their breath warms the air with a *pule* (prayer), followed by a chant to their ancestors, to the people who crossed to Kaho'olawe before them, and to the pantheon of their gods— Kū, Lono, Kāne, and Kanaloa. As they invoke guidance and strength, their words weave a cloak of spiritual protection to guard them in what could be a four-hour pull across the channel.

Unless you go by helicopter, the passage across 'Alalākeiki Channel is the primary way to reach Kaho'olawe, a 28,000-acre island the U.S. Navy used for fifty years for bombing practice. The federal government stopped shelling it in 1990 and four years later returned the island to the State of Hawai'i. By then the upper third of the island had been devastated by the bombardment and the animals that had overgrazed the land before the bombing began. Unexploded ordnance made the rest of the island—already a parched desert—too dangerous to cross on foot. Nonetheless, many Hawaiians considered it a blessing when the island was returned. For almost twenty years they had prayed and protested and negotiated to end the bombing.

During those two decades, Kaho'olawe was more than a symbol of Western abuse of the lands that had once sustained the people of the Hawaiian nation. During monthly "accesses" coordinated with the Navy, Kaho'olawe became a sanctuary, a place where Hawaiians could be Hawaiian and revive and practice their religion far from judgmental eyes. Today, state law has decreed that the island shall be reserved for traditional Hawaiian uses, with no commercial activity.

This essay was previously published as "Ho'omana: Religion," in *Nā Mamo: Hawaiian People Today* (Honolulu: 'Ai Pōkahu Press, 1996), 193–217.

When Craig Neff first landed on the island, in 1983, two years after the Navy began to allow Hawaiians access, he thought he knew what it meant to be Hawaiian.

When I was growing up, I was always locked into being Hawaiian. That was one thing I liked and I felt strong about. I was listening to Hawaiian music. I tried to see things Hawaiian. I thought walking around with your Hawaiian T-shirt, having one Hawaiian flag on the back of your car, paddling, whatever, was making you Hawaiian. But when I went over to the island, it really hit me what being Hawaiian was.

   When you're off [Kaho'olawe], you don't have to like the guy walking on the street because you don't know him. But on the island, anybody walk by, you tell'em "howzit" or something like that. It's a different feeling because you're dependent on this person. If you get hurt, he has to do something to take care of you. It's a different way of thinking.

The first time Craig visited Kaho'olawe, the sun and stars shone in clear skies for three days. But on the last night, after he had taken part in a ceremonial walk across the island, after prayers and offerings to the god Lono, clouds moved over the island, and it rained and rained—life-giving rain for the thirsty land. "That's what we were asking for, hoping for," Craig remembered,

and we stayed up the whole night talking story 'cause it was just too wet to even sleep. And the next day it was a nice, beautiful day. As we left the island we had to swim out and jump on this big catamaran, and I looked back and I just started to cry, and I told the person who went over with me, "What I went through, that was one for the Hawaiians."

Afterward, Craig decided Kaho'olawe was the place to be.

This is the key to get into what I was looking for. It wasn't going around beating up people, or yelling at people. That's not the goal of being Hawaiian. [It was] going over [to Kaho'olawe and helping to restore the island] and learning. When I came back and seen O'ahu, the streets and everything paved [for the first time] I could feel the ground under the asphalt just suffocating. It's a living thing, and if you put concrete or asphalt over it, you're killing, you're suffocating it. I could feel that when I was driving on the road [Kaho'olawe] and its people really changed the way I thought.

In 1976, Hawaiians formed an association, the Protect Kaho'olawe 'Ohana, to try and stop the bombing; protesters landed on Kaho'olawe, and the military arrested them for trespassing. During the next four years, the 'Ohana persevered through repeated landings and arrests, protests, negotiations, and a court case. George Helm, the charismatic 'Ohana leader, and his friend Kimo Mitchell disappeared in the rough seas of 'Alalākeiki Channel while paddling from Kaho'olawe to Maui. In 1980, the Navy granted the 'Ohana a four-day monthly access to the island ten times a year—forty days altogether—for religious, educational, and scientific activities; during an "access," the military would suspend bombing.

The 'Ohana wanted to perform religious ceremonies on Kaho'olawe. Their elders advised them to go to the island, believe their 'aumakua and gods, and call on the deities for help in restoring the island. At first, it was a self-conscious effort. The 'Ohana had to find teachers, kupuna who had living experiences healing the land; then they had to research, learn, and practice the rites for the annual Makahiki rituals, seeking to reenact the ceremonies as closely as contemporary realities allowed. Makahiki is the ancient four-month celebration of Lono, the god of fertility and agriculture. Traditionally, the season began in November; when Makali'i, the Pleiades constellation, appeared in the night sky with the new moon, it was time for the chiefs to suspend war, collect tributes, and hold festivals with hula and physical competitions. For the 'Ohana, the Makahiki became a time to rest and remember the past, plan for the future, and ask Lono's help in restoring the island of Kaho'olawe. But the consequences of the public ceremonies—the first in more than a century—extended beyond Kaho'olawe. The courage of the 'Ohana led other Hawaiians to ignore criticism and incorporate religious rites from past generations into modern ceremonies. Their efforts reminded Hawai'i that the 'āina, the land, has a spiritual life force; it has cultural value that is perpetuated through love, respect, responsibility, and proper cultivation of food and medicinal plants.

The 'Ohana conducts the opening and closing Makahiki ceremonies during two of its monthly accesses to Kaho'olawe, in November and January. Generally, the accesses last four days; they begin Wednesday evening or in the early morning hours on Thursday. The 'Ohana and up to eight people leave Maui from Mā'alaea Harbor or Mākena in fishing boats, outrigger canoes, or tourist catamarans and cross 'Alalākeiki Channel to Hakioawa Bay on Kaho'olawe. They double-wrap their gear in trash bags sealed with duct tape. After the crossing, the boars anchor offshore and everyone transfers in small groups to a Zodiac to motor closer to the shorebreak. Then people jump into the surf and join a human chain passing bags and people to the beach. The ocean is cold in the darkness, and it sometimes breaks with a ferocity that reminds newcomers they could easily drown without the help of others, without confidence in themselves, without an understanding of the ocean and the island.

For the next three nights, people camp near the beach, within an area the Navy has cleared of bombs. During most accesses, the 'Ohana and its friends spend their days working on trails, erosion control, or projects such as building a *pā*—a *hula* platform. During the entire Makahiki season, the 'Ohana focuses on honoring Lono. They trust him to provide gentle rains for the island to help turn it green again within their lifetimes.

The 'Ohana allows both men and women to prepare the *heiau* and shrine for the Makahiki ceremonies. But only the *mo'o* Lono, the men who devote themselves to the god Lono, conduct the formal ceremonies to the god. Women participate in the Lono rituals and, in addition, perform their own rites.

Efforts to restore the Hawaiian religion and the shrines of old have been difficult during the past fifteen years. The Navy accused the 'Ohana of revitalizing the Hawaiian religion on Kaho'olawe as a means of securing legal access to the island. Some Hawaiians, like Craig Neff's parents, could not understand what the young people were trying to do. Others dismissed the 'Ohana as crazy activists and said *kupuna* would keep secret the traditional rituals in order to protect their children from the consequences of awakening old *kapu*. But a few elders—Harry Kunihi Mitchell, Emma DeFries, and Mary Lee—encouraged the 'Ohana. Edith K. Kanaka'ole, a Big Island *kumu hula* who had grown up with the Hawaiian language and culture, urged 'Ohana members to go to Kaho'olawe during the Makahiki and perform the Lono rituals so the island would become green again. After she passed on, Aunty Edith's daughters helped teach the 'Ohana the traditional chants. Other people offered additional information. They gleaned what they could from books. All this, the 'Ohana said, was an intermediate step while more Hawaiians learned to speak the language and live the culture.

In ancient times, at the beginning of Makahiki the Hawaiians resurrected an image of Lono from a place of refuge and carried it in procession clockwise around an island, stopping at every district boundary. Each community presented offerings to representatives of the high chief. The people were then free to celebrate the remainder of the festival season with competitions and games. This is difficult in the twentieth century, because work schedules and logistical problems in traveling around Kaho'olawe force the 'Ohana to modify its rituals. During the closing ceremony, in January, Lono's image is carried across the middle of the island to the westernmost point, Laeokealaikahiki, the place where long-ago voyages to Kahiki, the ancestral homeland, began. At sunset the 'Ohana launches the Lono image in a ceremonial canoe filled with offerings. These will accompany the god back to Hakioawa for two days of Makahiki games, discussion, and personal reflection before returning to their lives across the channel.

Before each Makahiki officially begins, the 'Ohana asks everyone on-island to participate in an ocean purification ceremony, called *hi'uwai*. The ceremony usually takes place before dawn, but the 'Ohana decided to hold the November 1989 *hi'uwai* after dinner Friday night. The purification began with the sounding of the *pū*, a conch-shell trumpet, in the darkness. It signals *kapu*, and silence must be maintained. By the light of the moon and stars, people silently crossed the sand and lined up on the beach to receive from a *mo'o* Lono a sip of water mixed with *limu kalawai*, a freshwater algae symbolizing forgiveness, and *'olena*, a ginger root, for cleansing. Then, wearing swimsuits or nothing at all, they waded into the cold shorebreak and immersed in the sea.

The next time the *pū* sounded, ending the *kapu*, the people would celebrate by shouting the name of the god, "Lono-i-ka-Makahiki." Until then, many arms and legs tensed and curled up for warmth against the ocean chill, as people waited for their minds to relax and their bodies to float in rhythm with the sea. The water washes away ill and negative feelings, the sins and wrongs known as *hewa*. And with purification comes peace. It was a peace too brief for some; the *pū* sounded and people cheered "Lono-i-ka-Makahiki" as they splashed through the water, hugging one another. A bonfire was lit on the beach, and people huddled close to warm themselves and watch sparks float up to the stars. In the blazing firelight, their eyes glowed with happiness.

Purified by the ocean and warmed by the fire, everyone went to their camps to dress. They returned to the beach when the *pū* announced it was time for the procession to place offerings to Lono in the *imu*, an underground oven. Earlier, 'Ohana members had prepared ti-leaf bundles of fish, pig, *'awa, kalo*, breadfruit, banana, coconut, and sweet potato—all sacred to the god. For this Makahiki, the 'Ohana had selected ten men and ten women to carry the offerings. After cooking the ti-leaf bundles in the *imu* Friday night, they would remove the offerings and rewrap them in fresh ti leaves before Saturday's predawn Makahiki ceremonies at the Hale o Papa *heiau* and Hale Mua, the fishing shrine. Then, after an arduous hike to the top of the island, the 'Ohana would present a third set of offerings to Lono at another *lele* at Pu'u Moa'ulaiki.

For the *imu* procession, the 'Ohana dressed the ten men and ten women in simple unbleached muslin. The men wore *malo* and stood in a column to the left; the women were in *kikepa* on the right. Two spearsmen, also barefoot and in *malo*, separated them from the crowd. The *mo'o* Lono stood before the presenters, their bodies bare except for the muslin *malo* that covered their loins. One of them carried the image of Lono, which was raised high above the procession on a tall, wooden pole, its cross-piece festooned with *kapa*, feathers, and ferns. The men selected to blow *pū* preceded Lono's image, the sound of their conch shells trumpeting through the darkness, announcing the god's return to Kaho'olawe.

The procession moved slowly beneath the full moon. It crossed the beach and the dry streambed, moved up the slope through the main camp and beneath the *kiawe* grove, past Ka'ie'ie, the *pā* for hula, to the *imu*. Each presenter silently handed an uncooked ti-leaf bundle to a *mo'o* Lono, who passed it to another, then to another, until the last one placed it among the roasting stones in the *imu*. When all the offerings rested inside, the *mo'o* Lono covered the *imu* with burlap and dirt, and the cooking began.

Then everyone intoned a chant they had practiced the day before:

E hō mai ka 'ike mai luna mai e
I nā mea huna no'eau o nā mele e
E hō mai—e hō mai—e hō mai.

The people repeated the verse, gaining confidence, giving the message strength as the sound of their voices rose into the trees.

Different people have different opinions about the ceremonies taking place on Kaho'olawe. In the past, protocol has changed to meet the limitations of a specific access. Purification ceremonies in the ocean have taken place at varying times—before dawn, before midnight, or in the early evening. Some people want to see traditional ceremonial conduct more strictly enforced. Others want to see women in the role of *mo'o* Lono. As with all religions, the worshipers here have differing perceptions of their gods. One woman believes if she does not worship and feed her gods every day, they will consume her. Another believes that all gods, including Lono, lead to one supreme deity who watches over everyone, regardless of whether people use the name Akua, God, Allah, or Jehovah.

"For us who live in today's society, we don't have all the [ceremonial] answers," Craig said.

> We cannot go to somebody and ask them what the correct way is. We have to research. We have to ask a lot of people. Everybody has a different opinion of what went on, and our ceremony is not exactly as it would be in our ancestors' days, because of the circumstances that we are under. Half of the people are gonna agree with you and half might not. You can't worry about the roadblock, you just gotta keep moving forward.

The last night on the island, everyone sat in a circle and shared his or her impressions and feelings about the trip to Kaho'olawe. Participation in this *kūkākūkā* is mandatory, and the newcomers usually talk about their changed perception of the island. On this particular night, some 'Ohana members were angry. They had been videotaped during Friday night's purification ceremony and the dawn procession on Saturday. They believe videotaping violates the *kapu*. They want people to experience the island firsthand. Sitting in a room on another island and watching a tape, they say, dulls the Kaho'olawe experience and the goals of the 'Ohana.

The 'Ohana had granted permission for a documentary to be produced about the island. The person with the video camera, a Hawaiian, said he felt compelled to tape the rituals so more people could see the Hawaiian religion being practiced. That, he said, was more important than the objections of a few people who regarded it as an invasion of privacy.

The 'Ohana later decided to exclude the controversial scenes from the documentary, but disagreement about the taping is just one of several conflicts that surface in discussions about religion. Some Hawaiians oppose worship of the old gods, and others—including orthodox traditionalists—are critical of certain aspects of the 'Ohana protocol that they consider to "Christian."

During the *kūkākūkā*, Chris Peters listened to the arguments and thought about disagreements and conflict being an inherent part of religion. Chris was one of three Native Americans visiting Kaho'olawe from the Seventh Generation Fund. The U.S. Supreme Court denied his tribe's petition to prevent the construction of a logging road through pristine forest where members of the tribe went for purification ceremonies. Tribal elders questioned Chris and other young people about their reasons for reviving ceremonies no one had practiced for fifty years. Why, some elders asked, did the young people want to go back to the Stone Age?

Chris said Christianity has not helped all Native Americans cope with the abuse they suffer nor with modern American life in general. Many people need the old rituals to revive and restore their spirits. Although more tribes are performing the old ceremonies, people attack the reconstructed rituals—as in Hawai'i with the 'Ohana—for not being true to the past. Chris believes they are true for those who participate in them. If the rituals are stopped, "You stop their believing. You kill them. In some places, it is just a memory. It is past. It is no longer practiced. This," Chris said, gesturing toward the Hakioawa base camp where people laughed together as they prepared dinner, "is life."

A prominent Hawaiian scholar dismisses the 'Ohana as a minority of a minority—weekend Lono worshipers who put on *malo* and *kikepa* and chant memorized lines because they think that is what their ancestors did. The scholar sees Hawaiians becoming true to their culture only when they conduct themselves with a Hawaiian consciousness every moment of their lives, particularly when they cope with the westernized Hawai'i that awaits them beyond Kaho'olawe. And that, he said, requires a commitment few people are capable of making.

Craig has formulated his own ideas about Hawaiian worship.

The island knows who [we] are, and the island knows what [our] intent is in being there, and when you talk on that island, it hears you and it knows what you're about . . . not just the island, the *kūpuna* who are there, your ancestors if they're there, your *'aumākua* if they're there. They know it's not something you turn off and on. Nowadays, you say "*aloha 'āina*," it's a buzz word. For me *aloha 'āina* is just caring for not only the land but for everything around you. It's the ocean. It's the trees. It's the air. It's everything, and treating it as if it's a living thing. It's not dirt. It's not a rock. It's another form of life. It lives. It grows. It dies. Just like you. And if you take care of it, it's gonna take care of you. I don't care what religion you are, you don't have to believe in what I believe. It's a different road but the concept of *aloha 'āina,* or caring for the land, is a real simple thing. When you go back to your own home, that's the only thing you have to practice."

Making repeated journeys to Kaho'olawe helped Craig decide to give up his job at the Ala Wai Golf Course. He now focuses full-time on custom silkscreening for others and designing Hawaiian images for clothing printed under his logo, The Hawaiian Force. "Everybody said, 'Don't quit; you'll regret it." Especially my mom. For her, you work for the city, you put in your thirty [years], you got your benefits, you got everything. But for me, I thought about it a lot, and I prayed on it, and I'm just going with my feelings."

Whenever Craig Neff gets a chance, he goes to Kaho'olawe to refocus. "When you go there, you're not influenced by the car going by, by the radio; you can really concentrate on what's around you," Craig said.

You just look around and you can actually see a stone that was put there by a Hawaiian, by your ancestors, many years ago, a long time back, and it hasn't been moved. It hasn't been destroyed. It hasn't been influenced or tainted by anything. You can feel the *mana* around you in that area, what it was used for. If it was bad *mana,* you feel bad *mana.* If it was used for something good, you feel good *mana.*

"You can't learn being a Hawaiian from a book," repeated Craig.

A lot of people try, but being a Hawaiian is the way you think. It's your values and what you do every day. See, Hawaiians didn't have a real word for religion because it wasn't something that you turned off and you turned on, and you did on Sunday and you turned it off and you went home. It was a lifestyle. It's every day you live. It's everything you do. That's your religion. That's your life.

CHAPTER 22

Recognizing Native Hawaiians: A Quest for Sovereignty

Davianna Pomoaika'i McGregor

Native Hawaiians comprise a distinct and unique indigenous people with a historical continuity to the original inhabitants of the Hawaiian archipelago who exercised sovereignty as a nation centuries before the beginning of continuous European and American contact in 1778.

Native Hawaiian Health Care Improvement Act of 1992 (42 U.S.C. 1994)

The Hawaiian people remain determined to preserve, develop and transmit to future generations their ancestral territory, and their cultural identity in accordance with their own spiritual and traditional beliefs, customs, practices, language, and social institutions.

Public Law 103-150, Senate Joint Resolution of Apology, November 23, 1993

The truth and significance of these statements of findings by the U.S. Congress in the Native Hawaiian Health Care Improvement Act and Public Law 103-150 is at the heart of the most important human rights issue facing Hawai'i's people in the new millennium.

The U.S. Supreme Court, in the *Rice v. Cayetano* case, ruled on February 23, 2000 that elections for the trustees of the State of Hawai'i Office of Hawaiian Affairs (OHA), in which only Native Hawaiians were allowed to vote, used unconstitutional race-based qualifications.[1] The majority of the members of the court ruled that the Native Hawaiian OHA election violated the 15th Amendment of the U.S. Constitution which states that the right to vote cannot be denied on account of race or color.[2] Subsequently, in the November 2000 election for the trustees of the Office of Hawaiian Affairs, all registered voters, regardless of Native Hawaiian ancestry, were allowed to cast votes and to run for these offices.

The U.S. Supreme Court, in its ruling, stated that Native Hawaiians have a shared purpose with the general public in the islands and that the Constitution of the United States has become the heritage of all the citizens of Hawai'i, including Native Hawaiians. In addition, the court

331

raised questions about whether or not Native Hawaiians are, in fact, a distinct and unique indigenous people with the right of self-governance and self-determination under the U.S. law or whether they are, instead, an ethnic or racial minority. Under the U.S. Constitution, indigenous Native American tribes are recognized as domestic dependent nations, with inherent powers of self-governance and self-determination, for whom the U.S. federal government sustains a trust responsibility.[3] This status has been extended to Eskimos, Aleuts, and Native Alaskans under the Alaskan Native Claims Act. However, ethnic and racial minorities within the fifty U.S. states do *not* enjoy the status of nationhood, they do *not* have the right of self-governance and self-determination, and the federal government does *not* have a trust responsibility for them.

In the ruling, a majority of the Supreme Court justices also raised, but did not resolve, four fundamental questions regarding the status of Native Hawaiians. May Congress treat the Native Hawaiians as it does the Indian tribes? Has Congress in fact determined that Native Hawaiians have a status like that of Indians in organized tribes? May Congress delegate to the State of Hawai'i the authority to preserve that status? Has Congress delegated to the State of Hawai'i the authority to preserve that status?[4] A negative answer to any of these questions could result in a determination that Native Hawaiians do not qualify under U.S. law for the rights and protection afforded other indigenous peoples within the fifty states. The majority of the Supreme Court Justices also seemed to open the door to future legal challenges on the status of Native Hawaiians when it stated,

> It is a matter of some dispute, for instance, whether Congress may treat the native Hawaiians as it does the Indian tribes. Compare Van Dyke, The Political Status of the Hawaiian People, 17 Yale L. & Pol'y Rev. 95 (1998), with Benjamin, Equal Protection and the Special Relationship: The Case of Native Hawaiians, 106 Yale L.J. 537 (1996). We can stay far off that difficult terrain however."

Suddenly, the status, rights and entitlements which Native Hawaiians had enjoyed throughout the 20th century could be legally challenged out of existence. Moreover, the Supreme Court ruling seemed to contradict the policy of the U.S. Congress toward Native Hawaiians.

Beginning in 1906 and through 1998 the U.S. Congress, in effect, recognized a trust relationship with the native people of Hawai'i through the enactment of 183 Federal laws that explicitly included Native Hawaiians in the class of Native Americans.[5] Some of the laws extended federal programs set up for Native Americans to Native Hawaiians, while other laws represented recognition by the U.S. Congress that the United States bore a special responsibility to protect Native Hawaiian interests.[6] Although the operational policy of the U.S. Congress has been to exercise a trust responsibility with Native Hawaiians similar to Native Americans, none of the laws passed extended an explicit and formal recognition that Native Hawaiians are a sovereign people, with the right of self-governance and self-determination. Without such an explicit law, Native Hawaiians stand to lose the special benefits, entitlements, and protection that the U.S. Congress has extended to Native Hawaiians beginning in 1906.

In light of the ruling by the U.S. Supreme Court, Hawai'i's congressional delegation, led by Senators Daniel Akaka and Daniel Inouye, drafted and introduced legislation (called The Akaka Bill) to explicitly and unambiguously clarify the trust relationship between Native Hawaiians and the United States. Although the bill failed to pass in 2000, the Hawai'i congressional delegation reintroduced the bill for passage in 2001. When passed, the bill would formally and directly extend the federal policy of self-determination and self-governance to Native Hawaiians, as Hawai'i's indigenous native people. The legislation provides a process for the recognition by the United States, under the Secretary of the Department of Interior, of a Native Hawaiian governing entity.[7]

Opponents of Native Hawaiian recognition successfully lobbied Republican congressmen to oppose the bill in 2000. They continued their efforts to prevent its passage in 2001. Calling themselves "Aloha For All," the group is supported by the National Coalition for a Color Blind America. On their Web page, which lists four members, they state that they are, "creating web pages, speaking to Rotary clubs, Exchange Clubs and other organizations, writing letters to the editor and presenting op/ed articles to the media, testifying before legislative bodies, and litigating."[8] The Web page also states their opposition to the Akaka Bill, as follows:

> This legislation is dangerous to the people of Hawai'i and to the sovereignty of the United States. It is an attempt to divide the thoroughly integrated people of Hawai'i along racial lines. It would partition the State of Hawai'i by setting up an apartheid regime to which only *kanaka maoli* (the name Native Hawaiians prefer to call themselves) could belong . . . One of the most troubling aspects of the Akaka bill is its attempt to create an Indian tribe where none currently exists. It would be the first time in history when Congress recognizes a currently non-existent political entity and then puts in place a procedure to populate it."[9]

The Aloha For All group claims that all residents of Hawai'i are Hawaiian and that the limitation of any benefits to those who are "racially Hawaiian" is discriminatory and violates the 14th Amendment of the U.S. Constitution.[10]

The developments outlined above, which challenge Native Hawaiian status, rights, and entitlements sets the scene for this article. In the first part of this article, I review the indicators which show that Native Hawaiians continue to be a distinct people with a unique language, culture, economic life, and national lands. In the second part of this article I review the historical and political basis for the recognition of Native Hawaiian sovereignty and the organized efforts of Native Hawaiians to re-establish a government to exercise sovereignty.

CONTEMPORARY CONDITIONS OF NATIVE HAWAIIANS

In 1988, approximately 218,000 Native Hawaiians comprised 20.7 percent of the overall Hawai'i population. Of that amount, only 10,000 were pure Hawaiian and another 70,000 were estimated to have half Hawaiian ancestry or more. Thirty-two percent of all Native Hawaiians still lived outside of O'ahu on neighboring islands.[11]

In 1990, Native Hawaiians earned low incomes comparable to the most recently arrived immigrant groups, held low-status jobs, and had the highest rate of unemployment of all the ethnic groups in the islands. By contrast, the descendants of Caucasian, Japanese, and Chinese immigrants earned high incomes and held a greater portion of the managerial and professional jobs in Hawai'i. Moreover, a significant portion of the Native Hawaiians earned incomes that were insufficient to provide for their families and thus received public assistance to supplement their incomes. Among these, some depended entirely upon welfare support to meet their day-to-day needs.[12]

In 1992, 35 percent of the adult inmate population in state correctional facilities were of Native Hawaiian ancestry.[13]

In 1980, Native Hawaiians had the lowest life expectancy among the ethnic groups in Hawai'i, at 67.6 years compared to 73 for Caucasians, 77 for Japanese, 72 for Filipinos, and 76 for Chinese.[14] In 1989, the Native Hawaiian infant mortality rate was 11.8 per thousand. This represented 44 percent of the infant deaths in the state in 1989. Heart disease was the major cause of death among Native Hawaiians. While Native Hawaiians did not have the highest incidence of cancer, they had the highest mortality rates for most cancers. Native Hawaiian men had the highest incidence of lung cancer and Hawaiian women had the highest rates of breast cancer. Native Hawaiians over age 65 had the highest incidence of chronic diseases and were disproportionately afflicted by diabetes.[15]

These socioeconomic statistics reflect a disparity in the standard of living between Native Hawaiians and Caucasians, Japanese, and Chinese in Hawai'i. They also indicate a high degree of alienation from the social system and the political power structure of modern Hawai'i. On one hand, it represents the effect of institutionalized cultural barriers that prevent equal access to opportunities in the educational system, equal access to health care delivery systems, and adequate representation in the judicial system.[16] On the other hand, it reflects the persistence of Native Hawaiian cultural customs and practices in rural-based Hawaiian communities where Native Hawaiians did not assimilate into Westernized Hawai'i society.

These statistics reflect the individual and collective pain, bitterness and trauma of a people whose sovereignty has been and remains suppressed; who are dispossessed in their own homeland; and who lack control over the resources of their ancestral lands to provide for the welfare of their people. Sovereignty is looked to as a means of providing control over key resources to enable the Native Hawaiian people to be uplifted.

SURVIVAL OF THE NATIVE HAWAIIAN CULTURE

The present generation of Native Hawaiians stand upon the threshold of history as no previous generation of Native Hawaiians. Since first contact with Europeans and Americans, generation after generation of Native Hawaiians have faced the specter of decline, displacement, and impoverishment. However, the possibility of extinction as a people with a distinct language, culture, and land base has never been so imminent and real as it is for Native Hawaiians today. Action or inaction on their part will determine whether the Native Hawaiian language, culture, religion, subsistence farming, and fishing and land base will survive or gradually disappear with the passing away of their *kupuna* (elders).

At each critical juncture of Hawai'i's history, Native Hawaiians were challenged by changes that would undermine their traditional culture. Some Native Hawaiians chose to accept those changes. They passively accommodated and adjusted to Western society. Many actively assimilated and participated in Western political, social, and economic activities. Others chose to stand firm, reject, and resist change—actively or by withdrawing from mainstream economic and political activities.

Of singular importance to the perpetuation of the Native Hawaiian people are isolated and undeveloped rural communities that were historically bypassed by the mainstream of social and economic development. Native Hawaiians in these rural areas did not fully assimilate into the changing social system. Instead, they pursued traditional subsistence livelihoods in which they applied cultural customs, beliefs, and practices. They also sustained extended family networks through sharing and exchange of food, work, and services.

Rural Hawaiians still acquire the basic necessities for their families through subsistence activities upon the land by employing traditional knowledge and practices passed down to them from their *kupuna*. Family knowledge about prime fishing grounds and the types of fish that frequent the ocean in their district at different times of year usually assure Native Hawaiian fishermen of successful fishing expeditions.

Many Native Hawaiians in rural districts continue to cultivate fish in ponds and the open ocean by regularly feeding the fish in conjunction with making offerings at the *ku'ula* (fish deity) shrines that marked their ocean fishing grounds. Taro and other domestic crops are planted by the moon phase to assure excellent growth. Rural families take advantage of seasonal fruits and marine life for their regular diet. Native plants are still utilized for healing of illness by traditional methods that involve both physical and spiritual cleansing and dedication.

Cultural knowledge attached to the traditional names of places, winds, and rains of their district informed rural Hawaiians about the effect of the dynamic forces of nature upon the ocean and the land in their area. Legends and chants inform them about how their ancestors coped with such elements.

Thus, in these rural communities, Native Hawaiian custom, belief, and practice continue to be a practical part of everyday life, not only for the old people, but also for the middle-aged and the young. By contrast, such customs and beliefs have assumed an air of mystery and superstition for urban Native Hawaiians whose day-to-day lives depend solely upon wage-earning activities in a modern commercial economic system.

An analogy that conveys a sense of the significance of these areas can be found in the natural phenomena in the volcanic rainforest. Botanists who study the volcanic rainforest have observed that eruptions which destroy large areas of forest land, leave oases of native trees and plants which are called *kipuka*. From these natural *kipuka* come the seeds and spores for the eventual regeneration of the native flora upon the fresh lava. Rural Native Hawaiian communities are cultural *kipuka* from which Native Hawaiian culture can be regenerated and revitalized in the contemporary setting.

Beginning in the 1970s Native Hawaiians engaged in a cultural renaissance that reaffirmed the consciousness of, pride in, and practice of

Native Hawaiian cultural and spiritual customs and beliefs. In rallying around protection of the island of Kaho'olawe from bombing by the U.S. military, the traditional practice of *aloha 'aina* gained prominence and the importance of these rural Hawaiian communities as strongholds of traditional Native Hawaiian subsistence lifestyles was recognized.

Rural Hawaiian communities threatened with development organized to protect their landholdings and the surrounding natural resources in their districts from the assault of proposed tourist, commercial and industrial development. On the island of Hawai'i, Ka'u Hawaiians formed the Ka 'Ohana O KaLae to protect the natural and cultural resources of their district from a planned spaceport to launch missiles.[17] The Pele Defense Fund formed to protect the volcano deity Pele from the development of geothermal energy and electric plants.[18] On Moloka'i, the Hui Ala Loa, Ka Leo O Mana'e, and Hui Ho'opakela 'Aina are community groups which formed to protect the natural and cultural resources of Moloka'i for farming and fishing rather than for tourist resort development. On the island of Maui, the Hui Ala Nui O Makena organized to keep access to the ocean open for traditional fishing and gathering as well as recreation; Hana Pohaku developed community-based economic development projects on their *kuleana* lands in Kipahulu; and the Ke'anae Community Association worked to keep the water flowing to their taro patches rather than being diverted for development in Kula and Kihei or for hydroelectric plants. On Kaua'i island, the Native Hawaiian Farmers of Hanalei initiated community-based projects at Waipa and Ka Wai Ola organized to protect the shoreline of Hanalei from ruin by numerous tour boat operations. On O'ahu, community-based economic development projects were pursued on the Wai'anae Coast by Ka'ala Farms, the Opelu Project and Na Hoa'aina O Makaha. Malama I Na Kupuna O Hawai'i Nei, a statewide group, formed to protect and provide proper treatment of traditional Native Hawaiian burials.

Traditional navigational arts and skills were revived with the transpacific voyages of the Polynesian Voyaging Society on the *Hokule'a*, the *Hawai'i Loa*, and the *Makali'i*. *Halau hula*, the schools that teach traditional Hawaiian dance and chant, increased and flourished. *La'au Lapa'u*, traditional herbal and spiritual healing practices, were recognized as valid holistic medicinal practices. Hawaiian Studies from the elementary to university level was established as part of the regular curricula. Hawaiian music evolved into new forms of expression and gained greater popularity.

Perhaps the most remarkable development was the rejuvenation of the Hawaiian language. In 1987 there were only 2,000 native speakers of Hawaiian.[19] Most were in their sixties and seventies. Only thirty were under five years old. Extinction of the language because of America's colonial policy was imminent. However, Hawaiian language professors and students at the University of Hawai'i visited Aotearoa (New Zealand) and were inspired with the efforts of the Maori people to rescue their language through Maori language immersion preschools. They began Punana Leo Hawaiian language immersion preschools in Hawai'i and went on to establish Hawaiian language immersion classes in state schools throughout the islands. In the 1999-2000 school year, 1,750 students were enrolled in eighteen Hawaiian language immersion public schools.

All of these efforts, combined, reaffirmed the continuity and perpetuation of Native Hawaiians as unique and distinct with their own cultural and spiritual beliefs, customs, practices, language and ancestral national lands.

HISTORICAL AND POLITICAL BASIS OF NATIVE HAWAIIAN SOVEREIGNTY

Centuries before the beginning of continuous European and American contact, the Native Hawaiian people lived in a highly organized, self-sufficient, subsistence social system based on communal land tenure with a sophisticated language, culture, and religion. Hawaiian ancestral chants trace the origins from Papa, the earth; Wakea, the sky; Kane, springs and streams; Kanaloa, the ocean; and Pele, the volcano. *He Hawai'i kakou:* We are Hawai'i. Native Hawaiians are inseparable from the *'aina,* earth, sea, sky and the magnificent power of these life forces. Family genealogies link contemporary Native Hawaiians to astronomers, navigators, planters, fishermen, engineers, healers, and artisans who settled Hawai'i and constructed great walled fishponds, irrigated taro terraces, dryland agricultural systems, *heiau* (temples), *pu'uhonua* (refuge areas), adze quarries, coastal and inland trails, and extended family settlements. Native Hawaiians were a nation of people living in harmony and balance with the land, the *akua* (gods), and each other: *lokahi* (balance and harmony). Each *ahupua'a* valley system provided the families living within them the necessities of life: from abundant marine life in the ocean, to fresh water streams and springs, gentle sloping fertile lands for cultivation, and forests with trees for building houses and canoes, as well as plants for healing.[20]

After contact with the west, islanders began trading in cultivated food crops and sandalwood. As trade increased the Native Hawaiian people suffered periodic famine and were continuously exposed to devastating epidemics of foreign disease. A unified monarchial government of all the

Hawaiian Islands was established in 1810 under Kamehameha I, the first King of Hawai'i (1779–1819). Trade was conducted with China, England, and the United States on a regular basis. In 1819, Kamehameha died and his successors abolished formal observance of traditional religious ritual and ceremony. Rival chiefs defended the traditional gods but were defeated. In the following year, American missionaries began to settle Hawai'i and convert Native Hawaiians to Christianity. By 1823, after only forty-five years of contact, the Native Hawaiian people had declined from 400,000 to 135,000. Commercial whaling attracted increasing numbers of foreign settlers who demanded rights of citizenship and private ownership of land.[21]

By 1840, King Kamehameha II transformed the government into a constitutional monarchy, having signed a Bill of Rights in 1839 and a Constitution for the Kingdom of Hawai'i in 1840. In 1845, despite petitions of protest signed by 5,790 Native Hawaiians, foreigners were allowed to become naturalized citizens and to hold public office. Ka Mahele in 1848 established a system of private land ownership which concentrated 99.2 percent of Hawai'i's lands among 245 chiefs, the Crown, and the government. Less than one percent of the lands were given to 28 percent of the people, leaving 72 percent of the people landless. In 1850, foreigners were given the right to own land. From this point on foreigners, primarily Americans, continued to expand their interests, eventually controlling most of the land, sugar and pineapple plantations, banks, shipping, and commerce.[22]

Throughout the 19th century until 1893, the United States recognized the independence of the Hawaiian Nation and extended full and complete diplomatic recognition to that government. The United States government entered into treaties and conventions with the Hawaiian monarchs to govern commerce and navigation in 1826, 1842, 1850, 1855, 1875 and 1887.[23]

By 1887, Hawai'i had treaties and conventions with Belgium, Bremen, Denmark, France, the German Empire, Great Britain, Hamburg, Hong Kong, Italy, Japan, the Netherlands, New South Wales, Portugal, Russia, Samoa, Spain, the Swiss Confederation, Sweden, Norway, Tahiti, and the United States.[24] On November 28, 1843, Great Britain and France signed a joint declaration recognizing the independence of Hawai'i and pledging never to take possession of Hawai'i.[25] Hawai'i was also a member of one of the first international governmental organizations, the Universal Postal Union. It had established approximately a hundred diplomatic and consular posts around the world.[26]

In 1887, American planter interests organized a coup d'etat against King David Kalākaua, forcing him to sign the Bayonet Constitution, which took away his sovereign powers as king and the civil rights of Hawaiians. In 1889, eight men were killed, twelve wounded, and seventy were arrested in the Wilcox Rebellion, which attempted to restore the Hawaiian Constitution. By 1890, non-Hawaiians controlled 96 percent of the sugar industry and Native Hawaiians were reduced to only 45 percent of the population due to the importation of Chinese, Japanese, and Portuguese immigrant laborers by the sugar planters.

In the year 1893, the United States Minister assigned to the Kingdom of Hawai'i, John L. Stevens, conspired with a small group of non-Hawaiian residents of the Kingdom, including citizens of the United States, to overthrow the indigenous and lawful Government of Hawai'i.[27] In pursuance of that conspiracy, the United States Minister and the naval representative of the United States caused 162 armed naval forces of the United States to invade the sovereign Hawaiian Nation in support of the overthrow of the indigenous and lawful Government of Hawai'i and the United States Minister thereupon extended diplomatic recognition to a provisional government declared by eighteen conspirators, mostly American, without the consent of the native people of Hawai'i or the lawful government of Hawai'i, in violation of treaties between the two nations and of international law.[28]

Without warning or a declaration of war, this surprise attack upon a friendly and peaceful nation caught the government and its citizens totally unprepared to respond. Protesting the U.S. role in this conspiracy and receiving assurances of an immediate and fair investigation, the Queen, on January 17, 1893, trusted the "enlightened justice" of the United States and yielded, under protest, to the U.S. forces until an investigation could be completed and she could be restored. She wrote:

> I Lili'uokalani, by the Grace of God and under the Constitution of the Hawaiian Kingdom, Queen, do hereby solemnly protest against any and all acts done against myself and the Constitutional Government of the Hawaiian Kingdom by certain persons claiming to have established a Provisional Government of and for this Kingdom.
>
> That I yield to the superior force of the United States of America whose Minister Plenipotentiary, His Excellency John L. Stevens, has caused United States troops to be landed at Honolulu and declared that he would support the Provisional Government.
>
> Now to avoid any collision of armed forces, and perhaps the loss of life, I do under this protest and impelled by said force yield my authority until such time as the Government of the United States shall, upon the facts being presented to it, undo the action of its representative and reinstate me in the authority which I claim as the Constitutional Sovereign of the Hawaiian Islands.

Done at Honolulu this 17th day of January, A.D. 1893.[29]

Queen Lili'uokalani, the lawful monarch of Hawai'i, and the Hawaiian Patriotic League, representing the aboriginal citizens of Hawai'i, promptly petitioned the United States for redress of these wrongs and for restoration of the indigenous government of the Hawaiian nation, but this petition was not acted upon.

In a message to Congress on December 18, 1893, then President Grover Cleveland reported fully and accurately on these illegal actions, and acknowledged that by these acts, described by the President as acts of war, the government of a peaceful and friendly people was overthrown, and the President concluded that a "substantial wrong has thus been done which a due regard for our national character as well as the rights of the injured people requires that we should endeavor to repair." The following are excerpts from his report:

> The lawful Government of Hawaii was overthrown without the drawing of a sword or the firing of a shot by a process every step of which, it may safely be asserted, is directly traceable to and dependent for its success upon the agency of the United States acting through its diplomatic and naval representatives . . .
>
> But for the lawless occupation of Honolulu under false pretexts by the United States forces, and but for Minister Stevens' recognition of the provisional government when the United States forces were its sole support and constituted its only military strength, the Queen and her Government would never have yielded to the provisional government, even for a time and for the sole purpose of submitting her case to the enlightened justice of the United States . . .
>
> Believing, therefore, that the United States could not, under the circumstances disclosed, annex the islands without justly incurring the imputation of acquiring them by unjustifiable methods, I shall not again submit the treaty of annexation to the Senate for its consideration . . . I instructed Minister Willis to advise the Queen and her supporters of my desire to aid in the restoration of the status existing before the lawless landing of the United States forces at Honolulu on the 16th of January last, if such restoration could be effected upon terms providing for clemency as well as justice to all parties concerned.[30]

The Provisional Government refused to acquiesce to President Cleveland's request to restore the Queen to the throne. They continued to hold state power and lobby for annexation to the United States. Cleveland, not ready to shed American blood for the Hawaiian people and their Queen, took no further action.[31]

On July 4, 1894, the provisional government proclaimed the Republic of Hawai'i under a new constitution.[32]

On January 7, 1895, royalists organized an armed insurrection aimed at restoring the Queen to the throne. The restoration was crushed; 220 royalists, including the Queen herself, were arrested and charged as prisoners of war for treason and concealment of treason.[33]

On January 24, 1895, while being held prisoner in 'Iolani Palace, Queen Lili'uokalani was forced to sign a statement of abdication in favor of the Republic of Hawai'i. Once free, the Queen renounced the abdication, contending that she had signed the statement because it had been falsely represented to her that the royalists who had been arrested would be immediately released.[34]

In 1898, the United States annexed Hawai'i through the Newlands Resolution without the consent of or compensation to the Native Hawaiian people or their sovereign government. Native Hawaiians were thereby denied the mechanism for expression of their inherent sovereignty through self-government and self-determination, their lands and ocean resources.[35]

Through the Newlands Resolution and the 1900 Organic Act, the United States Congress received 1.75 million acres of lands formerly owned by the Crown and Government of the Hawaiian Kingdom and exempted the lands from then existing public land laws of the United States by mandating that the revenue and proceeds from these lands be "used solely for the benefit of the inhabitants of the Hawaiian Islands for education and other public purposes," thereby establishing a special trust relationship between the United States and the inhabitants of Hawai'i.[36]

From 1900 through 1959, Hawai'i was governed as a Territory of the United States. The official U.S. policy was to Americanize the multiethnic society of the Hawaiian Islands, beginning with the children through the American public school system. Hawaiian and other languages except English were banned as official languages or as a medium of instruction. An elite group of Americans who were the owners and managers of what was called the Big Five factories had monopoly control over every facet of Hawai'i's economy and social system.[37]

In 1921, Congress enacted the Hawaiian Homes Commission Act, which designated 200,000 acres of the ceded public lands for exclusive homesteading by Native Hawaiians, thereby affirming the trust relationship between the United States and the Native Hawaiians, as expressed by then Secretary of Interior Franklin K. Lane. Lane was cited in the Committee Report of the United States House of Representatives Committee on Territories as stating, "One thing that impressed me . . . was the fact that the natives of the islands who are our wards, I should say, and for whom in a sense were are trustees, are falling off rapidly in numbers and many of them are in poverty."[38]

In 1938 the United States Congress again acknowledged the unique status of the Native Hawaiian people by including in the Kalapana Extension Act a provision to lease lands within the extension to Native Hawaiians and to permit fishing in the area "only by native Hawaiian residents of said area or of adjacent villages and by visitors under their guidance."[39]

A plebiscite on statehood was held in 1940 by the territorial government. The question posed was, "Do you favor statehood for Hawai'i?"; 67 percent of the voters answered "yes." Almost one-third of the voters opposed statehood. In 10 of the 162 precincts the majority voted "no". Slightly more than 20 percent of those eligible did not vote.[40]

In 1946, the United States, as required under Chapter XI, Article 73 of the UN Charter, "Declaration Regarding Non-Self-Governing Territories," included Hawai'i on the list of its non-self-governing territories together with Alaska, American Samoa, Guam, Panama Canal Zone, Puerto Rico, and the Virgin Islands. By this action the U.S. accepted responsibility to assist the Territory of Hawai'i in achieving self-government. This was to be achieved when the inhabitants voted for one of the following three alternative statuses:

Complete independence from any other state.
Free association with another state.
Complete integration into another state.[41]

In 1959, in accordance with the Admission Act of March 18, 1959, a second statehood plebiscite was held. The plebiscite provided that the qualified voters of Hawai'i adopt or reject three propositions, all of which had to be adopted for Hawai'i to become a state: (a) "Shall Hawai'i immediately be admitted into the Union as a state?" (b) acceptance of the boundaries of the State, and (c) acceptance of all the provisions contained in the Statehood Bill. Any American citizen who had resided in Hawai'i for one year was eligible to vote. The result of the plebiscite was: 132,938 voters in favor of statehood and 7,854 opposed.[42]

For a plebiscite to be considered free and fair it must meet the criteria of (1) neutrality of the plebiscite area; (2) freedom from foreign occupation; and (3) control of the administration of the plebiscite by a neutral authority. Given these criteria, advocates of independence for Hawai'i charge that the 1959 plebiscite cannot be considered an adequate exercise in self-determination by the true residents of Hawai'i.

First, those who participated in the plebiscite could not be considered the correct "self," reflecting those citizens of Hawai'i or descendants of them who had been denied the continued exercise of their independent nation by the U.S. invasion in 1893. The U.S. government defined the qualifications for voting in such a way that it resulted in the exercise of an altered "self"-determination. By 1959, Hawai'i had been Americanized by years of transmigration from the United States of America and socialization through control over the media, the economy, and the educational, social, legal, and political system of Hawai'i. Following four generations of U.S. control over the society, the United States permitted the "qualified" voters in Hawai'i to become equal American citizens. Qualified voters were American citizens who were residents of Hawai'i for at least one year. Only U.S. declared citizens could vote. Those who resisted the American domination and insisted on their Hawaiian citizenship could not vote.

Second, the question, "Shall Hawai'i immediately be admitted into the Union as a State?" was unfair and fell short as a measure of self-determination. It failed to afford the people the range of choices from integration within the United States or to reemerge as an independent nation. The question, "Should Hawai'i be a free and independent nation?" should have been but was never asked.

Additional factors that make the 1959 plebiscite fraudulent as an exercise of self-determination were that the United States stated the question to be asked; supervised the plebiscite process; and counted the votes. The United States military maintained a strong presence in the territory when the plebiscite was conducted. Many in the U.S. military also participated in the plebiscite. The United States failed to carry out or to see that others carried out an educational program on the right to independence. In fact, the United States caused fear within the society by promoting a communist scare and a nuclear arms race scare which later proved, on both fronts, to have been fabrications of the government of the day. The United States did not inform the people of their right to self-determination or of the responsibility of the United States to the people regarding decolonization as called for under Chapter XI, Article 73 of the U.N. Charter.[43]

In 1959, after the Hawai'i statehood plebiscite, the U.S. removed Hawai'i from the U.N. list of Non-Self-Governing Territories. As evidence, the U.S. submitted a memorandum to the Secretary General, the text of the Congressional Act admitting Hawai'i into the U.S. as a state (1959 Admission Act),[44] a Presidential Proclamation, and the text of Hawai'i's Constitution. In response, the U.N. General Assembly, through Resolution 1469 (XIV) expressed the opinion that Hawai'i had effectively exercised the right of self-determination and had freely chosen its status as a state of the Union. This relieved the United States of further responsibility to report to the U.N.[45]

While the 1959 Admission Act incorporated Hawai'i and its multi-ethnic population into the United States of America as the fiftieth state, it also recognized and reaffirmed a trust relationship with the Native Hawaiian people.

Under the Admission Act, the United States mandated the new State of Hawai'i to assume responsibility for administration of 200,000 acres of Hawaiian Home Lands for the exclusive benefit of native Hawaiians. It also reaffirmed the trust relationship which existed between the United States and the Native Hawaiian people by retaining exclusive power to enforce the trust, including the power to approve land exchanges and legislative amendments affecting the rights of beneficiaries under the act.

Under the Admission Act, the United States also transferred responsibility for administration over portions of the ceded public lands trust not retained by the United States (approximately 1,200,000 acres) to the State of Hawai'i but reaffirmed the trust relationship which existed between the United States and the Native Hawaiian people by retaining the legal responsibility of oversight over the State for the betterment of the conditions of Native Hawaiians under section 5(f) of the Admission Act.

After 1959, Congress enacted over 100 pieces of legislation that addressed the special needs of Native Hawaiians ranging from healthcare and education, to economic development and cultural and natural resource preservation. Some examples of these include the Native Hawaiian Study Commission Act, Pub.L.No. 98-139, 97 Stat. 871 (1983); Native Hawaiian Health Care Act of 1988, Pub. L. No. 100-579, 102 Stat. 4181; and the Native Hawaiian Education Act, Pub. L. No. 103-382, 108 Stat. 3518 (1994).[46]

These laws culminated with the Apology Resolution of November 23, 1993, which directly acknowledged the inherent sovereignty of Native Hawaiians at the time of the overthrow of the Kingdom of Hawai'i. The Apology Resolution also acknowledged the vested rights of the Native Hawaiian people in the crown and government lands of the Kingdom of Hawai'i; and that Native Hawaiians continue to be a distinct people determined to preserve, develop, and transmit to future generations their ancestral territory and their cultural identity in accordance with their own spiritual and traditional beliefs, customs, practices, language, and social institutions.[47]

GOALS AND STRATEGIES

There are two distinct goals for Hawaiian governance: achieving nation-within-nation status, like other Native Americans, and achieving independence from the United States, under free-association status like the republics in Micronesia or as an independent state like island nations of the South Pacific.

Hawaiian groups tend to pose "nation-within-nation" and "independence" as two competing goals. However, it is my contention that these are actually complementary. In fact, we are really looking at one status that will address the unique and special conditions of the indigenous Hawaiian people and one status that will address the broader issues of the decolonization of Hawai'i as a whole for the indigenous Hawaiians in partnership with the "local" multi-ethnic population.

What is called nation-within-nation status is what has thus far been accorded to more than 550 Native American nations in the United States. It is important to emphasize that this status can and should be accorded to the indigenous Hawaiian nation whether Hawai'i is a part of or independent from the United States.

The process of decolonization toward total independence is a status for indigenous Hawaiians to pursue in conjunction with the broader "local" population, those who primarily identify culturally, socially, economically, and politically with Hawai'i as their homeland. This would include Hawai'i residents who distinguish themselves from America as well as from the nation from which their ancestors originated.

By the end of the twentieth century, the majority of indigenous Hawaiians seemed prepared to begin a process to re-establish Hawaiian sovereignty, but the broader local population appeared to need more time and education to unite in a process building toward decolonization.

A survey on support for sovereignty was conducted by SMS Research in February 1994. The survey asked the question, "Some Hawaiians have said that sovereignty can only be realized by declaring independence from the state, but others feel they can achieve sovereignty by working within the state and federal government. Which do you believe?" In response, 74 percent favored working within the system and 12 percent favored independence, while 14 percent were undecided.[48] The following was the breakdown by ethnic group:

	Total	Hawaiian	Caucasian	Japanese	Filipino
Within System	74%	73%	79%	70%	71%
Independent	12%	11%	8%	15%	14%
Undecided	14%	16%	13%	15%	15%

This poll is one indication of the broad support for recognition of Native Hawaiian sovereignty and the lack of support among the broad spectrum of Hawai'i's population, including Native Hawaiians, for the total independence of Hawai'i. If a vote had been taken in 1994, the majority of people born and raised in Hawai'i would probably have voted for Hawai'i to remain a state and for the recognition of Native Hawaiian sovereignty.

In July 1996 the Hawaiian Sovereignty Elections Council organized a Native Hawaiian Vote with funding from the Hawai'i State Legislature. The Council mailed out 81,507 ballots to registered Native Hawaiian voters which asked, "Shall the Hawaiian people elect delegates to propose a Native Hawaiian government?" A total of 30,423 ballots were cast, representing 37 percent of the registered voters. Of these, 22,294 (73.28 percent of the ballots cast) voted "yes" and 8,129 (26.72 percent of the ballots cast) voted "no."

There are numerous Native Hawaiian organizations working for the re-establishment and recognition of a sovereign Native Hawaiian nation. Native Hawaiians involved in these organizations seek to improve and uplift Hawaiian health, education, and standard of living. They also seek to protect and perpetuate the natural and cultural resources essential for religious, cultural, and subsistence custom, belief, and practice. Ultimately, Native Hawaiians seek full redress for past injustices; restitution of all of the territory of the Native Hawaiian nation; compensation for mismanagement and destruction of national lands and natural resources; and most significant, the re-establishment and recognition of a government to exercise sovereignty and self-determination.[49]

CONCLUSION

In the recognition of the status, rights, and entitlements of Native Hawaiian people as just, lies the future of human rights in Hawai'i. Many non-Hawaiians claim they bear no obligation to reconcile with the descendants of Native Hawaiians for the injustices that occurred decades ago by persons to whom they bear no relation. However, non-Hawaiians in Hawai'i benefit, while Native Hawaiians bear the burden of the results of those historical injustices. Moreover, the U.S. Congress and the President of the United States in Public Law 103-150 outlined a series of historical injustices for which they acknowledge responsibility and apologized "to Native Hawaiians on behalf of the people of the United States." The Apology Resolution also committed the Congress and all the people of the United States to a process of reconciliation with the Native Hawaiian people.

Among the reasons given by those who oppose Native Hawaiian entitlements is that the privileging of one ethnic group over the others is

unfair and will cause resentment and undermine the spirit of *aloha* in contemporary Hawai'i: *Aloha mai no, aloha aku* (when love is given, love
should be returned).[50] However, this *'olelo no'eau* means that *aloha* is reciprocal. Native Hawaiian people have given *aloha* to newcomers and their
descendants for generations. Now is the time for *aloha* to be acknowledged and returned to the Native Hawaiian people and their descendants. The Akaka Bill introduced by Hawai'i's congressional delegation
would provide an avenue for both the people of Hawai'i and the U.S.
Congress to correct the historic injustices they have suffered collectively
as a people, and enable them to exercise self-determination through self-
governance to heal as a people. While federal recognition would represent a culmination of a century-old trust relationship between Native
Hawaiians and the U.S. Congress, it would really constitute a small first
step in the re-establishment of a Native Hawaiian government since the
overthrow of the Hawaiian monarchy in 1893.

NOTES

[1] In the Apology Resolution, a Native Hawaiian (both words capitalized) is
defined as "any individual who is a descendant of the aboriginal people who,
prior to 1778, occupied and exercised sovereignty in the area that now constitutes
the State of Hawai'i." The Hawaiian Homes Commission Act and the Admission
Act use the term native Hawaiian (lower case n, capital H) to mean "Any descendant of not less than one-half part of the blood of the races inhabiting the
Hawaiian Islands previous to 1778. The term *"Kanaka Maoli"* is promoted as the
indigenous name for Native Hawaiians. However, *"Kanaka Maoli"* simply means
native or indigenous, while *"Kanaka Maoli Hawai'i"* means native or indigenous
Hawaiian. In the 1859 Civil Code of the Kingdom of Hawai'i, Chapter VIII,
"kanaka Hawai'i" is used to translate "native of the Hawaiian Islands" and *"ke
kanaka maoli"* is used to translate "native." In the 1878 Census of the Kingdom of
Hawai'i, *"He kane kanaka maoli* (Hawai'i)" was used for "Native Male" and *"He
wahine kanaka maoli* (Hawai'i)" was used for "Native Female." However, this must
have referred to pure Hawaiians only, as there was a category for "Half-Caste
Male" (*"He hapahaole kane"*) and "Half-Cast Female" (*"He hapahaole wahine"*). In
this article, I will use "Native Hawaiian" to refer anyone who has Hawaiian
ancestry, that is, who is descended from a *"Kanaka Maoli Hawai'i"* ancestor and
"native Hawaiian" to refer to those who are of half or more Hawaiian ancestry.
Under the law, thus far, only "native Hawaiians" are the beneficiaries of the
Hawaiian Home Lands and the ceded public lands trusts, as discussed below.

[2] No. 98-818, February 23, 2000. Kennedy, J. delivered the opinion of the Court,
in which Rehnquist, C.J., O'Connor, Scalia, Thomas, J.J. joined. Breyer, J. filed an
opinion concurring in the result, in which Souter, J. joined. Stevens, J. filed a dis-

senting opinion in which Ginsburg, J. joined as to Part II. Ginsburg, J. filed a dissenting opinion.

³ 1993–1998 / Federal Indian Policies / June 12, 1998.

⁴ These questions were raised in the following statement:
"If Hawaii's restriction were to be sustained under Mancari we would be required to accept some beginning premises not yet established in our case law. Among other postulates, it would be necessary to conclude that Congress, in reciting the purposes for the transfer of lands to the State—and in other enactments such as the Hawaiian Homes Commission Act and the Joint Resolution of 1993—has determined that native Hawaiians have a status like that of Indians in organized tribes, and that it may, and has, delegated to the State a broad authority to preserve that status. These propositions would raise questions of considerable moment and difficulty."

⁵ List of laws include the Older Americans Act; the Developmental Disabilities Assistance and Bill of Rights Act Amendments of 1987; the Veterans' Benefits and Services Act of 1988; the Rehabilitation Act of 1973, as amended in 1988; the Native Hawaiian Health Care Act of 1988; the Health Professions Reauthorization Act of 1988; the Nursing Shortage Reduction and Education Extension Act of 1988; the Handicapped Programs Technical Amendments Act of 1988; the Indian Health Care Amendments of 1988; and the Disadvantaged Minority Health Improvement Act of 1990.

⁶ Department of Interior and Department of Justice, "From Mauka to Makai: The River of Justice Must Flow Freely, Report on the Reconciliation Process Between the Federal Government and Native Hawaians," Washington, D.C., October 23, 2000, p. 56.

⁷ Statements on Introduced Bills and Joint Resolutions—April 6, 2001 (Senate—April 06, 2001) by Mr. Akaka (for himself and Mr. Inouye).

⁸ www.angelfire.com/hi2/hawaiiansovereignty; www.aloha4all.org.

⁹ Ibid.

¹⁰ Ibid., KITV News, June 4, 2001; *Honolulu Advertiser,* June 5, 2001, p. B-2.

¹¹ The difference in the two sources is due to the difference in handling persons of mixed parentage. The census did not have a mixed category and assigned persons of mixed ancestry to one of the categories on the basis of self-identification or the race of the father. The Health Surveillance Program bases it on birth statistics. The figure of 70,000 is from Office of Hawaiian Affairs, "Population Survey/Needs Assessment, Final Report" (Honolulu: Office of Hawaiian Affairs, 1986). In a study of the Health Surveillance Program data, the Office of Hawaiian Affairs estimated that there were 208,476 Hawaiians in Hawai'i in 1984, out of which 72,709 had 50 percent to 99 percent Hawaiian ancestry and 8,244 had 100 percent Hawaiian ancestry.

¹² Health Surveillance Program, 1988. According to the 1988 Health Surveillance Program, 18.9 percent of the Hawaiian families earned less than

$15,000 per year as compared to 12.5 percent of families in other ethnic groups. In the $60,000 or more category, only 13.6 percent of the Hawaiian families earned incomes at that level, while 21.4 percent of the families in other ethnic groups earned incomes at that level. According to the Research and Evaluation Division of the Department of Human Services, 20,487 Hawaiian families received public financial assistance and Medicaid in 1990. This represented 26 percent of all of the families in Hawai'i who received financial assistance and Medicaid in 1990. The same source reported that 14,956 Hawaiian families received Aid to Families with Dependent Children (AFDC) in 1990. This represented one-third (33.4 percent) of all of the families in Hawai'i who received AFDC in 1990.

[13] Department of Public Safety—Corrections Division, "Distribution of the Inmate Population By Ethnicity and Facility As Of June 30, 1992." The ethnic breakdown of the adult inmate population was as follows:Black (5.3 percent), Caucasian (22.9 percent), Chinese (0.9 percent), Filipino (7.9 percent), Hawaiian/Part Hawaiian (35 percent), Japanese (3.4 percent), Korean (0.9 percent), Samoan (3.9 percent), Other (16.1 percent)

[14] George S. Kanahele, *Current Facts and Figures About Hawaiians* (Honolulu: Project WAIAHA, 1982), p. 8.

[15] *Native Hawaiian Health Data Book* (Honolulu: Papa Ola Lokahi, 1992).

[16] Alu Like, "Summary of the Analysis of the Needs Assessment Survey and Related Data," 1976. Kamehameha Schools/Bishop Estate, 1983. Native Hawaiian Health Research Consortium, Mental Health Task Force, Alu Like, Inc. *E Ola Mau: Native Hawaiian Health Needs Study: Mental Health Task Force Report* (Honolulu: Native Hawaiian Health Research Consortium, Alu Like, Inc., 1985).

[17] "Sociocultural Impact Assessment" in the Environmental Impact Statement for the Commercial Satellite Launching Facility, Palima Point, Ka'u, Hawai'i, with Jon Matsuoka, 1991.

[18] Davianna McGregor, "Pele vs. Geothermal: A Clash of Cultures," in *Bearing Dreams, Shaping Visions: Asian Pacific Americans Facing the 90's* (Seattle: Washington State University Press, 1993).

[19] John Heckathorn, Ua Hiki Anei Ke Ola Ka 'Olelo Hawai'i?—Can the Hawaiian Language Survive? *Honolulu Magazine* 21, no. 10 (April 1987).

[20] E.S. Craighill Handy, "The Hawaiian Planter—Volume I: His Plants, Methods and Areas of Cultivation," *Bernice Pauahi Bishop Museum Bulletin* 161 (Honolulu: Bernice P. Bishop Museum, 1940); E.S. Craighill Handy and Mary Kawena Pūku'i, *The Polynesian Family System in Ka'u, Hawai'i*, (Wellington: Polynesian Society, 1958; reprint, Tokyo: Charles E. Tuttle Company, 1976); Samuel Kamakau, *Ruling Chiefs of Hawaii*, (Honolulu: Kamehameha Schools Press, 1961); Samuel Kamakau, "Ka Po'e Kahiko: The People of Old," *BPBM Spec. Publ.* 51., 1964; Samuel Kamakau, "The Works of the People of Old," *BPBM Spec. Publ.* 61, 1976; David Malo, *Hawaiian Antiquities,* trans. Dr. Nathaniel B. Emerson (Honolulu: Bishop Museum Press, 1971); T.G. Thrum (ed.), "Fornander Collection

of Hawaiian Antiquities and Folk-Lore," *BPBM Memoirs* 4, 5, 6 (1916–1920); Martha W. Beckwith, *Hawaiian Mythology* (Honolulu: UH Press, 1970); David Kalākaua, King of Hawaii, *The Legends and Myths of Hawaii: The Fables and Folklore of a Strange People* (Tokyo & Rutland: Charles E. Tuttle, 1973).

[21] Kamakau 1961; Ralph S. Kuykendall, *The Hawaiian Kingdom, Volume I, 1778–1854: Foundation and Transformation* (Honolulu: University of Hawai'i Press; 1938; reprint, Honolulu: The University Press of Hawai'i, 1980).

[22] Kuykendall 1980; Davianna McGregor, "Voices of Today Echo Voices of the Past," in *Malama Hawaiian Land and Water*, edited by Dana Naone Hall (Honolulu: Bamboo Ridge Press, 1985).

[23] A convention negotiated December 24, 1826, a Treaty of Commerce, declared that the "peace and friendship" between the United States and Hawai'i was "confirmed and declared to be perpetual." The Tyler Doctrine of 1842 included Hawai'i within the U.S. sphere of influence by stating that it "could not but create dissatisfaction on the part of the United States at any attempt by another power, should such attempt be threatened or feared, to take possession of the islands, colonize them, and subvert the native government." There was also the Treaty of Friendship, Commerce and Navigation, August 24, 1850; Rights of Neutrals at Sea, March 25, 1855; Treaty of Commercial Reciprocity, September 1876; Treaty of Commercial Reciprocity, November 9, 1887. See *Treaties and Other International Agreements of the United States of America*, V. 8.

[24] *Treaties and Conventions Concluded Between the Hawaiian Kingdom and Other Powers Since 1825.*

[25] Senate Ex. Doc. 52 Cong. 2 Sess., No. 57, p. 12.

[26] F.M. Hustat, *Directory and Handbook of the Kingdom of Hawai'i* (Honolulu: Polk, 1892).

[27] U.S. Congress, House, Report No. 243, "Intervention of United States Government in Affairs of Foreign Friendly Governments," 53rd Congress, 2nd Session, December 21, 1893 (Washington: Government Printing Office, 1893); U.S. Congress, Senate, Committee on Foreign Relations, "Hawaiian Islands," Report of the Committee on Foreign Relations With Accompanying Testimony and Executive Documents Transmitted to Congress from January 1, 1893 to March 19, 1894, Volumes I and II (Washington: Government Printing Office, 1894. Also referred to as "The Morgan Report"); U.S. Congress, Senate, Committee on Foreign Relations, Report No. 227, "Report from the Committee on Foreign Relations and Appendix in Relation to the Hawaiian Islands, February 26, 1894," 53rd Congress, 2nd Session (Washington: Government Printing Office, 1894); U.S. Department of State. "Papers Relating to the Mission of James H. Blount, United States Commissioner to the Hawaiian Islands." (Washington: Government Printing Office, 1893).

[28] Close to 5:00 P.M. on January 16, 1893, 162 U.S. naval forces with 80 rounds of ammunition each, one Gatling gun and one 37-millimeter revolving gun,

landed at the foot of Nuʻuanu Avenue and marched up Fort Street to Merchant Street. They were accompanied by a hospital corps with stretchers and medical supplies. Some troops were deployed to guard the U.S. consulate and some were sent to the U.S. legation. The main body of three companies ultimately took up quarters at Arion Hall near the government building and the palace. William De Witt Alexander, *History of the Later Years of the Hawaiian monarchy and the Revolution of 1893* (Honolulu: Hawaiian Gazette Co., 1896).

In a report to Congress on December 11, 1893 President Cleveland observed that:

There is as little basis for the pretense that such forces were landed for the security of American life and property. If so, they would have been stationed in the vicinity of such property and so as to protect it, instead of at a distance and so as to command the Hawaiian Government building and palace. Admiral Skerrett, the officer in command of our naval force on the Pacific station, has frankly stated that in his opinion the location of the troops was inadvisable if they were landed for protection of American citizens whose residences and places of business, as well as the legation and consulate, were in a distant part of the city, but the location selected was a wise one if the forces were landed for the purpose of supporting the provisional government. (Grover Cleveland, "Message of the President," December 18, 1893, in 53rd Congress 2nd Session, House of Representatives, Report 243, p. 7)

[29] Queen Liliʻuokalani, *Hawaii's Story By Hawaii's Queen* (Boston: Lothrop, Lee & Shepard, Co., 1898; reprint, Tokyo: Charles E. Tuttle Company, 1977), p. 387–388.

[30] U.S. House of Representatives, 53rd Congress, 2nd Session, December 21, 1893, p.13–14.

[31] Alexander 1896; Liliʻuokalani 1898.

[32] Ibid.

[33] Hawaiʻi State Archives, 1895 Insurrection File; Albertine Loomis, *For Whom Are the Stars?* (Honolulu: University of Hawaiʻi Press and Friends of the Library of Hawaiʻi, 1976).

[34] Liliʻuokalani, 1898.

[35] Robert M.C. Littler, *The Governance of Hawaii: A Study in Territorial Administration* (Stanford: Stanford University Press, 1929).

[36] U.S. Congress. 56th Congress, 1st Session 1899–1900. "Congressional Debates on Hawaii Organic Act, Together With Debates and Congressional Action on Other Matters Concerning the Hawaiian Islands." Washington, (photostat reproduction from the Congressional Record, v. 33, pts. 1–8), 1899–1900.

[37] Lawrence Fuchs, *Hawaii Pono: A Social History* (San Diego: Harcourt, Brace & World, Inc., 1961); Noel Kent, *Hawaii, Islands Under the Influence* (New York: Monthly Review Press, 1983); Andrew Lind, *An Island Community: Ecological*

Succession in Hawaii (Chicago: The University of Chicago, 1938; reprint, New York: Greenwood Press, 1968).
[38] U.S. Congress, House, Committee on the Territories, Report No. 839, 66th Congress 2nd Session. Seen in Hawai'i State Archives, Delegate Kalanianaole File on Rehabilitation.
[39] Act of June 20, 1938 (52 Stat. 781 et seq.).
[40] Roger J. Bell, *Last Among Equals: Hawaiian Statehood and American Politics* (Honolulu: University of Hawai'i Press, 1984).
[41] Rob Williams, esq., working paper for "Status and Entitlements of Hawaiian Natives" study, funded by the Ford Foundation, to the Native Hawaiian Advisory Council, 1992–1993; Hawaiian Sovereignty Advisory Council Report To The Legislature, January 1992; Presentation of Russell Barsh, esq., to the Hawaiian Sovereignty Advisory Commission, November 5–6, 1993, Hawai'i State Tower.
[42] Ibid.
[43] Ibid.
[44] "An Act to provide for the admission of the State of Hawai'i into the Union," approved March 18, 1959 (Pub.L. 86-3, 73 Stat. 4)
[45] Hawaiian Sovereignty Advisory Council Report To The Legislature, January 1992.
[46] Department of Interior and Department of Justice, "From Mauka to Makai: The River of Justice Must Flow Freely, Report on the Reconciliation Process Between the Federal Government and Native Hawaiians," Washington D.C., October 23, 2000, p. 56–57.
[47] Apology Resolution, Public Law 103-150.
[48] *Honolulu Advertiser,* February 22, 1994, pp. A-1 and A-4.
[49] Ka Lahui Hawai'i, claiming to represent 20,000 members, has held four constitutional conventions to establish their own national legislature, governor, and council of elders. As strong advocates for nation-within-nation status, Ka Lahui Hawai'i seeks recognition from the U.S. Congress and the State of Hawai'i as the nation of Hawaiians to exist within the nation of the United States of America. In the 1993 legislative session they introduced a bill calling for the transfer to their nation of all of the Hawaiian national lands controlled by the state government. The State Hawaiian Homes Association claims to represent 30,000 Hawaiians who are settled on Hawaiian Homelands. They seek immediate and direct control over the homestead lands they live on and use, seeking homerule over the Hawaiian Homelands. The statewide Association of Hawaiian Civic Clubs has traditionally represented the more conservative sector of the Native Hawaiian community. The clubs support Native Hawaiian sovereignty. There are several organizations that seek to totally decolonize Hawai'i. Smaller in number than the advocates of nation-within-nation status, they nevertheless comprise a very elo-

quent, determined, and militant sector of the community. Included among the organizations seeking total independence from the United States are the Institute for the Advancement of Hawaiian Affairs, the Nation State of Hawai'i, Ka Pakaukau, the Sovereign Kingdom of Hawai'i, the Hawaiian Patriotic League, and the Lawful Kingdom of Hawai'i.

[50] Pūku'i, 1983, no. 113, p. 15. *Aloha mai no, aloha aku; o ka huhu ka mea e ola 'ole ai.* When love is given, love should be returned; anger is the thing that gives no life.

Bibliography

Agard, L. K. 1982. *Politics, Hawai'i Sandalwood Trees and Hope*. Honolulu: L. K. Agard.

Ahlburg, Dennis A. 1994. Return Migration from the United States to American Samoa. *Pacific Studies* 17 (2): 71–84.

Alba, Richard. 1984. *Italian Americans: Into the Twilight of Ethnicity?* Englewood Cliffs, N.J.: Prentice-Hall.

———, and Reid M. Golden. 1986. Patterns of Ethnic Marriage in the United States. *Social Forces* 65:202–223.

Alexander, P. C., R. Neimeyer, and M. Follette. 1991. Group Therapy for Women Sexually Abused as Children: A Controlled Study and Investigation of Individual Differences. *Journal of Interpersonal Violence* 6:218–231.

Aluli, N. E., and H. K. O'Connor. 1988. The Moloka'i Heart Study and the Moloka'i Diet Study. *Nāa Pu'uwai*.

AMEA. 1993. AMEA Testifies before Congressional Subcommittee. *AMEA Networking News* 4 (5): 1.

Anderson, Charles H. 1970. *White Protestant Americans*. Englewood Cliffs, N.J.: Prentice-Hall.

Anderson, J., J. Martin, P. Mullen, S. Romans, and P. Herbison. 1993. Prevalence of Childhood Sexual Abuse Experiences in a Community Sample of Women. *Journal of American Academy of Child and Adolescent Psychiatry* 32 (5): 911–919.

Andrade, N. N. 1988. *A Statewide Native Hawaiian Community-Based Health Care System for the Delivery of Preventive Health Services*. Honolulu: E Ola Mau.

Annual Report of the U.S. Naval Governor of Guam. 1918.

Annual Report of the U.S. Naval Governor of Guam. 1919.

Annual Report of the U.S. Naval Governor of Guam. 1922.

[Anonymous]. 1775. *An Historic Epistle, From Omiah, to the Queen of Otaheite; Being His Remarks on the English Nation*. London: T. Evans. In Fuller Collection, Bishop Museum Library, Honolulu, Hawai'i.

Anzaldua, Gloria. 1987. *Borderlands/La Frontrera: The New Mestiza*. San Francisco: Spinsters/Aunt Lute Press.

Australia. 1984. *Report of the Committee to Review the Australian Overseas Aid Program*. Canberra: Australian Government Publishing Service.

Awatere, Donna. 1984. *Maori Sovereignty*. Auckland, N.Z.: Broadsheet.

Bachman, G., T. Moeleer, L. Bennett. 1988. Childhood Sexual Abuse and the Consequences in Adult Women. *Obstetrics and Gynecology* 71 (4): 631–642.

Bailey, Anne M. and Joseph R. Llobera, eds. 1981. *The Asiatic Mode of Production*. London: Routledge and Kegan Paul.

Bank of Hawaii. 1990. *Hawaii 1990: Annual Economic Report*. Honolulu: Bank of Hawaii Economics Department.

———— and Sir Joseph Dalton Hooker. 1896. *Journal of the Right Hon. Sir Joseph Banks: During Captain Cook's First Voyage in the H. M. S. Endeavour in 1768–71 to Terra del Fuego, Otahite, New Zealand, Australia, the Dutch East Indies, etc.* New York: Macmillan.

Barman, Jean. 1995. New Land, New Lives: Hawaiian Settlement in British Columbia. *Hawaiian Journal of History* 29.

Barrow, Tui Terrence. 1967. *Women of Polynesia*. Wellington, N.Z.: Seven Seas.

Barth, Fredrik. 1969. *Ethnic Groups and Boundaries*. Boston: Little, Brown.

Beaglehole, J. C., ed. 1967. *The Journals of Captain James Cook on His Voyages of Discovery*. Vol. 3, *Voyage of the Resolution and the Discovery, 1776–1780*. Cambridge: Published for the Hakluyt Society at the University Press.

Beckwith, Martha Warren. [1951] 1972. *The Kumulipo*. Honolulu: University of Hawai'i Press.

Bederman, Gail. 1995. *Manliness and Civilization: A Cultural History of Gender and Race in the United States, 1880–1917*. Chicago and London: University of Chicago Press.

Bedford, R. D. 1980. Demographic Processes in Small Islands: The Case of Internal Migration. In *Population-Environment Relations in Tropical Islands: The Case of Eastern Fiji*, edited by H. C. Brookfield. Paris: UNESCO.

Bennett, J. A. 1976. Immigration, 'Blackbirding,' Labor Recruiting? The Hawaiian Experience, 1855–1871. *Journal of Pacific History* 11.

Berger, Kathleen Stassen. 2001. *The Developing Person Through the Life Span*. New York: Worth Publishers.

Bertram, I. G., and R. F. Watters. 1985. The MIRAB Economy in South Pacific Microstates. *Pacific Viewpoint* 26 (3).

Bettis, Leland. 1993. Colonial Immigration on Guam; Displacement of the Chamorro People Under U.S. Governance. In *A World Perspective on Pacific Islander Migration*, edited by Grant McCall and John Connell (Kensington, N.S.W.: Centre for South Pacific Studies, University of New South Wales).

Bingham, Hiram. 1848. *A Residence of Twenty-One Years in the Sandwich Islands*. New York: Sherman Converse.

Birrell, Robert, and Tanya Birrell. 1987. *An Issue of People: Population and Australian Society*. Melbourne: Longman Cheshire.

Blaisdell, Kekuni. 1983. Health Section. *Native Hawaiian Study Commission Report*. Vol. 1. Washington: U.S. Government Printing Office.

———. 1985. Poisoning in Hawai'i Kahi'o, He Mau Nōnao Ola. *Ka Wai Ola O Ohiā.*

———. 1987. Panel on Native Hawaiian Health: Historical and Cultural Aspects. Hawai'i State Department of Health. 18 December.

Blake-White, J., and C. M. Kline. 1985. Treating the Dissociative Process in Adult Victims of Childhood Incest. *Social Casework* 66:394–402.

Blazic-Metzner, B. and H. Hughes. 1982. Growth Experience of Small Economies. In *Problems and Policies in Small Economies*, edited by B. Jalan. London: Croon Helm.

Blount, J. 1893. Report to US Congress: Hawaiian Islands. In *Executive Document No. 46, 53rd Congress*. Washington.

Bodnar, John. 1985. *The Transplanted.* Bloomington, Ind.: Indiana University Press.

Bodner, Michelle. 1982. *Princess Ruth.* Honolulu: University of Hawai'i Press.

Bollard, A. E. 1975. The Impact of Monetisation in Tonga. MA thesis, University of Auckland.

Book, Timothy, ed. 1989. *The Asiatic Mode of Production.* Armonk, N.Y.: M. E. Sharpe.

Borrie, W. D., and Geraldine Spencer. 1965. *Australia's Population Structure and Growth.* Melbourne: Committee for Economic Development of Australia.

Bougainville, Comte Louis-Antoine de. 1772. *A Voyage Round the World.* Translated by Johann Reinhold Forster. London: Royal Academy.

Breckenridge, Carol A. and Peter van der Veer, eds. *Orientalism and the Postcolonial Predicament: Perspectives on South Asia.* Philadelphia: University of Pennsylvania Press, 1993.

Brightman, Richard. 1995. Forget Culture: Replacement, Transcendence, Relexification. *Cultural Anthropology* 10 (4): 509–546.

Brookfield, H. C. 1972. Intensification and Disintensification in Pacific Agriculture. *Pacific Viewpoint* 12 (1): 30–48.

———. 1980. The Fiji Study: Testing the MAB Approach. In *Population-Environment Relations in Tropical Islands: The Case of Eastern Fiji*, edited by H. C. Brookfield. Paris: UNESCO.

———. 1984. Intensification Revisited. *Pacific Viewpoint* 25 (1): 15–44.

Brown, Richard P. C. 1998. Do Migrants' Remittances Decline over Time? Evidence from Tongans and Western Samoans in Australia. *Contemporary Pacific* 10 (1): 107–151.

Brownstone, David M., Irene M. Franck, and Douglass L. Brownstone. 1986. *Island of Hope, Island of Tears.* New York: Penguin.

Bushnell, J. A., J. E. Wells, and M. Oakley-Browne. 1992. Long Term Effect of Intrafamilial Sexual Abuse in Childhood. *Acta Psychiatr* (Scand.) 85:136–142.

Bushnell, O. A. 1966. Hygiene and Sanitation among the Ancient Hawaiians. *Hawaiian Historical Review* 2 (5): 13.

Campbell, I. C. 1989. *A History of the Pacific Islands.* Berkeley: University of California Press.

Chaliand, Gérard and Jean-Pierre Rageau. 1997. *The Penguin Atlas of Diasporas.* New York: Penguin.

Chambers, A. 1975. *Nanumea Report.* Wellington, N.Z.: Department of Geography, Victoria University.

Chappell, H. G. 1927. *Jaws and Teeth of Ancient Hawaiians.* Honolulu: Bishop Museum Press.

Cheng, Lucie and Edna Bonacich, eds. 1984. *Labor Immigration Under Capitalism.* Berkeley: University of California Press.

Chung, G. H. S., C. S. Chung, and R. W. Nemecheck. 1969. Genetic and Epidemiological Studies of Clubfoot. *American Journal of Human Genetics* 21:566.

Churchill, Ward, ed. 1983. *Marxism and Native Americans.* Boston: South End Press.

Cisco, Dan. 1999. *Hawai'i Sports: History, Facts, and Statistics.* Honolulu: Latitude 20 and University of Hawai'i Presses.

Clifford, James. 1994. Diasporas. *Cultural Anthropology* 9 (3): 302–338.

Cohen, Robin. 1997. *Global Diasporas: An Introduction.* Seattle: University of Washington Press.

Cohen, Ronald. 1978. Ethnicity: Problem and Focus in Anthropology. *Annual Review of Anthropology* 7:379–403.

Collins, Jock. 1988. *Migrant Hands in a Distant Land: Australia's Post-War Immigration.* Sydney.

Connell, John. 1980. *Remittances and Rural Development: Migration, Dependency and Inequality in the South Pacific.* Occasional Paper No. 22. Canberra: Development Studies Centre, Australian National University.

———. 1984a. *Diets and Dependency: Food and Colonialism in the South Pacific.* 2nd ed. Occasional Paper No. 1. Sydney: Freedom from Hunger Ideas Centre.

———. 1984b. Status or Subjugation? Women, Migration and Development in the South Pacific. *International Migration Review* 18 (4): 965–983.

———. 1985a. Islands on the Poverty Line. *Pacific Viewpoint* 26 (2): 463–473.

———. 1985b. *Migration, Employment and Development.* Country Report No. 25. *North America.* Noumea: International Labour Organisation and South Pacific Commission.

———. 1986. *Migration, Employment and Development in the South Pacific.* Noumea: International Labour Organisation and South Pacific Commission.

———. 1987. The Fatal Impact? Migration, Agriculture and Health in the South Pacific. In *The Effects of Urbanisation and Western Foods on the Health of Pacific Islands Populations.* Noumea: South Pacific Commission.

———, Graham Harrison, and Grant McCall. 1991. *South Pacific Islanders in Australia.* Report held at Bureau of Immigration, Population, and Multicultural Research Library, Melbourne.

——— and Grant McCall. 1989. *South Pacific Islanders in Australia.* Occasional Paper 9. Sydney: Research Institute for Asia and the Pacific.

The Contemporary Pacific. Journal published by the Center for Pacific Islands Studies, University of Hawai'i.

Cook Islands. 1983. *Cook Islands Development Plan, 1982–1985.* Rarotonga, Cook Islands.

Cooke, Amos Starr. 1937. *The Chiefs' Children's School.* Honolulu: Honolulu Star-Bulletin.

——— and Juliette Montague Cooke. [1941] 1987. *Amos Starr Cooke and Juliette Montague Cooke: Their Autobiography Gleaned From Their Journals and Letters.* Edited by Mary Richards. Reprint, Honolulu: Daughters of Hawai'i.

Cornell, Stephen. 1988. *The Return of the Native: American Indian Political Resurgence.* New York: Oxford.

Courtenay, John [pseud.]. 1775. *A Poetical Epistle, Moral and Philosophical, From an Officer at Otaheite. To Lady Gr**v*n*r.* London: T. Evans. In Fuller Collection, Bishop Museum Library, Honolulu, Hawai'i.

Cowling, Wendy. 1990. Motivations for Contemporary Tongan Migration. In *Tongan Culture and History,* edited by Phyllis Herda, Jennifer Terrell, and Niel Gunson. Canberra: Department of Pacific and Southeast Asian History, Australian National University.

Crèvecouer, Hector St. John [Michel-Guilliame-Jean] de. [1782] 1912. *Letters from an American Farmer.* New York: Dutton.

Crocombe, Ron G. 1978. Rural Development. *Pacific Perspective* 7 (1–2): 42–59.

———. 1979. Nepotism. In *Cook Island Politics: The Inside Story.* Auckland: South Pacific Social Science Association.

———. 1984. The Pan-Pacific Person: Staffing the Regional Organizations. *Pacific Perspective* 12:51–60.

———. 1992. *Pacific Neighbours: New Zealand's Relations with Other Pacific Islands.* Christchurch, N.Z.: Centre for Pacific Studies, University of Canterbury, and Suva, Fiji: Institute of Pacific Studies, University of the South Pacific.

———. 1993. Ethnicity, Identity and Power in Oceania. In *Islands and Enclaves: Nationalisms and Separatist Pressures in Island and Littoral Contexts,* edited by Gary Trompf, 195–223. New Delhi: Sterling.

Curson, P. 1979. Migration, Remittances and Social Networks Among Cook Islanders. *Pacific Viewpoint* 20 (2): 185–198.

Dagmar, Hans. 1989. Banabans in Fiji: Ethnicity, Change, and Development. In *Ethnicity and Nation-building in the Pacific,* edited by Michael C. Howard. Tokyo: United Nations University.

Daniel, G. Reginald. 1992. Passers and Pluralists: Subverting the Racial Divide. In *Racially Mixed People in America,* edited by Maria P. P. Root, 91–107. Newbury Park, Calif.: Sage.

Daws, Gavan. 1974. *Shoal of Time: A History of the Hawaiian Islands.* Honolulu: University of Hawai'i Press.

de Bres, J., and R. D. Campbell. 1975. Temporary Labour Migration between Tonga and New Zealand. *International Labour Review* 112 (6): 445–457.

Denoon, Donald, et al., eds. 1997. *The Cambridge History of the Pacific Islanders.* Cambridge: Cambridge University Press.

De Vos, George A. 1990. Conflict and Accommodation in Ethnic Interaction. In *Status Inequality: The Self in Culture,* edited by George A. De Vos and Marcelo Suárez-Orozco, 204–245. Newbury Park, Calif.: Sage.

Diaz, Vicente M. 1995. Bye Bye Ms. American Pie: The Historical Relations between Chamorros and Filipinos and the American Dream. *ISLA: A Journal of Micronesian Studies* (Rainy Season).

———. 2000. Into the Sunset (Boulevard): Tracking the Disturbing(ly) Familia(r) in Southern California. Conference paper presented 11–12 February at University of California, Santa Cruz.

——— and J. Kehaulani Kauanui. 2001. Introduction: Native Pacific Cultural Studies on the Edge. *The Contemporary Pacific* 13 (2): 315–342.

Dillon, Rosemary A. 1983. Hala-'o-vave: A Study of Settlement in a Low Lying Marsh Area of Nuku'alofa, Tonga. Dissertation for the Bachelor of Urban and Regional Planning, University of New England, Armindale.

Dinsmore, C. 1991. *From Surviving to Thriving: Incest, Feminism, and Recovery.* Albany, N.Y.: State University of New York.

Dirige, O., and C. K. Hughes. 1985. Nutrition/Dental Task Force Report. In *E Ola Mau: Native Hawaiian Health Needs Study.* Honolulu: Alu Like.

Dirlik, Arif, ed. 1993. *What Is In a Rim? Critical Perspectives on the Pacific Region Idea.* Boulder, Colo.: Westview Press.

Docker, Edward Wybergh. 1970. *The Blackbirders: The Recruiting of South Seas Labour for Queensland, 1863–1907.* London: Angus and Robertson.

Dorton, Lilikalā. 1986. Land and the Promise of Capitalism: A Dilemma for the Hawaiian Chiefs of the 1848 Māhele. Ph.D. dissertation, University of Hawai'i.

Dower, John W. 1986. *War Without Mercy: Race and Power in the Pacific War.* New York: Pantheon.

Du Bois, W. E. B. 1897. Strivings of Negro People. *Atlantic Monthly* 80 (August).

Dubanoski, Richard A., and Karen Snyder. 1980. Patterns of Child Abuse and Neglect in Japanese- and Samoan-Americans. *Child Abuse and Neglect* 4:217–225.

Dudley, Michael Kioni, and Keoni Kealoha Agard. 1990a. *A Hawaiian Nation.* Vol. 1, *Man, Gods, and Nature.* Honolulu: Na Kane O Ka Malo Press.

———. 1990b. *A Hawaiian Nation.* Vol 2, *A Call for Hawaiian Sovereignty.* Honolulu: Na Kane O Ka Malo Press.

Duncan, B. 1990. Christianity: Pacific Island Traditions. In *Religions of New Zealanders,* edited by Peter Donovan. Palmerston North, N.Z.: Dunmore.

Duncan, Janice K. 1973. Kanaka World Travelers and Fur Company Employees, 1785–1860. *Hawaiian Journal of History* 7.

Dunn, Stephen Porter. 1982. *The Fall and Rise of the Asiatic Mode of Production.* London: Routledge and Kegan Paul.

Durkheim, Émile. [1915] 1965. *Elementary Forms of the Religious Life*. New York: Free Press.

E Ola Mau. 1986–88. *Nā Mea Hou*. Newsletter.

Ellis, William. 1917. *A Narrative of a Tour Through Hawaii, or Owhyhee*. Honolulu: Hawaiian Gazette.

ESG submission. 1994. Submission by the English-Speaking Group (ESG) of Newton Pacific Island Church to the PIC Synod of the Presbyterian Church of Aotearoa New Zealand (PCANZ).

Ember, Melvin. 1964. "Commercialization and Political Change in American Samoa." In *Explorations in Cultural Anthropology*, edited by Ward H. Goodenough. New York: McGraw-Hill.

Emery, S. 1976. The Samoans of Los Angeles: A Preliminary Study of Their Migration from Pago Pago to the South Bary. Los Angeles: University of Southern California. Mimeographed.

Espiritu, Yen Le. 1992. *Asian American Panethnicity*. Philadelphia: Temple University Press.

———. 1995. *Filipino American Lives*. Philadelphia: Temple University Press.

Faces of the Nation. 1988. Produced by Nā Maka o Ka 'Āina for Ka Lāhui Hawai'i. Available from the Center for Hawaiian Studies, University of Hawai'i, or at www.namaka.com. Videocassette.

Fagan, Brian. 1984. *Clash of Cultures*. New York: W. H. Freeman.

Fairbairn, I. 1982. Second Thoughts on First Aid. *Islands Business* 8 (10): 32–36.

Firth, R. 1971. Economic Aspects of Modernization in Tikopia. In *Anthropology in Oceania*, edited by L. R. Hiatt and C. Jayawardena. Sydney: Angus and Robertson.

Fisk, E. K. 1966. The Economic Structure. In *New Guinea on the Threshold*, edited by E. K. Fisk. Canberra: Australian National University Press.

Flynn, Dennis O., Lionel Frost, and A. J. H. Latham, eds. 1999. *Pacific Centuries: Pacific and Pacific Rim History Since the Sixteenth Century*. London: Routledge.

Freeman, Derek. 1983. *Margaret Mead and Samoa: The Making and Unmaking of an Anthropological Myth*. Cambridge, Mass.: Harvard University Press.

Freeman, Gary P. and James Jupp, eds. 1992. *Nations of Immigrants: Australia, the United States, and International Migration*. Melbourne: Oxford.

Friedman, J. 1992. The Past in the Future: History and the Politics of Identity. *American Anthropologist* 94 (4): 841–845.

Fuchs, Lawrence H. 1961. *Hawai'i Pono*. New York: Harcourt, Brace and World.

Funaki, 'Inoke. 1993. Culture and Identity in the Pacific: A Personal Expression. Convocation address, BYU-Hawai'i.

Funderburg, Lise. 1994. *Black, White, Other: Biracial Americans Talk about Race and Identity*. New York: Morrow.

Gallimore, R., J. Boggs, and C. Jordan. 1974. *Culture, Behavior and Education: A Study of Native Hawaiians*. Beverly Hills: Sage.

Gibson, K. 1982. Political Economy and International Labour Migration: The Case of Polynesians in New Zealand. *New Zealand Geographer* 39 (2): 29–42.

Gifted and Brown, Tangata Music. 1994. So Much Soul. Soundtrack of *Once Were Warriors*. Auckland: Tangata Records.

The Golf War. 1995. Produced by Matt DeVries and Jen Schradie. Distributed by Bullfrog Films. Videocassette; also available through www.golfwar.org.

Goodman, B., and D. Nowak-Scibelli. 1985. Group Treatment for Women Incestuously Abused as Children. *International Journal of Group Psychotherapy* 35 (4): 531–544.

Goodyear-Smith, F. 1993. *First Do No Harm: The Sexual Abuse Industry*. Auckland, New Zealand: Benton-Guy Publishing.

Gordon, Milton M. 1964. *Assimilation in American Life*. New York: Oxford.

Gould, R. T. 1978. *Captain Cook*. London: Gerald Duckworth & Co. First published in 1935.

Gray, Ellen, and John Cosgrove. 1985. Ethnocentric Perception of Childrearing Practices in Protective Services. *Child Abuse and Neglect* 9:389–396.

Gray, Francine du Plessis. 1972. *Hawai'i: The Sugar-Coated Fortress*. New York: Vintage.

Gray, J. A. C. 1960. *Amerika Samoa: A History of American Samoa and Its United States Naval Administration*. Annapolis, Md.: U.S. Naval Institute.

Green, Harvey. 1986. *Fit for America: Health, Fitness, Sport and American Society*. Baltimore: Johns Hopkins University Press.

Greer, R. A. 1969. The Founding of Queen's Hospital. *Hawaiian Journal of History* 3:110.

Grossman, L. 1981. The Cultural Ecology of Economic Development. *Annals of the Association of American Geographers* 71 (2): 220–236.

Hall, Christine C. I. 1992. Please Choose One: Ethnic Identity Choices of Biracial Individuals. In *Racially Mixed People in America*, edited by Maria P. P. Root, 250–264. Newbury Park, Calif.: Sage.

Hall, Stuart. 1990. Cultural Identity and Diaspora. In *Identity: Community, Culture, Difference*, edited by Jonathan Rutherford, 222–237. London: Lawrence and Wishart.

———— and Bram Gieben, eds. 1992. *Formations of Modernity*. Cambridge: Polity Press, in association with Open University.

Handlin, Oscar. 1973. *The Uprooted*, 2nd ed. Boston: Little Brown.

Handy, E. S. Craighill, and Mary K. Pūku'i. 1972. *The Polynesian Family System in Ka'ū, Hawai'i*. Rutland, Vt.: Charles E. Tuttle.

Handy, E. S. Craighill, E. G. Handy, and Mary K. Pūku'i. 1972. *Native Planters in Old Hawai'i*. Bulletin no. 233. Honolulu: Bishop Museum Press.

Handy, E. S. Craighill, Mary K. Pūku'i, and K. Livermore. 1934. *Outline of Hawaiian Physical Therapeutics*. Bulletin no. 126. Honolulu: Bishop Museum Press.

Hanlon, David. n.d. Aloha for their Violence: Locating the NFL's Pro Bowl within Contemporary Hawai'i and the Deeper Hawaiian Past. Unpublished Paper.

Harlow, Barbara and Mia Carter, eds. 1999. *Imperialism and Orientalism: A Documentary Sourcebook*. Malden, Mass.: Blackwell.

Harré, John. 1966. *Maori and Pakeha*. London: Institute of Race Relations.

Hartwell, Jay. 1996. *Na Mamo: Hawaiian People Today*. Honolulu: 'Ai Pohaku Press.

Hau'ofa, Epeli. 1993. Our Sea of Islands. In *A New Oceania: Rediscovering Our Sea of Islands*, edited by Epeli Hau'ofa, Eric Waddell, and Vijay Naidu. Suva, Fiji: School of Social and Economic Development, the University of the South Pacific, in association with Beake House.

———. 1994. Our Sea of Islands. *The Contemporary Pacific* (Spring).

Hawaiian Kingdom Statistical and Commercial Directory and Tourist Guide of 1880–81. 1881. Honolulu: Polk.

Henderson, April. 1999. Gifted flows. Paper presented to the Out of Oceania conference, 22 October, Honolulu, Hawai'i.

Herman, J., and L. Hirschman. 1981. Families at Risk for Father-Daughter Incest. *American Journal of Psychiatry* 138 (7): 967–969.

Herman, J., and E. Schatzow. 1984. Time-Limited Group Therapy for Women with a History of Incest. *International Journal of Group Psychotherapy* 34:605–616.

Herman, J., D. E. H. Russell, K. Trocki. 1986. Long-Term Effect of Incestuous Abuse in Childhood. *American Journal of Psychiatry* 43 (10): 1293–1296.

Herodotus. 1942. *The Persian Wars*. Translated by George Rawlinson. New York: Random House.

Hezel, F. X. 1985. In the Aftermath of the Education Explosion. Truk: Micronesian Seminar. Mimeographed.

Hinckley, Gordon B. 2000. *Standing for Something*. New York: Random House.

Hirsch, Susan. 1958. The Social Organization of an Urban Village in Samoa. *Journal of the Polynesian Society* 67:266–303.

Hobbs, Jean. 1935. *Hawai'i: A Pageant of the Soil*. Stanford, Calif.: Stanford University Press.

Holmes, Lowell D. 1964. Leadership and Decision Making in American Samoa. *Current Anthropology* 66:301–38, 398–435.

———. 1974. *Samoan Village*. New York: Holt, Rinehart and Winston.

Houston, V. S. K. 1950. The Queen's Hospital. *Honolulu Advertiser*, 18–27 December.

Howard, Alan. 1961. Rotuma as a Hinterland Community. *Journal of the Polynesian Society* 70:272–299.

———. 1974. *Ain't No Big Thing: Coping Strategies in a Hawaiian-American Community*. Honolulu: University Press of Hawai'i.

Howard, Michael C., ed. 1989. *Ethnicity and Nation-building in the Pacific*. Tokyo: United Nations University Press.

Howe, K. R. 1984. *Where the Waves Fall: A New South Sea Islands History from First Settlement to Colonial Rule*. Honolulu: University of Hawai'i Press.

Ignacio, Lemuel F. 1976. *Asian Americans and Pacific Islanders: Is There Such an Ethnic Group?* San Jose: Pilipino Associates Inc.

Ito, K. 1978. Symbolic Conscience: Illness Retribution among Urban Hawaiian Women. Ph.D. dissertation, UCLA.

———. 1982. Illness as Retribution: A Cultural Form of Self-Analysis among Urban Hawaiian women. *Culture, Medicine and Psychiatry* 6:385–403.

Jacala, Jack. 1999. Personal conversation with author.

Jacobson, Matthew Frye. 1998. *Whiteness of a Different Color: European Immigrants and the Alchemy of Race.* Cambridge, Mass.: Harvard University Press.

James, Kerry. 1991. Migration and Remittances: A Tongan Village Perspective. *Pacific Viewpoint* 1 (4): 379–400.

Janes, Craig R. 1990. *Migration, Social Change, and Health: A Samoan Community in Urban California.* Stanford, Calif.: Stanford University Press.

Johannes, R. E. 1981. *Winds in the Lagoon: Fishing and Marine Lore in the Palau District of Micronesia.* Berkeley: University of California Press.

Jonassen, Jon. 1993. Former Executive Secretary, South Pacific Commission. Interviewed by Paul Spickard. Lāʻie, Hawaiʻi.

Josephson, G. S., and M. L. Fong-Beyette. 1987. Factors Assisting Female Clients' Disclosure of Incest during Counseling. *Journal of Counseling Development* 65:475–478.

Jury, Bill. 1947. Sweat Bowl Jamboree. *Navy News,* 14 December.

Kaeppler, Adrienne L. 1971. Rank in Tonga. *Ethnology* 10 (2): 174–193.

Kallen, E. 1982. *The Western Samoan Kinship Bridge: A Study of Migration, Social Change and the New Ethnicity.* Leiden: E. J. Brill.

Kalmijn, Matthijs. 1991. Shifting Boundaries: Trends in Religious and Educational Homogamy. *American Sociological Review* 56:786–800.

———. 1993. Trends in Black/White Intermarriage. *Social Forces* 72:119–146.

Kamakau, Samuel M. 1964. *Ka Poʻe Kahiko.* Special Publication 51. Honolulu: Bishop Museum Press.

———. 1976. *The Works of the People of Old.* Translated by Mary Kawena Pūkuʻi, edited by Dorothy Barrere. Honolulu: Bishop Museum Press.

Kamakawiwoʻole, Israel. "Lover of Mine." On *Iz in Concert,* ©1998 by Big Boy Record Company, Honolulu.

Kameʻeleihiwa, Lilikalā (*néee* Dorton). 1992. *Native Land and Foreign Desires.* Honolulu: Bishop Museum Press.

Kanahele, George Huʻeu Sanford. 1979. *Hawaiian Music and Musicians.* Honolulu: University Press of Hawaiʻi.

———. 1982. *Current Facts and Figures About Hawaiians.* Honolulu: Project WAIAHA.

———. 1986. *Ku Kanaka: Stand Tall: A Search for Hawaiian Values.* Honolulu: University of Hawaiʻi Press.

Kauanui, J. Kehaulani. 1999. Off-Island Hawaiians "Making" Ourselves at "Home": A [Gendered] Contradiction in Terms? *Women's Studies International Forum* 21 (6): 681–693.

Kavaliku, S. Langi. 1977. 'Ofa! The Treasure of Tonga. *Pacific Perspective* 6 (2): 47–67.

Keesing, Roger. 1989. Creating the Past: Custom and Identity in the Contemporary Pacific. *The Contemporary Pacific* 1:19–42.

Kelly, M. 1988. *Early Mission Impact on Hawaiians and Their Culture.* Honolulu: Church of the Crossroads.

Kent, Noel. 1983. *Hawaii, Islands Under the Influence.* New York: Monthly Review Press.

Kett, Joseph F. 1977. *Rites of Passage: Adolescence in America, 1790 to the Present.* New York: Basic Books.

Kilusang Magbubukid ng Pilipinas. 2000. Hacienda Looc Peasants Hit Malacanang Order. Press release, 17 August: http://www.golfwar.org.

Kimura, Larry L. 1983. The Hawaiian Language. *Native Hawaiian Study Commission Report.* Vol. 1. Washington: Government Printing Office.

Kitano, Harry H. L., Wai Tsang Yeung, Lynn Chai, and Herbert Hatanaka. 1984. Asian-American Interracial Marriage. *Journal of Marriage and the Family* 46:179–190.

Kittelson, David J. 1985. *The Hawaiians: An Annotated Bibliography.* Honolulu: Social Science Research Institute, University of Hawai'i.

Kluge, P. F. 1991. *The Edge of Paradise: America in Micronesia.* Honolulu: University of Hawai'i Press.

Koppel, Tom. 1995. *Kanaka: The Untold Story of Hawaiian Pioneers in British Columbia and the Pacific Northwest.* Vancouver: Whitecap Books.

Korbin, Jill E. 1987a. Child Abuse and Neglect: The Cultural Context. In *The Battered Child*, 4th ed., edited by R. Helfer and R. Kempe, 23–41. Chicago: University of Chicago Press.

———. 1987b. Child Maltreatment in Cross-Cultural Perspective: Vulnerable Children and Circumstances. In *Child Abuse and Neglect: Biosocial Dimensions*, edited by R. Gelles and J. Lancaster, 31–55. New York: Aldine.

Krader, Lawrence and M. M. Kovalevskii. 1975. *The Asiatic Mode of Production: Sources, Development, and Critique of the Writings of Karl Marx.* Assen: Van Gorcum.

Kuykendall, Ralph S. 1938–1957. *The Hawaiian Kingdom.* 3 vols. Honolulu: University of Hawai'i Press.

———. [1938] 1980. *The Hawaiian Kingdom, Volume I, 1778–1854: Foundation and Transformation.* Reprint, Honolulu: The University Press of Hawai'i.

Ladner, Joyce A. 1977. *Mixed Families: Adopting across Racial Boundaries.* New York: Doubleday.

Lal, Barbara. 1983. Perspectives on Ethnicity: Old Wine in New Bottles. *Ethnic and Racial Studies* 6 (2): 154–173.

Ledyard, John. 1963. *John Ledyard's Journal of Captain Cook's last voyage.* Edited by James Munford. Corvallis: Oregon State University Press.

Lee, E. S. 1966. A Theory of Migration. *Demography* 3:47–57.

Lee, Robert G. 1999. *Orientals: Asian Americans in Popular Culture.* Philadelphia: Temple University Press.

Leilua, T. T. 1988. Christian baptism, a sacrament of unity. B.D. thesis, Pacific Theological College, Suva, Fiji.

Leong, Russel C. 1998. Beyond "the lahar of coalitions": Filipino American Studies at UCLA. *Amerasia Journal* 14 (2):vi.

Levin, M. J. 1985. Pacific Islanders in the United States: A Demographic Profile Based on the 1980 Census. Paper presented at the Conference on Asian-Pacific Immigration to the United States, East-West Center, Honolulu, Hawai'i.

Lewis, Martin W. and Kāren Wigen. 1997. *The Myth of Continents: A Critique of Metageography.* Berkeley: University of California Press.

Lewthwaite, Gordon R., Christine Mainzer, and Patrick J. Holland. 1973. From Polynesia to California: Samoan Migration and Its Sequalae. *Journal of Polynesia History* 8:113–157.

Levy, Neil M. 1975. Native Hawaiian Land Rights. *California Law Review* 63 (4): 857.

Lieberson, Stanley, and Mary C. Waters. 1988. *From Many Strands: Ethnic and Racial Groups in Contemporary America.* New York: Russell Sage.

Lili'uokalani. 1898. *Hawai'i's Story by Hawai'i's Queen.* Boston: Lee and Shepard.

Lind, Andrew. [1938] 1968. *An Island Community: Ecological Succession in Hawaii.* Reprint, New York: Greenwood Press.

Linnekin, Jocelyn, and Lin Poyer. 1990. *Cultural Identity and Ethnicity in the Pacific.* Honolulu: University of Hawai'i Press.

Lonsdale, Roger, ed. 1984. *Eighteenth Century Verse.* Oxford: Oxford University Press.

López, Ronald W. 1970. The El Monte Berry Strike of 1933. *Aztlán* 1:101–112.

Lowe, Lisa. 1991. Heterogeneity, Hybridity, Multiplicity: Marking Asian American Differences. *Diaspora* 1 (1): 24–44.

Lyman, Sarah Joiner. 1979. *The Lymans of Hilo.* Hilo, Hawai'i: Lyman House Memorial Museum.

Lyons, R. 1980. Emigration from American Samoa: A Study of Bicultural Assimilation and Migration. Ph.D. dissertation, University of Hawai'i.

Ma, Sheng-Mei. 2000. *The Deathly Embrace: Orientalism and Asian American Identity.* Minneapolis: University of Minnesota Press.

Macdonald, B. 1982a. Self-Determination and Self-Government. *Journal of Pacific History* 17 (1): 51–61.

———. 1982b. *Cinderellas of Empire: Towards a History of Kiribati and Tuvalu.* Canberra: Australian National University Press.

Macpherson, Cluny. 1983. The Skills Transfer Debate: Great Promise or Faint Hope for Western Samoa? *New Zealand Population Review* 9 (2): 47–76.

Macpherson, Cluny. 1991. The Changing Contours of Samoan Ethnicity in New Zealand. In *Nga Take: Ethnic Relations and Racism in Aotearoa/New Zealand,* edited by Paul Spoonley, David Pearson, and Cluny Macpherson. Palmerston North, N.Z.: Dunmore.

———. 1995. Conceptualising and Explaining Ethnic Diversity among the Children of Samoan Migrants in New Zealand. Unpublished paper presented at the Ethnicity and Multiethnicity conference held at Brigham Young University-Hawai'i Campus, Lāi'e, Hawai'i.

——— and Richard D. Bedford. 1999. The Structural Roots of Transformation of Pacific Identity in Aotearoa. Paper presented to the Out of Oceania conference, 20 October, Honolulu, Hawai'i.

———, Paul Spoonley, and Melani Anae. 2001. *Tangata O Te Moana Nui: Changing Identities of Pacific Peoples in Aotearoa/New Zealand.* Palmerston North, N.Z.: Dunmore Press.

Malo, David. 1951. *Hawaiian Antiquities,* edited by N. B. Emerson. Publication no. 2. Honolulu: Bishop Museum Press.

Manners, R. A. 1965. Remittances and the Unit of Analysis in Anthropological Research. *Southwestern Journal of Anthropology* 21 (3): 179–195.

Marcus, George E. 1975. Alternative Social Structures and the Limits of Hierarchy in the Modern Kingdom of Tonga. *Bijdragen Tot de Taal- Land- En Volkerkunde* 131:35–66.

———. 1977. Succession Disputes and the Position of the Nobility in Modern Tonga." *Oceania* 47 (3): 220–241; 47 (4): 284–299.

———. 1980. *The Nobility and the Chiefly Traditions in the Modern Kingdom of Tonga.* Memoir no. 42. Wellington: Polynesian Society.

———. 1981. Power on the Extreme Periphery: The Perspective of Tongan Elites in the Modern World System. *Pacific Viewpoint* 22 (1): 48–64.

———. 1989. Chieftainship. In *Developments in Polynesian Ethnology,* edited by A. Howard and R. Borofsky, 175–209. Honolulu: University of Hawai'i Press.

Marsella, A. J., et al. 1985. Mental Health Task Force Report. *E Ola Mau Native Hawaiian Health Needs Study.* Honolulu: Alu Like.

Marshall, M. 1979. Education and Depopulation on a Micronesian Atoll. *Micronesia* 15 (1–2): 1–11.

Martin, J., J. Anderson, S. Ropmans, P. Mullen, and M. O'Shea. 1993. Asking about Child Sexual Abuse: Methodological Implications of a Two Stage Survey. *Child Abuse and Neglect* 17:385–394.

Mason, Leonard, and Pat Hereniko, eds. 1987. *In Search of a Home.* Suva, Fiji: Institute of Pacific Studies, University of the South Pacific.

Matsuoka, Jon and Terry Kelly. 1988. The Environmental, Economic, and Social Impacts of Resort Development and Tourism on Native Hawaiians. *Journal of Society and Social Welfare* 4.

McCall, Grant. 1994. *Rapanui: Tradition and Survival on Easter Island.* 2nd ed. Honolulu: University of Hawai'i Press.

McGregor, B., and D. Dutton. 1991. Prevalence Rates of Child Sexual Abuse With Populations Requiring Health System Intervention. In *Child Sexual Abuse: Critical Perspectives on Prevention, Intervention and Treatment,* edited by C. R. Bagley and Thomlinson. Toronto: Wall and Emerson.

McGregor, Davianna. 1985. Voices of Today Echo Voices of the Past. In *Malama Hawaiian Land and Water,* edited by Dana Naone Hall. Honolulu: Bamboo Ridge Press.

———. 1993. Pele vs. Geothermal: A Clash of Cultures. In *Bearing Dreams, Shaping Visions: Asian Pacific Americans Facing the 90's.* Seattle: Washington State University Press.

Mead, Margaret. 1930. *The Social Organization of Manu'a.* Bulletin no. 6. Honolulu: Bishop Museum Press.

Mecheril, Paul and Thomas Teo. 1994. *Andere Deutsche.* Berlin: Dietz Verlag.

Meiselman, K. 1978. *Incest: A Psychological Study of Causes and Effects with Treatment Considerations.* San Francisco: Jossey Bass.

Meleisea, M. 1987. *The Making of Modern Samoa: Traditional Authority and Colonial Administration in the Modern History of Western Samoa.* Suva, Fiji: Institute of Pacific Studies of the University of the South Pacific.

———, and P. Meleisea. 1980. The Best Kept Secret: Tourism in Western Samoa. In *Pacific Tourism: As Islanders See It,* edited by F. Rajotte and R. Crocombe. Suva, Fiji: Institute of Pacific Studies.

Merry, Sally Engle. 2000. *Colonizing Hawai'i: The Cultural Power of Law.* Princeton, N.J.: Princeton University Press.

Miike, L. 1976. Current Health Status and Population Projections of Native Hawaiians Living in Hawai'i. April. Washington: Office of Technology Assessment, U.S. Congress.

Miller, C. D. 1974. The Influence of Foods and Food Habits Upon the Stature and Teeth of the Ancient Hawaiians. Appendix E in *Early Hawaiians: An Initial Study of Skeletal Remains from Mokapu, Oahu,* edited by C. E. Snow. Lexington: University of Kentucky Press.

Miller, Stuart C. 1969. *The Unwelcome Immigrant: The American Image of the Chinese, 1785–1882.* Berkeley: University of California Press.

Misa, Pona. 1992. Interviewed by Paul Spickard. Lā'ie, Hawai'i.

Mishra, Sudesh and E. Guy, eds. 1997. *Dreadlocks in Oceania 1.* Suva, Fiji: Department of Literature and Language, University of the South Pacific.

Mishra, Vijay. 1996. The Diasporic Imaginary: Theorizing the Indian Diaspora. *Textual Practice* 10 (3): 421–447.

Mitchell, Donald D. Kilolani. 1982. *Resource Units in Hawaiian Culture.* Honolulu: Kamehameha Schools.

Mitchell, J. Clyde. 1959. The Causes of Labour Migration. *Bulletin of the Inter-African Labour Institute* 6:12–47.

Morauta, L., and M. Hasu. 1979. Rural-Urban Relationships in Papua New Guinea: Case Material from the Gulf Province on Net Flows. IASER Discussion Paper no. 25. Port Moresby: Institute of Applied Social and Economic Research.

Mortimer, George. 1975. *Observations and remarks made during a voyage to the Islands of Teneriffe, Amsterdam, Maria's Island near Van Diemen's Land, Otaheite, Sandwich Islands, Owhyhee, the Fox Islands on the north west coast of America, Tinian, and from thence to Canton in the brig Mercury commanded by John Henry Cox.* New York: Da Capo Press.

Morton, Helen. 1996. *Becoming Tongan: An Ethnography of Childhood.* Honolulu: University of Hawai'i Press.

———. 1998. Creating Their Own Culture: Diasporic Tongans. *Contemporary Pacific* 10 (1): 1–30.

Mossman, M., and P. Wahilani. 1975. Kulia i lokahi i ke ola! Mimeographed.

Multiracial Americans of Southern California. 1993. *Spectrum* 7 (4).

Munoz, Faye Untalan. 1974. Pacific Islanders: A Perplexed, Neglected Minority. *Church and Society* (January-February): 15–23.

Murphy, Brian. 1993. *The Other Australia: Experiences of Migration.* Melbourne: Cambridge University Press.

Nagata, Judith. 1974. What Is a Malay? Situational Selection of Ethnic Identity in a Plural Society. *American Ethnologist* 1:331–350.

Nash, Gary B. 1968. *Red, White, and Black in Colonial America.* Englewood Cliffs, N.J.: Prentice-Hall.

Native Hawaiian Health Data Book. 1992. Honolulu: Papa Ola Lokahi.

Ne, Harriet, with Gloria L. Cronin. 1992. *Tales of Molokai.* La'ie, Hawai'i: Institute for Polynesian Studies.

Neuman, Jacob, ed. 1910. *French and English Philosophers.* New York: Collier.

Nokise, Uili Feleterika. 1990. History of the P.I.C.C. In *Religions of New Zealanders,* edited by Peter Donovan. Palmerston North, N.Z.: Dunmore.

Nordyke, Eleanor C. 1989. *The Peopling of Hawai'i.* 2nd ed. Honolulu: University of Hawai'i Press.

Office of Hawaiian Affairs. 1986. Population Survey / Needs Assessment, Final Report. Honolulu: Office of Hawaiian Affairs.

Okamura, Jonathan. 1998. *Imagining Filipino American Diaspora: Transnational Relations, Identities and Communities.* New York: Garland Publishing Inc.

Oliver, Douglas. 1961. *The Pacific Islands.* 2nd ed. New York: Natural History Press.

Oriard, Michael. 1993. *Reading Football: How the Popular Press Created an American Spectacle.* Chapel Hill: University of North Carolina Press.

Osorio, Jonathan, and Kanalu G.T. Young. 1997. *Lei Mele No Pauahi: Music, Past and Present at Kamehameha Schools.* Honolulu: Kamehameha Press.

Pacific Islands Report. 1998. Pacific Islands Development Program: http://pidp.ewc.hawaii.edu/PI Report/1998/February/02-06-05.html.

Pacific Studies. Journal published by the Institute for Polynesian Studies, Brigham Young University-Hawai'i.

Paglinawan, L. 1972. *Ho'oponopono Project II.* Honolulu: Hawaiian Culture Committee, Queen Liliuokalani Children's Center.

————. 1980. Untitled paper. University of Hawai'i School of Social Work.

Parke, R. and C. Collmer. 1975. *Child Abuse: An Interdisciplinary Analysis.* Chicago: University of Chicago Press.

Patterson, Orlando. 1975. "Context and Choice in Ethnic Allegiance: A theoretical Framework and Caribbean Case Study." In *Ethnicity: Theory and Experience,* edited by Nathan Glazer and Daniel P. Moynihan, 305–349. Cambridge, Mass.: Harvard University Press.

Peattie, Mark R. 1988. *Nanyo: The Rise and Fall of the Japanese in Micronesia.* Honolulu: University of Hawai'i Press.

Peters, S., G. Wyatt, and D. Finkelhor. 1986. In *Sourcebook on Child Sexual Abuse,* edited by D. Findelhor and Associates. Newbury Park, Calif.: Sage.

Petersen, G. 1979. "External Politics, Internal Economics and Ponapean Social Formation." *American Ethnologist* 6 (1): 25–40.

Pitt, D. C. 1970. *Tradition and Economic Progress in Samoa.* Oxford: Oxford University Press.

Pitt, D. C., and C. Macpherson. 1974. *Emerging Pluralism: The Samoan Community in New Zealand.* Auckland: Longman Paul.

Plant, C. 1977. The Development Dilemma. In *Rotuma: Split Island,* edited by C. Plant. Suva, Fiji: Institute of Pacific Studies.

Pollard, B. 1978. The Problem of an Aid-Dependent Economy: The Case of Niue. In *South Pacific Dossier,* edited by G. Woods. Canberra: Australian Council for Overseas Aid.

Pollock, Nancy J. 1999. Where home is. Paper presented to the Out of Oceania conference, 20 October, Honolulu, Hawai'i.

Polson, S. 1983. Coconomics: Expert Agriculture Won't Pay the Bills. *Pacific Magazine* 8 (4): 21–24.

Pratt, G. 1893. *A Grammar and Dictionary of the Samoan Language.* London: London Missionary Society.

Pūku'i, Mary Kawena. 1983. *'Ōelo No'eau: Hawaiian Proverbs and Poetical Sayings.* Special Publication no. 71. Honolulu: Bishop Museum Press.

Pūku'i, Mary Kawena, E. W. Haertig, and Catherine A. Lee. 1972. *Nānā I Ke Kumu (Look to the Source).* Vol. 1. Honolulu: Hui Hānai.

————. 1979. *Nānā I Ke Kumu (Look to the Source).* Vol. 2. Honolulu: Hui Hānai.

Rennie, Sandra. 1987. Contract Labor Under a Protector: The Gilbertese Laborers and Hiram Bingham, Jr., 1878–1903. *Pacific Studies* 11(1).

Robertson, George. 1948. *The Discovery of Tahiti: A Journal of the Second Voyage of H. M. S. Dolphin Round the World Under the Command of Captain Wallis, R.N., in the years 1766, 1767, and 1768.* Edited by Hugh Carrington. London: Hakluyt Society.

Rolff, Karla. 1978. Fa'asamoa: tradition in transition. Dissertation thesis (Ph. D.). University of California, Santa Barbara.

Romanucci-Ross, Lola and George A. De Vos. 1995. *Ethnic identity: Creation, conflict, and accommodation.* Walnut Creek, Calif.: AltaMira Press.

Root, Maria P. P., ed. 1992. *Racially Mixed People in America.* Thousand Oaks, Calif.: Sage.

Rosenfield, Jean E. 1999. *The Island Broken in Two Halves: Land and Renewal Movements Among the Maori of New Zealand.* University Park, Penn.: Pennsylvania State University Press.

Rouse, Roger. 1991. Mexican Migration and the Social Space of Postmodernism. *Diaspora* 1 (1): 13.

Roux, J. C. 1980. Migration and Change in Wallisian Society. In *The Island States of the Pacific and Indian Oceans,* edited by R. T. Shand. Canberra: Development Studies Centre, Australian National University.

Sahlins, Marshall. 1985. *Islands of History.* Chicago: University of Chicago Press.

Sahni, Kalpana. 1997. *Crucifying the Orient: Russian Orientalism and the Colonization of the Caucasus and Central Asia.* Bangkok: White Orchid Press.

Said, Edward. 1978. *Orientalism.* New York: Random House.

Saloutos, Theodore. 1956. *They Remember America: The Story of the Repatriated Greek-Americans.* Berkeley: University of California Press.

San Juan, E., Jr. 1998. *From Exile to Diaspora: Versions of the Filipino Experience in the United States.* Boulder, Colo.: Westview Press.

Sardar, Ziauddin. 1999. *Orientalism: Concepts in the Social Sciences.* Buckingham: Open University Press.

Sawer, Marian. 1977. *Marxism and the Question of the Asiatic Mode of Production.* The Hague: Nijhoff.

Saxton, Alexander. 1971. *The Indispensable Enemy: Labor and the Anti-Chinese Movement.* Berkeley: University of California Press.

Scarr, Deryck. 1994. Deconstructing the Island Group in Pacific History. *Pacific History Association Newsletter* 31:7.

Schneider, Jane, ed. 1998. *Italy's "Southern Question": Orientalism in One Country.* Oxford: Berg Publishers.

Schoeffel, P. 1995. The Samoan Concept of Feagaiga and Its Transformation. In *Tonga and Samoa: Images of Gender and Polity,* edited by J. Huntsman. Christchurch, N.Z.: Macmillan Brown Centre for Pacific Studies, University of Canterbury.

Schwalbenberg, H. 1984. *Micronesians on the Move: Guam or Hawaii?* Compact of Free Association Memo No. 12. Truk: Micronesian Seminar.

Seers, D. 1983. *The Political Economy of Nationalism.* Oxford: Oxford University Press.

Senara, T. 1987. Samoan Religious Leadership: Tradition and Change. M.A. thesis, Religious Studies, University of Otago.

Sevele, F. 1973. Regional Inequalities in Socio-Economic Development in Tonga. Ph.D. thesis, University of Canterbury, Christchurch, New Zealand.

Shaban, Fuad. 1991. *Islam and Arabs in Early American Thought: Roots of Orientalism in America.* Durham, N.C.: Acorn Press.

Shankman, P. 1976. *Migration and Underdevelopment: The Case of Western Samoa.* Boulder, Colo.: Westview.

Shook, Victoria E. 1995. *Ho'oponopono.* Honolulu: East-West Center.

Shore, Bradd. 1978. Introduction. *New Neighbours . . . Islanders in Adaptation,* edited by Cluny Macpherson, Bradd Shore, and Robert Franco. Santa Cruz, Calif.: UC Santa Cruz Center for South Pacific Studies.

———. 1982. *Sala'ilua: A Samoan Mystery.* New York: Columbia University Press.

Simmons, A., S. Diaz-Briquets, and A. R. Laquian. 1977. *Social Change and Internal Migration.* Ottawa: International Development Research Centre.

Small, Cathy A. 1997. *Voyages: From Tongan Villages to American Suburbs.* Ithaca, N.Y.: Cornell University Press.

Snow, C. E. 1974. *Early Hawaiians: An Initial Study of Skeletal Remains from Mokapu, Oahu.* Lexington: University of Kentucky Press.

Spickard, Paul R. 1989. *Mixed Blood: Intermarriage and Ethnic Identity in Twentieth-Century America.* Madison: University of Wisconsin Press.

———. 1996a. Christians in a Multicultural America. *Christian Scholar's Review* 24:4.

———. 1996b. *Japanese Americans: The Formation and Transformations of an Ethnic Group.* New York: Twayne.

———. 1998. Twice Immigrants: Kibei in America and Japan and America, 1910–1950. Paper presented to Japanese American Experience Conference, 18 September, at Willamette University, Salem, Oregon.

———. 2001. Who is an Asian? Who is a Pacific Islander?: Monoracialism, Multiracial People and Asian American Communities. In *The Sum of Our Parts: Mixed Heritage Asian Americans,* edited by Teresa Williams Leon and Cynthia Nakashima. Philadelphia: Temple University Press.

———. n.d. What's Critical About White Studies? In *Uncompleted Independence: The Creation and Revision of American Racial Thinking,* edited by Paul Spickard and G. Reginald Daniel. Notre Dame, Ind.: University of Notre Dame Press. In press.

———, ed. 1994. Pacific Island Peoples in Hawai'i. *Social Process in Hawai'i* 36 (special issue).

——— and W. Jeffrey Burroughs. 2000. We Are a People. In *We Are a People: Narrative and Multiplicity in Constructing Ethnic Identity,* edited by Paul Spickard and W. Jeffrey Burroughs. Philadelphia: Temple University Press.

———, Debbie Hippolite Wright, Blossom Fonoimoana, Karina Kahananui Green, David Hall, Dorri Nautu, Tupou Hopoate Pau'u, and John Westerlund. 1995. *Pacific Islander Americans: An Annotated Bibliography in the Social Sciences.* La'ie, Hawai'i: Institute for Polynesian Studies.

Spoonley, Paul, David Pearson, and Cluny Macpherson, eds. 1991. *Nga Take: Ethnic Relations and Racism in Aotearoa/New Zealand*. Palmerston North, N.Z.: Dunmore.

Stade, Ronald. 1998. *Pacific Passages: World Culture and Local Politics in Guam*. Stockholm: Stockholm University.

Standing, G. 1982. *Circulation and Proletarianisation*. Working Paper no. 119. Geneva: International Labour Office and World Employment Programme.

Stannard, David E. 1986. Tourism Called a Phony "Happiness" Industry. *Honolulu Star-Bulletin*. 9 June.

———. 1988. *Before the Horror: The Population of Hawai'i on the Eve of Western Contact*. Honolulu: University of Hawai'i Press.

State of Hawai'i Data Book. 1983. Hawai'i Department of Planning and Economic Development.

Stavrianos, L. S. 1981. *Global Rift*. New York: Morrow.

Steiner, Stan. 1970. *La Raza*. New York: Harper and Row.

Stewart, C. S. 1970. *Journal of a residence in the Sandwich Islands during the years 1823, 1824, and 1825*. Honolulu: University of Hawai'i Press.

Stillman, Amy Ku'uleialoha. 1996. Hawaiian Hula Competitions: Event, Repertoire, Performance, Tradition. *Journal of American Folklore* 109:357–380.

Tagupa, W. E. H. 1981. Education, Change and Assimilation in Nineteenth-Century Hawai'i. *Pacific Studies* 5:57.

Tai, William. 2000. Interviewed by Vicente M. Diaz.

Takaki, Ronald. 1983. *Pau Hana: Plantation Life and Labor in Hawaii*. Honolulu: University of Hawai'i Press.

Taft, Ronald. 1966. *From Stranger to Citizen*. London: Tavistock.

Tatla, Darshan Singh. 1999. *The Sikh Diaspora*. Seattle: University of Washington Press.

Taule'ale'ausumai, F. 1990. The Word Made Flesh. Pastoral Theology thesis, Faculty of Theology, University of Otago, Dunedin, N.Z.

Thieselton, T. F. 1975. *Folklore of Women*. Williamstown, Mass.: Dorner House Publications.

Thiongo, Ngugi Wa. 1986. *De-Colonizing the Mind*. London: Heinemann.

Thomson, James C. et al. 1981. *Sentimental Imperialists: The American Experience in East Asia*. New York: Harper and Row.

Thomson, J. K. 1976. Economic Development in the South Pacific: Some Problems and Prospects. In *Oceania and Beyond: Essays on the Pacific Since 1945*, edited by F. P. King. Westport, Conn.: Greenwood.

Tiffany, Sharon W. 1974. The Land and Titles Court and the Regulation of Customary Title Successions and Removals in Western Samoa. *Journal of the Polynesian Society* 83:35–57.

Time. 1993. Special Issue: The New Face of America.

Tisdell, G., and I. Fairbairn. 1984. Subsistence Economies and Unsustainable Development and Trade: Some Simple Theory. *Journal Of Development Studies* 20 (2): 227–241.

Todaro, Michael P. 1976. *Internal Migration in Developing Countries: A Review of Theory, Evidence, Methodology, and Research Priorities*. Geneva: International Labour Office.

Tokai, Ferenc. 1979. *Essays on the Asiatic Mode of Production*. Budapest: Akademiai Kiado.

Tonganibeia, Bintonga Even. 1993. Kiribati, Development and Internal Migration. In *A World Perspective on Pacific Islander Migration*, edited by Grant McCall and John Connell. Kensington, N.S.W.: Centre for South Pacific Studies, University of New South Wales.

Trask, Haunani-Kay. 1983. An Historical Over-View of Hawai'i: Pre-Contact to the Present. *Native Hawaiians Study Commission Report*. Vol. 1. Washington: Government Printing Office.

———. 1985. E Ola Mau Native Hawaiian Health Needs Study. In Historical/Cultural Task Force Report. Honolulu: Alu Like.

———. 1993. *From a Native Daughter*. Monroe, Maine: Common Courage Press.

Trask, M. B. 1982. Report to the U.S. Secretary of the Interior and Governor of the State of Hawai'i. In *Federal-State Task Force on the Hawaiian Homes Commission Act*. Honolulu.

Tuifua, Brenda. 1992. Faka'apa'apa: A Historical Perspective. Paper presented to the Phi Alpha Theta Conference. Honolulu. 6 March.

Tuimaleali'ifano, Morgan. 1990. *Samoans in Fiji*. Suva, Fiji: Institute of Pacific Studies, University of the South Pacific.

Tukuitonga, Colin. 1999. Discussion Paper for the National Health Committee. In *Primary Healthcare for Pacific People in New Zealand*, 3–4. Retrieved November 4, 2000 from the World Wide Web at http://www.nhc.govt.nz/pub/phc/phcpacific.html.

U.S. Bureau of the Census. 1983. *1980 Census of Population. 1B. General Population Characteristics. United States Summary* (PC80-1-B1). Washington: Government Printing Office.

U.S. Bureau of the Census. 1992. *1990 Census of Population. General Population Characteristics. United States* (CP-1-1). Washington: Government Printing Office.

U.S. Congress. 1988. *Congressional Record—House, 12 October*. Washington: Government Printing Office.

Uyematsu, Amy. 1971. The Emergence of Yellow Power in Asian America. In *Roots: An Asian American Reader*, edited by Amy Tachiki, Eddie Wong, and Franklin Odo. Los Angeles: UCLA Asian American Studies Center.

Vancouver, George. [1798] 1967. *Voyage of Discovery to the North Pacific Ocean and*

Round the World. Edited by John Vancouver. Reprint, New York: Da Capo Press.

Van Hear, Nicholas. 1998. *New Diasporas: The Mass Exodus, Dispersal, and Regrouping of Migrant Communities.* Seattle: University of Washington Press.

Vasconcellos, José. [1925] 1979. *La Raza Cósmica.* Translated by D. T. Jean. Fullerton, Calif.: California State University, Centro de Publicaciones.

Vitarelli, M. 1981. *A Pacific Island Migration Study: Palauans in Hawaii.* Honolulu: Pacific Islands Development Program, East-West Center.

Wakefield, Wanda Ellen. 1997. *Playing to Win: Sports and the American Military, 1898–1945.* New York: State University of New York Press.

Walker, M. 1988. Features of Counseling Work with Adult Survivors of Child Abuse. *Counseling: The Journal of the British Association for Counseling* (July): 15–18.

Wallace, William Kauaiwiulaokalani III. 1993. Interviewed by Paul Spickard, La'ie, Hawai'i.

Wallerstein, Immanuel. 1974–89. *The Modern World-System.* 3 vols. New York: Academic Press.

Wallman, S. 1977. The Bind of Migration: Conditions of Non-Development in Lesotho. In *Perceptions of Development,* edited by S. Wallman. Cambridge: Cambridge University Press.

Walsh, A. C. 1969. A Tongan Urban Peasantry: A Conjecture or Reality? In *Pacific Peasantry,* edited by I. G. Bassett, 87–107. Manawatu: New Zealand Geographical Society.

Ward, R. G. 1961. Internal Migration in Fiji. *Journal of the Polynesian Society* 70 (3): 257–271.

Waters, Mary C. 1990. *Ethnic Options: Choosing Identities in America.* Berkeley: University of California Press.

Watters, Ray. 1987. MIRAB Societies and Bureaucratic Elites. In *Class and Culture in the South Pacific,* edited by Antony Hooper, Steve Britton, Ron Crocombe, Judith Honisanan, and Cluny Macpherson, 32–55. Auckland, N.Z.: Centre for Pacific Studies, University of Auckland; and Suva, Fiji: Institute of Pacific Studies, University of the South Pacific.

Wei, William. 1993. *The Asian American Movement.* Philadelphia: Temple University Press.

Wendt, Albert. 1965. Guardians and Wards: A Study of the Origins, Causes, and the First Two Years of the Mau in Western Samoa. M.A. thesis, Victoria University, Wellington, N.Z.

Wendt, Albert. 1973. *Sons for the Return Home.* Honolulu: University of Hawai'i Press.

Wilton, Janis and Richard Bosworth. 1984. *Old Worlds and New Australia.* Ringwood, Victoria, Australia: Penguin.

Wittfogel, Karl A. 1957. *Oriental Despotism*. New Haven, Conn.: Yale University Press.

Wong, D. 1987. False Allegations of Child Abuse: The Other Side of the Tragedy. *Pediatric Nursing* 13 (5): 329–332.

Wong, Sau-ling C. 1995. Denationalization Reconsidered: Asian American Cultural Criticism at a Theoretical Crossroads. *Amerasia Journal* 21 (1/2): 1–27.

Wright, Debbie Hippolite and Paul Spickard. n.d. Pacific Islander Americans and Asian American Identity. In *Intersections and Divergences: Contemporary Asian Pacific American Communities*, edited by Linda Trinh Vo and Enrique Bonus. Philadelphia: Temple University Press. In press.

Yang, Y. H. 1982. Agricultural Performance, Food Availability and Dietary Change in Asia and the Pacific. Paper submitted to Agri-Energy Roundtable, Maui.

Young, B. 1980. The Hawaiians. In *Peoples and Cultures of Hawaii: A Psychocultural Profile*, edited by J. McDermott, W. Tseng, and T. Maretzki, 5–24. Honolulu: University Press of Hawai'i.

Zambucka, Kristin. 1982. *Princess Kaiulani*. Honolulu: Mana.

Zhao, Xiaojian. 2002. *Remaking Chinese America: Immigration, Family, and Community, 1940–1965*. New Brunswick, N.J.: Rutgers University Press. In press.

Contributors

Keoni Kealoha Agard was educated at Chaminade University and the University of Hawai'i School of Law. He is an attorney and a Hawaiian sovereignty activist living on the island of O'ahu, and co-author of *A Call for Hawaiian Sovereignty* (Nā Kāne O Ka Malo Press, 1990).

Melani Anae earned a Ph.D. at the University of Auckland, where she is a Lecturer in Anthropology and a member of the Centre for Pacific Studies. She is co-editor of *Tangata O Te Moana Nui: The Evolving Identities of Pacific Peoples in Aotearoa/New Zealand* (Dunmore Press, 2001).

Kekuni Blaisdell, a writer, speaker, and Kanaka Maori sovereignty activist, is a member of the faculty of medicine at the University of Hawai'i.

John Connell teaches anthropology at the University of Sydney. His many books on the Pacific include *The Last Colonies* (Cambridge University Press, 1998) and *Writing of Passages: Migration and Literature* (Routledge, 1995).

Wendy Cowling holds a Ph.D. from Macquarie University and is a Lecturer in Anthropology and Convener of Pacific Studies at the University of Waikato.

Vicente M. Diaz teaches in the Program in American Cultures at the University of Michigan. Having earned a Ph.D. from the University of California, Santa Cruz, he has published several articles on Pacific Islander issues and has produced a video, *Sacred Vessels: Navigating Tradition and Identity in Micronesia*.

Michael Kioni Dudley is a scholar and activist for Hawaiian rights. He holds a Ph.D. from the University of Hawai'i, and has taught there and at Chaminade University. He is co-author of *A Call for Hawaiian Sovereignty* (Nā Kāne O Ka Malo Press, 1990) and author of *Man, Gods, and Nature* (Nā Kāne O Ka Malo Press, 1990).

Diana Fitisemanu graduated from Brigham Young University-Hawai'i and Columbia University. She is currently in business in Aotearoa/New Zealand.

'Inoke Funaki holds degrees from Church College of Hawai'i and Brigham Young University in Utah. He is Professor of Psychology at Brigham Young University-Hawai'i.

Lupe Funaki earned a B.A. at Brigham Young University-Hawai'i. She is a college administrator at Brigham Young University in Utah.

Karina Kahananui Green was educated at Brigham Young University-Hawai'i. She and her family live in California.

David Hall graduated from Brigham Young University-Hawai'i and is a computer specialist working in Auckland.

Jay Hartwell is a graduate of Colorado College and the Columbia School of Journalism. A former journalist and author of *Nā Mamo: Hawaiian People Today* ('Ai Pōhaku Press, 1996), he is an administrator at the University of Hawai'i.

Debbie Hippolite Wright holds degrees from the University of Waikato and Brigham Young University (in Hawai'i and in Utah). She is chair of the Social Work Department at Brigham Young University-Hawai'i. Her publications include *Pacific Islander Americans: An Annotated Bibliography in the Social Sciences* (Institute for Polynesian Studies, 1995).

Craig R. Janes earned a Ph.D. in medical anthropology at the University of California, San Francisco. He teaches anthropology at the University of Colorado, Denver. He is the author of many articles on medicine and culture in Asia and the Pacific, and of *Migration, Social Change, and Health: A Samoan Community in Urban California* (Stanford University Press, 1990).

The late **George H. S. Kanahele** was a scholar (Ph.D. Cornell), community leader, and businessman. His many books include *Kū Kanaka Stand Tall: A Search for Hawaiian Values* (University of Hawai'i Press, 1986) and *Hawaiian Music and Musicians* (University Press of Hawai'i, 1979). One of the founders of the Native Hawaiian Tourism and Hospitality Association, he died in 2000.

Davianna Pomoaika'i McGregor earned a Ph.D. at the University of Hawai'i. She is Associate Professor of Ethnic Studies at the University of Hawai'i at Manoa and a leading speaker for Hawaiian sovereignty. She is co-editor of *Our History, Our Way: An Ethnic Studies Anthology* (Kendall/Hunt, 1996).

Brucetta McKenzie graduated from Brigham Young University-Hawai'i.

Helen Morton, Ph.D. Australian National University, is a Lecturer in the School of Social Sciences at Australia's La Trobe University. She is the author of many articles on Pacific Island topics and a book, _Becoming Tongan_ (University of Hawai'i Press, 1996).

Dorri Nautu holds degrees in political science from the University of Hawai'i and Brigham Young University-Hawai'i, and is a public servant in O'ahu.

Tupou Hopoate Pau'u earned a bachelor's degree from Brigham Young University-Hawai'i. She and her family live in California.

Asesela Ravuvu is Professor and Director of the Institute for Pacific Studies at the University of the South Pacific in Suva. Among his many books are _Vaka I Taukei: The Fijian Way of Life_ (Pacific Island Books, 1983), _The Fijian Ethos_ (Institute for Pacific Studies, 1987), and _Development or Dependence_ (University of the South Pacific, 1988).

Carolina Robertson holds a Ph.D. from Indiana University. She is Professor of Music and Coordinator of Graduate Studies in Ethnomusicology at the University of Maryland. She is editor of _Musical Repercussions of 1492_ (Smithsonian Institution, 1992) and author of many other works.

Joanne L. Rondilla is a graduate of the University of California, Santa Barbara, and a student in the Ph.D. program in Ethnic Studies at the University of California, Berkeley.

E. Victoria Shook received her M.A. degree in communication from the University of Hawai'i. Her research interests include the comparative study of conflict resolution in Asia and the Pacific, with particular emphasis on mental health applications.

Paul Spickard is Professor of History and Asian American Studies at the University of California, Santa Barbara. He was educated at Harvard and the University of California, Berkeley. Among his many books on racial matters in the United States and Hawai'i are _Revealing the Sacred in Asian and Pacific America_ (Routledge, 2002) and _We Are a People: Narrative and Multiplicity in Constructing Ethnic Identity_ (Temple UP, 2000).

Haunani-Kay Trask is a poet, Professor of Hawaiian Studies at the University of Hawai'i at Manoa, and one of the most visible proponents of Hawaiian sovereignty. Her Ph.D. is from the University of Wisconsin. Among her many writings are _Eros and Power: The Promise of Feminist Theory_ (University of Pennsylvania Press, 1986) and _From a Native Daughter: Colonialism and Sovereignty in Hawai'i_ (University of Hawai'i Press, 1999).

Index

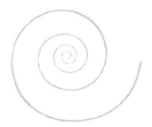

381